Collected Wheel Publications

Volume XXIX

Numbers 448 to 464

Buddhist Publication Society
54 Sangharaja Mawatha
PO Box 61
Kandy
Sri Lanka

http://www.bps.lk

First edition: 2015

Copyright (©) Kandy; Buddhist Publication Society.

Publication Data Individual Wheels:

Wheel 448/49: 1st ed. 2002. *Wheel 450/52*: 1st ed. 2002. *Wheel 453/54*: 1st ed. 2003. *Wheel 455/57*: 1st ed. 2003. *Wheel 458/60*: 1st ed. 2004. *Wheel 461*: 1st ed. 2006. *Wheel 462*: 1st ed. 2006. *Wheel 463*: 1st ed. 2006. *Wheel 464*: 1st ed. 2007.

National Library of Sri Lanka-
Cataloguing in Publication Data

Collected Wheel Publications Volume XXIX: Numbers 448–464.- Kandy: Buddhist Publication Society Inc., 2014
BW 29 - 528p.; 22cm.

ISBN 978-955-24-0412-2

i. 294.3 DDC 23
1. Buddhism

ISBN: 978-955-24-0412-2

Typeset at the BPS in URW Palladio Pali

Printed by
Creative Printers & Designers,
Bahirawakanda, Kandy.

Contents

KEY TO ABBREVIATIONS

A	Aṅguttara Nikāya
Ap	Apadāna
Bv	Buddhavaṃsa
Cp	Cariyāpiṭaka
D	Dīgha Nikāya
Dhp	Dhammapada
Dhs	Dhammasaṅgaṇī
It	Itivuttaka
Ja	Jātaka verses and commentary
Khp	Khuddakapāṭha
M	Majjhima Nikāya
Mil	Milindapañha
Nett	Nettipakaraṇa
Nidd	Niddesa
Paṭis	Paṭisambhidamagga
Peṭ	Peṭakopadesa
S	Saṃyutta Nikāya
Sn	Suttanipāta
Th	Theragātha
Thī	Therigātha
Ud	Udāna
Vibh	Vibhaṅga
Vin	Vinaya-piṭaka
Vism	Visuddhimagga
Vism-mhṭ	Visuddhimagga Sub-commentary
Vv	Vimānavatthu

The above is the abbreviation scheme of the Pali Text Society (PTS) as given in the *Dictionary of Pali* by Margaret Cone.

The commentaries, *aṭṭhakathā*, are abbreviated by using a hyphen and an "a" ("-a") following the abbreviation of the text, e.g., *Dīgha Nikāya Aṭṭhakathā* = D-a. Likewise the subcommentaries are abbreviated by a "ṭ" ("-ṭ") following the abbreviation of the text.

The sutta reference abbreviation system for the four Nikāyas, as is used in Bhikkhu Bodhi's translations is:

AN	Aṅguttara Nikāya
MN	Majjhima Nikāya
J	Jātaka story
Mv	Mahāvagga (Vinaya Piṭaka)
Cv	Cullavagga (Vinaya Piṭaka)
SVibh	Suttavibhaṅga (Vinaya Piṭaka)
DN	Dīgha Nikāya
SN	Saṃyutta Nikāya

Talks on Buddhist Meditation

by

Godwin Samararatne

Compiled from five lectures

Edited by

A.G.S. Kariyawasam

The Wheel Publication No. 448/449

First published 2002

PREFACE

What we give to our readers as the wheel number 448/449 is a collection of lectures on Buddhist meditation given by the well-known Sri Lankan meditation master the late Mr. Godwin Samararatne in 1998 at the Chin Lin Nunnery, Hong Kong.

In a series of five talks on the subject he takes the meditator along the lengthy road of Buddhist meditation indicating in his clear and pragmatic style of presentation why Buddhist Meditation is becoming popular throughout the world today thereby introducing the practiser to one of the most important exercises taught in Buddhism for developing the mind and reaching mental concentration or *samādhi,* which is the primary aim of Buddhist meditation leading to both *samatha* and *vipassanā*.

Next he takes on the four meditations of "divine abodes" or *brahmavihāras* which are discussed in great detail citing instances from everyday life as to how these can be properly practised. His practical guidelines such as treating mindfulness of breathing as one's "friend" and calling for its help in problematic situations as a "trump card" reminds one of the dictum in the game of bridge "when in doubt play a trump."

The importance of awareness (*sati*) and of loving kindness (*mettā*) is highlighted showing their true significance in the practice of Buddhist meditation. The application and the value of self-criticism is another valuable point of advice as also the method of dealing with unpleasant emotions which are quite common in our day-to-day activities. The inadvisability of meditating with the aim of something particular in return is also such a guideline.

These lectures, These lectures were naturally were naturally quite full of repetitions and therefore had to be extensively edited to suit the literary form needed for a printed book. Of course, editing was done without the least prejudice to the preservation of the catachistic nature of the talks.

All in all, these exercises in meditation can be described as "lessons from Buddhism" which, if followed carefully, can make the contemporary world, torn apiece into antagonistic factions and mini-powerblocks, get most of its wounds healed and make the earth a more congenial place for human habitation.

It is also welcome news to see and hear that more and more Westerners are turning to the Buddhist way of thinking and living owing to the efforts of people like Godwin Samararatne.

As per information about the author we are reproducing an appreciation of him written by Ven. Bhikkhu Bodhi.

—Editor, BPS

In Memoriam

Acharya Godwin Samararatne

(1932 – 2000)

In late March death snatched from our midst, too soon, one of Sri Lanka's most beloved Buddhist teachers, Godwin Samararatne. For close to twenty years, Godwin had been the resident meditation teacher at the Nilambe Meditation Centre near Kandy. He had also taught meditation within Kandy itself, at the Lewella and Visakha Meditation Centres (two affiliates of Nilambe), at the University of Peradeniya, at private homes, and at the Buddhist Publication Society. But Godwin did not belong to Sri Lanka alone. He belonged to the whole world, and he was loved and esteemed by people clear across the globe. Thousands of people from many lands came to Nilambe to practise meditation under his guidance, and they also invited him to their own countries to conduct meditation courses and retreats. Thus over the past two decades Godwin, in his own quiet way, had become an international Buddhist celebrity, constantly in demand in countries ranging from Europe to Hongkong and Taiwan. He was also a regular visitor to South Africa, where he conducted his last meditation retreat earlier this year.

What was so impressive about Godwin, however, was not what he did but what he was. He was above all a truly selfless person, and it was this utter selflessness of the man that accounts for the impact he had on the lives of so many people.

I use the word "selflessness" to describe him in two interrelated senses. First, he was selfless in the sense that he seemed to have almost no inner gravitational force of an "I" around which his personal life revolved: no pride, no ambition, no personal projects aimed at self-aggrandisement. He was completely humble and non-assertive, not in an artificial self-demeaning way, but rather as if he had no awareness of a self to be effaced. Hence as a meditation teacher he could be utterly transparent, without any trips of his own to lay upon his students.

This inward "emptiness" enabled Godwin to be selfless in the second sense: as one who always gave first consideration to the welfare of others. He was ready to empathise with others and share their concerns as vividly as if they were his own. In this respect, Godwin embodied the twin Buddhist virtues of loving kindness and compassion, *maitrī* and *karuṇā*. Even without many words, his dignified presence conveyed a quietude and calm that spoke eloquently for the power of inner goodness, for its capacity to reach out to others and heal their anxiety and distress. It was this deep quietude and almost tangible kindness that drew thousands of people to Godwin and encouraged them to welcome him into their lives. The trust they placed in him was well deposited, for in an age when so many popular "gurus" have gained notoriety for their unscrupulous behaviour, he never exploited the confidence and good will of his pupils.

Though Godwin taught the practice of Buddhist meditation, particularly the way of mindfulness, he did not try to propagate "Buddhism" as a doctrine or religious faith, much less as part of an exotic cultural package. His inspiration came from the Dhamma as primarily a path of inner transformation whose effectiveness stemmed from its ability to promote self-knowledge and self-purification. He saw the practice of meditation as a way to help people help themselves, to understand themselves more clearly and change themselves for the better. He emphasised that Buddhist meditation is not a way of withdrawing from everyday life, but of living everyday life mindfully, with awareness and clear comprehension, and he taught people how to apply the Dhamma to the knottiest problems of their mundane lives.

By not binding the practice of meditation to the traditional religious framework of Buddhism, Godwin was able to reach out and speak to people of the most diverse backgrounds. For him there were no essential, unbridgeable differences between human beings. He saw people everywhere as just human beings beset by suffering and searching for happiness, and he offered the Buddha's way of mindfulness as an experiential discipline leading to genuine peace of heart. Hence he could teach people from such different backgrounds — Western, Asian, and African; Buddhist, Hindu, Christian, and Muslim; Sri Lankan Theravadins and Chinese Mahayanists — and all could respond favourably to his guidance.

If it was not for a chronic liver condition that he had patiently endured for years, with hardly a word of complaint, Godwin might well have lived on to actively teach the way of mindfulness for at least another decade. But this was not to be, for in late February, almost immediately upon his return from a teaching engagement in South Africa, his illness flared up and a month later claimed his precious life. Those of us who have been touched by him will long bear in our hearts the memory of his calm, gentle personality, and of the impact his life had on our own.

May he quickly attain the Supreme Bliss of Nibbana.
Ven. Bhikkhu Bodhi

1. Why Is Meditation Becoming Popular?

GODWIN: Firstly, I like to welcome each one of you. I am very happy to be back and I am also very happy to see some of my old friends here. It's also nice to see some new faces.

I will give a short talk and there will be time for questions and then we can do some meditation together and wind up with some chanting, both in Chinese and Pali. When I arrived here this time, my friends told me that now there is more interest in meditation here and that there have been many teachers and many masters, also visiting this country. I was very happy to hear this and in a way, it did not surprise me because I know that everywhere in the world there is more and more interest in meditation now, especially in western countries. So a question arises: Why is there this interest in meditation in the present world? We can think of different reasons but a general reason is, I think, there is more and more suffering in this world. So human beings, at least some of them, are finding ways and means of finding some peace, a way out of the suffering. So I'll be presenting some aspects of meditation which will help us, as I said, to experience more peace and to find a way out of suffering.

In this modern world, one of the things that is happening because of mechanisation and industrialisation is that human beings are also becoming more and more machine-like, automatic. Here meditation offers two very important solutions.

One is that when human beings start becoming more more machine-like, they more or less become machines. They do not seem to have feelings and one result of this lack of feelings is that they become more and more violent, more and more violent towards themselves and towards others and also towards the environment, the surroundings wherein we live. This is why the problem of environment and ecology has also become very serious in the present world. Accordingly, meditation of loving kindness and of compassion is extremely helpful in dealing with this lack of feelings, lack of warmth.

A phrase that I often like to use is that 'meditation of loving kindness helps ourselves to be our best friend'. If you can be your best friend then naturally your behaviour will be not unskilful, and unwholesome to you and you create more and more happiness for yourself as well as for others. Thus, meditation on loving kindness helps us to open our hearts to ourselves as well as to others.

Another way meditation of loving kindness can help us is in regard to what I call 'wounds,' wounds created due to different reasons, from the past, wounds in relation to what you have done to others, and what others have done to you. I think that there is no human being who has not been wounded in one's life. A great source of suffering in the modern world is holding onto these wounds which can generate lots of suffering for oneself as well as for others. Meditation on loving kindness helps us to heal these wounds by learning to forgive ourselves as well as others. It is only when we can heal these wounds that we really experience joy and peace in ourselves. When we experience this joy and peace in ourselves, this can become infectious and it can even affect others.

So these are some very important aspects of meditation of loving kindness which the modern world needs very badly. I would suggest that this is the only way to work with global violence, violence that we are faced with in this modern world.

Another important aspect of meditation which can help us to work with human beings who are becoming more and more mechanical is the practice of awareness, the practice of being present. It is a practice of being alert and awake and like the meditation of loving kindness, this aspect of being aware also has many benefits. One is that it helps us to be conscious and to know what is happening in us, in our mind and body from moment to moment as far as possible. This awareness can help us to develop insight, to see what are we doing to ourselves and to others. It helps us to see how we create suffering in ourselves and in others. What awareness helps us to experience is that sometimes, or most of the time, how we create our own suffering. When you see quite clearly, how we create our own suffering, then it becomes clear that it is only we who can free ourselves from the suffering that we have created. Sometimes I like to define meditation as a way of discovering the medicine for the sickness that we ourselves create.

Another aspect of awareness is that it helps us to experience the present moment. It is interesting that most of the time, we live either in the past or in the future, and we hardly know this fact because it happens habitually, mechanically, sometimes unconsciously. Thus here again awareness helps us to realise how we are using the past and the future which again can create problems for ourselves and for others.

So we need to use the past, we need to use the future. One simple way of using the past and the future is to learn from whatever has happened in the past as a learning experience, as a teacher. Whatever mistakes we have committed in the past, instead of holding onto them feeling guilty and suffer from them, it is better if we can ask ourselves: "what can I learn from my past mistakes?" It can be a very useful way of coming to terms with the past. Otherwise we carry the past as a burden. In a way this type of thinking and practice enables us to let go of this burden that we are carrying all the time.

In the same way, we must use the future also as a friend. Very often when we think of the future, sometimes what happens is that we feel anxious, or insecure. But if we can make friends with the future and learn to be open to the future, we will be learning to relate ourselves to the future in a much more creative way. With awareness, we can thus learn to experience the present moment when we breathe consciously, and in relation to the past and the future, we can see the past as a teacher and the future as a friend. This will be really beautiful, creating a happy and a peaceful way of living.

Another way by which we can use awareness is to use awareness to learn, to discover, to explore, and to investigate what is happening in our mind and body. A real problem we have in everyday life is how to relate ourselves to unpleasant emotions. A problem modern man is confronted with is the problem of stress, which is universal. Now people are finding ways and means of working with stress. It is interesting that there are now workshops called "stress management courses," Here they do not try to get rid of stress but to manage and control it. Awareness helps us to find out under what circumstances do we feel stressed, and also what really happens to us mentally and physically, when we experience stress. In this way we can explore, learn and investigate any unpleasant emotion that we experience.

Everyone here must be familiar with unpleasant emotions like anxiety, fear, sadness, guilt etc. which are quite familiar to us. When we experience them, we nomally have no way or tools to work with them. Human beings have thus become helpless victims of these unpleasant emotions which really control, overwhelm and affect us. In meditation there are techniques and ways to deal with these unpleasant emotions. In fact there has been a very interesting book that has come out recently, "Emotional Intelligence." Has anyone heard of this book? The author, who is a Buddhist, says that human beings are trying to develop more and more high I.Q., but what is more important is not to develop a high I.Q. but to discover an intelligent way of working with emotions. This has become a bestseller and there has been lots of workshops on this problem because in the modern world, unpleasant emotions have become a real challenge.

Here again meditation, specially the aspect of awareness, helps us to work with such emotions. One method is not to repress them, not to control them, nor to express them but just to be aware of the emotions when they are there. We cannot prevent these emotions from arising but what we can learn is how to work with them when they arise rather than continue to suffer as a result of them.

Maybe another aspect of meditation is that it helps us to learn to be our own teacher, to be self-reliant, to have complete confidence in ourselves. This is a hard teaching but it is very important. It teaches you to develop your own resources, your own self-reliance, your own tools and how to work with suffering when it arises. So what arises from that is that we learn to take responsibility for what is happening in us, without blaming others or your surroundings. When there is a change taking place in your mind, you will be able to handle whatever that arises in a particular environment, whichever it may be.

I like to conclude by presenting a Buddhist symbol which shows how we can live in any environment and learn how not to be affected by that environment. This symbol is the lotus flower. As you know, the lotus flower grows in muddy waters and though it is surrounded by muddy and dirty water, it is able to remain unaffected by what is around it.

Thus in this modern world, there can be lots of challenges, lots of difficult situations, lots of problems that might arise but with the practice of meditation, we'll still be able to see them as challenges and learn like a lotus, still not being affected by the surroundings in which we are placed.

Questions

QUESTION: When joy and bliss arise during meditation and when the body starts to tremble, is that O.K?

GODWIN: I'm happy you are experiencing joy and bliss. It is very important to experience joy and bliss in meditation. When joy and bliss arise, and the body trembles, just know that the body is trembling and just try to find what exactly is the sensation you are experiencing and just learn to be with the sensation. What is important is not to hold on to them, when we have these positive emotions.

QUESTION: How to use our future in a proper way? For example, in the office when I deal with my boss, at first I may find that my boss has got some incorrect or improper views and then I have this anxiety that the situation may turn bad in the future and I become emotional. Then I try to alter my boss's attitude thinking that the situation maybe O.K. But afterwards, I find that I have not handled the situation properly. I could have done better. So my question is: How can I ensure that what I am doing at the present moment is the correct way to handle the situation rather than having done it first and then look back and regret for what I have done?

GODWIN: Just a few practical suggestions: How to work with such bosses? One thing you said is that you would like to change the attitude of the boss in which you can never succeed. Arising from that what you should learn to do is to change your attitude towards the boss. That is to use the boss as your spiritual friend because the boss is teaching you something through which you can look at your own mind. As I have said this is the importance of awareness. So the emphasis is not on what the boss is saying or doing but on your own mind, how you are relating yourself to what the boss is saying or doing.

Thus it will be interesting to start experimenting with your boss. So rather than feel angry with him or seeing him as a problem, you must learn to see him as a spiritual friend by finding out the emotions that arise in you when you are with the boss: "How long will these emotions stay with me? Now today, this is what happened with the boss. Now let me see what happens with him tomorrow?" So you are looking forward to be with the boss because it is a very valuable learning experience for you. You can really feel grateful that you have such a good boss, that he is really showing you a mirror to watch your own mind. Thus, without giving a minus to the boss or to yourself, you can give pluses both to yourself and to the boss.

These suggestions that I have offered can be used in any situation in relation to people: it need not necessarily be the boss.

QUESTION: Master, normally people practise meditation by sitting down with their legs crossed: but what happens if, as I am a little bit old and having a kidney problem making it difficult to sit too long to practise meditation, whether I can do meditation by lying down on my back?

GODWIN: There is still hope for you. You can just sit down on a chair with your spine erect and as you rightly said, you can use the lying down posture but what is important is that in that posture you have to be very alert and awake because from lying down you might start snoring but it is still interesting to learn to meditate in the lying down posture.

I am very happy that you have asked some very good practical questions. Now let us take a short break for about five minutes and during this time, please see how you can be aware of whatever you are doing. Whether you are standing or walking, whatever you are doing, please try to slow down your movements and just try to practise awareness as far as possible. Being silent will be helpful in practising this awareness.

So please come back after five minutes if there's a need to go outside.

GODWIN: The meditation which you are going to do is something very simple. In my talk, I emphasised the importance of being aware, being mindful, being awake. So let us develop this very important skill during this sitting. We can try to be aware, mindful and alert from moment to moment as far as possible, just knowing what is happening in our mind and body from moment to moment.

In my talk I also emphasised the importance of friendliness and gentleness. We will try to combine awareness with friendliness and gentleness, feeling friendly and gentle to whatever is happening in our mind and body as far as possible. This is something very simple that we are going to do now.

You can close your eyes. If you are having thoughts, just know what thoughts you are having very sharply, very clearly. If you are experiencing sensations, just know what sensations you are experiencing from moment to moment. You can experience the present moment, just feeling the peace and the stillness in this room, feeling what it is to sit with your body completely still. If the body is still, the mind may become still and you can feel the stillness around you, feeling friendly and gentle towards our mind and body.

Final remarks

Now please do not think that meditation is over. Please continue to know what is happening in your mind and body from moment to moment. In a way, there is no beginning or ending of meditation. This is the importance of awareness, of knowing. Thank you very much for sitting so peacefully and calmly.

Please make an effort to put in practice some of the suggestions that I have made: learn to be your best friend and also to be a friend of others. Learn to forgive yourself and others and then heal any wounds that you are carrying: make an effort to live consciously, with awareness and with a mind that is fully awake. As I have suggested, try to work with unpleasant emotions when they arise: try to find a new direction in your life, a new way of living where you will live in such a meaningful way that you will be not creating any suffering for yourself and for others. And may you experience more joy, more peace and friendliness to oneself.

2. Ānāpāna-sati and its Advantages

Godwin: I would like to firstly welcome each one of you. Now please listen to my talk. The subject that has been suggested to me is to speak about the benefits of meditation on breath. We can reflect as to why the Buddha chose 'breath' as an object of meditation.

A very important aspect of meditation is developing awareness, mindfulness. Here we can use our breath to develop awareness. In Pali this technique is called *ānāpāna-sati*, developing awareness, mindfulness in relation to the in-breath and the out-breath. We can use the breath always to develop the practice of mindfulness because we are breathing all the time so that as it is with us all the time we can make use of that to develop awareness. Ahjan Chah, one of the meditation masters in Thailand, has said that if you remember to breathe, then you remember to meditate. If you have time to breathe, then you have time to meditate. So this is the first point I want to make as to why the Buddha might have chosen breathing as a technique of meditation.

Another important aspect of meditation is learning to experience the present moment, the here and the now. Here again, it is very interesting that when we breathe, we always breathe in the present. Sometimes I like to refer to our breath as our friend. If you make a connection with your breath as a friend, then whenever we think of our friend, the friend will help us to experience the present moment. Whenever we are lost in thoughts about the past and the future and there is confusion and disorder in our minds, you have only to think of your friend and immediately you can experience the present moment.

There is another important aspect to it, namely when we are at times affected by our thoughts, when the thoughts control us, our friend can help us to learn to let go the thoughts, and to control them rather than allow the thoughts to control us. With the help of our friend we can experience the present moment by letting go the thoughts about the past and the future.

Related to our thoughts are our emotions and there is a very strong connection between our thoughts and emotions. Sometimes thoughts can create emotions and then with thinking, we can make them bigger. Hereagain if we can remember our friend and seek his help it will help us immediately to recover ourselves from emotions because it will help us to find some space in our mind, which space can help us to recover from whatever emotions that we are experiencing. We can experiment with this for ourselves.

Another useful thing that our friend can show us is the state of our mind. We all know what happens to our friend when we are affected by a strong emotion like anger, fear, excitement, stress or insecurity. What happens to our breath? As we know, it moves very very fast. Hence, it can be a very useful and a reliable signal to show us what is happening in our minds. If someone has problems with his emotions like anger, our friend will immediately show us from the way the breathing moves that we are getting angry. So it can be a very very useful signal as I said and then if you can listen and heed the signal, you will be able to recover from that emotion immediately.

In the same way, when our mind is calm, relaxed and still, what happens to our friend? The breath also becomes calm and sometimes so subtle that you do not even realise that you are breathing. Thus, if we can learn to make a connection with our friend, the friend will always tell us what is happening in our mind. Some of the friends we have can be sometimes wrong but you will realise that this social friend is always right and reliable.

Our friend also teaches about our body. Hereagain the way we breathe can indicate to us the state of our physical and mental well-being. If you can focus attention on the breath, you will sometimes realise that breathing can be very relaxing. Sometimes it can be very deep or shallow. When you realise that it is shallow, it will always show that you are having some tension in your body, and naturally it will create an emotion and will indicate the connection between tension and emotions. The only way or one of the ways of letting go this tension is by using our friend. In such a situation if you can take some deep breath immediately you might be able to relax your mind and body to a great extent.

In Buddhist meditation, there are two aspects as the aspect of experiencing calm or tranquillity, which is called Samatha and the aspect of developing Vipassanā, insight or wisdom. It is interesting that the object of meditation is relevant to both these aspects. When we are aware of the in-breath and the out-breath and if we can learn not to react to what is happening, then the mind becomes calm and tranquil. Thus this technique also helps us to develop wisdom or insight, *vipassanā*.

One aspect of *vipassanā* is to experience the fact of impermanence or change. When we are aware of the breath we will realise that whatever is happening in our mind and body, including breathing, it changes from moment to moment. You will immediately realise how thoughts are arising and are passing away. This becomes quite clear with our breath. Hereagain if we can be aware of the sensations, we will realise how variations of sensations are taking place and are changing from moment to moment. Thus we learn to be open to any changes that will be taking place in our mind and body from moment to moment. And this insight which you develop by becoming open to change and impermanence internally, will help you also to be open to the fact of impermanence when it happens externally.

As we know, sometimes we have no control of what is happening externally regarding certain events in our life. Suffering arises when we resist this change, when we resist impermanence. Thus if we can really be open to impermanence and understand the nature of impermanence, it will be a very powerful way of overcoming suffering. Then we can develop this very important insight: how suffering is created by resisting change and how we can overcome suffering by being open to change and by understanding the nature of impermanence.

Another important insight that can arise in relation to our breath is the realisation that there is only the breathing that is taking place within us as its rise and the fall and that there is no ego or a sense of "I" or "me." There is only the process of breathing from moment to moment.

Another very important insight to be realised is that we are all inter-connected, inter-related and inter-being, despite which we think that we are separate and foreign to one another in a sense. But when we reflect on breathing, we realise that what is common to all beings is this fact of breathing. This should enable us to develop a feeling of oneness with beings around us because what unites us, what is common to all beings is this fact of breathing. We have to realise that we breathe the same air as we cannot separate the breath and say "the air that I am breathing is mine." Hence there is this universality.

According to a Buddhist text, those who have meditated on this object can easily remember the breath at the time of death if they are conscious. I know some people who are working with dying people and help them to die by getting them to breathe at that time and thereby to learn to be conscious of the breathing at that time. So when we are dying, if we can experience the present moment with our friend, we have a good chance of dying peacefully. So our good friend helps us to live peacefully and to sleep peacefully. Before you fall asleep if you can spend some time just to relax your mind and body with the breath, you can sleep peacefully. And then if we can die peacefully, is there anything more that we need in this world to live peacefully?

Questions

QUESTION: Yesterday we heard from you that some people are teaching other people how to manage tension and you were saying that it is best to get rid of it and I am very glad to hear you just followed up on what you said yesterday by telling us to get rid of tension and other emotions through watching the breathing or having smooth and deep breathing. Can you elaborate more on this because it is very useful. Thank you.

GODWIN: So as I said, when we have an emotion, an unpleasant emotion, what makes it worse is our thinking, our thoughts. It is very interesting that when we have an emotion, if we have the space of mind to watch our thoughts, we will realise how thoughts come so quickly at the time and from which we can create a big story. Sometimes a small emotion can really blow up through just this process of thinking.

For example, if someone has made you angry or at least you think that someone has made you angry, then what happens to us? You will be using thoughts about that person, how that person has been behaving in the past etc., so that our whole attention is about that person and with negative thoughts about that person our anger becomes worse and worse. In such a situation, we loose control. Actually at that moment the emotions and the thoughts really control and overwhelm us. If you can spend some time with the breath, just the in-breath and the out-breath, completely being with it, then at least for a few minutes this brewing up of that emotion will become less severe.

In relation to tensions in our body also if we can do some deep breathing consciously and deliberately it can also help us to deal with that tension. In a way, being with the breath or just being with the sensation can be the same because we are experiencing the present moment with the help of the breath and the sensation.

An interesting process to be discovered is as to how thoughts and emotions are involved in creating tension. Supposing someone is afraid of dogs. When such a person sees a dog, the thought comes: "Ah, the dog is there, may be the dog is going to bite me." That thought immediately gives rise to emotions—emotions of fear, anxiety, insecurity etc. and that can give rise to tension in the body. If we can see this process taking place slowly, it can be very very useful. There can be very important discoveries that we can make. And again the process continues. We react to the tension with thoughts which then become emotions. So it really becomes what can be called a vicious circle.

So how can we interrupt and break this vicious circle? One very powerful way is to spend some time with the breath because then immediately your mind comes to the present and then to all these things. There can be some space that is created by this focusing on our friend.

I took some time to explain in this way because I think we all can relate ourselves to what I have been saying. Therefore, what I would suggest is to experiment with what I am saying and just find out for yourself whether it works.

QUESTION: Some people have mentioned that there should be four steps in this breathing technique. These are soft, shallow, smooth and long and when I tried to follow these four steps, I found that my heart beats faster and when I counted the breathing, I found that even my breathing becomes faster. So how to deal with this situation?

GODWIN: I am not surprised because it seems that you are trying to force the breathing in an artificial way. What is important is to spend some time just allowing the body to breathe naturally. Our friend knows very well how to breathe. Even when we are asleep our friend continues to breathe. In fact this is what will be emphasised when we try to experiment with this technique: to spend some time firstly just allowing the body to breathe naturally, without being controlled, manipulated or interfered. Then it becomes a very simple and a natural way, just knowing, just being aware of what is happening to the body when the body is inhaling and exhaling. So it is a very simple technique but we are very good at complicating a simple technique.

It is interesting that the text says that when you realise that the breath is long, you just know that the breath is long, when you realise the breath is short, you know that it is short. So whatever is happening naturally, you just know it. So I like to suggest to you to try out the way I will be presenting the technique and after you finish, come and tell me what your experience was.

QUESTION: Master, when we are doing meditation, very often we cannot meditate well. Our body, our mind or breathing is not peaceful and calm. What should we do? Shall we just stop and do something else?

GODWIN: It is a very useful question and I like to offer a few suggestions. When we sit to meditate, please do not have any expectations of what should happen or what should not happen. If we can just know whatever is happening what is important is not to judge, not to give a plus, not to give a minus but just knowing from moment to moment what is happening in your mind and body with openness.

The whole idea of meditation is to experience freedom from suffering. Sometimes when we try to meditate with expectations, the meditation itself creates suffering for us. When we have an expectation that the mind should be calm, that there should be only positive experiences etc., if they arise, we hold on to them. When we are unable to hold on to them, that creates suffering. Then, when the mind is not calm and relaxed, you will think that you are not meditating rightly and that too creates suffering. So without this positive and negative ideas of duality just be open, just be friendly to whatever is happening from moment to moment with awareness. That can give us immediate freedom. I shall be emphasising this aspect when presenting this technique.

Now please take a short break and try to develop awareness. When you are moving, try to move slowly and consciously as far as possible. What can help us is the practice of complete silence during this short break.

Meditation instructions

Let us begin the meditation without any expectations of what should or should not happen. We will begin with what is called the "beginner's mind." Let us begin by being aware of our body, the different sensations, the different movements in our body. Let us learn to feel friendly towards our body and also to feel what it is to sit with our body completely still. See if you can feel the stillness around you and now please allow the body to breathe naturally. The body knows very well how to breathe and therefore just allow the body to do what it likes. Now please find out what happens in the body when the body is breathing naturally and also the different movements and sensations in the body when the body is breathing. Let us just be with the different sensations and movements in our body from moment to moment.

3. Four Sublime States — I

Today and tomorrow, we are going to talk about a very important aspect in Buddhist meditation. It relates to the development of four very important spiritual qualities within ourselves. They are called "The Four Sublime or Beautiful States (*brahma-vihāra*)" Also known as "Divine Abodes," we can be like divine beings or gods when we develop them. I like to see that these four qualities as our friends because if we can encourage them to be with us most of the time, this will help us to experience a lot of joy and lightness which will help us to give joy and lightness to others also. To put it in another way, when these four friends are not with us, it can create lots of suffering for ourselves as well as for others. These four qualities in Pali sound so soothing, so nice, as you can see. They are *mettā, karuṇā, muditā* and *upekkhā*. *Mettā* is loving kindness or friendliness; *karuṇā* is compassion; *muditā* is sympathetic joy and *upekkhā* is having a non-reactive and an equanimous mind. Let us today talk about the first two qualities, the first two friends.

Mettā in simple terminology means just 'friendliness.' Hence the interesting question is: "where do we begin this friendliness"? It is psychologically interesting that we are to begin in ourselves. I think it is difficult to be friendly to others unless you are friendly to yourself. A phrase that I like to use is:

mettā enables us to be our best friend. Sometimes we do not realise that we can be our own worst enemy. Generally speaking, we see enemies outside ourselves and all our life we are trying to find and get rid of the external enemies without realising that we can be our worst enemy.

In what way do we become our worst enemy? One is that we can be extremely critical and hard on ourselves. It can become a very strong habit in us, to give ourselves minuses. When we have this habit of giving ourselves only minuses, we will also be giving minuses to other people as well. So we can create a hell where only minuses exist. However, meditation of loving- kindness helps us to see this very clearly, how we become our own enemies by giving ourselves and others minuses and also we learn to see more and more positive qualities in us and others.

In this connection there is a beautiful word that is used in the Dhamma which is "rejoicing" in our own good qualities, in the positive aspects in ourselves. Thus everyone of you can rejoice that you have made a commitment as meditators. In this way, to see more and more the positive side in us is to learn to rejoice in our own goodness. This can bring lots of joy and lightness to us and when we experience more and more joy and lightness in us, then it also can be infectious to others. It can influence and inspire others also to experience more joy and lightness.

In the Dhammapada, one of the very important books on the Buddha's teaching, there is a very interesting idea that we should try to overcome our suffering through joy because at times we try to overcome suffering through suffering. When suffering arises and we experience unpleasant emotions it becomes very easy to handle them when we experience more and more joy and lightness.

Another aspect of rejoicing is when we take to meditation as a part of our spiritual life, when we learn to lead a harmless, skilful and a wholesome life, not creating suffering for ourselves and others. This comes under an ethical behaviour very much emphasised in the Buddha's teaching wherein there is a beautiful phrase, expressed by the Pali words *anavajja-sukha*, which is joy and bliss that come from harmlessness, joy and bliss that come from a skilful wholesome way of living. Thus one can see how clearly we can learn to be our best friend from being our worst enemy.

Another way whereby we can be our own enemy is when we hold on to the wounds that we carry in relation to what has happened in the past. Wounds can be generally created by what you have done to others and *vice versa*. In relation to what you have done to others, a very destructive emotion that we can be holding on to is guilt and remorse, while in relation to what others have done to you, the emotion that assumes this role is hatred and ill will.

When we have these unhealed wounds, it can affect us in many ways, even our body sometimes. We can have psychosomatic illnesses which are created by psychological reasons. It can also affect our body wherein it can create certain tensions. Its also can affect our sleep and we will be having dreams in relation to some of these unhealed wounds. So we can be experiencing sadness, fear and guilt even while we are sleeping. At the time that we die, some of these unhealed wounds can surface in a very strong way so that we will not be able even to die peacefully.

So it is extremely important for us to learn how to heal these wounds. Hereagain meditation of loving kindness can be extremely helpful in learning also to forgive yourself as well as others. Forgive ourselves by realising that we are human, that we are still not enlightened, that we are still imperfect. In the same way forgive others by realising that they are human, that they are also imperfect like you. This is also a way of learning to let go of the past so that we do not carry this past as a very heavy burden that we are holding on to. It is only when we can really heal these wounds and let go of the past and the burden that we can really experience joy, peace and more compassion for ourselves and others.

Now I like to say something about our second friend, *karuṇā*,which becomes associated when you see suffering in other people. It is extremely important to learn to do something, to have friendliness when you see suffering in other people. In this world, there can be more and more suffering in particular situations. Thus we need to develop this important spiritual quality of compassion where we need to do something, even small things when you see someone suffering. One of the spiritual teachers has said that it is not so important to do big acts of loving kindness to others when you see suffering but it is small mercies that we can and should do.

This reminds me of again a quotation from the Buddha where he was emphasising the importance of loving kindness when he was addressing a group of monks. He told them that if they can practise loving kindness during the time it takes to snap your fingers, they are worthy of being monks. This shows that even practising loving kindness for a few minutes is worthy.

In the same way, doing little acts such as even talking to or smiling with a person even for a few minutes constitute a way of developing this quality. When you develop this quality, you are bound to see such opportunities everywhere, even while travelling in a bus or going on the road, so that you can be of some help and show some kindness to others.

I also like to suggest that regarding this quality of *karuṇā*, one should also learn to relate it to oneself. When you see yourself suffering, when you realise that you are suffering yourself, you will be your worst enemy if you just allow yourself to continue to suffer in this way. So having *karuṇā* for yourself is trying to do something about this suffering.

Now we realise that these qualities are called beautiful and divine because they help us to do something about our own as well as about the suffering of others. Here too, like loving kindness, when you develop this quality of *karuṇā* and when you see that whatever help you have given is having the desired effect, you can be very happy about it. When you see that you can do something about your own suffering, this can develop lots of self-confidence and you can be happy that you have found a way to deal with your suffering and also found a way to eradicate the suffering of others.

Questions

QUESTION: I would like to ask if there is any limit for compassion and loving kindness. For example, I have a friend who asked me to lend him some money because he said he was poor but in fact I later found out that he went gambling. Even when I came to know this I gave him money a second and third time and stopped. Thus there is a limit to forgiveness, loving kindness and compassion.

GODWIN: Very good question, because in everyday life we sometimes have to face such situations. It is very important to realise that loving kindness does not mean allowing others to exploit you. This can be considered as "idiotic compassion." In this connection there is a very interesting story. It is one of my favourite stories, which I like to share with you. It comes from the Indian tradition and the story is about a cobra who was practising loving kindness.

There was this cobra practising loving kindness in the forest saying: "may all beings be well, may all beings be happy, may all beings be peaceful." An old woman who was collecting firewood saw this cobra and mistaking it to be a rope she used the cobra to bundle the firewood that she was carrying. As the cobra was doing loving kindness, it allowed this woman to do anything and the woman carried the bundle of firewood home and the cobra escaped with lot of physical pain and wounds.

It went to meet its teacher and said: "See what has happened to me. I was practising your loving kindness and see the wounds and all the pain that I am experiencing in my body. The teacher said very calmly: "You have not been practising loving kindness: you have been practising "idiotic compassion" because you should have shown that you were a cobra. You should have at least hissed." Thus in relating yourself to people like the person you described, we have to learn to hiss whereby you will be doing a service for him.

QUESTION: Master Godwin, I have a problem which I like to present here. A couple of times in my life, in fact recently, lots of things were going wrong: things like losing control and it was just like my being in the eye of a hurricane, spinning and spinning or like a rat climbing on the wheel trying to keep up with the spin and I don't understand that my own mind should create such a horror. I want to know whether you have any idea what really is causing it, and how to get out of it.

GODWIN: Anyway I would like you to, if you don't mind, meet me personally and I like to get more details on what exactly is happening but in the meantime, I might try to offer one or two suggestions.

The first suggestion I like to offer is learning to make friends with unpleasant experiences. When we have unpleasant experiences, whether it is physical or mental pain, what normally happens is we don't like it, we resist it and then the result is we start hating ourselves for that. By hating, resisting and disliking them, sometimes we might be giving them more power and energy. Here, loving kindness can be used by making friends with this situation, which you are experiencing. A phrase

I like to use sometimes is just to tell yourself: "It is O.K. that I don't feel O.K." This is the first suggestion I like to offer.

The second suggestion is making friends with it and becoming open to it. Then you can explore, investigate and learn about what you are going through. Sometimes we may have such an experience when we have unrealistic goals in life, when we have expectations about how you should behave, how others should behave, how life should be etc. Sometimes in a way, we can be making strong demands of how things should be and when these demands are met, you are happy but when not met, we start to suffer and to hate ourselves, others and life itself. So with friendliness, you can learn to find out, learn and explore more about what you are really going through.

The third suggestion I like to offer is something related to the second suggestion. That is to find out whether this condition is created by thought, emotion or sensation. Sometimes when we have such unpleasant experiences, it is a very good practice to spend some time with the sensations or the breath which technique can help you to create some space when you will realise that these sensations are changing all the time. If one can really be open to the sensations and become open to the change, one will be able to relate oneself to it in a different way.

The last suggestion I like to offer is to find out the time when you do not have unpleasant experiences. It is extremely important in everyday life to find out if you are bothered by a particular emotion and to know the times when that emotion is not there. Perhaps if you can be open to that, you might be surprised that during the day, there are moments when this condition that you are describing is completely absent. I am sure you are not experiencing that now because I can see you smiling.

So I would suggest to try to use some of these tools and still if they do not work, you can either call me or come and see me.

Another last point is that if we can learn to see such experiences as valuable opportunities to learn, then it is a beautiful way to live. Learning from unpleasant experiences and negative conditions is to exploit them as opportunities for our spiritual growth.

QUESTION: Usually when nothing happens, it is very easy to say "let's have loving kindness to ourselves and to others," but when things happen, for example, somebody saying or doing something around us which makes us very unhappy, my experience is that I get very very angry, to such an extent that I completely forget everything about loving kindness and I find that I cannot even sleep for a few nights and this hatred remains for a few days. I want to know whether you have had any such experience before. If you have, how did you handle it?

GODWIN: Very good question, very good question. I am very happy that you are presenting very practical questions relating to everyday life. Firstly I will share with you how I work with such situations and that will help you to work with what you have described.

The first point is: do not be surprised, because we are still human, and imperfect. As long as we are human and imperfect, we are bound to get angry. So why should we be surprised?

The second point is: do not give yourself a minus because you are getting angry. By giving yourself a minus, what you are doing is getting angry about the anger and you are hating yourself because you have anger.

The third point is that, if you are unable to observe the anger at the time it arises, to do so at least later, when you can start reflecting on as to what happened: "Why did I get angry? Why did I use those words? What really made me lose my control?" So our failures can become very valuable spiritual friends. This kind of reflection has to be done in a very friendly, gentle way rather than in a very hard way, beating yourself and unnecessarily experiencing guilt and remorse in relation to what has happened. Also, as I said in my talk, you can forgive yourself with the thought that you are still human: "Let me see when I meet that person next week, I will see how I will be reacting to that person." Thus you willl be learning from and experimenting with such experiences.

If we need to have an ideal, the ideal should be not to get angry. A more realistic ideal we can have in relation to anger is is to see how soon we can recover from that anger. This is the importance of practising awareness in everyday life. If you can practise awareness and if you can have a connection with your breath, then as you are getting angry, the breath will tell you that you are getting angry, and with that awareness, you can notice how you can really recover from that anger.

I met a woman having a terrible temper, anger was her big problem. I gave her a simple suggestion which worked very well. I told her to carry a mirror in her pocket and whenever she got angry, to look at the mirror, without opening her mouth but just to look at the mirror. When she did it she was shocked to see her own person. Whenever she did that she felt bad about how she looked like because she was concerned about her appearance. There was an immediate recovery from the anger and sometimes she was able to laugh at her own anger.

[*Now follows a short interval during which the meditators were asked to move slowly with awareness and also to maintain silence and enjoy the space that silence creates in one's mind and to come back after a few minutes.*]

One must feel grateful that one has this body, that we can use this body for our practice.

Can you see yourself as your best friend and really feel it too? Feel it in every part of your body, your whole being, in the area of your heart and allow your heart to open up to yourself, like a flower? Feeling yourself as your best friend, can you forgive yourself for any mistakes you have made in the past? In forgiving yourself, can you really say to yourself and feel these words: "May I be well, may I be happy, may I be peaceful, may I be free of suffering"? For anyone who does not have such wounds, you can feel happy that you have healed your wounds. For those who have wounds in relation to what others have done to you, let us also learn to heal these wounds by learning to forgive others, and to let go of the past, learning to let go of any hatred or ill will that you have been carrying.

Can you think of these and others and also wish them that they also be well and happy, that they be peaceful and free of suffering? In healing our wounds, may we experience more joy, more lightness, more friendliness to oneself and to others.

Let us learn to rejoice that we are learning to develop
loving kindness to oneself and to others.

4. Four Sublime States — II

According to the Buddha's teaching, when we develop the four spiritual qualities of *mettā, karuṇā muditā* and *upekkhā* we can become god-like. That is why they are sometimes called "the divine abodes." I like to see them as four of our very beautiful friends. When we have these four friends within us, they will make us beautiful, they will make us experience more joy and lightness and this can also infect and affect others around you. Last time I spoke of two of these qualities, *mettā*, loving kindness and *karuṇā*, compassion.

Mettā can be seen very briefly as learning to be your best friend and also to be a friend to others. *Mettā* helps us to open our hearts to ourselves as well as to others. *Karuṇā* is when you see suffering in us and in others, doing something to overcome such suffering. In this modern world, as there is lot of suffering which manifests itself in different ways, it is extremely important to develop this quality of *karuṇā* in relation to one's own as well as others' suffering. In this connection, the Buddha has said: "Helping others is helping yourself: helping yourself is helping others, and eventually you see no difference between ourselves and others."

Today I like to deal with the third and the fourth qualities, which are *muditā*, sympathetic joy and *upekkhā*, having an equanimous and non-reactive mind.

It is interesting to see that while *karuṇā* is responding to suffering in whatever way it turns, *muditā* is when you see others happy, you also become happy because others are happy. This is sometimes not easy because the opposite of this quality of *muditā* is jealousy and envy, specially when you see others doing better than yourself. Is it possible for us to really be happy and joyful that others are experiencing happiness and joy?

Another aspect of *muditā* is making an effort to make others happy. In a way one can relate it to *karuṇā* because when you see others suffering, trying to do something about it and then getting them to experience some joy and lightness from their suffering is *karuṇa*. When that happens, you can be extremely happy about that, which is *muditā*.

This sympathetic joy or *muditā* has another interesting aspect, which is learning to rejoice and to be happy about your own happiness. Though this sounds simple, sometimes for some people, it is not easy in practice. There are some people when they experience happiness and joy, they would say: "I don't deserve this. I am such a bad person that I don't deserve to be happy." Yet others would say: "How can I feel happy? I feel guilty because there is such a lot of suffering around me and how can I experience joy? When I experience joy, I feel guilty about it." Thus, it is extremely important to learn to develop this quality as it is quite interesting: to rejoice in your own happiness and goodness and in seeing more and more the positive in you and in others.

Everyone of you right now should rejoice because you have made a commitment to follow a spiritual path by being meditators. You should rejoice that you have made a commitment to lead a harmless life, learning not to harm yourself and others. You should also rejoice that meditation sometimes or most of the time is an attempt to work with our unpleasant experiences, whether physical or mental. How many people in this world are really prepared to do this? Try to learn from them and ask the question: "What can I learn from this?" I'm very happy to find that some of you have been coming for these talks regularly. You can rejoice yourself that you have this motivation, this interest.

Being hard and critical about ourselves and giving ourselves minuses may come sometimes for some people quite naturally. That is why we need to deliberately and consciously cultivate this positive quality of rejoicing in some of the qualities that I have mentioned. Sometimes I reflect that we, all human beings, have the potentialities to become free which means that these qualities of freedom are just within us. Meditation can be seen as a way of acknowledging and realising this and allowing these factors of enlightenment to arise in us. I hope you realise the importance of this beautiful quality, the divine-like quality of *muditā*, sympathetic joy, in relation to ourselves and to others.

The last quality of equanimity, of having a non-reactive mind also is something we have to cultivate. Therefore, when we meditate and do formal sitting meditation, whenever a pleasant feeling occurs, if you are having a non-reactive mind you can learn just to relate yourself to it without giving it a plus and thereby wanting to continue with it. When we have an unpleasant experience to physical or mental pain, the immediate reaction is giving it a minus and not liking it, resisting and disliking it. Thus with an equanimous mind you just learn to see things just as they are without giving pluses and minuses.

As we are still human, there are moments when we like or dislike, with commensurate reactions. Hereagain I would suggest that if you are reacting, just to realise that you are reacting and then to find out, in your own experience, how suffering is created for you when you like something and continue holding on to it. And also when you are resisting and disliking something, how it again creates suffering. Thus we can learn from our reactions, from our reactive minds.

When you react just know that you are reacting and it is a learning experience. When you do not react just know that you are not reacting and see for yourself the results, the benefits of it. Thus, if we can really learn to be open, and see the difference between the reactive and the non-reactive minds that can be considered something very important.

This is how we can try to practise when doing formal meditation. We must learn to do this in everyday life as well, which may be more difficult but that should be the practice. If you can be observant and aware in the different situations in everyday life, you can catch yourself how in certain situations you like certain things, which you like to continue and to which we give pluses and in other situations which we don't like and we like to get rid of them. Hence, when doing formal meditation in everyday life, when you like and identify yourself with something, try to see for yourself what happens to you, what it does to you. Then you will realise that you are making a very very important discovery, namely, that we cannot be demanding from life how things should be. In a way what we are doing is making demands from ourselves as to how we should behave in making demands from others, how they should behave in demanding from life, how life should be according to our own terms. Making demands is one thing and the reality is another. This is a simple way of seeing as to how we create our own suffering. Hereagain, it is very important in everyday life just to see how we create our own suffering with the demands we are making.

This brings us to what the Buddha discovered as the Four Noble Truths, the first of which is the fact of suffering. There is no human being who is not familiar with the first noble truth, for everyone here, including myself, has experienced the first noble truth. Maybe some of you are experiencing it even now.

Here an interesting question arises: Why is suffering a noble truth? What is noble in suffering? It is an interesting and a useful question to reflect. I suggest that it is noble because, from suffering, if you can go to the second noble truth, you can find a way out of suffering. In everyday life when you are suffering, if you can tell yourself: "I am experiencing the first noble truth," that is an interesting way of saying about suffering. Then what happens to most people is they just stick only in the first noble truth, only in suffering.

The second noble truth is more difficult sometimes because you have to find out how you are creating your own suffering by your likes and dislikes, by the demands that you are making. I would suggest that this is a very very important realisation for us because if we can see that we are creating our own suffering, then you have the realisation that only you can free yourself from the suffering that you create yourself. This brings us to the third and the fourth noble truths.

Questions

QUESTION: I don't understand the relationship among the Four Sublime States that you have mentioned. For example, when you mentioned about equanimity, you said that we should not distinguish between liking or disliking or any such outside circumstances but when you talk about loving kindness, compassion and sympathetic joy, we have to feel for others and external circumstances; so we have to get involved in what happens outside. So how can you reconcile the three qualities where we have to get involved with what happens outside while the fourth quality is that we should not distinguish.

GODWIN: Very good question. I like practical examples. So let us take a practical example where you are walking on the road and you see someone fallen on the road. If you have loving kindness and compassion, there is a need and an urge to respond. Here again there are two very important words: 'reacting' and 'responding.' Reacting would be getting emotionally involved, having fear, insecurity, and even start crying. And if there is a reaction, you will not be able to respond clearly as what to do about that person. This is how the four qualities come together.

Thus with an equanimous mind you learn to do something about it, just responding without reacting. I hope it is clear.

QUESTION: If we only handle the situation as you have just said, then if we go on this way, I feel that we may get cold and very indifferent to what is happening outside. Only handle the situation and do not feel anything. So what is your suggestion?

Godwin: Yes. Well this is why my response to the earlier question was that you have to have *mettā, karuṇā,* when you see the person fallen on the road. If there is no *mettā* and *karuṇā,* you will just see the person fallen on the road and you just walk by. It is only because of *mettā* and *karuṇā* that this person felt the need to do something, to act, to show some concern and care for that person. It is that sense of concern and care that makes you act. This is what is beautiful when you cultivate these qualities. When there is a need to use them in such situations, there is just the response. I hope the answer is clear.

QUESTION: How can we cultivate these four qualities during meditation?

GODWIN: Another good question, practical question. This is how it can be done. Now what I suggest sometimes is to choose one of these four qualities. May be today we can do what we did yesterday, by choosing loving kindness.

If one wants to develop *karuṇā,* then supposing when you are sitting there you get physical pain and suffering. So rather than continue to suffer try to do something about it, learn to be friendly in relation to that, and to let go that. That would be practising *karuṇā* in relation to meditation. Then you can immediately perhaps experience sympathetic joy, to feel happy. Instead of suffering you tried to do something about it and now there is a change taking place. Now you can experience joy and happiness about it. Then you can experience the last quality by realising that you should not hold on to this joy and have a non-reactive attitude. Thus you see one particular simple situation and develop *mettā, karuṇā, muditā,* and *uppekhā,* all the four qualities. Today when we meditate, I might try to offer some guidelines regarding all these four aspects.

QUESTION: Can I just come back to the big qualities *mettā, karuṇā.* Are they not reactions and feelings that one would have when one sees a child fallen on the road?

GODWIN: I again repeat the same point and take the example of the child. When you walk on the road and you see a child fallen instead of a man, here too it is the same principle because with a child, you can really react, you can even start crying, and feel sad: "Oh, see what has happened to the child?" When you get involved like this, you will not be in a position to help that poor child. Thus, like doing something to the person who has fallen, here you show some concern also and then you would do something about the child.

This is why I used the two words, please get the two words very clear: reacting and responding. If we react emotionally, we can again learn form that also. What made me become so sad, depressed and insecure? It could be a thought like this "may be my own child would be like this." Thus we can create a huge story from that typical incident. If that happens, you can reflect on that: "Oh why am I reacting?" Hence that becomes an object of meditation.

And may be in another situation, you might be able to respond, very clearly and calmly, with a still mind as to what has to be done. So you see the difference very clearly: "Ah, see what happens when I react and see what happens when I respond." Just see the difference.

The same principle applies to what is happening internally. Here it applies to some external event as when we are meditating, someone who is very habitually reactive, can be reactive to what is happening in meditation also. To take an example, supposing your knees are in pain. You can say "my knees are in pain, who knows my knees might break." I know some meditators who have broken their knees and in like manner you can create a huge story from the pain in the knees. And from the pain in the knees, you can have anxiety, fear, insecurity and all such unpleasant emotions. So responding would be just observing the pain and learning to make friends with it and if it becomes unbearable, you change the posture. Now let me thank you very much for asking questions and take a small break.

Meditation on the Four Sublime States.

We will try to radiate lots of friendliness in all directions. "May all beings be well, happy and peaceful and free of suffering." Let us now think of the people whom you know are suffering, whether physical or mental. Let us feel for those people who are suffering, let us feel concern for them. "May they be free of the suffering that they are experiencing." Can you really wish this from your heart? Can you now feel happy that you are trying to develop qualities of loving kindness and compassion for others? Rejoice in doing so. Can you be happy with yourself that you are trying to develop these qualities of the heart?

Let us now try to develop the important quality of a non-reactive mind. Whatever is happening in our mind and body right now, can you relate yourself to that without liking or disliking? Or if we are experiencing physical pain and discomfort, can we relate ourselves to it without reacting? If your mind is not calm, can you just know that the mind is not calm and not react to it, not give it a minus? Also if you are experiencing pleasant experiences, can you like it and relate yourself to it without liking it and giving a plus?

Just be open to whatever is happening and learn to see things just as they are.

5. Meditation in Everyday Life

GODWIN: I like to welcome each one of you for this one day meditation programme. The first point I want to make is that everyone of you should feel very happy because being a Sunday and a holiday you have the motivation to come here and spend the whole day in meditation. Everyone of you should rejoice and should feel very happy about this.

One of the things that we have been emphasising in the talks as a very important aspect in meditation is the practice of awareness, mindfulness. So today we will make a special effort to develop this very very important skill, the skill of being conscious. And also related to that, we will try to have continuity of awareness from moment to moment as far as possible. Whether you are sitting, standing, walking, eating, doing *yoga* or whatever you are doing, whether going to or doing something in the toilet, please make an effort just to know, just to be conscious of what is happening in your mind and body from moment to moment.

It is also important to learn to use awareness with friendliness and gentleness. There is a very interesting Mahayana text in which watching and observing yourself is compared to a mother, who keeps on just watching and observing, just noticing her child whatever the child is doing. In the same way, if you can watch, observe and find out what is happening in your mind and body with awareness and friendliness, this combination becomes extremely important. Another important aspect of awareness is experiencing the present moment, the here and the now. So today let us make an effort just to forget whatever has happened in the past, which we cannot change, because it is gone. And then let us not think of the future because the future has not yet come. Thus, in a way, thinking of the past and the future is not being one with reality and today we will make a special effort to use awareness and friendliness to experience the present moment as much as possible.

A very important area wherein we need to work is that of emotions, especially emotions like sadness, fear, insecurity, shame, guilt etc. that create suffering in everyday life. So I'll be presenting techniques which will help you to work with these unpleasant emotions. It is also important to know when these unpleasant emotions are absent. Here too what will be helpful to us is the practice of awareness because if you know how to be aware, then you know what unpleasant emotions you are having and not having. I will present one or two tools which will help you to work with them.

Thus it is important to have self-confidence by knowing when these unpleasant emotions would arise and how to deal with them. We need not be afraid of them and you will discover some of these tools and I really hope that you will develop this self-confidence in you and trust in the Dhamma so that you know what to do with them when they arise. Knowing how to recover from them is extremely important.

In conclusion, I like to suggest that you make a real effort to make full use of your stay today. In a way you have made a big sacrifice in coming here on a holiday. So let us make an effort to make full use of the opportunity and get a glimpse and a taste of what meditation is about and then to have the confidence that through your own efforts, you can find a way out of the suffering you yourself have created.

Sitting Meditation

Let us begin by just feeling friendly and gentle towards our mind and body. Can you see yourself as your best friend? Can you really feel it in every part of your body, your whole being? And being your best friend, you have complete confidence and trust in yourself. Now let us just be mindful, aware, alert and awake of what is happening in our mind and body from moment to moment.

Please realise that what we are doing is not developing concentration but just learning to be aware, to be conscious and to be alert. Please don't try to achieve anything but just know what is happening in your mind and body. If you are aware you know that you are sitting completely still and that you will feel the stillness in this room.

Now we will use our awareness to become aware of our breath. So please allow your body to breathe naturally and just be aware of the sensations and movements you experience in the body, in your breath. You know when the body is inhaling and also when it is exhaling. Feel friendly towards your thoughts and just return to your breath. Experience the present moment with the help of your friend, the breath. When the breath is long you know that the breath is long. When it is short you know that it is short. When it is deep you know that it is deep. When it is not deep you know that it is not deep. Feeling the stillness in the room, you inhale. Feeling the stillness in the room, you exhale. If there are unpleasant sensations in the body, just learn to feel friendly and gentle towards them. Don't see them as disturbances or distractions. Let us now end with meditation of loving kindness and take a short break.

Please don't think that the meditation is over. Please continue to know from moment to moment what is happening in your mind and body. We can meditate in four postures which are sitting, standing, walking and lying down. We will be exploring three of these postures, sitting, standing and walking. Now let us do some standing meditation and when you stand, please stand slowly, observing every movement when you are standing and observing the intention to stand. Also learn to stand slowly so that you will not be disturbing persons around you.

Now just feel what it is to stand. Feel the different sensations and movements in your body when you are standing. When thoughts come, gently let them go off and come back. Experience the present moment with the help of your body. Note carefully and sharply how sensations in the body change from moment to moment. Feel what it is to stand with your body completely still. Then you can feel the stillness around you and try to remains not thinking about the past or the future but experiencing the present moment with the help of the sensations and stillness. Whatever you experience in the body, just see them as just sensations arising and passing away from moment to moment.

Walking Meditation

Here you should be aware of all the movements in your body while you are walking. It is experiencing the present moment with the help of conscious walking. You must feel the different sensations and the movements in your body while you are walking. You can look at the feet of the person in front and let go your thoughts gently and come back to walking and just enjoy conscious walking without looking around. You should walk as if you are walking on lotus flowers, conscious of each step that you are taking. You must feel the sensations in your knees and of the feet touching the floor.

You can try to slow down the walking so that you are really conscious of each step that you are taking from moment to moment and let go your thoughts gently and come back to walking. Now you can stand wherever you are and close your eyes.

Now let us do a short sitting before yoga: so you walk slowly with moment to moment awareness to where you were seated and then we will do a short sitting. So continuity of awareness from walking to sitting is very important. This is going to be a very short sitting so we will try to sit with a mind that is really alert and awake from moment to moment, and as it is a short sitting, you must learn to sit without moving.

Discussion

We can discuss what we have been trying to do today. What we will try to do is to go over some of the things we did today followed by a question time.

The first technique we practised was just being aware of whatever was happening. Does anyone have any question in relation to this?

QUESTION: When I practised the walking and standing meditation, I was able to be aware of the sensations and what happened at the time but when I practised sitting this morning, I had many passing thoughts and was carried away by these passing thoughts. Later if we are going to have sitting again this afternoon then, if I am again carried away by the passing thoughts, can I do standing meditation instead of sitting or what other suggestion you would give me?

GODWIN: Yes. Very clear question. In that technique I have presented, it is something very simple just to observe the passing thoughts and to know very clearly, and sharply, what thoughts are arising from moment to moment. Having passing thoughts should not be a problem when we have this awareness of whatever is happening.

QUESTION: Thank you for your teaching. Now I know that my suffering comes from my expectations but this is my habitual pattern, this is my bad habit. How can I stop this bad habit from coming back again. That is the first question. The second part is should I deal with this situation with sympathetic joy or with equanimity? And the third part of the question is if I deal with it with equanimity, would there be another expectation of what I have to do?

GODWIN: Well, it is quite right to say that suffering is created by our expectations and that it is a strong habit in us and this is where awareness becomes important. With awareness, you catch yourself immediately when your habitual pattern arises and realise that it is just a habit and not reality. Again, to repeat, being aware and catching the habit when it arises in whatever form and then learning to let go it, knowing that it is just a habit, is what is required. If you can catch it as it arises it will be great because then you will be really handling it effectively. As I have often said, as we are human, sometimes we might fail to catch it as it arises and we might become victims of this habit. When that happens again reflect on what has happened when the event is over and then learn from what has happened and learn to experiment with such situations. The best technique to work of course is to be aware and be equanimous as you have pointed out, learning to have a non-reactive mind to whatever is happening.

Whether to have a non-reactive mind is another expectation to be realised: I am trying to be non-reactive but sometimes it might succeed, sometimes not so that if you can have that openness, there is very little likelihood of it becoming a strong expectation. I am very happy that you have made a very important discovery and I would like to say that with such a tendency for discovery I am sure you have confidence for more and more discoveries and I feel that eventually you will succeed in working with this habitual pattern. Another thing you were doing was focusing on breathing.

QUESTION: When I walk normally in the streets, there is no problem, very natural but when I try to practise walking meditation and place mindfulness on the feet, then I find that my walking becomes unstable.

GODWIN: Actually my question was about focusing on breathing, but it is alright that you asked a question about walking. You are making a very interesting point because in meditation also we have to do things naturally. This is why in the meditation of breathing one has to learn to breathe naturally. In the same way when doing the walking meditation, it is only slowing down but in slowing down one is learning to walk naturally. But if you try to do it differently and not naturally, then naturally you will have problems in both cases.

A very interesting point that arises from that question is that when we are meditating, we feel that we should do something different, something special. So if you try to do something special, as if it is something different, then there will be special problems. Therefore please realise that meditation is not something special. It is something very natural. It was so beautiful when I had a session with a group of children, so natural, simple and uncomplicated.

QUESTION: I usually meditate in the night around 1.00 a.m. and I find that when I breathe my eyes appear to be pulled inwards. When I meditate during the daytime there is no such problem. So I would like to know whether there is a difference between meditating at night and during daytime.

GODWIN: It depends. If you are getting up at 1.00 a.m. I feel that you may be trying too hard. I am very happy that you are so motivated to start meditating at 1.00 a.m.which is a big plus. I like to suggest to you to try to meditate between 3.00 and 4.00 in the morning, may be 3.30 or 4.00 and the problems that you were describing may not happen then. In most meditation centres in Sri Lanka, we get up around 3:30, 4:00 or 4:30. I think it is very important that we should get enough sleep, of course depending on the individual.

QUESTION: When we meditate and focus on the breath sometimes we may find that the air around us is polluted. For example, when somebody is cooking nearby and there are smells, the focusing would be disturbed by the smells or the polluted air. So what should we do under those circumstances? Should we stop meditating or what?

GODWIN: No I would suggest you to continue with the meditation because it might be difficult to find a place where there is no pollution. The problem is not with the smell of food but with ourselves. If we can find ideal places where there is nice air without smell of food that is very good. But does that mean that we should not meditate in places where there is smell of food and not very pure air? In relation to the smell of food, when you get that smell what you can observe is as to what the thoughts that you have in relation to the smell of food. It will be a very good insight that when you get the smell of food there is only smelling and no reaction to the smell. If this happens, you have a very important insight, a glimpse, that the problem is not with what is happening externally but what is happening inside us. What is beautiful about meditation is the so-called distractions and disturbances. They become your teachers. Rather than wasting such situations, we should learn to confront such situations and see how far you can meditate. This will give you a lot of self-confidence which will be a very very important breakthrough.

If we meditate in a place where there is pure air, where there is no smell of food, do we think there won't be any problems for us? There we might have other problems.

Thank you very much for the useful questions that have been asked but what struck me was all the questions were asked by ladies. I hope the men do not have any problems.

Discussion with Another Group

GODWIN: Do you have any questions about what we have been trying to do today?

QUESTION: When we sit, is there a posture which we must stick to?

GODWIN: I would say the ideal posture will be the cross-legged posture wherein too there are variations. The lotus posture is one. Anyway, whatever the cross-legged posture be what is important is to have your spine erect because when you have your spine erect, it is very easy to become alert and awake and really be conscious. So this is where *yoga* exercises can help you sometimes to work with your posture. In the afternoon session, if you have any difficulties with the sitting posture, please ask the *yoga* Master and he will help you with the sitting posture. Here again what is important is to have your posture wherein you can feel relaxed. It is very very important to be mentally and physically relaxed when you meditate.

QUESTION: When I meditate and after I have completely relaxed, I find my eyes usually become moist and tears coming out. I would like to know as to what happens here.

GODWIN: I am happy to hear that you do feel relaxed when you meditate. When you are relaxed if something is happening in the eyes, just know that it is happening. When we meditate, we really do not know what is going to happen in our mind and body. Many different things can happen in our mind and body. If you ask the question: "Why is this happening to me? Is it the right or the wrong thing?" etc., it can create more problems and more suffering. So in meditation whatever is happening, you just observe, you just know, and then continue. Something else is bound to happen next.

QUESTION: I would like to ask questions not about meditation but about the Four Sublime States. I work in a coroner's court as a clerk and whenever I read reports on the cases, in each case there is a deceased person. He or she may have been killed in an accident or might have committed suicide. Whatever the cause of death, when I read the reports, I have to write down his or her age, occupation, address, reason for death etc. and there is a code for each age, occupation and when I do this, I find that no matter whether a person is young or old, man or woman, there has been a lot of suffering and it is because of such suffering that they have committed suicide or because of some negligence that they were involved in accidents. Whenever I write down a code in the file, I feel pain in my heart and sometimes what I do is reciting some formula like *namo tassa* and then the pain would become a little bit less. I also found that my mind expands, thinking that the person who has committed suicide must have suffered a lot before committing the act and even thereafter in his next life, he may have to go to a place where he has to continue with the suffering. Thus I become very unhappy. I would like to know how to handle this situation. Should I try to lessen the pain or should I just allow the pain to go on?

GODWIN: I will give a simple suggestion. You can think of the particular without the details such as age, the circumstances and then think of him or her that wherever that person may be, wish him or her to be well, happy, be peaceful and free of suffering. So in place of pain, grief and suffering, you will be developing loving kindness for that person. It will be good for both you and that person.

QUESTION: Most of the time when I meditate, I find that it is very difficult to relax because there are many passing thoughts. What is your suggestion?

GODWIN: What is wrong with passing thoughts? There is nothing wrong with them. Or do you think that you should not be having passing thoughts when you complain that you cannot relax? As I have repeatedly mentioned, please make friends with your thoughts, emotions and sensations. I cannot understand why meditators hate their passing thoughts. When we do not meditate passing thoughts are no problem and when we meditate they are not welcome. So when you do not meditate, you feel very relaxed despite the passing thoughts and when you meditate you cannot relax because of them. Are not we very funny? See what we are doing in the name of meditation. Please understand this very clearly.

QUESTION: Previously, I have practised some other kind of breathing where my breathing is not natural. Now I would like to practise natural breathing and then I found that because of this change of my breathing pattern during the sitting, my body became stiff and even my skin got affected. I would like you to give some suggestions as to what I should do.

GODWIN: Now when you are seated in this posture, I am sure you are breathing. Is that creating a problem? No. So when you sit, there is nothing special. Thus, most of the questions are very interesting for me and for you they are different and something special. There is a meditation Master in Sri Lanka who tells that when you sit and if you aim for something special, you will have special problems. Please realise that meditation is a way of living. Please realise that meditation is involved not only when you are sitting but whether it is sitting, standing, walking, lying down or in any situation, one has to have meditation of just being aware. Then meditation becomes natural and all these questions about what happens in sitting may not arise.

QUESTION: The first question is that when I was younger, I was able to sit cross-legged but now I am much older and I cannot sit cross-legged. So I would like to ask whether I can meditate in the posture in which I am now sitting. The second question is that I practise visualisation and I visualise some deity or Bodhisatta so that I have seen a deity coming down from the sky. I would like to ask whether this phenomenon is O.K. or not.

GODWIN: First question. You are looking very beautiful, very peaceful when you are sitting on the chair.

QUESTION: So when I sit like this, can my feet touch the ground?

GODWIN: The way you are sitting now is perfect.

QUESTION: I am now 91 years old.

GODWIN: I am very impressed and inspired that at 91 you could be sitting so beautifully on the chair and that you could so clearly ask these questions.

About the second question, I am very sorry I have not practised "visualisation meditation." I am sure you must have a teacher who is teaching you about visualisation. I think you should ask the question from the teacher concerned. I am very sorry.

QUESTION: The teacher who taught me visualisation has passed away.

GODWIN: Then I will try to offer some suggestions. So when you visualise, when you have pleasant or unpleasant visualisation, just try to have a mind that is equanimous in both situations. I am sure you will be able to do that.

Discussion with Another Group

QUESTION: When we have negative feelings and thoughts when in meditation, how can we be friends with them and deal with them?

GODWIN: Please see it as an opportunity, as a learning experience because it is extremely important and valuable for us to learn about unpleasant emotions.

The second suggestion is, as I have been saying this morning, how far can we make friends with them, saying they are O.K? The third suggestion is to try to find out what exactly is negative and unpleasant about them. Is it a thought, a sensation or an emotion? Try really to look deeply into what you consider as negativity. Another tool is to think of our friend, the breath. Breathing whilst standing and just becoming conscious of the sensations in the body: just being with the breath and the sensations. Then you might be having less thoughts and this will help you really to create a space around that unpleasant emotion troubling you. The next tool is for us to realise that 'whatever arises passes away.' What is funny is that if you have an unpleasant emotion and tell it "don't leave me, don't go," what will happen? It won't stay. Or if you say: "stay with me" it will change. Thus we have no control. These things arise and pass away. It is just to be open to that important aspect is what the Buddha has taught.

Another very important point is that when these unpleasant emotions are not there you should know that they are not there. As emotions are subject to change sometimes we have pleasant emotions and sometimes unpleasant emotions. We cannot be having all these pleasant emotions nor all these unpleasant ones. So again one should be open to both and know when they are there and when they are not there. The last tool is to realise that these are visitors that come to our mind. So you must be a very good host.

Let these visitors come and go. When they come, as a good host you must say: "Hello, welcome" and make friends with them and talk to them. You must try to find out as to why they have come and try to learn from them. When they leave, say: "Good bye, come back." In this way, we can sometimes learn to play with their coming and going. Rather than see them as problems, look at them as very interesting situations and challenges and to work with them. And it is a very deep Buddhist insight to know that they do not belong to us. The problem arises when we think that they belong to us thereby creating sadness and anxiety in us. I hope you will wait for these visitors to come and then learn to use some of these tools. When you develop lots of self-confidence, you know what to do when they arise.

QUESTION: At the beginning, I think it may be difficult for us to welcome unpleasant experiences . When they come, we will not like them and here reflection is very important. After the unpleasant experience has gone, we can reflect on the situation and gradually we will discover that we can really learn a lot from such experiences and they are really our great teachers. Then gradually we will even welcome unpleasant experiences. So I think reflection is very important.

GODWIN: So I hope that those who have problems with unpleasant emotions will have the experience of learning to make friends with them.

QUESTION: When I meditate, it is not important that there are unpleasant or pleasant sensations. Sometimes there are practical questions which arise and need to be answered. For example, in daily life there are things which we should handle. As you said, we should respond but not react. So when those questions arise, should we think about the solution during the meditation because it is very natural that when such questions arise, we need to think how to handle them. Can we think whilst we meditate?

GODWIN: Yes, a useful question. This brings up an important technique in meditation which is called "reflection" which is using thoughts in a very creative way. Usually we use thoughts destructively to create our own suffering but here when you use thoughts creatively, you are using them to work with all kinds of suffering. So, what is important is with a mind that is calm and clear, you start to reflect on the problem you are supposed to be having. A very interesting exercise is to see that problem from different angles. Usually we see only one or two aspects of the problem but when we reflect in this way, we can see many more areas and aspects of the problem. This in itself, as I said, becomes a meditation and from this, a solution to the problem may arise.

QUESTION: Master, when we practise a non-reactive mind, we have a negative feeling, which we try to overcome: say worries and things like that, which are negative emotions. Would we become pieces of wood or lose interest in life or lose the ambition to succeed? Is there a problem here?

GODWIN: In relation to unpleasant emotions, I offered many tools. When I offered the tools, I never spoke about a non-reactive mind. In working with unpleasant emotions, you should not have the idea that you will have a non-reactive mind, in which case, I should have just said that there is only one tool, a non-reactive mind. I did not say that. In Sri Lanka there are many people who are grief-stricken through having lost sons in the war. I just cannot ask them just to have a non-reactive mind. It does not work. So I would tell them to realise that it is natural that you have grief inside. We all have grief in us, and it is natural then to try to work with them with the different tools that I have mentioned. I think the problem is with the term, 'non-reaction,' a feeling that you do not need any action. Is that the problem you have? Is that what is worrying you?

QUESTION: No. If we are non-reactive to things and outside circumstances there may be a danger that we would have no feelings and as a result, not interested in anything else.

GODWIN: For a few days I have been speaking about *mettā, karuṇā, muditā,* and *upekkhā*. I said that they are really making an effort to open our hearts because they are all qualities of the heart. So firstly, when you have *mettā,* you learn to open your heart to yourself, feeling for yourself. Then when you have *mettā* for others, you really open your heart to others. So you are relating yourself to others with warmth. The second quality that I mentioned was *karuṇā* which means really feeling for the suffering, concern and care for others. If you do not have feelings, you cannot care and have concern for others. In the same way, if you do not care for yourself, then you do not have *karuṇā* for yourself. I have been emphasising so much the importance of joy and lightness, which are nothing but the area of your heart, of your feelings. A non-reactive mind may be described as "to be cool without being cold." So I like to tell my friend not to use the word "non-reactive" but to use the words, "cool but not cold." Is it clear now? Thank you.

QUESTION: Can you give us some idea as how to maintain your joy, compassion and warmth to negative people whom you meet day in and day out. I find it very difficult. I get swallowed up in their negativity after a while and I cannot help them and then I cannot help myself.

GODWIN: Although it is time for *yoga,* I will still respond to that question because it is a very important question. I think everyone here can relate oneself to that question specially in everyday life. Sometimes we are forced to see people whom you consider as negative, may be starting with your husband or wife or probably your boss. What do we do then? Fortunately or unfortunately, you cannot avoid them or escape them. Then what do we do? I will give some suggestions. First suggestion is not to be surprised. Why? They and you all are unenlightened beings. It is very very important to realise that we are living in a world which is full of imperfect human beings including yourself. To put it in a stronger language, according to the Buddha, "until we are enlightened, we are all crazy." We are crazy in the sense that no one can claim that we can always see things as they really are. We all see things subjectively and not objectively. In this sense, we are all crazy. As we are lving in a crazy world please don't be surprised when you see imperfections everyday, both in yourself and in others.

The second suggestion is that when you see imperfections in others, try to remind yourself: "I am also imperfect like that person." Otherwise, we have a self-righteous attitude: "I am perfect, the other person is negative. I am positive, the other person is negative." Is there anyone here who is always positive? Are you always positive? So just realise: "now the other person is negative and I too can also be behaving like that." Then you become more and more humble.

The third suggestion is to try to see them as your *gurus* and teachers, as your "masters." I like to mention now that I have been called a "master" but I like to see myself as a "spiritual friend" and not as a "master." When you see negative people, please see them as masters. Why? The master is showing you a mirror. What we do when we are angry is to look at our face in the mirror. So whichever way the master is behaving, look at your own emotions. "What are the emotions that are coming? I am giving that person a minus. Thus I am getting angry, annoyed and agitated." See all the emotions that arise are thankfully due to the master. The function of a good master is to try to test whether you are good meditators. This master is testing whether you are a good meditator.

Let me suggest something very difficult and very interesting: try to see the master as if it were for the first time. Sometimes we come to the conclusion that he is a negative person. Every time you see that person, you will be with that conclusion, prejudice and bias. Sometimes we see what we want to see. So poor master, even if he is behaving in a positive way, he looks negative because we only want to see what we want to see.

The last suggestion is to ask the master as to the negative things he can see in you. That will be very revealing. Thank you very much. Enjoy your *yoga*.

GODWIN: We will now try to meditate on our thoughts because in the discussion there were people who were having difficulties with thoughts. Let us learn to meditate on thoughts. Just learn to observe and to watch the thoughts that arise and pass away in our minds. Let us learn to make friends with our thoughts and to observe them very sharply, very clearly. Let us see how far we can observe the thoughts without judging them, without awarding pluses or minuses, just letting thoughts come and go. If you judge the thoughts, just know that you are judging them and see the difference when you are judging and when you are not judging them.

If some of you are having difficulties with unpleasant emotions, can you just allow them to arise—emotions such as sadness, fear, anxiety, depression, whatever you do not like—let them arise now.

If there are no such unpleasant emotions, just know that they are not there and if they are there, just know that they are there and then make friends with them.

I will now offer some suggestions as how to integrate meditation in daily life. One can see meditation as medicine for the sicknesses we create for ourselves. The first point that needs to be very clear in your mind is: "Are you really interested in taking the medicine? Have you really made a commitment to take the medicine?" If you have really made a commitment to take the medicine, one can never say that he forgot to take the medicine or that he had no time to take it. You all have different priorities in life but where does this taking medicine figure in that list? This is a very important point to be clear and it is the first point I like to make.

The second point is the importance of just knowing, just being aware, just finding out what is happening to us, especially in our daily life. One has to make a sincere effort during the day to make a conscious effort to try to be aware, to be conscious of what is happening to you. May be a good time to do this is in the morning. Just as we wake up in the morning, one may have lots of things to do but can you just spend a few minutes just lying down on your bed? I mean it would be ideal if you can do some sitting meditation in the morning even for a short time, at least lying down and spending even five minutes in the lying down posture. You may start the day with loving kindness meditation by just feeling friendly towards yourself and radiating thoughts of loving kindness. It is useful to have just a wish, "may I get an opportunity to practise loving kindness, *karuṇā*, *muditā* and other things that we have been discussing." This is a beautiful way to begin the day. It won't take more than five minutes.

There are certain things that we have to do in the morning. However much you are busy, everyone will brush their teeth in the morning. No one will say "I do not have time to brush my teeth." Here again, can we just practise a little awareness, (mindfulness) when we are brushing our teeth? What happens when we brush our teeth? Again, we have thoughts, we hardly know that we are brushing our teeth. This becomes a very very strong habit in us. As it is a strong habit, thoughts will come. So just learn to let go the thoughts and come back to conscious brushing of your teeth.

However much you are busy, you are bound to go to the toilet. It is interesting that the Buddha has described how we should develop awareness when you are even in the toilet. Try to be aware and conscious of what is happening when you are in the toilet. I call this 'toilet meditation.' If you are really interested, motivated and really want to take the medicine you will have time to do at least toilet meditation.

You will definitely be having breakfast. I won't be telling you to eat breakfast in silence because it is not possible. At least by spending one minute before you start eating breakfast you can feel grateful towards the person who has prepared it for you. It is beautiful to feel grateful for that person or even if you have prepared the breakfast yourself, just feel grateful thinking "today I prepared my breakfast and now I am eating it." Just developing this quality of feeling grateful is a very important aspect, a very important spiritual quality. You also must at least make an effort at least occasionally to come back to awareness in tasting, swallowing and chewing. Just make an effort to do that.

What happens next? May be you have to go to work, which is a very interesting place where interesting challenges crop up. A very important aspect there in your everyday life is the problem of human relations. How to relate yourself to people around you.? As we live in an imperfect human world all the time, we have to encounter and to have relationships with imperfect human beings. Here what we can try to do is to try to learn from them. There lies the importance of meditation and of awareness in trying to watch your own mind relating to others. Here, it is natural to have unpleasant emotions. This is the importance of awareness, of watching and of learning. We can see how to work with the emotions, to understand them and to let go of them.

Supposing at that time, we are unable to do that and we get angry and annoyed and then we show and express our anger. What happens when we do this? Again, please do not be surprised and learn not to give yourself a minus. This is very very important. If you do not have time there, when you go back home or when you have a little space, what you can do is to reflect on what really happened. This is learning to reflect and this reflection, this exploration, has to be done in a very very friendly and a gentle and not in a harsh way, its being an extremely critical attitude to yourself and seeing yourself as a failure.

So this would be a very creative way of living where we really learn from our mistakes. Our mistakes become an area for our spiritual growth. I like to suggest that rather than giving yourself a minus, please give yourself a plus for this. You deserve a big plus because you are learning from this, you are trying to use them as part of your spiritual growth. So should not we rejoice for this learning and growing and our effort to do this. Again one should feel grateful for such an opportunity.

Here it does not mean allowing others to do what they like to do, namely allowing yourself to be exploited. Sometimes, in certain situations, we need to be assertive and firm because some people understand only that language. Here again very deliberately and consciously you must say "now I'm going to be very firm, I'm going to be assertive in relation to this person." You do it with complete awareness. I know some meditation masters who pretend that they are getting angry with their students in order to awaken their students. So it can be used as a tool, as a device.

I also would like to suggest that during this day, specially if you are very busy, just try to take very brief times when you can spend some time on yourself. You do not have to leave the place of work but still be seated on your chair and you can even have your eyes open so that no one really knows what is happening. Please spend some time with your friend, the breath, at least for five minutes. It will create space in your mind. The build-up that is happening in your office, or whatever you are doing, there can be some recovery even for five minutes, and this will really help you. Of course you have the freedom when in the office also to do some toilet meditation where you can be completely alone, secluded. So during the day, whatever emotions and states of mind that would arise, they are bound to arise in a busy place. What we have to do is to make them the objects of meditation.

When you go back home, you might be too tired to meditate and as such spend at least ten minutes, either in the cross-legged posture or just lying down on a chair and just go on reflecting on how you spent the day. Try to do this reflection in a very friendly and a gentle way: "Now how did I spend the day today? What were the times when I had unpleasant emotions? What were the times when they were not there"? This is equally important. Sometimes you might be surprised that for the whole day you were angry only once. This can really help you to understand and to discover about yourself, about how you are relating yourself to others. This can naturally bring about a transformation in oneself.

Another point related to this which is a really powerful, very practical and a direct practice is to see the Four Noble Truths in everyday life. It will be really excellent and wonderful when you are suffering during the day, if you can remind yourself "here I am experiencing the Buddha's first noble truth." If you can tell yourself all this, you will be relating yourself to that suffering in an entirely different way. Then if you can really move from that to the second noble truth "Now let me see, in what way am I creating my own suffering?" Then you can use the third and the fourth noble truths also in this way. During the day, just find out when you are free, when there is no suffering and then find out as to why there no suffering"? If you can really learn to use the Four Noble Truths in daily life in this practical, simple and direct way, you will be living in the Buddha's teaching whether you are suffering or not. Isn't that a beautiful way to live?

A few more practical suggestions may be given. In the Buddha's teaching, spiritual friends are very much emphasised. So you are very fortunate here that you have many groups doing meditation. It is good to join one such group and to cultivate friendships with spiritual and noble friends. Spiritual friendship is learning to grow together. I was speaking about relationships earlier wherein you can see them as spiritual friends. It is a very positive way of relating to one another. If there are meditation groups, please join one of them.

Another helpful suggestion is to read about the Buddha's teaching. Here again there are some very valuable books that have been translated and I think some of them are already distributed here. It is good to read and reflect on them. This can really inspire us and be an incentive for us to practise by reminding ourselves of the importance of taking the medicine.

Questions

QUESTION: Master, I like to ask that when we are sick and suffering from great pain or other things, can we practise meditation spiritually because we are not in a fit state of mind.

GODWIN: If I understood the question correctly, it means that there are certain situations when we are really overwhelmed by emotions and where there is lot of suffering and it is not possible to think of meditation at such times. What I would suggest here is that you can wait until you recover from that state of mind. It does not matter how long it takes and then as I had suggested earlier, you can look back and reflect: "What really happened to me? What really made me go through the physical and mental suffering? What can I learn from that experience?" This is the importance of spiritual friends. At that moment, if you have a spiritual friend, it is something very wholesome and skilful just to share your suffering with another person. This is how we help one another.

QUESTION: I occasionally join talks on Buddhism like this one and I sit and meditate occasionally. There was an experience when I was sitting. I felt some force or very strong sensation in my abdomen towards my heart and it made me very uncomfortable and I cried. Can you comment on this phenomenon?

GODWIN: As I said this morning, when we meditate, we really do not know what is going to happen. As it happened to you, the most unexpected thing can happen. So when such things happen, please do not be surprised and blame yourself. Please do not give that experience a big minus and also do not try to understand it. Sometimes we cannot understand it intellectually but we can only know it. This is the beauty of awareness. This is why the Buddha has said that this is the only way. Just realise what is happening to you and just be with it. If it is very unpleasant, you can say: "I do not really feel O.K. but it's O.K. Just really feel it, just really say it.

The last point is something I consider as very important. It is that meditation is also learning to work with unpleasant experiences, as it does not mean having only positive and pleasant experiences, with which we are familiar. I like to repeat that such experiences are extremely valuable and useful, if you can really learn from them by seeing them as meditative objects rather than as something strange, unusual and so on. Please make such experiences the objects of meditation. Sometimes I consider such unpleasant experiences as more valuable than the so-called pleasant experiences, which do not create problems. So in that sense, such unpleasant experiences are valuable because you learn to handle them when they arise. This is exactly what happens in life. Suddenly when we find ourselves with an unexpected situation in life we use the same principle. So you see the importance of learning to handle such situations. If such events were to arise externally in meditation we learn to do the same. This is why in the Dhamma there is what is called internal and external. Here too it is the same principle, same solution.

QUESTION: I was told by somebody that it is very important for us to chose the right type of meditation. May I ask whether there are any schools of meditation which are evil and others which are not evil and how can we distinguish between these types of schools? What are the criteria for us to choose the right master?

GODWIN: I like to quote a very very inspiring text from the Buddha when he was asked the same question. People told the Buddha: "There are many teachers, there are many methods, we are confused. Please help us." The Buddha said: "Please do not accept anything just because it is said in the traditions, just because it is written down in the scriptures, just because it sounds logical and reasonable." This is the important point. Do not even accept when a teacher says something. Please do not accept what I am saying also. The Buddha said that only when you see it for yourself in your own experience only to accept any teaching. That is the right quality for you to practise. The teacher is ultimately your own experience, which should see whether the medicine is working or not. You have to see it for yourself. I am so amazed and inspired that it is a very radical teaching of the Buddha.

QUESTION: Can meditation cure insomnia?

GODWIN: I work with people who suffer from insomnia. This becomes interesting in meditation on loving kindness of which they speak of eleven benefits, three of which are related to sleep. With loving kindness, you sleep peacefully and wake up peacefully, you do not have unpleasant dreams, nightmares and so on. When I meet people who suffer from insomnia, what I tell them is to practise loving kindness before falling asleep and I have found that this generally helps in working with insomnia.

QUESTION: If we sleep very late, we feel very tired mentally and feel like going to sleep most of the time. In that situation, when tiredness is so overwhelming, is it right that we should not force ourselves to continue with the sitting and just go to sleep?

GODWIN: What I would suggest is that when you wake up and you find that you have not had enough sleep and you really want to meditate, what can be attempted is not to do sitting meditation straightaway, but to do some *yoga* exercises where you try to wake up physically and mentally through them.

Another suggestion is to take a very cold shower. This will also help you to wake up physically and mentally and then try to sit with your eyes open.

Dependent Origination

A Layperson's Perspective

By

Ron Wijewantha

The Wheel Publication No. 450/452

ACKNOWLEDGMENTS

This book would not have been possible but for the encouragement I received from many people.

Madawala Seelawimala Mahathera and Bhikkhu Bodhi Mahathera have been my primary sources of inspiration. The former, my mentor for encouraging me and providing me with access to his library and his deep knowledge of the suttas, and the latter by his continuing authorship of a vast number of tracts explaining important suttas in simple yet elegant and lucid language. To both of them I have much pleasure in dedicating this book.

My friend Sondra Jewel as well as Henepola Gunaratana Nayaka Thera (author of several books on meditation), Madawela Seelawimala Mahathera, and Prof Lily de Silva read through the script critically and pointed out inconsistencies and inaccuracies, and suggested appropriate corrections.

My three daughters, their spouses and my three grandsons helped me in many ways. So did Dr Udeni Balasuriya and Dr Jatal Mannapperuma. It is not possible to state in words how much I owe Sita, my dearest wife of nearly fifty years. She has given me much-needed encouragement at all times, and constantly prodded me to stay on track.

Mr A.G.S. Kariyawasam has enriched this presentation with careful editing.

Many people in the Sacramento-Davis-Woodland area participated in my *vipassanā* meditation programmes over the last seven years, and many others participated in the Friday meditation and discussion group at the West Sacramento Buddhist Temple. Their enthusiasm, comments and questions have in many ways acted as a catalyst to my comprehending many aspects of the Dhamma, which otherwise I had previously taken for granted.

This book is written in memory of my dear departed parents Arthur and Gertrude and our dear son Ajith. May their journey through *saṃsāra* be short and free of difficulties and dangers.

It is with much pleasure that I offer all those mentioned above my grateful thanks and the merit accruing from the writing of this book:

"The Gift of the Dhamma, exceeds all other gifts".

California, October 2002.
Ron W.

AUTHOR'S PREFACE

In this presentation, we shall proceed on a voyage of discovery. We shall first briefly discuss the fundamental philosophy and doctrine of the Buddha, and then try to discover ourselves. We shall see what we are really made of at the fundamental level. We shall then observe how the mind and body work in close association, and the pre-eminent position occupied by the mind in this process. Next we shall address the issue of our moral weaknesses and strengths, and discover how mindfulness can make us better members of society.

We shall discover the message underlying the doctrine of Dependent Origination or *Paṭiccasamuppāda* and then use such information as a tool to understanding that everything in this world is insubstantial, conditioned and that what we had understood as a permanent "I" is a mental illusion, and that everything in the universe is subject to decay, impermanence and suffering. This realization at the experiential level will encourage us to follow the Noble Eightfold Path as a way to escape from the *samsaric* round of births, deaths and rebirths.

At the end of each chapter, there will be some footnotes giving references to the texts as well as Pali words as they first appear in the texts. References to the Buddha's own words as quoted from the suttas have also been incorporated into the footnotes.

To make some of the explanations easily comprehensible, I have occasionally used examples from various scientific disciplines. Undoubtedly these could be replaced by even better examples as we continue expanding our scientific frontiers. Hopefully my attempts will suffice for the present.

Let us only keep in mind the timelessness of the Buddha-word.

The few pages on *vipassanā* meditation were based on the meditation practices of groups of participants and myself. They are certainly not meant to replace well-recognized meditation masters or the many excellent books on the practice. They are only for temporary guidance until a suitable meditation master is found. Some books on meditation are listed at the end of the book. However, meditation teachers and books can help only up to a point. Ultimately it is the readers them-selves who will have to do the work.

I make no claim to originality in what I have presented in this book. It is based on the discourses of the Buddha and the commentaries and essays thereon by various distinguished authors too numerous to enumerate. What is new is only the method of presentation which emphasizes the fact that escape from suffering and attainment of liberation is within our grasp, provided we make the attempt by comprehending the *dhamma* and gaining insight into the true nature of all conditioned phenomena through *vipassanā* meditation.

Finally, I take full responsibility for whatever omissions and errors there may be in the interpretation of the profound doctrine of Dependent Origination or *Paṭiccasamuppāda,* as well as in the rest of the presentation.

I wish you happy reading!

Ron W.

Namo tassa bhagavato arahato sammāsambuddhassa
(Homage to Him, the Exalted, the Worthy, the Fully Enlightened One!)

CHAPTER I

Preliminary

The *Paṭiccasamuppāda,*[1] also known as dependent origination and Causal Genesis, contains the central doctrine of the Buddha and complements His central teaching which is the Four Noble Truths. It is acknowledged by all to be a teaching that continues to be a challenge to students of Buddhism in their attempts at understanding it. However, a mere intellectual understanding of dependent origination is not enough. The truth contained therein must be directly grasped, personally experienced and intuitively penetrated if we are to reap the maximum benefits from it. In the text which follows, the term *paṭiccasamuppāda* and dependent origination will be used interchangeably.

There is yet another reason why we need to understand and comprehend it experientially, for it is eventually a direct way to the penetration and understanding of impermanence or inconstancy, unsatisfactoriness or distress, and non-self or no-soul—*anicca, dukkha* and *anattā*. It is with this combined understanding that we can achieve liberation which is the extinction of suffering and freedom from rebirth.

In the contemporary scene with so much interest in Buddhism in the West, it is perhaps opportune to offer a simple and an easily understandable book containing the basic tenets of Buddhism, plus an explanation of dependent origination and a method by which this knowledge could be used to achieve liberation. What is not called for is any previous knowledge of

---

1. *Paṭiccasamuppāda*: (Sanskrit: *pratītyasamutpāda*)–dependent origination; the twelve-factor cyclical process of causal conditioning affecting the perpetuation of *saṃsāric* existence which must be broken or transcended in order to make progress on the spiritual path to Nibbāna.

Buddhism. All that is required is an open, unprejudiced mind. This book will, therefore, lead the reader through an understanding of the doctrine of dependent origination to its intimate relationship with the Four Noble Truths and finally to insight into our very own selves through *vipassanā*[2] meditation.

This book is not meant for those who have a deep knowledge of the Dhamma,[3] whether they are erudite scholars or senior members of the Saṅgha[4] endowed with vast knowledge of this and other doctrines of the Buddha. It is meant only for those who are presently engaged in or intend to be vipassanā meditators, possessing perhaps only a modicum of knowledge of the Dhamma, but, having the enthusiasm to use whatever relevant information they acquire as an aid on their journey towards final liberation.

Nevertheless, a short list of books on dependent origination is provided at the end of the text for those whose interest in it is philosophical, intellectual or academic.

The Buddha

The Buddha to-be was born over 2500 years ago into the Sakyan Clan in a small state bordering India, which nestled in the Himalayan foothills in what we now call Nepal. He was heir to the Sakyan throne and lived a life of luxury in the capital city, Kapilavastu.

When he reached his late twenties, shielded by his father from life's natural phenomena of birth, decay, illness and death, the prince was suddenly exposed to four eye-opening experiences: A man weakened with age, a man decimated by sickness, decay and decrepitude, a corpse being carried on the shoulders of grieving relatives for cremation and an ascetic moving with measured step, downcast eyes and a serene countenance.

The prince thereafter became increasingly introspective and thoughts such as the following began to stir within him with increasing intensity: "Youth, the prime of life, ends in old age and

---

2. *Vipassanā* (*bhāvanā*): the systematic development of insight through the meditation method of observing the reality of oneself by observing sensations (feelings) within one's own body.
3. Dhamma: the teachings of the Buddha.
4. Saṅgha: the community of Buddhist monks and nuns.

man's senses fail him at a time when they are most needed. The hale and hearty lose their vigour and health when disease creeps in. Finally death comes perhaps suddenly and unexpectedly, and puts an end to this brief span of life. Surely there must be an escape from this unsatisfactoriness, from ageing and death.[5]

"Suppose that, being myself subject to ageing, sickness and death, to sorrow and defilement, I seek the unageing, unailing, deathless, sorrowless and undefiled state, the supreme security from bondage, Nibbāna."[6]

Accordingly, at the age of 29, on the day of the birth of his only child Rāhula, he left his kingdom, from home to homelessness, discarding the enchantment of the royal life, rejecting the joys and pleasures that most young people yearn for. He cut off his long hair with his sword, set aside his royal robes and putting on an ascetic's garb, retreated into sylvan solitude to seek a solution to those problems of life that had deeply stirred his mind - a solution, an answer to the riddle of life. A true, real and practical way out of unsatisfactoriness and suffering, leading to enlightenment[7] and Nibbāna.[8]

He then spent six long years in experimentation, self-mortification, reflection, contemplation and meditation. Although these efforts were ultimately helpful in formulating his doctrines in due course, they did not directly help in his quest for enlightenment and liberation. The *bodhisatta* (the name given to an aspirant before he attains enlightenment) now thought 'is there another way for me to strive towards enlightement?'

And he brought to mind an incident which took place just a short while back when a team of itinerant musicians and dancing girls had passed through the grove where he was in meditation. Unaware of his presence, they had played their instruments and one of the dancing girls had shouted out to the lute-player and asked him to play a tune, but warned him not to tune his lute too low nor too high. For, she said: 'good music can

---

5. Piyadassi Thera, *Spectrum of Buddhism*, 1991.
6. Bikkhu Bodhi, *The Buddha and His Dhamma*, 1999.
7. Enlightenment: "awakening,", achievement of supreme knowledge, and liberation. The enlightenment of a Buddha is called *sammā-sambodhi*- "perfect Enlightenment".
8. Nibbāna: (Sanskrit–*Nirvāṇa*): extinction, the ultimate reality, the unconditioned.

be made only when the lute is tuned to the correct pitch between these two extremes'. And here a lesson could be learnt, he thought.

"Self-mortification and self-indulgence are two extremes to be avoided."[9]

As a result, he decided then and there to adopt this middle way, one which balanced care of the body with sufficient time available for contemplation and deep investigation. One day when his physical strength had returned, he approached a lovely spot in Uruvelā by the banks of the river Neranjarā. There he prepared, underneath a Ficus tree (later to be called the Bodhi Tree - *ficus religiosa*), a seat of newly cut *kusa*-grass donated by a grass-cutter. He then sat on it cross-legged, making a firm resolution that he would not rise up until he had won the goal of liberation, Nibbāna.

As night descended he entered into deeper and deeper stages of meditation until his mind was perfectly calm and composed. In the first watch of the night there unfolded before his inner vision his experiences in many past births, extending over many cosmic eons; in the middle watch of the night he developed the "divine eye" by which he could see beings passing away and taking rebirth in accordance with their *kamma*[10] and in the last watch he directed his concentration and focused his mind to the penetration of the deeper truths of existence. Through this he gained insight into the *paṭiccasamuppāda* or the chain of conditioned existence encompassing the most basic laws of reality and thereby removed from his mind even the subtlest veil of ignorance. When dawn broke, He had achieved what he had been striving for. He had "awakened" from ignorance. He had reached Enlightenment. He was a Buddha who had in this very life attained the Deathless, the Unconditioned which is Nibbāna.[11]

He was now ready to share his discoveries, his Dhamma with one and all. Towards this end, he formulated his discoveries into four simple laws, which he called the Four Noble Truths, truths which, when fully and properly comprehended, ennobled

---

9. Wijewantha Ron, *The Life and Message of the Buddha*, 1990.

10. Kamma: Action, specifically an action performed by oneself that will have a repercussion in one's future.

11. Bhikkhu Bodhi, *The Noble Eightfold Path*, (B.P.S), 1994.

the practitioner by his realizing the goal of Nibbāna. (Hence the word 'Noble' which precedes the word 'Truths').

The Four Noble Truths

1. *Dukkha* - Suffering or unsatisfactoriness or distress
2. *Dukkha-samudaya* - The origin of suffering
3. *Dukkha-nirodha (Nibbāna)* - The cessation of suffering and
4. *Dukkha-nirodha-gaminī-paṭipadā*–The way to the end of unsatisfactoriness, which is the Noble Eightfold Path.

Thereafter, in many a sermon during his forty-five year ministry, he gave prominence to the Four Noble Truths.

> "It is because we have not understood, not penetrated the Four Noble Truths that we have wandered so long in this beginingless *saṃsāra*.[12] Those who fully penetrate the truths are freed from *saṃsāra* (D.ii, 90).
>
> To penetrate and comprehend these Four Noble Truths we need more information about them.

Suffering *(dukkha)*. *Dukkha* is the first Noble Truth. Although *dukkha* has often been translated as 'suffering', the words that encapsulate its meaning best are: unsatisfactoriness, distress or discomfort. The Buddha says that there is unsatisfactoriness in the world.

The 'world' in this case refers to us, the living beings, for the Buddha has often said that this fathom-long body of ours is the world. (A fathom in the ancient world was the distance from the tip of the middle finger of one outstretched hand to the tip of the middle finger on the other outstretched hand. -this incidentally is the height of that person.–Mariners consider a fathom as 6 feet in length).

The Buddha would often use the word 'world' when referring to what we recognize to be a person, as can be seen in the following incident where a novice monk appears confused and blurts out:

Novice monk: "The world, the world *(loka)*" it is said. "To what extent does the word 'world' apply"?

---

12. *Saṃsāra*: the conditioned; it is the round of existence of rebirths which is transcended with the realization of enlightenment.

The Buddha : "It disintegrates (*lujjati*) and therefore it is called the "world". Now, what disintegrates? The eye disintegrates. So also for ear, nose, tongue, body, consciousness and their corresponding sense data... It disintegrates, therefore it is called the 'world'". (S.xxxv.82).

All sentient beings live a life full of suffering, both physical and mental, and it is the mental aspect which can bring us most harm. For, in addition to our becoming emotionally upset when things go wrong, we can also, by reacting negatively, accumulate a lot of negative *kamma.*

Origin of Suffering *(dukkha-samudaya)* is the second Noble Truth. The origin of suffering is craving rooted in ignorance. Craving (*taṇhā)* can have a deeper meaning too. It is a combination of greed and selfishness rolled into one. When craving becomes intense it changes to clinging, *(upādāna).* Craving can be of various types. Sensual craving (*kāma-taṇhā*), craving for life (*bhava-taṇhā*) and even craving for the extinction of life *(vibhava-taṇhā).*

Cessation of suffering *(dukkha-nirodha)* or Nibbāna: Nibbāna is the third Noble Truth. It is the unconditioned, the undefinable, the ultimate truth, the steady state, the inactivated state where there is no more conditioning. It is timeless, without a past and without a future, the changeless state free from all causation, the transcendental condition.

The fourth Noble Truth is the path leading to the end of suffering (*dukkha-nirodha-gāminī paṭipadā).* It is the path, the way to the end of unsatisfactoriness. It is called the Noble Eightfold Path, which if followed will lead to Nibbāna. This path is beautifully summarized by the Buddha when answering a deity[13]: "Tangled within, tangled without, mankind is entangled in a tangle. I ask this question, Gotama: Who disentangles this tangle?" asked a deity.

"When the wise man established in virtue (*sīla*) develops concentration (*samādhi*) and wisdom (*paññā*), then as a *bhikkhu* ardent and prudent, he disentangles this tangle" replied the Buddha. (S.i.13).

As it can be seen from the above, the Buddha shows that these eight steps of the Path can be arranged within three

---

13. Deity *(deva*): a heavenly being.

groups. Virtue or morality (*sīla*), concentration (*samādhi)* and wisdom *(paññā)*.

The eight factors of the Noble Eightfold Path are:

1.	Skilful Understanding	wisdom or *paññā* group
2.	Skilful Thought	
3.	Skilful Speech	virtue/morality or *sīla* group
4.	Skilful Action	
5.	Skilful Livelihood	
6.	Skilful Effort	concentration or *samādhi* group
7.	Skilful Mindfulness	
8.	Skilful Concentration	

This eight-fold path is called the Middle Path as it avoids the two extremes of self-indulgence and self-mortification. It must be borne in mind that, although as a training programme one is expected to graduate from virtue/morality to concentration and then to wisdom, in actual practice they overlap or they are interdependent and inter-related, and the further we progress, the more interrelated they appear to be.

'Concentration (meditation), O Monks, supported by virtue brings much fruit, brings much advantage. Wisdom supported by concentration brings much fruit, much advantage. The mind supported by wisdom (right understanding) is wholly and entirely freed from the intoxication of sense desires, from becoming, wrong views and ignorance' (D.16).

It is useful at this stage to briefly explain the eight factors that make up the Noble Eightfold Path. We shall start with morality/virtue (*sīla).*

Morality or *sīla* group

Skilful Speech: Along with skilful speech we must also look at non-skilful speech such as slander, gossip, idle chatter, false and harsh speech. Once we remove these impurities, we are left with skilful speech.

Skilful physical action: Non-skilful physical action is when we hurt, wound or kill sentient beings. So also if we steal, borrow with no intention of returning, participates in sexual misconduct and use intoxicants. What will then remain is purity of action.

Intoxicants include, in the broader sense, various hallucinating drugs and any substance which causes people to lose their sense of proportion or their sense of values. A person could in fact become unskilful when intoxicated with power because of the position the person holds.

Skilful livelihood: It is important that we should abstain from earning a living by means which bring harm to others, such as dealing in intoxicants, fire-arms, running gambling dens, owning shares in casinos, prostitution and so on.

A good criterion for what is unskilful livelihood is motivation. If one's motivation is impure, then that living is unskilful. For example, if a practising physician were to wish that people in his community be frequently struck down by epidemics, necessitating medical intervention so that he could make more money, then his motivation is bad. Similarly, if a merchant were to wish for scarcities and non-availability of essential food items so that he could raise the price of his goods arbitrarily, then his motivation too is bad, and his livelihood is unskilful.

How can both these persons conform to skilful livelihood? One suggestion is that both of them change their attitudes and develop *mettā* or universal kindness first towards themselves and then towards the rest of the members of the community. Another is to set aside, in the case of the physician, perhaps a half day each week for treatment of disadvantaged members of the community and, in the case of the merchant, a certain percentage of his monthly profits for charity or to subsidize purchases made by disadvantaged persons in the neighbourhood.

2. The concentration or *samādhi* group

The first step is **skilful effort**. In our daily life, we are frequently told to take physical exercise when we feel weak. It is the same with the mind. While it is yet untamed, it requires plenty of good exercise. We could therefore do a number of things: First we must look at the mind and see whether it has any defilements.

i. If we see any defilement, (here we have to be honest with ourselves about it) we need to get rid of them.
ii. If there are no visible defilements, then we need to guard the sense-doors comprising the eyes, ears, nose, tongue, body and mind (thoughts).

iii. If we see virtues, try to retain and multiply them.

vi. If we see no good qualities, develop and cultivate them by keeping the sense-doors open, and by means of *vipassanā* meditation (see chapter 6).

Some of the advice, which the Buddha gave young novice Rāhula, his erstwhile son, on the above is relevant here. He said:

> "Develop the meditation on *mettā* (loving-kindness) Rāhula, for, Rāhula, by developing *mettā*, ill-will is abandoned.
>
> "Develop the meditation on *karuṇā* (compassion), Rāhula, for, Rāhula, by developing compassion, cruelty is abandoned.
>
> "Develop the meditation on *muditā* (appreciative joy), Rāhula, for, Rāhula, by developing muditā, aversion is abandoned.
>
> "Develop the meditation on *upekkhā* (equanimity), Rāhula, for, Rāhula, by developing equanimity, Rāhula, hatred is abandoned.
>
> "Develop the meditation on *asubha* (impurity), Rāhula. for, Rāhula, by meditating on impurity, lust is abandoned.
>
> "Develop the meditation on *anicca* (impermanence) Rāhula, for, Rāhula, by meditating on impermanence, pride of self is abandoned" (M.61).

The next is **skilful mindfulness**. This means present awareness, awareness of the present moment, not the moment before or the moment to come. This is what we do when we focus on the breath during *vipassanā* meditation. Awareness of everything happening as it is. Observing the truth as it is, nature as it is, and all sensations from the grossest to the most subtle. It is seeing reality, not imagination, and when observing, not reacting to gross sensations, but just observing without identifying any of them as belonging to us.

Skilful concentration is the third step in this group. During *vipassanā* meditation, we learn from experience that we can concentrate on both good and bad thoughts! It is unskilful when we concentrate on the past or on the future. These thoughts are counter-productive. They lead to illusions, delusions and confusion. It is skilful concentration that purifies the mind, freeing it from aversion and attachment. It is continuous awareness of reality within the framework of the body.

Wisdom or *paññā* group

What is wisdom (*paññā*)? Before discussing this, let us keep in mind that the morality (*sīla*) group comprises the first three steps on our journey along the path to liberation. It also helps us to avoid negative actions, which harm both others and ourselves.

Concentration (*samādhi*) group

Equally important is the second group of three steps: the concentration (*samādhi*) group, which helps to develop our mastery over the mind and lays the foundation for developing *paññā* or wisdom. It is wisdom (*paññā*) that is absolutely necessary to attain the liberation of Nibbāna.

With the help of the first two groups, we can remove some impurities on the surface of the mind. However, while doing so, instead of getting rid of gross negativities, we actually push most of them into the unconscious or deeper level of the mind where they are called *anusaya*. It is here that they accumulate like dormant volcanoes, ready to erupt when given the proper time and circumstance. These volcanoes are the old stock of defilements called 'klesha'. It is by developing wisdom and insight[14] that we can ultimately remove even the last traces of impurities from the mind. This allows us to stop generating negative *kamma*.

Wisdom or paññā is of three types called *sutamaya-paññā*, *cintāmaya-paññā* and *bhāvanāmaya-paññā*. They are progressive steps:

Sutamaya-paññā is wisdom from reading appropriate texts, listening to discourses and participating in discussions. But this is other people's learning! We therefore have to be careful that we do not accept everything we hear or read, for we can become

---

14. Insight: is the intuitive exposing of the truth of impermanency, suffering and impersonal nature of all corporeal and mental phenomena of existence. It is by *vipassanā* meditation that this *vipassanā-paññā* (insight-wisdom) is developed and revealed.

conditioned and turn to blind faith. The Buddha has advised against blind faith.

Advising the Kālāma people He said. "... Now look you Kālāmas, do not be led by reports, or tradition, or hearsay. Be not be led by the authority of religious texts, nor by mere logic or inference, nor by considering appearances, nor by the delight of speculative opinions, nor by seeming possibilities, nor by the idea: 'this is our teacher'. But, O Kālāmas, when you know for yourselves that certain things are unwholesome and wrong and bad, then give them up...And when you know yourselves that certain things are wholesome and good, then accept them and follow them"(A. Vol, 1.p189).

Cintāmaya-paññā is what we conclude by analysis, contemplation and reflection on what we have heard. It is wisdom acquired through one's own thinking but based on what one had heard. And here it is appropriate also to keep in mind the four reliances:

> "Do not rely on individuals, rely on the teachings
> Do not rely on the words, rely on the meanings
> Do not rely on the adapted meanings, rely on the ultimate meanings
> Donotrelyonintellectualknowledge,relyonwisdom"[15].

The third is ***bhāvanāmaya-paññā***. This is insight or experiential wisdom that can lead us to liberation, to Nibbāna. However, we should remember that the first two have played, and will always continue to play a very important role, for it is these two concepts that directed us to the third. The three factors are like a three-legged stool. Take away one leg and the stool will collapse. It is wisdom through meditation that helps us to loosen all the knots that we have been tying every day of our lives, and it helps us to eradicate all impurities, particularly the three root causes of our wandering in *saṃsāra* - *lobha, dosa,* and *moha* (greed, hatred and delusion) and thus to open our minds to direct wisdom.

Let us look deeper into the two specific steps of the Path within the Wisdom group.

The first is **skilful thought**. Our thought processes are most of the time coloured by illusions, delusions, confusion and wrong

---

15. Dalai Lama, *A Flash of Lightning in the Dark*, 1994.

thoughts. This is called *ayoniso manasikāra*. We need to change it to thinking in the proper way called *yoniso manasikāra*. We slowly begin to get an inkling of the truth by removing defilements first at the surface level of the mind. By practising *vipassanā* meditation we start noticing bad and impure thoughts as they arise and surface. But, by simply observing them with equanimity and letting them go, they can be eradicated. Now our thought patterns change to thinking in the proper way and we are ready to go to the final step of the path, namely skilful understanding.

Skilful understanding: Proper thoughts now start appearing. This is possible because we can now look deeper into the unconscious layers of the mind. By thinking in the proper way, we start seeing reality as it is, without illusions, delusions and confusion. We see nature with its true characteristics, as it really is. We are now able to progress through the three types of wisdom discussed above.

We see the 'bigger-picture' now: that there is no real 'I', but merely processes which come to be and die, that all beings are inter-connected and subject to conditionality, and that the underlying theme is the need for harmony, kindness, and compassion if one is to progress to wisdom and ultimately take the first transcendental[16] step to Nibbāna.

We conclude the discussion of the Path with the Buddha's own words:

> From skilful understanding proceeds purity of thought
> From skilful thought proceeds purity of speech
> From skilful speech proceeds purity of action
> From skilful action proceeds purity of livelihood
> From skilful livelihood proceeds purity of effort
> From skilful effort proceeds purity of awareness
> From skilful awareness proceeds purity of concentration
> From skilful concentration proceeds purity of wisdom
> From skilful wisdom proceeds liberation.

---

16. Transcendental/Supramundane: That which is beyond even the concept of reality,–that which transcends all thoughts.

CHAPTER II

Prerequisites to Understanding the Paṭiccasamuppāda

The Buddha, while unequivocally stating that the way to liberation is to follow the Noble Eightfold Path, has also provided us with complementary pathways to help us reach this same goal.

Thus on a certain occasion when visiting the Kuru[17] people He expounded the Mahā Satipaṭṭhāna Sutta[18]. In the introduction itself he has said, "This is the only way *(ekāyano maggo)* for the purification of beings, for the surmounting of sorrow and lamentation, for the abandoning of pain and grief, for reaching the Right Path and realizing Nibbāna, that is the setting up of the Four-fold Mindfulness" (M.10).

On another occasion He has stated, "He who sees dependent origination sees the Dhamma, He who sees the Dhamma sees the dependent origination" (M.28).

The purpose of this book is to explore the latter, viz., dependent origination.

We cannot liberate ourselves from suffering (*dukkha*) merely by the intellectual understanding of this profound doctrine. On the contrary, we shall see as we proceed that we can truly understand it only by total immersion in this doctrine. This understanding is progressively structured. The first level of knowledge is by reading, listening and studying the suttas[19] and is called *sutamaya-paññā*. This is followed by analytical knowledge known as *cintāmaya-paññā*. We can then carry it to the final level of knowledge, which is experiential wisdom known as

---

17. Kuru: The people inhabiting a market town called Kammās-sadhamma.

18. Mahā Satipaṭṭhāna Sutta: A discourse on the four-fold mindfulness, containing detailed instructions on insight meditation and the assurance that following and practising the instructions will lead to liberation from suffering

19. Suttas: The discourses of the Buddha.

bhāvanāmaya-paññā and reached only by insight (*vipassanā*) meditation. It is at this stage that we achieve wisdom and insight into the interconnectedness of all phenomena, of their impermanence and distress, leading finally to our realization of the Truth. Thus, by comprehending experientially this most difficult doctrine, the gateway to at least the first stage of liberation, that of Stream-winner (*sotāpanna*), will be opened to us.

It is essential that those who start on this journey equip themselves first with a factual working knowledge of the Dhamma so that the journey of discovery becomes easier. Such 'knowledge' will be of immense benefit in understanding each of the links or factors comprising the *paṭiccasamuppāda*..

The subjects, which we shall presently study, are:

1. Saṃsāra.
2. Nibbāna.
3. The 5 Aggregates comprising mind and matter.
4. Kamma and Rebecoming (Rebirth).
5. The three universal characteristics of all conditioned things,–impermanence (*anicca*), suffering (*dukkha*) and non-self (*anattā*).
6. Conditionality
7. The four steps to liberation which are that of stream-winner (*sotāpanna*), once-returner (*sakadāgāmi*), non-returner (*anāgami*) and finally the fully liberated person, the arahat.

Saṃsāra

Saṃsāra is the process of birth and death without beginning. *Saṃsāra* means 'the round of rebirth' or more literally 'the wandering around' continuously. According to classical terminology, it could be said that *saṃsāra* extends over manifold worlds (*loka*) and involves rebirth into various planes of existence, based on one's *kamma*. The Buddha has said: "Bhikkhus, this *saṃsāra* is without conceivable beginning. No first point is discerned of beings roaming and wandering (in *saṃsāra*), bonded by ignorance and fettered by craving..." (S. II, 178, 182). Our aim should therefore be to terminate this cycle of birth, death and rebirth

In Buddhist texts, the word used to denote the cosmos or universe is 'loka'. Its uses are as numerous as the English word 'world'. The early Buddhist texts do not state that the major world-systems are all there in the universe. The question of whether the world is finite or infinite is left unanswered. The standpoint of early Buddhism was to state that the universe was "without a known beginning" and that it is 'conditioned'.

As for the end, this will occur only at the end of an epoch or an aeon, called *kappa*. Several similes are given to illustrate what an immensely long period an aeon is. One such passage reads as follows: 'Suppose there was a city of iron walls one *yojana* in length, one in width and one high, filled with mustard seeds, from which a man were to take out at the end of every hundred years a mustard seed. That pile of mustard seeds would in this way be sooner done away with than an aeon, so very long is an aeon. And of aeons thus long, more than one has passed, more than a hundred, more than a thousand, more than a hundred thousand' (S.11.182).

Nibbāna

We have discussed Buddhist cosmology briefly in order to understand *saṃsāra* better,–the unbroken and continuing process of rebirth which can occur in any plane of existence in the cosmos, depending on one's performance. All such rebirths, it is important to note, are "conditioned".

There is on the other hand a blissful state of complete spiritual freedom. This is the state of Nibbāna. It is an unconditioned state, a peaceful state, and a state totally free of greed, aversion and delusion. It is a state, which once reached, prevents the person from returning to the round of *saṃsāra*.

But to arrive at this state of Nibbāna, one has to follow a path of purification. Only a supremely enlightened being, namely a Buddha, can show such a path to us. Our aim should be to realize the bliss of Nibbāna by following his instructions. These instructions were laid down by him in his very first discourse, and are contained in the Fourth Noble Truth as the Noble Eightfold Path.

It is a path, which leads to emancipation and complete freedom from the conditioned. The Buddha assures us that by following this path with mindfulness, wisdom and proper application Nibbāna can be realized here and now.

The Five Aggregates[20]

At the conventional level we know that we have a body and a mind, but at the supra-mundane or transcendental level[21] we can go deeper and redefine them. The Buddha found that by penetratingly examining his own nature, he could comprehend the reality within himself.

He realized that every sentient being is a composite of five processes, which he called aggregates (*khandha*) four of which are mental, which He called *nāma*, and the other physical, called *rūpa*. He found that mentality and materiality always work in unison. There is mutual interaction between the physical base and mental activity. They are interconnected and have a cause and effect relationship. However, at the same time the Buddha has emphasized that it is the mind that is foremost:

> 'Mind is the forerunner of all phenomena.
> Mind is chief, everything is mind-made.
> If one speaks or acts with an impure mind,
> Suffering follows one, as the cartwheels
> follow the foot of the draught-animal.'
>
> ... If one speaks or acts with a pure mind,
> ... Happiness follows one as a shadow that never leaves.

(Dhp 1-2).

What is this thing known as the mind or *nāma*? The Buddha has observed that the four aggregates comprising the mind were fundamentally nothing but four processes in constant interaction with one another. They are:

Sensation or feeling *(vedanā)*
Perception, sense-impressions and concepts *(saññā)*

---

20. For an elegant, simple essay on this subject, read "*The selfmade private prison*" by Prof Lily de Silva, BPS, Bodhi Leaves, No.120.

21. Supra-mundane: transcendental *(lokuttara)*. This is a term for the 4 paths and fruits of *sotāpanna, sakadāgāmi, anāgāmi and arahat*. As opposed to this is 'mundane, (*lokiya*)', which refers to all states of consciousness arising in the 'worldling'. Mundane thoughts can also arise in the Noble Ones but not *vice-versa*. When mundane thoughts arise in the Noble Ones such thoughts are not associated with the supra-mundane paths and fruition. (Nyanatiloka, *Buddhist Dictionary*).

Reaction/ mental formations, cognative activities *(saṅkhāra)*
Consciousness *(viññāṇa)*

The first three of the aforementioned mental processes are considered as concomitants or adjuncts of the fourth, consciousness, which is defined as the primary factor of mental life. To picture the way these four processes interact and work together, we have to look at familiar examples. Consider our own endocrine system. It is a group of specialized organs and body tissues that produce, store and secrete chemical substances known as hormones. As the body's chemical messengers, hormones transfer information and instructions from one set of cells to another. Because of the hormones they produce, endocrine organs have a great deal of influence over the body.

These organs are sometimes called ductless glands because they have no ducts connecting them to specific body parts. The hormones they secrete are released directly into the bloodstream. The primary glands that make up the human endocrine system are the hypothalamus, pituitary, parathyroid, adrenal, pineal and the reproductive glands. The pancreas, an organ often associated with the digestive system, is also considered part of the endocrine system.

The hypothalamus, found deep within the brain, directly controls the pituitary gland. It is often described as the coordinator or the conductor of the endocrine system. When information reaching the brain indicates that changes are needed somewhere in the body, nerve cells in the hypothalamus secrete chemicals that either stimulate or suppress hormone secretions from the pituitary gland. Acting as liaison between the brain and the pituitary gland, the hypothalamus is the primary link between the endocrine and the nervous systems.

Now consider a musical sextet or a string quartet. Here too, the individual musicians have to be coordinated under a single leader, a conductor or lead-player in order to produce harmonious music. As in these examples, our mind requires a lead-player, and it is consciousness which plays this part. It is also consciousness which ensures the continuity of the individual through the duration of a single life. When a person is in an inactive state, like when he is sleeping or unconscious, this life-continuum consciousness lies dormant in what is called a *bhavaṅga* state. But when a sense organ makes contact (*phassa*) with a sense object, then the appropriate sense consciousness is activated as shown below, producing the desired effect:

contact	*phassa*
consciousness	*viññāṇa*
sensation	*vedanā*
perception	*saññā*
conceiving	*vitakka*
differentiation	*papañca*
reaction	*saṅkhāra*

One mind-moment

It will be noted from the above that in addition to the functioning of the four aggregates comprising the mind, two other activities of thought-perception and differentiation take place immediately after perception and before reaction or mental formation(*saṅkhāra*). In the Madhupiṇḍika sutta (M. 18), the complete process is described as follows: "...Dependent on the eye and forms, eye-consciousness arises. The meeting of the three is contact. With contact as a condition there is feeling. What one feels, that one perceives. What one perceives, that one thinks about. What one thinks about, that one mentally proliferates. What one has mentally proliferated as the source, perceptions and notions tinged by mental proliferation beset a man with respect to past, future and present forms cognizable through the eye. ..."

One mind-moment takes only a nano-second and is immediately followed by another and still another. At a maximum, seventeen mind-moments are needed for a single thought process to be completed. It is only after numerous mind-moments that *saṅkhāras* or mental formations result in fruition as a reaction. Hence it would not be incorrect to say that there is always consciousness to monitor everything that is happening, while triggering the other three aggregates to produce the desired effect. Thus, from the moment a person is born upto his last breath or mind-moment, these four processes occur continuously.

Perhaps we can better understand how the four aggregates of the mind work by means of a practical example. Suppose a man opens his front door, looks outside and sees an object moving in his direction.

i. He is first aware in a general way of an approaching object. This is consciousness (*viññāṇa).*
ii. He then, taking past experiences of the approaching person into consideration, will either like or dislike the person. But if that person is unknown to him, he will remain neutral about liking or disliking. This is sensation (*vedanā).*
iii. He then recognizes the object/subject (by instantaneously comparing it against previous experiences). This is perception (*saññā).*
iv. Immediately thereafter, he will react (*cetanā*) with either pleasure or displeasure, or with no reaction (indifference), which will be followed by appropriate action. This is reaction (*saṅkhāra).*

Once this mind-moment is completed, it will be followed immediately by the next mind-moment and then another and so on. This is the pattern, which will be followed throughout life, except when one is asleep or rendered unconscious.

Hence, human experience can be considered to be a rapid sequence of mind-moments, which occur, in a fixed sequence of sensation, perception and reaction within the framework of consciousness. When the sensation phases become concentrated through this repetition of mind-moments, the reaction takes on a physical or a mental aspect. For instance, in the above example, the man may welcome the approaching person with kind words or, if he dislikes the person, the welcome could be a negative one. Finally, if the approaching person is a stranger, the welcome could be indifferent, such as 'may I help you?'

Citta: A single act of consciousness is called a *citta.* It is made up of many components. The principal factor in each *citta* is consciousness itself. Its function is the basic experiencing of the object and is itself given the name of the whole act viz, *citta.* Besides the aggregates themselves, there are the 'mental factors' such as emotions, which influence and give the *cittas* their distinctive character. The most important of these are the acts of consciousness (*cittas*) influenced by the mind when it is subject to the three defilements of greed, aversion and delusion, or to their opposites-non-greed, non-hate and non-delusion.

We have so far examined the way in which a thought-process operates by drawing on the *suttas.* Now, with this knowledge of how the mind works, we could give some more consideration by studying it in more detail, as explained in the Abhidhamma Piṭaka.[22]

Abhidhamma and consciousness

Our consciousness receives signals all the time from within ourselves or from outside. The functional continuity of the consciousness of a person, as stated before, is ensured throughout that person's existence in this life from conception to death. This consciousness is called *bhavaṅga*. Whenever an object impinges on any sense-door, this *bhavaṅga*-consciousness is arrested, thus setting the stage for the cognitive and related processes such as perception, sensation and reaction to perform their respective functions. This is followed by volition *(saṅkhāra)*. This is the stage, which is most important from an ethical point of view, since it is here that wholesome and unwholesome thoughts *(cetanā)*, which are kammically effective, occur. This latter stage is given the name *javana* in the Abhidhamma.

It must be remembered that *bhavaṅga* supervenes immediately after each cognitive process until the next cognitive process arises. "Arising and persisting at every moment during the passive phase of consciousness, the *bhavaṅga* flows on like a stream, without remaining static even for two consecutive moments."[23] The thought-processes that interrupt *bhavaṅga* - consciousness operate through the five sense doors (eyes, ears, nose, tongue, body and the mind).

Reaction/cognitive activities *(saṅkhāra)*

We have been examining *saṅkhāra,* the fourth aggregate, only as far as it denotes all those factors which accompany conscious

---

22. Abhidhamma-piṭaka. The third 'basket' or 'piṭaka' comprising the collection of higher teachings, i.e. the systematic philosophical exegesis of the Dhamma (the Buddha's doctrine). The first 'piṭaka' or basket is the Sutta *piṭaka* (the collection of the discourses of the Buddha); the second *piṭaka* or 'basket' is the *Vinaya-piṭaka* (rules of discipline for monks and nuns). The name given to all three of the above is 'Tripiṭaka'—literally, "' three baskets".

23. *Comprehensive Manual of Abhidhamma,* Bhikkhu Bodhi Ed., BPS, 1999.

volitional activities. There are, however, other definitions of *saṅkhāra* as well, but they are not directly relevant to understanding how the four aggregates of mentality work together. We need to remember that all four of the above psychological states, namely consciousness, perception, sensation and reaction are causally conditioned by various factors such as one's physical and social environment, by the physiological state of the body, our upbringing and previous experiences and so on. A gradual development of awareness (*sati*) by *vipassanā* meditation reveals to us these intricate relationships. "It also reveals the fact that the mind itself dissolves into a stream of *cittas* flashing in and out of being, moment to moment, coming from nowhere, yet continuing in sequence without pause"[24]

Lets us also remember that a human being's stream of consciousness has a conscious and an unconscious component. Our conscious mental activity gets into the 'unconscious' and accumulates in it, continuing to influence our conscious behaviour. In the unconscious state are the latent tendencies of the mind called the *anusayas.* These are the tendencies to satisfy our desires, our egoistic impulses or aggression, as well as the beliefs we cling to in the unconscious mind, such as doubt, wrong views, conceit, ignorance, arrogance and pride, just to name a few. These are factors, which need to be eradicated during our journey through *saṃsāra* .

Matter

Matter is all of the visible components that make up our body (*rūpa*), and at the ultimate level consists merely of four primary elements (*dhātu*). It is very difficult to define *dhātu* in modern terms and language, for they mean much more than what we know as elements of the periodic table and as 'particles' of current particle-science). For, in its original form, this word also conveys its characteristics.

They are:

Solid (*paṭhavi*) element.
Liquid (*āpo*) element.
Heat/fire (*tejo*) element.
Air/wind (*vāyo*) element.

---

24. *Comprehensive Manual of Abhidhamma*, Bhikkhu Bodhi ed., BPS, 1999.

We can understand them better by looking at their characteristics:

Solidity for the solid element.
Fluidity and cohesion for the liquid element.
Heat or caloricity for the heat element.
Movement for the wind/air element.

These four primary elements manifest themselves in the human body in various permutations and combinations. But at the fundamental level they are sub-atomic particles in constant motion, arising and vanishing in unimaginably rapid succession. Ultimately matter is nothing but crystallization of energy, thus giving them an apparent false reality. Our skeletal structure has a preponderance of the solid element with small quantities of the others. Our circulatory and lymphatic systems are filled mainly with the fluid element, and the lungs and respiratory system are filled with the air element. Digestion and body warmth is performed by caloricity, and we can move about by a combination of the air and the fluid element.

In addition to the above, combinations of these primary elements are considered to have various types of secondary qualities such as colour, odour, taste and nutritive essence. The five aggregates, which we discussed above, cover the entire range of experience of a sentient being. Form covers all physical phenomena, both within one's body and without. The four remaining categories of mentality cover all mental events: feelings are characterized by pleasure, pain and neither pleasure nor pain, regardless of whether they are based on physical or mental sensations. Perception denotes the mental act of applying labels or names to physical or mental events. Mental formations cover the verbal and mental processes of concocting thoughts, questions, urges or intentions in the mind, while consciousness covers the act of consciousness at any of the six sense-doors: the eyes, ears, nose, tongue, body and intellect (mind).

It is by understanding the complex inter-relationships among these aggregates that one is led into the area of dependent origination. As one's understanding grows more sensitive, the point is driven home that all clinging to these phenomena should be abandoned.

Kamma and Rebirth

Let us take kamma first. It is the law that every action has some effect, some reaction.

We may have experienced and also realized that our actions affect the quality of our mind.

Each of our actions has an impact on our mind, and thus the quality of our mind has a direct influence on the quality of our life. The teaching of kamma, however, goes much deeper and gives a more thorough explanation of the whole process. Society is usually accustomed to measure the quality of actions predominantly by the impact they have on its surroundings. In the teaching of kamma we instead focus *on the effects our various actions have on ourselves.*

All actions performed through the three doors of body, speech and mind are kamma. More precisely, kamma is the volition, the intention—*cetanā*—behind the action. These *kammic* volitions have the inherent potential to bring about a corresponding type of result, a *kamma-vipāka*. Volitions have often been compared to seeds and the results they bring forth as the fruits. By kamma we mean the whole accumulated potential of all present and past volitions which have not yet produced their results.

The teaching of kamma is somewhat similar to the physical law of the preservation of matter and energy. Kamma might be considered an example of this law–the conservation of the positive and negative energy, which we generate, from the visible realm of matter into the more subtle dimensions of the mind. But we need to emphasize that while the physical law of action and reaction is mechanical, the law of *kamma* and *kamma-vipāka* rests on volition. For, each of our volitions leaves behind an imprint or dormant bud of energy in our minds, and when these *kammic* impulses ripen under suitable external conditions, they will bring forth some result.

Let us remember that mental processes or mental impulses are very significant. Think of the minds, which created the microchip or sent man to the moon. Truly the mind, as the Buddha said, is the forerunner of all actions. To impress on us the dynamics of kamma, let us bring to mind Newton's third law of motion; "For every action there is an equal and opposite reaction". The law of kamma is an impersonal energy dynamic, for when its effects are personalized or, in other words, experienced from the point of view of the personality, they are experienced as a reversal in that direction, *a coming back to the intender of the energy of his or her intention.* Those who can recollect playing with a 'Newton's cradle' will remember this vividly.[25]

In these examples the person who develops hatred for others experiences hatred from others. On the other hand, the person who develops love for others experiences love from others and so forth. In other words, *you receive from the world what you give to the world; what goes around comes around!* However, we should always keep in mind that "although we used physical energy systems for ease of comprehension of kamma and *kamma-vipāka*, there is a distinct difference between the law of *kamma* and the law of physics. In the law of kamma, volition plays a critical role, and in the absence of greed, hatred and delusion, *kammic* energy is not generated. Further, with the attainment of Arahatship, no more *kammic* energy is generated for this very reason."[26]

We should remember that kamma is an immanent law, which governs the balancing of energy in our continuing existence. It is impersonal, yet a law, and the balancing of energy does not always occur within the span of a single lifetime. It is not a simple tit-for-tat kind of law. Therefore, without some knowledge of rebirth along with that of kamma, it is not possible for a person to understand the significance or the meaning of events in his or her own life.

Let us take a hypothetical example: Classmates of a student give him a derogatory nickname. He is quite unhappy and feels frustrated, and he does not understand that this experience is simply bringing to completion an impersonal process. The wrongs other people do to him are the direct result of one's own past actions, both in previous as well as in this present existence. But the student is not aware of this. Consequently, he could become, for example, angry or vengeful or depressed, or withdraw into sorrow to suffer in silence. Each of these responses creates kamma, another imbalance of energy, which in turn must be balanced sometime in the future. In this way, one *kammic* debt has been paid, so to speak. Unfortunately, without his realizing it,

---

25. *Ibid.*
26. H. Gunaratana Mahāthera, in a personal communication.

the student has created another *kammic* debt! (Incidentally, so have his tormentors).

Let us now look at the ethical side. Volitional actions may be 'morally wholesome', 'morally unwholesome', or morally neutral, and they may be actions which find expression in physical, verbal or mental behaviour.

The morally wholesome and unwholesome actions are said to give rise to appropriate consequences: They may find expression in this life, the next, or in lives to come unless their potentialities are extinguished or they do not find an opportunity for fruition. And the word kamma is used to denote volitional acts, which find expression in thoughts, words and deeds.

If the volition, or intention behind an action is governed by the three unwholesome roots of greed, aversion or delusion (*loba, dosa, moha*), the ensuing kamma is unwholesome and will bring forth unsatisfactory, undesirable, unpleasant results. If our volition is governed by non-greed (generosity, selflessness), non-hatred (kindness, friendliness), and non-delusion (clear understanding, insight, wisdom), then the kammic force will be wholesome, bringing forth happiness and other desirable results.

It must be kept in mind that the teaching of Buddhism is not that of continuing to perform good kamma for the sake of rewards in continued *saṃsāric* existence. On the contrary, it is the elimination of the effects of kamma by spiritual progress towards liberation.

Re-becoming (rebirth)

What happens to a person when he/she dies? To the average person, the material and mental constituents of what we call a 'person' disintegrates - ashes to ashes dust to dust. But is that all? According to Buddhist understanding, the accumulated, and yet unused *kammic* energy gives impetus to the start of a new life. To put it in another way, the stream of mind-movements, driven forward by craving, conditions the initiation of a new series of consciousness, which continues in a new life form. Thus a new life comes into being.

Therefore, in the ultimate sense, our present life is a series of mind-moments rapidly rising and passing away, based on a single physical organism which too is subject to constant change. After death, this series of mind-moments of the consciousness continues, finding support in a new physical organism. The last moment of this life is followed by the first mind-moment at rebirth or re-becoming in a new existence. We may perhaps be uncertain as to whether there is a difference between re-birth and re-becoming. The word used to describe the evolution from existence to existence is re-becoming (*bhava*). Rebirth in this sense continues to take place until a person has spiritually evolved to the state of an Arahat.

One may then ask, 'is it I who is reborn, or is the being in the next existence someone else?' Before we answer this question, we need to understand more clearly 'who am I'? Perhaps the easiest way to comprehend this would be to look at your old photograph album. Compare the baby you were in your first year of life, then the child at 5 years of age, then at 10, next at 16, and so on to the present. Are they the same person or not? It is hard to say, and you may probably think that they, frankly, are not the same. Compare last month and now, and what about yesterday and today, then an hour ago? In fact you are not exactly the same person now as when you started to read this chapter, because from moment to moment we are not exactly the same, yet neither are we entirely different.

As another example, let us take a stream and a person bathing in it. The stream when he started to bathe and the stream when he finished bathing were not the same, for the water in the stream had constantly flowed by. In fact we would be also correct when we say that the person who bathed in the river is not the same as the one who left the stream for dry land. He too has changed considerably, with many biochemical and developmental changes having taken place during the interim period. Rebecoming means exactly the same thing. The being of the last existence and the being of the present life and the one due to arise in the future are not quite the same, but also not entirely different. According to Buddhism, 'he is neither the same nor another' (*na ca so, na ca añño*) when we give a strictly accurate description, although in common parlance we may say that he is the same person.

When we look at life, we see that no physical matter—what we call materiality—from the dying body passes over to a new life. Neither does any part of the mind or aggregate of mentality (be it consciousness, or perception, or sensation) pass from the old life to the new. What connects the past existence with the present one is the same link that connects yesterday and today, and today and tomorrow. It is not a real 'I' but simply the sequence of cause and effect. It is important to see the relationship between kamma and rebirth in terms of the Dhamma, for it is kamma and rebirth which show us the principal laws of conditioned existence. These we shall study in the next chapter.

Kamma should never be understood as a kind of unchangeable fate. The most important and far-reaching result of our past kamma is re-becoming itself, re-becoming in a particular plane of existence. The plane of existence into which rebirth will occur is determined by the consciousness that arises just prior to death. In the case of human life, it refers to the place of birth, the country, the family and the parents. These crucial circumstances of our life occur in accordance with our past kamma.

Therefore, the only way to escape this wandering is by getting rid of as much defilements as possible. It is necessary for us to remove greed, hatred and delusion and develop the opposites of these, namely greedlessness, hatelessness or non-aversion and wisdom (non-delusion), respectively. These will eventually bring about a happy and an equanimous disposition conducive to morality, compassion, appreciative-joy and universal-kindness. With such positive mental qualities, it should be possible for us to proceed successfully along the Eightfold Path, ending finally in wisdom and liberation.

The arising of mind and body at conception and its continuity during the course of life is the result of our past volitions. More particularly, our mental and bodily features, our personality traits, propensity towards health or illness, beauty or ugliness, the quality of our sense faculties, our intelligence, popularity, social status and skills,–all these are fundamentally rooted in our past actions.

The three universal characteristics

According to the Dhamma, there are three universal characteristics common to all living and non-living things in the Universe.

They are:

1. the characteristic of impermanence
2. the characteristic of unsatisfactoriness
3. the characteristic of selflessness

These three characteristics are always present in, or connected with, existence and they tell us about the nature of existence.

As a result of understanding these three characteristics, we can learn to develop detachment. Once we understand and comprehend the fact that impermanence, unsatisfactoriness and non-self universally characterize all existence, we can eliminate our attachment to continued existence and enter the threshold of total liberation. This is the purpose of understanding these three characteristics: it removes attachment by identifying delusion and confusion—the misunderstanding that existence is permanent, pleasant and has something to do with the self.

This is why understanding the three characteristics is called wisdom.

i. Impermanence (*Anicca*)

The fact of impermanence should be obvious to anyone who looks objectively at life and the world in which we live. Everything is ever changing, subject to destruction, unstable, unreliable and constantly decaying. No matter how much we try to hold on to something, it is not the same as it was moments ago,—just like the person bathing in the stream that we examined earlier.

Another useful exercise is to closely observe and analyze in our minds the flame of a burning candle. We take note of the flame and we see five unique characteristics: the flame's arising, developing, continuing, flickering and dying out completely. This is what we should see as happening to all of us. For ours too is a cycle of impermanence of birth, growing up, being young and strong, ageing, decaying and finally passing away. Similarly, our mental states are also impermanent. At one moment we are happy, and at another sad. As infants, we hardly understand anything: as adults in the prime of life, we understand a great deal more and in our old age, we lose the power of our mental faculties and become like infants once again.

Human impermanence is well described by Shakespeare (1564-1616) in what he calls "the seven ages of man".

> ... At first the infant,
> Mewling and puking in the nurse's arms.
> And then the whining school- boy, with his satchel,
> And shining face, creeping like snail

Unwillingly to school. And then the lover
Sighing like furnace, with a woeful ballad
Made to his mistress' eyebrow. Then a soldier,
Full of strange oaths, and bearded like a pard,
Jealous in honour, sudden and quick in quarrel,
Seeking the bubble reputation
Even in the cannon's mouth. And then the justice,
In fair round belly with good capon lin'd,
With eyes severe, and beard of formal cut,
Full of wise saws and modern instances;
And so he plays his part. The sixth age shifts
Into the lean and slipper'd pantaloon,
With spectacles on nose and pouch on side,
His youthful hose well sav'd a world too wide
For his shrunk shank; and his big manly voice,
Turning again toward childish treble, pipes
And whistles in his sound. Last scene of all,
That ends this strange eventful history,
In second childishness and mere oblivion,
Sans teeth, sans eyes, sans taste, sans everything.

From: "As You Like It".

ii. Suffering or unsatisfactoriness (*Dukkha*)

The Buddha has said that whatever is impermanent is suffering and whatever is impermanent and suffering is also non-self. I need not elaborate on suffering or dissatisfaction as we have dealt with this topic in chapter one. Briefly, we can say that birth, decay, bodily and mental illness, death, sorrow, lamentation, despair, separation from loved ones, non-fulfillment of wishes, association with unpleasant people, living under stressful circumstances and so on are suffering. We could even say that dissatisfaction/unsatisfactoriness can take place when worldly happiness comes and goes, and we crave for more.

iii. Non-self (*Anattā*)

The third universal characteristic of existence is non-self, impersonality or insubstantiality. This is one of the distinct and unique features of the teachings of the Buddha. The Buddhist doctrine of non-self denies a permanent entity or soul which runs through different existences without change of identity, while it does not deny the continuity of an evolving consciousness—a stream of consciousness determining its state of re-becoming in different forms of cosmic existence.

Briefly, we could perhaps understand that everything in this world could be considered as self-less because we cannot find a part in anything that can be called the self; nor can we tell our body not to get sick or to stop ageing. This so-called being is composed of just five components - body, feeling, perception, mental function and consciousness. None of these components can be called the self and even outside of these five factors there is no permanent 'self'. If just one of these components is removed, nothing remains. Since all things are changing all the time, including ourselves, there is no rationale for us to believe that there is a permanent self.

Before we leave these three subjects, let it be emphasized that the truth of impermanence must not only be accepted intellectually, but it must be experienced as a reality within ourselves during *vipassanā* meditation. By directly understanding impermanence, as well as non-self and unsatisfactoriness, we reach true insight, which leads to liberation. However, the Buddha realized and taught that full liberation comes only when the three fundamental evils of desire, hatred/aversion and delusion/ confusion are extinguished. Then only one is freed from the bondage of 'self' with the destruction of ignorance.

Cause and effect

This too is a universal law. We can best understand it by way of examples. You see on TV that a poor child died in a car accident, and you send a modest cheque towards the burial fund. Cause and effect. Your grandson is mishandled on the playing field, and you scold the coach. Cause and effect. You learn and practise *vipassanā*, and you become a kinder and gentler person. Cause and effect. You see with surprise that people like you more. Cause and effect. Our neighbour shouts at another neighbour, and he retaliates in kind. Cause and effect.

Another example:

"For want of a nail, the shoe was lost,
For want of a shoe, the horse was lost,

For want of a horse, the rider was lost,
For want of the rider, the battle was lost."

Benjamin Franklin (1706-1790).

The best example of cause and effect can be found in the Four Noble Truths. Suffering, the first Noble Truth is the *effect* and craving the second Noble Truth is the *cause*. Wisdom, the fourth Noble Truth is the *cause* and the attainment of Nibbāna the Third Noble Truth is the *effect*. Thus every effect has a cause behind it

Conditionality

If we were to carefully examine phenomena in this world, we would see that everything is conditioned. Everything, both animate and inanimate, has arisen because of conditions and consequently is subject to impermanence.

We wish to have a home of our own. A new house. We find a developer and give him a plan for a house. He starts by first laying the foundation; then he brings all sorts of building materials to the site and constructs the house. We first see the skeletal framework of the building, and in stages the construction is completed. It is ready for occupation. When we move in, the house becomes a home. But if we dismantle the house, it gets reduced once again to its component parts. There is nothing permanent in it. The parts are impermanent. So is the house. It came to be because of conditions. There is nothing substantial or permanent to be called a home, either.

In fact, this very universe or cosmos itself and everything in it are subject to conditionality. The ultimate truth about us is that we too are conditioned and subject to impermanence, suffering or unsatisfactoriness, and have no permanent self or 'I'. In these circumstances it is seen that we urgently need to be liberated from this suffering, this distress by realizing Nibbāna.

The Path to Liberation

The path to Nibbāna lies through the understanding of *saṃsāra*, and the state of mind that realizes Nibbāna is called liberation (*vimokkha*). The three contemplations leading to Nibbāna are called doors to liberation (*vimokkha-mukha*). If the door to liberation is the contemplation of impermanence, the signless liberation (*animitta-vimokkha*) arises. If it is the contemplation of suffering, the desireless/wishless liberation (*appaṇihita-vimokkha*) arises. If it is the contemplation of non-self, the voidness/emptiness liberation (*suññatā-vimokkha*) arises. The signless liberation focuses upon Nibbāna as devoid of the 'signs' determinative of a conditioned formation; the wishless liberation as freedom from the hankering of desire; and the emptiness liberation as devoid of a self or any kind of substantial identity. These three liberations signify precisely the contemplations of the three universal marks of the conditioned: impermanence, suffering, and selflessness.

In each case, the understanding of the conditioned and the realization of the unconditioned are found to lock together in direct connection, so that by penetrating the conditioned to its very bottom and most significant features, the aspirant passes through the door leading out of the conditioned to the supreme security of the unconditioned, which is Nibbāna. The breakthrough to the unconditioned comes in four stages called the four-supramundane paths. (next page). Each momentary path-experience eradicates a specific group of defilements ranked in degrees of coarseness and subtleness.

The Buddha saw humans as shackled by the chains of their own weaknesses. Destruction of all the shackles (fetters) will deliver one from the wheel of rebirths and it will be the end of the road leading to the blissful state of Nibbāna. There are in all ten such shackles or fetters. Destruction of all the shackles will deliver one from *saṃsāra* or round of renewed births and it will signal the end of the road leading to the blissful state of Nibbāna.

The ten fetters (*saṃyojana*)

1. Delusion of self or personality view
2. Doubt
3. Clinging to rules and believing in the efficacy of ceremonies and rituals
4. Sensuality
5. Ill will
6. Passion for earthly life
7. Desire for fine-material and immaterial existece

8. Conceit
9. Restlessnesss
10. Ignorance

The four supramundane paths of *sotāpanna, sakadāgāmi, anāgami* and *arahat* cut off the above defilements in gradual stages. The path to Nibbāna consists of these four distinctive and progressive steps. Progression through each step indicates the eradication of a specific group of defilements ranked in degrees of coarseness and subtleness. With the first supramundane path the aspirant eradicates the first three of the above fetters. Thereby he/she becomes a 'stream-winner' (*sotāpanna*). This person is bound for deliverance in a maximum of seven more lives passed in the human or heavenly worlds. He will take rebirth among gods and men for a maximum of seven lives after which he will attain Nibbāna.

The second supramundane path attenuates fetters four and five to the point where they no longer arise frequently or obsessively. With such attainment the aspirant advances to the stage of a 'once-returner' (*sakadāgāmin*), one who is due to return to the sense sphere world only one more time. By eliminating the two fetters of sense desires and aversion or ill will, the aspirant attains the supramundane state of 'non-returner' (*anāgami*). The *anāgamin* is no longer bound to the sense sphere but is heading for rebirth in a pure divine abode (*suddhāvāsa*), where he/she will attain the final goal of Nibbāna.

The fourth of the supramundane paths cuts off the remaining five fetters. With such attainment the aspirant becomes an *arahat*, who has destroyed all the defilements and reached the state of perfection.

Chapter III

Paṭiccasamuppāda: The Doctrine

The Buddha followed the expounding of the Noble Eightfold Path with many other discourses, including those on *kamma* and rebirth and other related subjects to explain the nature of reality in a very encompassing way: in a way to make known the unsatisfactory and untenable predicament of all beings in *saṃsāra*. These dangers are very apparent when we consider the workings of the immanent law of *kamma*. In this way he made people to reflect on whether there was a reasoned and acceptable method for escape from this spiral of continuing existence. The Buddha, as a skilled teacher, adopted diverse styles of presentation of His Dhamma, depending on his audience - whether they were *devas,*[27] *Saṅgha*, lay-disciples or non-believers. Because He laid stress on the importance of dependent origination,[28] the Buddha in many later suttas (as recorded in the Tripitaka[29]) has explained the dependent origination in many ways.

Determining that the manner in which this profound doctrine would later be presented required the vast and unlimited intelligence that is possessed only by a Buddha, He needed a mode of presentation that was simple enough to memorize but not so simple as to distort the teaching. It should be kept in mind that over two thousand five hundred years ago, during the time of the Buddha, reading and writing was the exclusive right of the priestly Brahmin class. Hence an oral tradition had been developed to keep the Dhamma alive. He also needed words that would point to the immediate realization of awareness in the listener's mind. Finally, He needed a framework for the teaching as a whole so that those who wanted to pursue specific points

---

27. Devas–see ch1. f.n.14

28. *Pratītya-samutpāda*—The Sanskrit spelling of the Pāli word *paṭicca-samuppāda* as it appears in Mahāyāna sūtras

29. Tripiṭaka. Literally, "three baskets" or collections of the teachings of the Buddha, namely: 1. The Sutta-piṭaka—the collection of discourses, (2). The Vinaya-piṭaka—the collection of monastic rules for Buddhist monks and nuns. And 3. The Abhidhamma-piṭaka—the collection of higher teachings or philosophical exegesis of the Dhamma.

could also keep track of the larger picture. The result was the *Paṭiccasamuppāda* —dependent origination, which was, of course, the Dhamma which the *bodhisatta* had penetrated and brought to fruition on the night of his awakening in becoming a Buddha, the Enlightened One.

Consequently, over the last 25 centuries the basic structure of this doctrine has come down to us undiluted and unchanged. Many have mastered it, and those of us who wish to do the same must follow the very same path used by our predecessors. At the outset, the Buddha warned people that it was a profound and difficult subject to comprehend. When Ānanda, His constant companion told him, "It is wonderful and marvelous, sir, how this dependent arising is so deep, yet to myself it seems as clear as clear can be". The Buddha replied, "Do not say so, Ānanda! Do not say so, Ānanda! This dependent arising, Ānanda, is deep and it appears deep." (Mahā Nidāna Sutta).

By announcing this doctrine as deep, He would stir the imagination and interest of the public, and people were bound to inquire why this discourse was so deep. Then they would, more often than not, want to study it. In a similar way, we too would like to understand and comprehend the Dhamma as contained within this discourse. For, in this age of advanced information technology, we now have many special facilities to help us and at the end of the rainbow is the proverbial pot of gold - Insight leading to liberation, and such release from suffering and the round of *saṃsāra* is the attainment of Nibbāna.

You will recollect that in chapter one we discussed what the Buddha discovered on the night of the day of His Enlightenment, namely the Truth of conditioned arising. He did this by reflecting on birth and death and the need to find the reason why one wanders in *saṃsāra* with no end in sight. This he did by examining himself, both his body and his mind, at the experiential level. As he went deeper and deeper into reflection and meditation, he saw that it was clinging to the five aggregates, i.e. the 'form' and the four components of the mind-consciousness, perception, sensation and reaction, which He called the 'five-aggregates of clinging, (*pañca-upādānakkhandha)*, rooted in craving and born of ignorance that led to misery and suffering. Craving, clinging and attachment at the surface level, He observed, are augmented by greater misery at deeper levels.

People may be happy with what they have, but they always want something more. They develop attachment and become addicted to craving resulting in endless misery. It is like a bottomless pit, for, before long, one is attached to material things and identifies them as 'I, mine'. People do not stop there; they become attached also to beliefs, views, various theories and traditions and such among other things.

The Buddha out of compassion for the world exclaimed that the people of this world fall into trouble and sojourn on and on in *saṃsāra,* not knowing how to escape from their misery. There must be an escape, which can be discerned. The Buddha then looked at this age-old problem 'with careful attention, resulting in a breakthrough with wisdom' He asked himself as to why was there sorrow, lamentation, pain, grief, ageing, decay and death. He saw that it was because of birth. He next asked himself, 'Why birth? How does it come about?' The reason for this too was very clear. It was due to becoming, the urge to exist, to become, to come into being.

Let us look at these steps in the form of a chart, with ageing, decay and death at the bottom, and then trace each link upwards;

'How did consciousness come about?' He realized that it was due to a specific condition, namely volitional activities. Mental volitional formations resulting from negative and positive intentions which is also equated to *kamma*. It is the sum-total of all of the unspent *kammic* energy which had been generated and accumulated in previous existences, the energies which had not been used up previously. 'Then why does one participate in volitional activities'? He asked himself, and He saw with insight and wisdom that it was due to ignorance (*avijjā*).

Beings act without realizing or knowing the consequences of their intentions and actions. In fact they do not know, nor understand the Four Noble Truths. They are also ignorant of the natural law of cause and effect, and ignorant of the consequences of negative *kamma*. Due to craving and clinging they are also ignorant of the ever-present dangers. It is the ignorance of the fact that there is no permanent entity called 'I' or self that is the root cause. This was as far as He needed to go.

The riddle of birth, life and death

Craving is conditioned by ignorance, while intense craving acts as a catalyst to ensure that one continues in the *saṃsāric* round of births and rebirths. Let us pause for a while and discuss feeling, craving and clinging a little more. Feelings are of three types: pleasant, unpleasant and neutral.

Craving. If there were no feelings or sensations, there would be no craving. This ideal situation is attained when one becomes a Noble One. But the rest of us are subject to greed, thirst, desire, longing, yearning and sensual wants. It is this craving that is the root cause of rebirth. Craving is of three types, namely:

craving for sense-pleasures
craving for rebecoming or existence
craving for an end to existence.

"Where does craving arise and take root? Where there is the delightful and the pleasurable, there craving arises and takes root. Where there are forms, sounds, smells, tastes, bodily contacts and ideas, which are delightful and pleasurable, there craving arises and takes root." (D.22)

Craving is conditioned not only by the pleasant, but by the unpleasant as well and those who suffer, be they the poor, the unloved, the sick, the aged, the disabled, the unwanted–all crave freedom from their suffering. Even the affluent and the healthy are not free from craving. They crave for more and more. Man's appetite for more and more is truly insatiable.

Clinging: Clinging or attachment is four-fold. There is attachment to sense-desires, to wrong or negative views, to rites and rituals as a saving grace and finally there is attachment to the self as an unchanging and continuing personality.

Clinging is not the mere attachment in a reasonable way to one's possessions and views, but the overly attachment and overly grasping and the consequent selfishness not to let go under any circumstance. Of the above the most dangerous and pernicious is the belief in an abiding self or an ego or 'I'. If this wrong notion is not got rid of, the discernment of the other two characteristics of existence, namely imperma-nence and suffering, becomes extremely difficult. On the other hand, if the wrong notion of a permanent 'self' is removed by proper application, the other wrong notions cease automatically. The Buddha saw no abiding indestructible soul or *attā*. He denied the existence of such an entity in the five aggregates: in this world of body and mind, or elsewhere.

> "All this is void of an *attā* or derivatives thereof"
> *suññaṃ idaṃ attena va attaniyena vā* (M.22).
>
> "O Mogharāja, ever mindful–see the world as void
>
> Having eradicated the notion of a self (*attā*) so may one overcome death:
>
> *sunnatā lokaṃ avekkhassu–Mogharāja sadā sato*
> *attānudiṭṭhiṃ vohaccu–evaṃ maccutaro siyā* (Sn.1119).

We left the Buddha at the end of His conclusion that 'volitional activities are conditioned by ignorance'. We can now continue from there: He then looked at what He had discovered in reverse order as well, and it confirmed His findings: "**W**hen there is no birth, ageing and death do not come to be. With the cessation of becoming, comes cessation of ageing and death. When there is no becoming, birth does not come to be. With cessation of existence, comes cessation of birth".... (And so on.).........up to ignorance. In other words, ageing and death resulted because of birth, which was because of becoming, the process of being born because of (and is conditioned by) clinging.... .

These findings are what we know as dependent origination - *Paṭiccasamuppāda*. Let us read a few of the Buddha's own words on this subject as given in the *Nidāna Saṃyutta*.

i. *Origination*

"Bhikkhus, before my enlightenment, when I was yet a bodhisatta, not yet fully enlightened, it occurred to me: "Alas, this world has fallen into trouble, in that it is born, ages and dies, it passes away and is reborn, yet it does not understand the escape from this suffering (headed by) ageing-and-death?'

"Then it occurred to me: 'when what exists does ageing-and-death come to be? By what is ageing-and-death conditioned?' Then, bhikkhus, through careful attention, there took place in me a breakthrough by wisdom: 'When there is birth, ageing-and-death comes to be; ageing-and-death has birth as its condition.' "Then, bhikkhus, it occurred to me: 'when what exists does birth come to be? By what is birth conditioned? ... Then, bhikkhus, through careful attention, there took place in me a breakthrough by wisdom: 'When there is becoming, birth comes to be; birth has becoming as its condition..."

"Then, bhikkhus, it occurred to me: "Thus with ignorance as condition, volitional formations (come to be); with volitional formations as condition, consciousness..." Such is the origin of this whole mass of suffering. 'Origination, origination'–thus, bhikkhus, in regard to things unheard before there arose in me vision, knowledge, wisdom, true knowledge and light".

ii. *Cessation*

"Then, bhikkhus, it occurred to me: 'when what does not exist does ageing-and-death not come to be? With the cessation of what does the cessation of ageing-and-death come about?' Then, bhikkhus, through careful attention, there took place in me a breakthrough by wisdom: 'When there is no birth, ageing-and-death does not come to be; with the cessation of birth comes cessation of ageing-and-death.' "Then, bhikkhus, it occurred to me: "Thus with the remainderless fading away and cessation of ignorance comes cessation of volitional formations: with the cessation of volitional formations, cessation of consciousness ... Cessation, cessation–thus, bhikkhus, in regard to things unheard before there arose in me vision, knowledge, wisdom, true knowledge, and light." *Nidāna Saṃyutta.*

Dependent Origination (in direct order, *anuloma*)

From ignorance come volitional actions (leading to rebirth)
From volitional actions comes (rebirth)—consciousness
From (rebirth)—consciousness comes name and form (personality)
From name and form come the five senses and mind-base
From the five senses and mind-base comes contact
From contact come feelings (sensations)
From feelings (sensations) comes craving/desire
From craving comes clinging/grasping or attachment (to continued existence)
From clinging/grasping comes becoming
From becoming comes birth
From birth come ageing and death, sorrow, lamentation, pain, grief, and despair. Thus there is the origination of this whole mass of suffering.

Dependent Origination (in 'reverse' order: *paṭiloma*)

If ignorance is absent (there will be) no volitional activities
With no volitional activities, no rebirth-consciousness
With no rebirth-consciousness no name and form
With no name and form, no five senses and mind-base
With no senses and mind-base, no contact
With no contact, no feelings/sensations
With no feelings/sensations, no craving
With no craving, no clinging
With no clinging, no becoming
With no becoming, no birth
With no birth, ageing and death cease, and sorrow, lamentation, pain, grief and despair. Thus there is the cessation of this whole mass of suffering.

Another discovery of the Buddha was that consciousness finds nutriment in mind-and-matter, and mind-and-matter in turn finds nutriment in consciousness. They show a symbiotic relationship. This is reminiscent of the relationship between certain species of fungi and algae which can live together symbiotically by developing into lichens, which can then live even under harsh climatic conditions, but cannot survive independent of each other.

"... Therefore, Ānanda, this is the cause, source, origin, and condition for mentality-materiality, namely, consciousness. ..... Therefore, Ānanda, this is the cause, source, origin, and condition for consciousness, namely, materiality-mentality" ...(Mahā Nidāna Sutta). In the same Sutta the Buddha emphasized the importance of specificity as a linking factor in this chain of conditionality:

" ... Ānanda, if one is asked: 'Are ageing and death due to a specific condition?' one should say: 'They are'. If one is asked 'Through what condition is there ageing and death?' one should say: 'With birth as condition there is ageing and death'. Ānanda, if one is asked: 'Is birth due to a specific condition?' one should say: 'it is'. If one is asked: 'through what condition is there birth?' One should say: 'With becoming as condition there is birth'... "Thus, Ānanda, with mentality-materiality as condition there is consciousness; with consciousness as condition there is mentality-materiality; ... and with birth as a condition ageing and death, sorrow, lamentation, pain, grief, and despair come to be. Such is the origin of this entire mass of suffering."

When we looked at the diagrammatic representation of the twelve factors of dependent origination, we saw that each was conditioned by the preceding factor, which in turn conditioned the next and so on. Thus, for volitional formations the causal condition was ignorance. For consciousness it was volitional formations and so on. The Buddha explained it in this manner for the ease of memorisation and of compre-hension. However, he has stated elsewhere that there are in fact twenty-four other conditions *(paccaya)* also contributing in various combinations to condition each of the twelve factors of dependent origination. It would suffice for our current discussion merely to note these relationships, feed back loops and dependence of its twelve factors by way of the twenty-four modes of conditionality[30].

We can now see that dependent origination is a teaching of conditionality, which encompasses everything in the cosmos,

---

30. *Paccaya*: The 24 conditions. 'Condition' is something on which something else, the so-called 'conditioned thing' is dependent, and without which the latter cannot be. For a full explanation and table of the 24 modes of conditionality, see *Buddhist Dictionary* by Nyanatiloka, BPS, 1990.

and that this teaching is the essence of the Buddha's Dhamma. Dependent origination and conditionality are facts of life.

If one were asked to summarise dependent origination, the obvious choice of words would be none other than those used by Arahat Assaji (one of the Buddha's first five disciples) when answering Upatissa's[31] query as to what was the Buddha's doctrine:

Ye dhammā hetuppabhavā -
tesaṃ hetuṃ tathāgato āha
Tesaṃ ca yo nirodho -
evaṃvādī mahāsamaṇo.

'Whatever from a cause proceeds,
Thereof the Tathāgata has explained the cause:
Its cessation too He has explained:
This is the teaching of the Supreme Sage"

Vin.1. Mahāvagga

Conditionality goes on forever, uninterrupted and uncontrolled by any external agency or power of any sort.

31. Later, Arahat Sāriputta.
(** Alternately you can replace 'from' with 'dependent on' and 'comes' with 'arises').

CHAPTER IV

Understanding the Paṭiccasamuppāda

In the previous chapter was presented the doctrine of dependent origination the way the Buddha discovered it and in the manner in which he explained it. This was based on a number of discourses of the Buddha. We left aside the more complex details, for our purpose was simply to get the feel of this important subject.

The Buddha emphatically declared that the first beginning of existence is inconceivable. It is impossible to think or believe in a first beginning because no one can truly trace the ultimate origin of anything, not even of a grain of sand, let alone of human beings,–despite what present-day cosmologists are wont to say.

It should be realized that life is just a 'becoming'. It is merely a conflux of mind and body subject to conditionality. According to the Buddha, all conditioned or compounded things come into being, presently exist and then cease–*uppāda, ṭhiti* and *bhaṅga*.

However, for us to fully understand this profound subject, we need to review the information and explanations given in chapter 2, plus the additional information given below. Even then, no explanation can be expected to give a full and final understanding of the process of dependent origination. Nevertheless, the information contained here can be used to probe the process while at the same time train the mind to come to a reasonable understanding of this profound and fundamental doctrine.

One of the links of the *paṭiccasamuppāda* which frequently bothers people is the difficulty in visualizing how "volitional formations/*kamma* in one life conditions consciousness" in the next. Consciousness is the most subtle and deep point which is difficult to grasp and comprehend, for it is this link that explains rebecoming and rebirth. And this is what He told Ānanda: "If consciousness were not to descend into the mother's womb, would mentality-materiality take shape in the womb?" "Certainly not venerable Sir."

"If, after descending into the womb, consciousness were to expire, would mentality-materiality be generated into this present state of being?" "Certainly not, venerable Sir."...

"Therefore, Ananda, this is the cause, the source, the origin, and condition for mentality-materiality, namely, conscious-ness:" *Mahā Nidāna Sutta.*

The rebirth-consciousness, which we are discussing here is explained in the Abhidhamma as follows: For rebirth consciousness to take place, it must be preceded by death in the immediate previous existence. Death-consciousness or *cuti-citta* is the very last consciousness to occur at the moment of death. It is the *citta* which marks the exit from a particular life. Death-consciousness is of the same type as the rebirth-linking consciousness and moment-to-moment consciousness *(bhavaṅga),* and like them it pertains to the process-freed side of existence, the passive flow of consciousness outside an active cognitive process. Death-consciousnss is followed by a rebirth-linking consciousness called the *paṭisandhi-citta* which occurs only once in any individual existence. It is at the moment of rebirth and is conditioned immediately by the previous death-consciousness.

This rebirth-linking consciousness is followed by the usual moment-to-moment consciousness *(bhavaṅga),* which continues to be present throughout a person's life. It is different from the consciousness which arises when the six-sense bases in a live person come into contact with their respective sense-objects as follows:

"With eye and forms arises visual consciousness
With ear and sounds arises auditory consciousness
With nose and odours arises olfactory consciousness
With tongue and flavours arises taste consciousness
With body and tangibles arises tactile consciousness
With mind and mental objects arises mind-consciousness"

(M,I,111-112).

At that time, when perception, sensation and reaction are operative, the *bhavaṅga* consciousness lies dormant and comes into effect immediately thereafter. (Please also see chapter 2). In the proposition, volitional formations/*kamma* conditions consciousness, we have to understand that *saṅkhāra* is equated to *kamma* and that the consciousness referred to here is rebirth-consciousness.

To understand this subject better, it is necessary first to have an understanding of energy systems. We are aware that every phenomenon in the cosmos is based on energy and accordingly we generate energy whenever we think or do anything. This energy is what we can equate to *kamma* and this accumulated *kammic* energy gets attenuated to different degrees when a person attains the three transcendental paths of stream-winner, once-returner and non-returner respectively. It comes to an end with the attainment of the fourth transcendental path, which is Arahatship.

However, for the life processes to continue too, energy is necessary. And we know that mitochondria, which generate energy for vital activities are in all the cells of our body. And such energy falls within the domain of physical energy.

In the case of human conception too, like in all human activities, energy is necessary, which fact embryologists know when they carry out *in-vitro* fertilization. Perhaps the same type of system prevails in the human body too when *in-vivo* fertilization takes place. In other words, energy is required at the point of conception. The question then is, 'where does this energy come from'? Is it from within the uterus, or could it be from the energy of rebirth-consciousness and *kamma*?

So let us picture what may perhaps happen when a person is about to die. According to dependent origination, it is the accumulated kamma of the previous birth that acts as the specific condition for rebirth-linking consciousness in the next. The consciousness, which we are now discussing is the rebirth-linking consciousness which is the first consciousness that appears in the new life, i.e. in the zygote at the moment of its initiation.

According to the Dhamma, three conditions must be present for a new life to come into being. They are the viable spermatozoon of the father, a viable ovum (oocyte) of the mother and the 'person-to-be-born'. The energy to trigger the start of a new life is presumably provided by the person-to-be-born, called *gandhabba* in the *Mahātaṇhāsaṅkhaya Sutta*.

Some sutta-commentators believe that *gandhabba*[32] is simply a term for rebirth-consciousness or *paṭisandhi viññāṇa*. It

---

32. *Gandhabba*. Often thought to be the rebirth-linking or very first consciousness of the being to be born.

is this energy potential released at the time a person dies in the previous birth and conditioned by craving is the desire for becoming. This energy is so formidable that it attracts itself to another appropriate existence. It is the last thought-process that carries with it this grasping force (energy) and the unused kamma and, like a flash of lightning, it enters the mother's womb, and perhaps enters the oocyte simultaneously with the spermatozoon and energizes the male and female pro-nuclei in the zygote to undergo the first mitotic cell division, thus laying the foundation for the start of a new life. The two-celled embryo then divides itself into a four, eight, and sixteen-cell embryo and so on.

Unless rebirth-consciousness links up with the zygote at its initiation, there can be no start of a new life. Along with this consciousness the rest of the factors of mentality, as well as the physical factors of materiality, begin to manifest.

"This reciprocal conditional relationship between consciousness and name-and-form (*nāma-rūpa*) continues throughout the entire course of life; consciousness infuses the whole mental and material structure to make them participants in all experience; and the mental and material structure provide a footing for consciousness to grow and flourish." Bhikkhu Bodhi.

In ancient commentaries this transfer of consciousness and *kamma* is compared to what happens when one lighted candle is used to light another candle. Nothing substantial moves from one candle to the other, but the light does.

In understanding the above example we should keep in mind that nothing of the five aggregates (which we call a 'being'), moves from the previous life to the present one. Only conditionality exists. The Buddha has emphasized this as shown in the following incident:

Sāti was a recalcitrant monk who had insisted on misconstruing the Buddha's words. Sāti had insisted that consciousness is a persistent transmigrating entity. The Buddha had then reaffirmed His previous statement that consciousness is dependently arisen in that it arises in dependence of conditions and that apart from conditions there can be no origination of consciousness *(aññātra paccayā natthi viññaṇassa sambhavo).*

Getting back to human development, it is seen that once the embryo is initiated, it will start developing rapidly and by the third week will show the initiation of the heart and circulation system as well as the start of the formation of the brain and the nervous system. This is followed rapidly by the formation of the five physical sense-organs and consciousness, namely the eyes, ears, nose, tongue, body and the mental-base (*ajjhattika*), and their respective external (*bāhira*) bases which are: visible objects, sound, odour, taste, body and mind objects. The ensuing mind-body phenomenon reaches foetal maturity at the end of nine months.

The arising of the above primordial mind-body combination during embryonic and foetal development, as well as the continuing development during the course of life, is called the 'round of results' (*vipākavaṭṭa*), and is the result of our past volitions-*kamma*. The microscopic zygote thus finally develops into a human being equipped with a six-sense base, during the foetal-embryonic stage. It is perhaps useful to remember that when we referred to rebirth-linking consciousness, we did not imply that this consciousness is a permanent entity, which continues in the same state without change throughout the cycle of existence. Consciousness too is conditioned and is therefore not permanent. It comes into being, performs and passes away yielding place to a new consciousness. It is explained as a perpetual stream that goes on until the final cessation of 'becoming'. When one gives it more thought, one realizes that in effect there is no 'being' in this world in the absence of consciousness, and in a way, consciousness is existence, the will to live, to continue and to become (*bhava*).

We can now see that the *paṭiccasamuppāda* is a teaching of conditionality of everything in the world. It goes on forever, uninterrupted and uncontrolled by any external agency or power of any sort.

Let us make a chart once again of the twelve links forming the chain, the spiral of continuing existence. The following list (reading downwards) denotes the conditional relationship between the 12 links of dependently arising phenomena.

1. Ignorance
2. Volitional formations
3. Consciousness
4. Mentality-materiality
5. Six Senses
6. Contact

7. Feeling
8. Craving
9. Clinging
10. Becoming
11. Birth
12. Ageing and death

In the doctrine of dependent origination, we refer to three periods of time: the past, the present and the future. This is in order to exemplify how the twelve factors act upon the consecutive sequence of lives. Ignorance and volitional formations belong to the previous birth, the next eight links to the present, and the last two links, birth and ageing and death belong to the next existence. Now, how can this chain of cause and effect be broken in order to reach liberation? Unless we can break the chain, we will surely drift forever in *saṃsāra*, in a stream of birth, death and rebirth.

The Buddha in his wisdom explored all the possibilities and realized that there were, in fact, two points along this chain where it could be broken. Of these, the first is 'ignorance' and the other is at the point of 'craving.' He therefore, had to find a way to stop craving. He recollected that by meditating with insight, wisdom and equanimity, one could develop total awareness of every sensation which occurs in the body. When one sees every sensation without greed, hatred or delusion, one does not react to situations.

The Buddha has also shown us a way out of ignorance, which in turn will prevent the arising of fresh reactions. This is by means of *vipassanā* meditation, for, with continued *vipassanā* meditation it is possible for us to develop mindfulness and insight. Then will arise wisdom with which we can successfully eradicate ignorance. Liberation follows.

This is how an enlightened being, an Arahant, faces all incidents in his day-to-day life: with wisdom and without volition. Having eliminated conceiving the Arahant no longer finds delight in the objects he encounters. He no longer pursues pleasure and enjoyment and in the absence of delight and craving, there is no condition for the renewal of *saṃsāric* existence. At the end of his present life, he concludes his journey in *saṃsāra* and brings an end to it.

We have so far depicted dependent origination as a chain of causes and effects strung over time. However, this is not necessarily the best way to show causal inter-connectedness.

The Buddha has said:

> When this is, that is.
> From the arising of this, that arises.
> When this is not, that is not.
> From the ceasing of this, that ceases.

Mahātaṇhāsaṅkhaya sutta.

A recent commentator sees in the above: "an inter-play of synchronic and linear principles". The linear principle connects events over time as follows:

> When this is, that is
> When this is not, that is not.

On the other hand, the synchronic principle is also evident as follows:

> From the arising of this, that arises
> From the ceasing of this, that ceases.

It is then evident that the two principles intersect so that any given event is influenced by two sets of conditions, those acting from the past, and those acting from the present."[33]

Dependent Origination and the Four Noble Truths

There are many ways to show the interconnectedness between the twelve links of the Dependent Origination and the four Noble Truths. For instance, in one analysis it is shown that the first Noble Truth, (the existence of suffering or unsatisfactoriness), is related to the links of consciousness, name and form, the six-sense bases, contact, sensation, birth, ageing and death. The balance five links of ignorance, reaction, craving, clinging and becoming are related to the second Noble Truth (the origin of suffering).

We can then say that the latter set of five are the causal factors, while the former set of seven are the effective factors. We

33. Thanissaro Bhikkhu, *The Wings of Awakening,* 1996.

thus see that it is the origin of suffering which causes suffering, for suffering is dependent on its origin and will not exist in its absence.

It is also possible to show that, in the doctrine of dependent origination, all four Noble Truths are embodied: "The *paṭiccasamuppāda* in its order of arising manifests the process of becoming (*bhava*): in other words, the appearance of suffering (the First Truth); and how this process of becoming or suffering is conditioned (the Second Truth). In its order of ceasing, the *paṭiccasamuppāda* makes plain the cessation of this becoming, this suffering (the Third Truth), and how it ceases (the Fourth Truth)."[34]

34. Piyadassi Mahathera, *The Spectrum of Buddhism.*

CHAPTER V

Paṭiccasamuppāda and the Upanisā Sutta

To study and comprehend the *paṭiccasamuppāda*, it is important that there be a total immersion in this *sutta*. It requires a "paradigm shift". We need to look at it not merely as a doctrine but as something personal, which one can experience. By doing so, it comes alive. We also need this focus not only in regard to this doctrine, but also to all doctrines of the Buddha, for He spoke only of 'suffering and how to end suffering.' In fact, when we look at the twelve links, we see that the last few words in the *sutta* refer to 'this whole mass of suffering'.

Hence, the purpose of understanding this *sutta* is to find a solution, a way to end this otherwise ceaseless wandering in *saṃsāra*. If we lose track of this fundamental point, we would only be looking at the byways and not at the main highway to Nibbāna.

Let us examine what we have learnt and understood by looking at the twelve links in the standard descending order, as if we are the live participants in this *saṃsāric* process of the rounds of rebirths. In the discussion which follows, 'I' and 'we' are used in the conventional sense merely as expedients (much like the way the Buddha referred to his previous births).

Starting with ignorance, we looked at how we had perhaps conducted ourselves in our previous birth, which, for purposes of discussion, we assumed was here on earth. We believed that conditioned by our ignorance of the dangers inherent in the three fundamental evils of greed, aversion and delusion, and not understanding the three eternal verities of impermanence, suffering and the absence of a permanent 'I' or 'self', we remained unaware that there was no permanent self or 'I'. We also had no knowledge of the working of the immanent law of *kamma* and rebirth. In fact, we did not know the four Noble Truths. As a result, we accumulated a considerable amount of negative *kamma*.

On the other hand, although we were not aware of the above factors of defilements, we were inherently good people, for we had perhaps been kind, compassionate, sharing, forbearing, patient and also morally above reproach in our previous birth. Consequently, we did spiritually evolve a little more and became 'eligible' for an earth life because the accumulated positive *kamma* outweighed the negative *kamma*. Therefore, when we died, we received another chance to spiritually evolve further by birth in this world of sentient beings. We are now reaping some of the 'benefits' of our *kamma*, as *kamma-vipāka* or in other words the consequences of our previous actions in *saṃsāra*.

This earthly life did not come about fortuitously, but conditioned by our previous volitions *(kamma)*. We now have a chance to progress in our evolution and hopefully can move closer to liberation if we get rid of ignorance, greed, hatred and delusion, and practise generosity, morality and the four sublime states of loving-kindness, compassion, participating joy and equanimity. We now also have the opportunity to understand dependent origination as a way out of ignorance.

It has become clear to us how rebirth-consciousness appears at the time of conception in the mother's womb in this re-becoming and we then pictured how mind-and-matter develops in the embryo and the foetus, followed by the development of the six-sense organs and the related six-sense-consciousnesses. We then came to appreciate that although we had considered ourselves as unique entities we are, in fact, nothing but body and mind, which together comprise the five aggregates of clinging. There is no permanent 'I'.

We saw how, because of the six-fold contact of our senses with their respective objects, we started to have feelings, which turned to craving and then clinging and how we could become enslaved to our cravings and clingings. We also saw how the energy so generated would lead to our wanting survival or becoming or existence: in other words, giving way to the atavistic tendency for survival and perpetuation of the species.

If during this lifetime we are to find a way out of the *saṃsāric* round, we need to mend our ways. We need to not only get rid of our inherent tendency towards craving, but to eradicate it totally.

> 'Just as a tree with roots untouched and firm in the ground
> Though felled, puts forth new shoots,
> If the habit of craving and aversion is not uprooted,
> Suffering arises over and over again' (Dhp 338).

If we do not get rid of attachment, craving, clinging and hatred along with our delusion of a permanent self, we will at the end of this existence be merely drifting once more in *saṃsāra* and be subject to the whole mass of suffering. We, therefore, have understood that we need to step back and mindfully change direction, change course and adopt one of the proven methods of the Buddha to develop wisdom and thereby attain liberation.

However, to develop wisdom, it is necessary to understand the Dhamma, and this we can do by reading or listening to the Dhamma and practising it, which would result in *sutamaya-paññā.* (In the present context it is repeatedly reading and understanding this book). Then by reflection and contemplation, we can gain the wisdom called *cintāmaya-paññā.* This will finally lead us to insight or *vipassanā* meditation and, through insight meditation, we should be able to achieve wisdom–*bhāvanāmayā-paññā* and comprehension of the Dhamma (Ch.1).

How can we, after studying and understanding the *paṭiccasamuppāda,* take the next step? How can we get rid of ignorance, craving and clinging and achieve liberation? Fortunately, the Buddha has indeed shown us how this can be done stepwise. He has shown us how we can move from mundane dependent origination to the supra-mundane state by a series of interconnected links leading to liberation *(vimutti).*

Upanisā sutta

This advice is found in the *Upanisā sutta* of the *Saṃyutta Nikāya.* In this *sutta,* the Buddha begins with the words, "The destruction of taints, monks, is for one who knows and sees, not for one who does not know and does not see..."

Taints are what are commonly called *āsavas* in the *suttas,* and there are four groups of them:

> sense-desires–*kāma-āsava*
> desire for existence–*bhava-āsava*
> holding narrow views–*diṭṭhi-āsava*
> ignorance–*avijjā-āsava*

What are the benefits of removing these taints? It is the realization of Nibbāna.

It is said that with stream-entry - *sotāpanna,* the taint of wrong-views is destroyed. Through the path of Non-returning -

anāgāmi, the taint of sense-desire is destroyed, and through the path of *Arahantship* the rest of the taints of existence and ignorance are finally destroyed.

The relevant portion of the *Upanisā sutta* reads as follows:

... "Thus, bhikkhus, with ignorance as the proximate cause, volitional formations (come to be); with volitional formations as proximate cause, consciousness; with consciousness as proximate cause, name-and-form; with name-and-form as proximate cause, the six sense bases; with the six sense bases as proximate cause, contact; with contact as proximate cause, feeling; with feeling as proximate cause, craving; with craving as proximate cause, clinging; with clinging as proximate cause, birth; with birth as proximate cause, suffering; with suffering as proximate cause, confidence; with confidence as proximate cause, gladness; with gladness as proximate cause, rapture: with rapture as proximate cause, tranquillity; with tranquillity as proximate cause, happiness; with happiness as proximate cause, concentration; with concentration as proximate cause, knowledge and vision of things as they really are; with knowledge and vision of things as they really are as proximate cause, revulsion; with revulsion as proximate cause, dispassion; with dispassion as proximate cause, liberation; with liberation as proximate cause, the knowledge of destruction (of the *āsavas*)".

It is seen from the above that the way to liberation begins with confidence initially supported by ***ignorance*** and ends with *āsavakkhaya-ñāṇa,* meaning the wisdom for the destruction of taints by attaining *vimutti,* liberation or *Arahantship.*

To study transcendental dependent origination, we can depict the links in the *Upanisā sutta* in the same manner in which we displayed the twelve links of the *paṭiccasamuppāda* in chapter 3:

The Upanisā Sutta

Part1. Mundane dependent origination

Ignorance *(avijjā)* leads to ... *kamma* formations *(saṅkhāra)*
Kamma leads to ... consciousness *(viññāṇa)*
Consciousness leads to. ...mentality-materiality *(nāma-rūpa)*
Mentality-materality leads to ... six-fold sense bases *(salāyatana)*
Six-fold sense bases lead to ... contact *(phassa)*
Contact leads to ... feeling *(vedanā)*
Feeling leads to ... craving *(taṇhā)*
Craving leads to ... clinging *(upādāna)*
Clinging leads to ... existence *(bhava)*
Existence leads to ... birth *(jāti)*
Birth leads to ... suffering *(dukkha)*

Part 2. Supra-mundane dependent origination

Suffering leads to ... confidence *(saddhā)*
Confidence leads to ... joy/gladness *(pāmojja)*
Gladness/Joy leads to ... rapture *(pīti)*
Rapture leads to ... tranquillity *(passaddhi)*
Tranquillity leads to ... happiness *(sukha)*
Happiness leads to ... concentration *(samādhi)*
Concentration leads to ... knowledge and vision of things as they really are *(yathābhūta-ñāṇadassana)*
Knowledge and vision leads to ... revulsion/disenchantment *(nibbidā)*
Revulsion-disenchantment leads to ..dispassion *(virāga)*
Dispassion leads to ... liberation *(vimutti)*
Liberation leads to ... destruction of cankers or taints *(āsavakkaya-ñāṇa)*

When we look at the *Upanisā sutta* in the above form, we see in part one, the now familiar twelve links of dependent origination, which we had studied before in chapter 3. The only difference is in the 12th link, where the Buddha has purposefully replaced "death and decay" with "suffering". For it is this substitution, which helps to lead to the second application (part 2) of dependent arising, which is to show a path leading to liberation.

Part two begins with, confidence *(saddhā)*, i.e., confidence in the Buddha and his doctrines, and then leads up to tranquillity and happiness. From there on are shown the progressive steps leading finally to liberation and with it the destruction of taints. This second application of 'dependent arising' has been given the name 'transcendental or supramundane dependent arising' as it leads to transcendence[35].

It appears that in the second part of this *sutta*, the Buddha is telling us not to stop but to move forward till we are fully liberated (*vimutti*) and all cankers/taints (*āsava*) are destroyed. For, by now, having comprehended the doctrine of dependent origination, and understood conditionality experientially, the learner is suffused with confidence and acceptance of the Truth in the Buddha Dhamma. He should now wish to go forward. This decision in turn will generate joy or gladness in the meditator, who also knows that he is proceeding in the right direction.

At this stage, the meditator would check within him as to whether his morality is completely above reproach and whether he is practising the *sīla* portion of the Noble Eightfold Path. When this is self-confirmed, the meditator will be suffused with rapture and will make a determined effort to proceed intensively through the concentration and wisdom groups of the Noble Eightfold Path.

He would now realize that further progress is not possible without *vipassanā* meditation. The links of joy, rapture, tranquillity, happiness, concentration, knowledge-and-vision-of-things as-they-are, disenchantment and dispassion- (*pāmojja, pīti, passadhi, sukha, samādhi, yathābhūta-ñāṇa-dassana, nibbidā and dispassion* respectively (as shown in the *Upanisā sutta*), are states of mind. They are sequential steps in spiritual development leading to transcendence. They also act as signposts, which help identify our progress along the path to liberation (*vimutti*).

We should also understand that each of the above steps arises in dependence on the previous one, and hence represents dependent origination, and demonstrates in the *Upanisā sutta* how they lead to dispassion and liberation.

There are also a number of *suttas* scattered in the *Sutta Piṭaka,*[36] which show steps similar to those shown in the *Upanisā sutta* leading to liberation, but with individual variations, for,

---

35. *Transcendental Dependant Origination*—Bhikkhu Bodhi, Wheel Publication Nos. 277/278. BPS, Kandy, Sri Lanka.

36. *Sutta-piṭaka:* the discourses of the Buddha as contained in the *Tripiṭaka*.

there are many ways to reach the goal. Some of the pathways are long and some are short. But the main signposts along the way remain the same, for we already know (chapter 3) that the Buddha varied his methods of teaching according to circumstances. The *Upanisā sutta* was directly addressed to his bhikkhus, who we can assume were already familiar with *vipassanā* meditation. All he needed therefore to do was merely to highlight the most important steps leading to liberation and leave it to the bhikkhus to fill in the gaps.

Vipassanā meditation

We are now living in a different era separated from the time of the Buddha by well over two thousand five hundred years. Hence it is difficult to find genuine *vipassanā* meditation masters. Two renowned 20th century masters were the late Mahasi Sayadaw[37] and the late Ñāṇārāma Mahāthera[38]. They had researched a vast amount of Buddhist literature including the *suttas,* commentaries and sub-commentaries on them as well as the monumental classical works, *Vissuddhi magga*[39] *and the Paṭisambhidā magga*[40] and incorporated such information into their own experiences in insight meditation practices before offering practical courses in *vipassanā* meditation.

The progressive steps in *vipassanā* meditation as taught and practised by them are given below in the form of a table. The steps are longer than those shown in the *Upanisā Sutta.* This is understandable; the present generation readers and meditators could very well benefit from more detailed instructions than their counterparts of twenty-five centuries ago, who had direct access to the Buddha or His Arahants.

---

37. Mahasi Sayadaw, *Practical Insight Meditation,* B.P.S. 1991.
38. Ñāṇārāma Mahathera, *The Seven Contemplations of Insight* B.P.S, 1997.
39. *Visuddhimagga, The Path of Purification,* Translated by Bhikkhu Nanamoli, 1993 Ed.
40. *Paṭisambhidāmagga,* (PTS).

Comparing steps to liberation through insight (*vipassanā*) meditation

(i) Mahasi Sayadaw

1. Analytical knowledge of mind and body
2. Knowledge by discerning conditionality
3. Knowledge of comprehension
4. Knowledge of corruption of insight
5. Knowledge of dissolution
6. Awareness of fearfulness
7. Knowledge of misery
8. Knowledge of disenchantment
9. Knowledge of desire for deliverance
10. Knowledge of re-observation
11. Knowledge of equanimity about formations
12. Insight leading to emergence
13. Knowledge of adaptation
14. Maturity knowledge
15. Path knowledge
16. Fruition knowledge
17. Reviewing knowledge
18. Attainment of fruition

(From: *The progress of insight*—Mahasi Sayadaw)

(ii) Ñāṇārāma Mahathera

1. *Stage of viewing*

i. Discerning delimitation of mind and matter
ii. Discernment of conditions
iii. Purification by overcoming doubt
iv. Full understanding of the known

2. *Stage of comprehension*

i. Knowledge of comprehension of the three characteristics (impermanence-distress-no 'I')
ii. Immature stage of knowledge of rise and fall of phenomena
iii. Knowledge of corruptions of insight
iv. Knowledge of right and wrong paths
v. Mature knowledge of rise and fall of phenomena
vi. Awareness of fearfulness
vii. Purification by knowledge and vision of the way

3. Stage of gaining insight

i. Knowledge of dissolution
ii. Knowledge of fearfulness
iii. Knowledge of danger
iv. Knowledge of disenchantment/revulsion
v. Knowledge of desire for deliverance
vi. Knowledge of reflection i.e., reviewing the three characteristics.
vii. Knowledge of equanimity towards formations
viii. Knowledge of conformity of all phenomena to the three characteristics
ix. Knowledge of change of lineage from mundane to supramundane (lineage of the noble ones)
x. Knowledge of path of stream-entry
xi. Knowledge of fruition

(From: *The Seven Contemplations of Insight*—Ñāṇārāma Mahāthera)

Voyage of Discovery

It is now time to re-state what we have discovered on our voyage through our body and mind, and what more needs to be done to achieve liberation.

Primary

a. Understood how mind and matter worked.
b. Learnt to cultivate mindfulness.
c. Changed lifestyle so as to ensure adherence to the *sīla* group of the Noble Eightfold Path and became appreciative of the benefits of non-greed, non-hatred and non-delusion.
d. Commenced cultivating the sublime states of universal-kindness, compassion, unenvious-joy and equanimity (*mettā, karuṇā, muditā* and *upekkhā*).
e. Studied the *paṭiccasamuppāda* and understood its interconnectedness to the Four Noble Truths and the doctrine of *kamma* and rebirth.
f. Made the *paṭiccasamuppāda* come alive during contemplation and discovered within it impermanence, unsatisfactoriness and the non-self nature of all

phenomena at the transcendental level.
g. Practised reflection and contemplation.

Secondary

a. Developed a desire to go forward, and therefore discovered the *Upanisā Sutta* which shows the road to transcendence.
b. Understood and comprehended the *Upanisā Sutta* at the *sutamaya* and *cintāmaya* levels.
c. Realized that the links in the second part of the *Upanisā Sutta* directed us towards liberation and that insight (*vipassanā*) meditation is essential for further progress.

Tertiary

a. Realized that we have still some way to go on our journey to fruition.
b. Realized that *vipassanā* meditation required intensive application.
c. Looked around for a recognized teacher and/or books on *vipassanā* meditation, and commenced *vipassanā* meditation proper.
d. Observed that after reaching the 'concentration' stage, it was necessary to open one's mind to all phenomena as they appear and disappear.
e. Saw superficially the appearance and disappearance of phnomena.

* * *

Some practical instructions on *vipassanā* meditation and how our knowledge and insight into the *paṭiccasamuppāda* could help us to complete our journey to liberation are offered in the next chapter.

CHAPTER VI

Paṭiccasamuppāda and Vipassanā Meditation

We are now ready for the final part of our journey, for we now know and understand that everything in the universe is conditioned and subject to impermanence, distress and unsatisfactoriness and that there is no such thing as a continuing self or 'I'.

Life is a continuing process of evolution. Each of us has the potential to evolve morally and spiritually. In fact, we have been doing so during our journey through *saṃsāra* every time we have had an earthly life. We now have the added advantage of a time period in which the Buddha's Dhamma is available to guide us. This opportunity is not accidental but a result of the *pāramis*[41] which we had developed to a certain level in previous births.

If this were not true, we would not even have had the inclination or the opportunity to select this book for reading, let alone studying and comprehending its contents.

We now have complete confidence in the Buddha and the Dhamma, and are eager to experience the truth embodied in the *paṭiccasamuppāda*, for we have realized that craving, clinging and attachment are the byproducts of ignorance, which ensure our continuing journey in *saṃsāra*.

A special effort is needed to truly comprehend and realize the supramundane in a short series of steps. These steps are incorporated into the practice of *vipassanā* meditation, but to take these steps we have to promise ourselves that we shall make a sustained effort, for we are now well aware of the rewards that lie ahead. We can therefore perhaps repeat what the poet Robert Frost (1874–1963) said:

---

41. *Sati-sampajañña–sati* is mindfulness, and *sampajañña* is thorough understanding or comprehension, the two together, *sati-sampajañña* is defined as 'mindfulness with clear comprehension.'

"But I have promises to keep,
... And miles to go before I sleep"

From: "Stopping by Woods on a Snowy Evening".

The time has come for this effort. However, this last part of the journey has to be crafted carefully and followed conscientiously.

The Buddha has repeatedly emphasized the importance of contemplation and meditation as a way, in fact an essential requirement, to achieve liberation. The classical *suttas* in this regard are *The Mahā Satipaṭṭhāna sutta* (M) we referred to in chapter 2, the *Ānāpānasati sutta* (M) and the *Upanisā sutta* with which we became familiar in the previous chapter.

There are now numerous meditation centers in the USA, UK, Europe and Asia that conduct courses on a regular basis in the Theravada tradition and are popularly known as *vipassanā* meditation centers. The focus is on strictly following the instructions as contained in the *Satipaṭṭhāna Sutta*. The courses range from 1-3 months of total immersion, or shorter retreats of ten days' total immersion, as well as still shorter workshops. The teachers at these centers are second or third generation descendents of the original *vipassanā* meditation masters who are said to have individually 're-discovered' *vipassanā* meditation techniques in Myanmar *(Burma)* and used them with success to attain liberation.

The need for the earnest student to find a suitable meditation teacher must be emphasized. Even if the reader is very knowledgeable in the Buddha Dhamma, the fact remains that one is now journeying along an unfamiliar path. Consequently, there will be many occasions when one could benefit from the advice and instructions of a competent, experienced meditation master.

It is also advisable for the student to enquire whether such a teacher uses an understanding and contemplation of the *paṭiccasamuppāda* with its twelve links as an essential part of the *vipassanā* practice, for we can recollect from our previous studies what the Buddha has said in this regard:

"He who sees dependent origination sees the Dhamma, He who sees the Dhamma sees the dependent origination" (M28).

Then by inference, could we not perhaps say 'one who does not see dependent origination does not see the Dhamma' and 'he who does not see the Dhamma does not see dependent origination'?

But while the reader is searching for a teacher, he may perhaps find the information given below sufficient to start meditating in the *vipassanā* way. *It should however be kept in mind that these instructions are poor substitutes for a competent and proven meditation guide.* The instructions given below are drawn from the limited experiences of my fellow meditators and myself.

Preliminary steps in meditation

The beginner must first feel sufficiently motivated to proceed on his own. He should dedicate himself earnestly to the task ahead. Next he has to select a place suitable for his daily meditation and decide on a time frame for each meditation session. (He can of course change this as he moves along and as his competency improves). Further, he has to select a suitable place relatively free of disturbances. Then, by experimentation, he must choose a suitable posture in which he can remain for a considerable length of time with the minimum of bodily movements. He also needs to have the patience to continue in the practice even when there are no visible signs of progress. In summary, the meditator needs to find each day, the time followed by the following 6 p's:

Time - **p**lace - **p**osture - **p**ractice - **p**atience - **p**erseverance - and still more **p**ractice!

A person may find it beneficial to start a meditation session by first looking inwards and ensuring that he is skilful in speech, action and livelihood (steps in the Noble Eightfold Path).

The usual practice is then to arrive at a sublime and a tranquil state of mind by wishing himself and all sentient beings to be happy and well. By doing so, he is able, at least for the duration of the meditation session, to suppress the negativities of anger and greed. The tool to be used is often called an 'invocation' or a 'wish'. The meditator himself can formulate it, or the following model (or a modification) could be used instead. Most *vipassanā* teachers suggest this kind of invocation to be used by their students.

A Wish For Happiness

May I be well. May I be happy and peaceful. May no harm come to me.

May I be free from greed, selfishness and jealousy. May I be able to meet the ups and down of life with patience, courage and understanding.

May my parents, teachers and family be well. May they be happy and peaceful. May no harm come to them. May they be free from greed, selfishness and jealousy. May they be able to meet the ups and downs of life with patience, courage and understanding.

May my friends and all the people in this city be well. May they be happy and peaceful. May no harm come to them. May they be free from greed, selfishness and jealousy. May they be able to meet the ups and downs of life with patience, courage and understanding.

May everyone in this country be well. May they be happy and peaceful. May no harm come to them. May they be free from greed, selfishness and jealousy. May they be able to meet the ups and downs of life with patience, courage and understanding.

May those who dislike me be well. May they be happy and peaceful. May no harm come to them. May they be free from greed, selfishness and jealousy. May they be able to face the ups and downs of life with patience, courage and understanding.

May all sentient beings be well. May they be happy and peaceful. May no harm come to them. May they be free from greed, selfishness and jealousy. May they be able to meet the ups and downs of life with patience, courage and understanding.

He now tells himself to exercise self-restraint in respect of his six-sense faculties: eyes, ears, tongue, nose, body and mind, and after gathering inward confidence to commence meditation. If he were now to focus his mind on one or more of the 'sublime states' (*brahma-vihāra*) of universal kindness (*mettā*), compassion (*karuṇā*), participating joy (*muditā*) and equanimity (*upekkhā*), he would find that his mind would settle down and reach a high degree of tranquillity and serenity conducive to meditation, because:

Universal kindness or friendliness promotes good-will and therefore reduces ill-will.

Compassion results in reducing the pain and misery of others in a practical way. It helps abandon cruelty, while encouraging us to be merciful and helpful.

Participating joy fosters absence of envy and helps abandon hatred and dislike.

Equanimity helps us to regard all persons with tolerance and it generates goodness in us.

These four emotions, as we can see, are the embodiment of goodness. That is why they are called 'sublime'.

William Shakespeare (1564–1616) was not far off the mark when he said:

> "The quality of mercy is not strained
> It droppeth as the gentle rain from heaven
> Upon the place beneath: it is twice blessed
> It blesseth him that gives and him that takes".

We only need replace the word 'mercy' with friendliness, compassion, sympathetic joy or equanimity respectively.

And, when we reflect even for a moment on the ups and downs of life, we will undoubtedly agree with the nineteenth century anonymous poet who wrote:

> "Life is mostly froth and bubbles,
> Two things stand like stone:
> Kindness in another's troubles!
> Courage in your own."

From. 1866 - 'Ye wearie wayfarer
Hys Ballad. In Eight Fyttes'

Now with a non-agitated mind, the meditator can take the next step, which is to develop concentration.

Concentration

Since the meditator is firmly established in morality (*sīla*), and has a tranquil mind, he can now select a subject on which to fix his attention to the exclusion of other thoughts during a meditation session. One of the most popular subjects used for developing concentration is one's breath, for when it comes to the breath, one does not associate it with anything, not even with oneself or 'I'. One considers the breath as something that has always been there from the day of birth to the last breath on the day of his death.

In the meditation on the breath, the posture is particularly important. If one does not adopt an upright cross-legged, or semi-cross-legged posture sleepiness can often hinder one's efforts. (Western meditators may find that they are unable to adopt this posture for physiological or other reasons, in which case, sitting upright on a straight-backed chair with the feet firmly placed on the ground has been found by present day meditation teachers to give comparable results). The meditator now focuses his attention on his normal breath and watches how the air flows in and out through his nostrils. He follows the breath only at the point of entry and exit. Following points will be useful:

i. The first step is to find it. What we are looking for is the physical sensation of the air that passes in and out of the nostrils. This is usually just inside the tip of the nose, and less frequently on the upper lip. You find your 'point' by taking a deep breath and noticing where you have the most distinct sensation of the in-breath. Repeat with an out-breath and confirm this point. It is from this point that you will follow the whole breath. *Once you have located this 'breath point,' don't deviate from it.*

ii. Make no attempt to control the breath.

iii. Observe the breath closely. There are delicate variations. Long breaths, short breaths, deep breaths, shallow breaths, smooth breaths and ragged breaths. They also combine in various ways - like the notes in a piece of music.

iv. Next, do not observe only the outline of the breath. Observe the beginning, middle and the end. So also in the out-breath.

v. Study the above phenomena and move on. Return your attention to the breath, over and over again.

vi. Do not let the monkey-mind syndrome and distractions bother you. Be equanimous. All novice meditators will pass through this phase during their early meditation practice. They find the mind wandering and not remaining fixed on the object of meditation, which in this case is the breath. The mind is like the proverbial attention-deficit monkey who can rarely stay still for more than a few seconds. He will jump from one branch of a tree to another all the time, in spite of the fact that the branch on which he sits is full of luscious tender leaves and edible ripe fruits. He is constantly on the lookout for 'greener pastures'. There are several well-known ways out of this conundrum. The first is the counting method. A novice will start counting the breath when he notices that the mind is wandering, but he does so only up to ten.[42] If the mind continues to wander he will repeat this exercise as many times as is necessary for him again to focus exclusively on the breath.

The second method is to 'label' all distractions as soon as they appear by identifying each distraction with just a single word. For example, 'car', 'TV', 'dog', 'thinking' and so on, and then letting go of the distraction and getting back to mindful meditation on the breath.

vii. Having got rid of distractions and having learnt to keep the mind from wandering, it is *wordless* observation of the breath.

viii. *Vipassanā* meditation is an active function. It is awareness through one-pointedness.

ix. As your concentration deepens, you will have less trouble with an agitated mind.

x. Your breathing will now slow down and you will be able to follow it more and more clearly with fewer interruptions. You will begin to experience a state of great calm in which you enjoy complete freedom from physical irritants such as greed, lust, envy, jealousy and hatred. These are beautiful, clear, blissful states of the mind.

xi. These blissful states are, however, temporary and will end when the meditation session ends.

However, in spite of all our efforts there is a class of hindrances that can affect our progress. These are called *nīvaraṇa*. For instance, we may experience impatience with lack of progress, or aversion in the form of anger, or depression because progress seems slow. Sometimes lethargy overwhelms us, and we doze off as soon as we start to meditate. Sometimes we may be so agitated that we fidget or find excuses to avoid meditating. At other times scepticism undermines the will to

---

42. The counting method has several variations depending on the teacher.

continue, unreasoning doubts about the methodology or about your teacher, or even about our own ability to meditate.

At such moments we must understand that these hindrances have arisen only in reaction to our success in practising mindfulness with clear comprehension (*sati-sampajañña*)[1]. If we persevere, they are bound to disappear gradually.

The five *nīvaraṇas* (hindrances) really are all in the mind. They are:

1. Sensual desire
2. Aversion or anger, ill will and hatred
3. Sloth and torpor or lethargy, which simply is mental laziness.
4. Agitation (restlessness)
5. Doubt.

We must remember that all the five hindrances are mental factors. They are not self, just impersonal factors functioning in their own way.

In the *suttas* we find a simile illustrating the effect of these different obstructions. Imagine a pond of clear water where a rare gem lies at the bottom. We now add a number of bright dyes to the water, which then takes on beautiful psychedelic patterns. We become entranced with the beauty and intricacy of the colours and do not penetrate to the depths. This can be compared to sensual desires. Anger, ill will and aversion can be compared to boiling water. Water that is boiling, as in a geyser, is very turbulent and we cannot see through to the bottom. Sloth and torpor are like the pond getting covered by a dense layer of algae. One cannot possibly penetrate to the bottom. Restlessness and worry are like a wind-swept pond. The surface is agitated and the bottom is impenetrable. Doubt is like the water when muddied; the bottom is obscured.

Now, how can we deal with these enemies?

Happily, there are specific ways to deal with them as they confront us along the path. The first is to recognize them, to see them clearly every moment they appear. This very recognition is the most powerful and effective way of overcoming them. Recognition leads to mindfulness and mindfulness means not clinging, not condemning and not identifying oneself with the object. All hindrances are impermanent mental factors. They arise and pass away. If we are mindful of them as soon as they arise, do only note them without reacting, (in fact, decline to identify ourselves with them); then they would pass through the mind without creating 'waves'. Mindfulness is the best and most effective way of dealing with them.

We can then see the bottom of the pond clearly and we will find no difficulty in picking up this rare gem, which as you already would have guessed, is 'wisdom'. As we know, this wisdom leads to insight and insight in turn leads to liberation.

Three steps in *Vipassanā* meditation

Once a novice meditator has learnt to concentrate on the breath, or any other subject of his choice for a reasonable period of time and to stay focused, he is ready to be introduced to insight or *vipassanā* meditation proper. *Vipassanā* or insight is the experiential understanding of the real nature of all phenomena in one's own mind and body. It is the very same model, which the Buddha adopted on the day of his Enlightenment. It is to observe with a clear unclouded and non-judgmental mind each and every thing happening in this fathom-long body.

We need to follow this same method and observe and develop insight within ourselves experientially. The universal method of insight meditation consists of a three-fold, graduated course corresponding to three stages of insight development.[2]

Step 1 - Walking meditation

The meditator will choose a subject such as the breath, or walking, to discriminate mentally and recognize the subtle differences in the ultimate constituents of actuality *via* the chosen subject of meditation. Let us assume that he has selected walking meditation.

In *vipassanā* meditation, a crucial factor is learning to concentrate and to be mindful. You will remember that previously, we learnt to concentrate and be mindful of the breath while in the sitting posture. Walking meditation too can lead to concentration as well as awareness. With proper walking meditation one can even gain insight into mind and matter and their impermanence.

A meditator should practise walking meditation with full awareness of the manner in which the steps are taken. At this introductory stage, he should note as 'left' when he takes a left step and when taking a right step, to note it as 'right'. The mind must observe the movement of the foot. He should lay stress on awareness, sharp awareness of the movement of the foot. To do walking meditation, he will need a private place with enough space for about eight or more paces. He will be walking back and forth very slowly.

The physical directions for walking meditation proper are simple. Start at one end and stay for the time it takes to breathe two or three times. Your arms should be held in a way that is comfortable in front, behind or at your sides. Lift the heel of one foot, then rest that foot on its toes. Next lift the foot and carry it forward slowly in a short step and then bring it down. Next shift your weight onto this leg and then slowly repeat with the other foot. Continue till you come to the end of the walk and stop for the time it takes you to breathe twice. About-turn clockwise, very slowly and mindfully, (this is in keeping with the Buddhist tradition of circumambulation). On completion of the turn, remain stationary for two breaths, then proceed walking in the previous fashion till you come back to your starting point. Repeat this slow walking with mindfulness and total concentration until it is time to end your meditation session. Remember to keep your head up and your neck relaxed. Keep your eyes open to maintain balance, but in a rather unfocussed manner so that you are not looking at anything in particular. Walk naturally but at the slowest pace that is comfortable. Watchout for tensions as soon as you spot them. Your objective is to attain total alertness, heightened sensitivity and a full, unblocked experience of the motion of walking.

You will now observe that a step, which appeared to be smooth and continuous, is in fact composed of a complex series of tiny activities. Try not to miss anything. You can break down each step to many component parts. At the start you can notice at least four of these: lifting of the foot, moving the foot forward, dropping it down and shifting the body weight onto that foot.

You will also see that with good concentration you will not be aware of the form of the foot. Nor will you be aware of the body or bodily form. What you know is just movement of the foot. You will in fact find yourself fully immersed in a fluid, unbroken awareness of motion.

If your mind wanders, note the distraction in the usual way, then return your attention to walking. *Don't think, just feel. Register the sensations as they flow.* The *vipassanā* walking technique is designed to flood your consciousness with simple sensations, and to do it so thoroughly that all else is pushed aside. When you do so over a period of time, many things are revealed to you.

Let us discuss the practice of walking meditation a little more. We started by trying to be mindful of the act of stepping, then we moved onto focusing on two stages of walking. Stepping and putting the foot down, stepping, putting down. We then started to note mindfully four stages in each step. Raising our heel, lifting our foot, moving it forward and finally placing it on the ground. We progressed to the point where we noted five stages: Raising, lifting, moving, placing (frequently called 'pressing'), and shifting your weight.

By now you should have realized that when you were mindful of these five stages when taking a single step, you were naturally slowing down your walking, which came automatically. This slowing down is particularly beneficial because it is only then that you can be truly mindful and fully aware of all the movements. Whereas previously you thought that when taking a step it was a continuous movement, you now realize that this is not so. The raising movement of the heel is not mixed with the lifting movement of the foot and the lifting movement of the foot is not mixed with the moving forward movement, and so on. You will observe all movements clearly and distinctly.

As *vipassanā* meditators, you will notice much more as you continue with the practice. When you lift the foot you will experience the lightness of the foot. When you push the foot forward you will notice movement from one place to another. When you put the foot down you will feel the heaviness of the foot because the foot becomes heavier and heavier as it descends. When you put the foot down and shift your weight, you feel the touch of the ground as either hard or soft.

When you observe these four processes you are perceiving the four primary particles - they are the solid, liquid, heat/caloricity and finally air particles.

Let us go into a little more detail about the characteristics of these primary elements during walking meditation. In the first movement of lifting the foot when you felt lightness, you perceived caloricity. This energy allows us to raise the foot and move it forward, but in the lifting and carrying forward of the foot there was also movement. Movement is one aspect of air and it is dominant as we move the foot forward. When you move the foot down, there is a kind of heaviness in the foot. Heaviness is a characteristic of liquid. Thus you have perceived the liquid element. Finally when pressing the foot down and shifting your weight onto that foot, you perceive the hardness or softness of the ground. You have now felt the characteristic and the nature of solidity and have seen, experientially, the composition of the aggregates of *rūpa* or matter.

We thus see that in just one step, we can perceive many processes. Only those who practise walking meditation can ever hope to see these things.

When you continue to practise walking meditation you will come to realize that with every movement, there is also the noting mind, the awareness of movement. There is the lifting movement and the awareness of the lifting movement, then the movement and the awareness thereof, and so on. You then come to realize that both the movement and the mind (which is aware of the movement) arise and disappear in that very moment. Movement, awareness, disappearance. The moment of awareness is in the mind, whereas matter achieves the movement of the foot. In other words, mentality and materiality are working together.

Another thing, which you discovered, is that an intention precedes every one of the movements. You lift your foot because you want to. You move it forward because you want to, and so on. You thus realize that an intention has always preceded a movement, and you understood from practical experience that, as the Buddha said, "mind is the forerunner of all phenomena". This discovery by actual experience and practice during *vipassanā* meditation is the first of the *vipassanā* insights. It is called *nāma-rūpa-pariccheda-ñāṇa*, or insight knowledge of how mind and matter always work together.

You now understand that there is a cause or a condition for every movement, and in this case, the condition is the intention preceding each movement. You thus finally comprehend the relationship of conditioning and the conditioned, cause and effect. With this understanding, you have taken a giant step forward in your meditation.

Meditation on the Breath

If you have selected the breath as the preferred subject for meditation, you will begin the practice as outlined in the foregoing pages. You will, instead of letting go of disturbances and thoughts, address them with equanimity as they appear, and only let them go after contemplation and realizing that they are nothing but phenomena which arise, stay awhile and then pass away *(uppāda, ṭhiti, bhaṅga)*.You will also realize that they are at the fundamental level, void or empty of a permanent core.

Taking stock

We are now well on our way: a voyage within our own body and mind to find the truth unclouded by the delusion of a self-perpetuating 'I'. However, before we proceed to the next step in *vipassanā* meditation, it is useful to take stock of how far we have progressed in the development of the mind, for we need to make sure that we have removed all negative feelings and emotions which would otherwise impede our progress. If we continue to harbour hatred, aversion, greed, selfishness and sensual desires, it will virtually be impossible for us to proceed towards the development of insight.

There are many known methods for getting rid of these negativities permanently. One proven method is for us to look inwards during a meditation session and see with an open, non-judgmental mind whether we indeed have these negative characteristics within ourselves or not. Another recommended way is to contemplate on the opposite positive factors, namely the four sublime states or *brahma-vihāras* of universal kindness, compassion, participating joy and equanimity. When we do so, taking one subject at a time, we can see whether even the tiniest of their opposites are yet in our minds or not.

The Buddha has laid down a method for developing the sublime states: "Here, monks, a disciple dwells pervading one direction with his heart filled with loving-kindness, likewise the second, the third and the fourth direction; so above, below and around; he dwells pervading the entire world everywhere and equally with his heart filled with loving-kindness, abundant, grown great, measureless, free from enmity and free of distress." (DN 13). He repeats the same advice for the other three sublime states as well. We need only replace the word loving-kindness with either compassion or participating joy or equanimity.

In 'pervading' and 'directions', one's thoughts should be directed first to the east, then to the west, next to the north and then to the south. This should be followed by directing one's thoughts to the areas in between and finally to the zenith and the nadir, i.e., above and below, including the skies and birds and the seas and fish and so on.

In practising meditation using loving-kindness as a model, we first repeat the 'invocation' or 'wish' as given earlier and then we direct such thoughts to those we love, and so on (as described in the invocation) till we come to disagreeable people. This of course is the hardest task, but as true meditators we can breakdown the remaining barriers by heroic effort. We make no discriminations in our pervasive thoughts of loving-kindness, and extend our thoughts of loving-kindness equally to all. (There is a Sinhala saying which comes to mind: "when serving rice, do so to everyone using the very same spoon")[43].

At this point of proper practice, we should have come to a higher stage of concentration, and we would in fact have reached access-concentration *(upacāra-samādhi)*. Further progress will lead to full concentration (*appanā*) reaching fruition as the first *jhāna,* then onto the higher *jhānas*. The ultimate aim of attaining the *jhānas* relating to the four sublime states is to produce a state of mind that can serve as a firm foundation for the development of liberating insight into the true nature of all phenomena as being impermanent, subject to suffering and being void. A mind that has achieved meditational absorption induced by the *Brahma-vihāra* (sublime states) will now be pure, tranquil, firm, collected and largely free of negativities. A meditator is then well prepared for the final effort, which is aimed at deliverance.

Meditative development of the sublime states will be aided by repeated reflection upon the benefits they bring and the dangers of their opposites. As the Buddha has said 'What a person considers and reflects upon for a long time, to that his mind will bend and incline.'[5]

---

43. Sinhala: The main race and language of Sri Lanka.

Step 2 of *vipassanā* meditation

As persons who have made a study of the *paṭiccasamuppāda* in the previous chapters, it would be appropriate to use it as the subject for our advanced *vipassanā* meditation. This is also particularly appropriate because of the fact that the Buddha on his road to enlightenment used this very subject for His awakening. The Buddha categorically says that this was His eye-opening discovery in one sentence: 'He who sees Dependent Origination sees the Dhamma. He who sees the Dhamma sees Dependent Origination (MN 28). The Arahat Assaji was the first to see this clearly, as was shown earlier.

Meditating on the *Paṭiccasamuppāda*.

The meditator will now look at the *paṭiccasamuppāda* as part of his personal experience from different angles. He contemplates, reflects and analyzes it. He finds that whichever way he looks at it, the inevitable conclusion in the ultimate sense is that there is no being or individual, but only a continuity of conditioned, dependent phenomena occurring in what appears as a causal chain constantly undergoing origination and dissolution.

With further application of concentration focused into laser-sharpness, he looks again at the twelve links of the *paṭiccasamuppāda* in the forward and reverse directions. Forward contemplation shows us the existence of suffering. He first sees how ignorance sets in motion the life cycle. Ignorance thus conditions action, and action conditions consciousness. From consciousness he proceeds to contemplation of name-and-form, then the six senses and so on. Finally he sees that craving leads to clinging and then to becoming. With becoming he sees that birth is inevitable. Now with insight he sees that birth is always followed by sickness, ageing and death - all of which cause considerable suffering. Contemplating the twelve links in this manner will lead him to a profound understanding of mind-matter phenomena called an individual (*puggala*).

He would then practise the reverse contemplation, but he should not do so by starting with the twelfth link and proceeding backwards to the first link. On the contrary, he should start in this case too with ignorance, for, once there is no ignorance, there will be no deluded action. When actions are not governed by greed, hatred and delusion, he sees that there is no defilement of consciousness. He proceeds in this manner till he comes to becoming, birth and death—thus seeing with insight how this whole chain of becoming ceases. He then realizes that he has been gradually engaging the Eight-fold Path (the Fourth Noble Truth) of skilful understanding, skilful thought, skilful action and so on, to put an end to the chain of suffering.

He next sees that this five-aggregate 'person' is at the ultimate level nothing but a combination of the five formations or the five groups of clinging (*pañcupadānakkhandha*) which are subject to decay, suffering and death. He also sees with insight that he cannot find a permanent core or entity in the entire conditioned dependent chain. He finds only phenomena and becomes detached from them, and with this detachment he comprehends the fact of non-self or *anattā.*

The meditator now spreads his focus to other phenomena and sees clearly that all formations, which he looks at, along with their causes and conditions, originate and dissolve before his very eyes. They are all impermanent, *anicca*.

At this point of self-realization, a meditator is often beset by certain corruptions of insight called *vipassanā upakkilesa.* These are extraordinary experiences that arise when insight meditation begins to gather momentum. Examples are the perception of one or more of the following: bright lights, an aura around the meditator, a sharp increase in understanding, happiness, rapture, or a feeling of being energized. While these are useful indicators telling the meditator that he is now progressing well, they become corruptions or *kilesa* when he begins to get attached and proceeds to enjoy and dwell in them, thinking that he is now liberated.

The meditator should instead, recognize them merely as imposters and examine these experiences with equanimity and according to the three universal characteristics of all conditioned phenomena, namely as impermanent, subject to suffering and non-self. With this insight he will then let go and proceed with renewed enthusiasm.

In the second stage of insight meditation we have used the subject of *paṭiccasamuppāda* because of our familiarity with it. There are, in addition, numerous topics that are suitable for advanced meditation. In fact, in the *Mahā Satipaṭṭhāna Sutta* itself, the Buddha has recommended four subjects as suitable for insight meditation, which are:

The body (including the breath)—*kāyānupassanā*
Feelings or sensations—*vedanānupassanā*
The mind—*cittānupassanā* and
Mental formations—*dhammānupassanā*.

Out of all of these, the breath often takes precedence as the subject most suitable for meditation. However, it is the meditation teacher who will be the most competent person to suggest a meditation subject to the novice meditator, and he will do so according to his assessment of the novice's individual aptitudes.

Step 3 in *vipassanā* meditation

The meditator who has practised insight meditation successfully at stage two for some time, will now continue self-examination with added zest and energy. He will observe non-judgmentally everything happening within his body, while at the same time not allowing proliferation of thoughts. He will merely observe phenomena: their appearance, short existence and immediate dissolution (*uppāda, ṭhiti, bhaṅga*), unconnected to anything else.

He will then be following the instructions that the Buddha gave the advanced meditator, Bāhiya Dārucīriya–an injunction so deep that it brought Bāhiya to enlightenment right on the spot:

"In the seen there will be only the seen; in the heard there will be only the heard; in the sensed there will be only the sensed; in the cognized there will be only the cognized. This is how you must train yourself, Bāhiya" (*Udāna*, 1:10).

The meditator now sees with insight that all formations within himself, as well as in the whole universe, are indeed characterized by impermanence, unsatisfactoriness and devoid of 'self'. (see foot-note 5). He fixes his mind on just one of the above characteristics and quite soon is able to make a break-through to full understanding. Noble Path-consciousness arises, and he transcends the mundane and passes to the supramundane, which is the peace of Nibbāna, for the first time.

On the other hand, if he is contemplating and reflecting on the *paṭiccasamuppāda*, he would be fixing his mind on all three characteristics simultaneously, and it will not be long before he too is able, as in the previous example, to transcend the mundane, pass onto the supramundane peace of Nibbāna for the first time. He then completes the experiential understanding of the Four Noble Truths by attaining the knowledge of the Path of stream entry, *sotāpatti-magga-ñāṇa*. He has totally uprooted and discarded forever the three fetters, the of false view of personality, doubt and attachment to rites and rituals.

He rounds up his effort by achieving the knowledge of fruition (*phala-ñāṇa*) and the blissful peace of Nibbāna. It is at this stage that there arises in the meditator the reviewing knowledge of the Path and the Fruit (table 5.2. item 16*)* by which the meditator reviews the defilements that have been eliminated and those that yet remain.

A noble disciple may perhaps not stop now. What is left is only the need to eliminate the remaining seven defilements or fetters in order to become an Arahat—the fully liberated person.

CHAPTER VII

Concluding Remarks

We have now completed our journey of discovery, for we have explored the 'world',–our body and mind in the light of the Dhamma.

The Buddha has shown that the first critical step on our way to liberation is to first understand and comprehend the doctrine of dependent origination: "It is through not understanding, not penetrating this doctrine that this generation has become entangled like a tangled ball of string unable to pass beyond the round of *saṃsāra*." (M.ii.55). The final step is to practise the Dhamma *via* the Four Noble Truths, for we now realize that liberation is not possible until we eradicate ignorance (*avijjā*) and the three root defilements of greed (*lobha*), hatred (*dosa*) and delusion (*moha*) by following the Noble Eightfold Path, and *vipassanā* meditation.

When we do so, it can be as rewarding an experience for you, as it has been for me. We would perhaps have also realized that *vipassanā* meditation when targeted towards liberation entails an intensive and dedicated practice, for:

> "The heights by great men reached and kept
> Were not attained by sudden flight,
> But they, while their companions slept,
> Were toiling upward in the night." Longfellow 1807–82.

Nevertheless, a meditator should not over-strain himself whilst meditating. Here the importance of equanimity must be stressed. The meditator will then realize that meditation can be a pleasant and rewarding experience. This is why members of the *Ariya Saṅgha*–The Noble Ones, all had smiling faces.

When we 'live' the Dhamma in all of our waking hours, we will in effect be meditating, reflecting in the proper way *yoniso-manasikāra* and contemplating with total awareness and mindfulness all the time. It is with this paradigm shift, that meditation, like one's breath, becomes 'second nature' to us.

Insight and the development of understanding come when the mind is quiet. When we have an open and non-judgmental mind and see everything happening in our own body and mind from moment to moment with insight, the true Dhamma unwinds before our very eyes, and we commence to see the truth. How fast we progress thereafter depends solely on our individual efforts and abilities.

Let us not regret the past but let go of it and remember that we have the rest of our lives to achieve liberation.

> *"A fellow went to a Zen master and said,*
> *If I work very hard, how soon can I be enlightened?*
> *The Zen master looked him up and down and said, 'ten years'.*
> *The fellow said, 'No, listen, I mean if I really worked hard at it, how long?'*
> *The Zen master cut him off 'I am sorry I misjudged, twenty years.'*
> *'What!' said the young man, "You don't understand! I'm...'*
> *'Thirty years,' said the Zen master.*

From *Buddhism Plain and Simple* by Steve Hagen.

This brings us to the end of the presentation. It is the hope and fervent wish of the author that readers benefit from its perusal, which, for maximum benefit, should be accompanied by earnest contemplation, reflection, meditation and last but not least, genuine dedicated application.

May all beings develop insight and realize liberation!

BIBLIOGRAPHY (SEQUENTIAL)

1. Piyadassi Mahathera, *The Spectrum of Buddhism*, 1991.
2. Bhikkhu Bodhi, *The Buddha and His Dhamma*, 1999.
3. Narada Mahathera, *The Buddha and His Teachings*, 1997.
4. Walpola Rahula Mahathera, *What the Buddha Taught*, 1959.
5. Ron Wijewantha, *The Life and Message of the Buddha*, 1990, Limited Edition.
6. The Dalai Lama, *A flash of Lightning*.
7. K.N. Jayatilleke, *The Message of the Buddha*, 1979.
8. Bhikkhu Bodhi, *A Comprehensive Manual of Abhidhamma*, 1999.
9. Peter Della Santina, *The Tree of Enlightenment*, 1997, Taipei. Taiwan.
10. Tanissaro Bhikkhu, *The Wings of Awakening*, (*An anthology of the Pali Canon*), 1996.
11. Bhikkhu Bodhi, *Transcendental Dependent Origination*, 1980.
12. John Walters, *Mind Unshaken*.
13. Bhikkhu Bodhi, *The Great Discourse on Causation*, 1995, BP211S, BPS, Kandy, Sri Lanka.
14. Mahasi Sayadaw, *Practical Insight Meditation*.
15. Nyanatiloka, *Buddhist Dictionary*, 1980, BPS, Kandy, Sri Lanka.
16. Ñāṇārama Mahathera, *The Seven Contemplations of Insight*, 1997, BPS.

Other Recommended Reading

1. Piyadassi Mahathera, *Dependent Origination*.
2. U. Pandita, *In This Very Life*, 1992.
3. Bhikkhu Bodhi, *The Noble Eightfold Path*, 1994.
4. Bhadantacariya Buddhaghosa, *The Visuddhimagga, The Path of Purification*, Translated by Bhikkhu Nanamoli. BPS. 1991.

Books on Vipassanā Meditation

1. *Practical Insight Meditation,* (Basic and Progressive Stages), Mahasi Sayadaw, 1991, BPS, Sri Lanka.
2. *The Progress of Insight,* Mahasi Sayadaw, 1994, BPS, Sri Lanka.
3. *The Art of Living,* (Vipassanā meditation), William Hart, (As taught by S.N. Goenka), 1987, Harper Row.
4. *Mahā Satipaṭṭhāna Suttam,* 1993, (Goenka's translation), Vipassana Research Publication, Dharmagiri, Igatapuri, Maha Rashtra, India.
5. *In This Very Life,* U Pandita, 1992, Wisdom.
6. *Mindfulness In Plain English,* Henepola Gunaratana Mahathera, 1991, Wisdom.
7. *The Four Foundations of Mindfulness,* U. Silananda, 1990, Wisdom.

Some texts containing material on *Paṭiccasamuppāda*

1. *Visuddhimagga-Path of Purification,* Chapter 17, Trans. Bhikkhu Nanamoli.
2. *Paṭisambhidāmagga,* (PTS). *Paṭisambhidamagga Aṭṭhakathā* (Sinhala script, Simon Hewavitarana Bequest).
3. *Sutta pitaka,* (PTS).
4. *The Sālistamba Sutra,* N.Ross Reat, Motilal Banasidass Publishers Pvt.Delhi.
5. *Paṭṭhāna of the Abhidhamma Piṭaka.*
6. *The Wings of Awakening,* Tanissaro Bhikkhu, 1999, Corporate Body of the Buddhist Educational Foundation, Taipei, Taiwan, R.O.C.s
7. *The Tree of Enlightenment,* Peter D.Santina, 1998, Corporate Body of the Buddhist Educational Foundation, Taipei, Taiwan, R.O.C.
8. *Mahā Nidāna Sutta, The Great Discourse on Causation and its Commentaries,* Translation plus a long introductory essay, Bhikkhu Bodhi, BPS. 1984.

Woman in Buddhism

Studies on her Position and Role

by

Professor Dhammavihāri Thera

The Wheel Publication No. 453/454

First published 2003

PREFACE

Does woman need to be a subject of ceaseless controversy and debate? Thousands of years ago, back in Indian history, the *Manusmṛti*, the Grand Law Book of India, recorded that women were created for the generation of humanity [*Prajānārthaṃ striyaḥ sṛṣṭāḥ*]. It was argued therefore that she was entitled to equal justice with man [*Tasmād sādhāraṇaḥ dharmaḥ saha patnyā udīritaḥ* (Manusmṛti IX.96). This means: "Therefore an equal *dharma*, to be shared with the wife, has been laid down."

We also know that in early Vedic India the woman was entitled to attend to the *gārhya-patya* [i.e. the domestic sacrificial fire] in the absence of her husband from the home. But she was not to remain there long and enjoy that justifiably owned position. It was soon widely made known to people that it was unpleasant to the gods to see women at the sacrifices. She could not on her own make offerings to the gods [*Nāsti strīnāṃ pṛthag yajṭaḥ: Na vrataṃ nāpyupoṣathaṃ*. Manu V. 153]. There was no religiousness for woman, apart from humiliating subservience to her husband, which could do her any good [*patiṃ śuśrūyate yena tena svarge mahīyate.* Ibid.].

Buddhism ceaselessly challenged these religious inroads to social attitudes and approaches. Gender difference is not to stand in the way of women in religion or society. *Itthibhāvo no kiṃ kayirā?* "What will our being women matter?" The Buddhist nun Somā roared back in this manner at a heckling Māra. Spiritual profundity of nuns like Dhammadinnā and Vajirā should remain undiminishing sources of inspiration to women anywhere in the world.

Know ye the culture of your past - your achievements and the heights you have reached. In these essays, I have endeavoured to give you an insight into them. With your vision clear and aware of the goal you wish to achieve " Go ye forward and retrace not your steps" - *Mā nivattha, Abhikkama.*

May the generous contributors to this *dhamma-dāna,* living and dead, receive their blissful rewards.

Dhammavihāri 2002

International Buddhist Research and Information Center

WOMAN IN INDIA: DISCRIMINATED AGAINST OR NOT?

Concepts like women's liberation and feminist activists are nothing new in the world which we have inherited. This part of the world where we live is unquestionably known to have had a highly developed culture of its own, dating back to more than two and a half millennia. Where bondage exists and wields a crushing power, the concept of liberation, associated with or without violence in speech and action, seems necessarily a must. In ancient India, through various epochs of its history, with diverse religious and cultural traditions having their impact on society, both liberation and domination are equally well known. Through a very rigid vertical division of society into what was then known as the four castes or *catur varṇa* in the Puruṣa Sūkta of the Rig Veda, with its unjustifiable [except through doctrinaire religious teachings] social gradations, those who were higher up in the human community thus placed through religious sanctions, did definitely dominate over those below them. This clearly did happen with the Brahmins dominating over the Śūdras.

Likewise, men and women were separated apart, with serious gradations of high and low, superior and inferior, and stupidly enough at times, even clean and unclean [with an antithesis between male and female and high-castes and low-castes]. Any one who has enough patience to study the relevant literary sources of this period, from the early to the late, together with their religio-cultural emphases, should also have enough honesty to lay bare their contents with regard to these very vital sociological considerations. Re-writing of ancient history has become a very fashionable art to-day [more in support of very parochial aspirations and a measure of obviously necessary self-defence]. At the same time, there is also the very clearly evident new interpretations of theological positions. But these are by no means adequate to make amends for some of our mistakes of the past. That is why some of the old garrisons of religion are being assailed and their walls are seen crumbling down. And to-day, even people who attempt to formulate universal value systems for the benefit of humanity, seem to lack an adequate knowledge of the past which they plan to analyze and assess. They also seem to go more by hearsay and wishful thinking. Obviously, some of this background knowledge of the ramified past is either not known to them or is deliberately shut out from them.

My endeavour before this august assembly to-day is to pick out a few unquestionable authenticated positions in history, irrespective of the faiths and creeds to which we belong, and analyze them with dignified detachment, in order to be able to serve the cause of humanity at large. We are well aware that in this area we cannot have computer-designed products to sell to the world. They must naturally emerge from history, through revision and mod ification of some, and perhaps a total rejection of other patterns of thinking and social institutions which we have set up and inherited. Let me begin with ancient India, with more than two thousand year old traditions, even prior to the birth of Gotama in India in the sixth century B.C. As Buddhists, we begin by paying the highest tribute to the woman as the mother in the home. Literally, that is where we begin. As for the need of test-tube babies, even if we can get them without a mother, let us adequately be honest about our own motivation.

Woman in India / her position of respect and recognition

Perhaps it may be said with a fair degree of accuracy that the oldest and boldest statements regarding the glory of the woman in the human community had their origin in India, and that even more than two thousand years before the commencement of the Christian era. They are traceable back to the contents of those venerated volumes of the Rig Veda where we are told that in the unbroken continuity of the domestic sacred fire or the *Gārhya-patya*, the wife of the householder had to rightly step in and keep tending it until his return. There were no known grounds then, religious or social, on which to keep her out. The world apparently had not yet come to such a state of decadence to necessitate the setting up of a CEDAW - Convention on the Elimination of Discrimination Against Women.

In the sociology of that part of the then known world [i.e. in the sub-continent of India], a cataclysmic event of the magnitude of the glacial age was being set in motion about this time.

Human institutions where women held honoured and elevated positions, well founded on justice and fair play, were being assailed by sectarian groups with vested interests. These seem to have come out like volcanic eruptions, with or without warning rumblings, we do not know. Unknown and unseen authority of religion was being invoked and was good enough for any of these anti-humanist actions. Historians have studied what happened during this process. Their observations need to be studied with due detachment, unmindful of the invariable chastisement we are liable to get in the process for the sins of those who preceded us.

Here is Professor Altekar, an eminent historian, analyzing this social disaster which came upon women via a religious tornado.

> The prohibition of *upanayana* amounted to spiritual disenfranchisement of women and produced a disastrous effect upon their general position in society. It reduced them to the status of Śūdras. What, however, did infinite harm to women was the theory that they were ineligible for them [Vedic sacrifices] because they were of the status of Śudras. Henceforward they began to be bracketed with Śudras and other backward classes in society. This we find to be the case even in the Bhagavadgītā [IX. 32].
>
> *The Position of Women in Hindu Civilization*, p, 204.

Religious discrimination on the basis of sex

In the Manusmṛti which is a work of the Dharma Śāstra literature of India, we witness the cruel infliction of domestic subservience on the woman. The road to heaven is barred to her and there is hard bargaining with her for the offer of an alternative route. She can have no worship or prayer on her own [*Nāsti strīnāṃ pṛthag yajño na vrataṃ nāpyupoṣathaṃ*]. Matrimony and obedience to the husband [*patiṃ suśrūyate yena*] are the only means whereby a woman can hope to reach heaven [*tena svarge mahīyate*].

> *Nāsti strīnāṃ pṛthag yajño na vrataṃ nāpyupoṣathaṃ*
> *patiṃ suśrūyate yena tena svarge mahīyate.* Manu. V. 153

> No sacrifice, no vow, no fast must be performed by women [apart from their husbands]. If a wife obeys her husband, she will for that [reason alone] be exalted in heaven.
>
> *The Laws of Manu* Tr. by G. Buhler
> SBE. Vol. XIV. p.196. Ch.V. *v.* 155

The above is a beautiful study in historical contrast. The Vedas and the Manusmṛti we quoted above both belong to what we would in India call the Brahmanic tradition. But what a cleavage from the Vedas to the Dharma Śāstras and what a sharp contrast in attitudes. The woman is mercilessly and perhaps jealously, dragged down from her pedestal and virtually spat at. This calculated degradation of woman is seen being openly worked out even through the Brahmanas. She is ruthlessly reviled as being impure in the eyes of the gods, both physically and religiously. Painfully humiliating rituals [being treated as a draught animal with straw wrapped round her waist] are prescribed for her admission to the sacrificial ritual and restoration to the normal society of men and women. It is said to be the gods who seem to make the fuss about it. Or it is more likely that the masters of the rituals seem to compel the gods to do so.

One of the most atrocious acts of discrimination against the woman, man being placed in a very highly privileged position, is seen once again in the Manusmṛti [SBE. XXV quoted above, p. 196. *vv.* 157, 168].

Women are also said to be very much circumscribed in their intellectual and spiritual capacities. In their social life, stunning blocks have been placed on their way. On the death of her husband, a widow is not allowed, according to the Dharma Śāstras, even to think of the name of any man.

> *Na ca nāmā'pi gṛhṇīyāt patyau prete parasya tu.*
>
> Manu.

> At her pleasure let her emaciate her body by [living on] pure flowers, roots and fruit; but she must never even mention the name of another man after her husband has died.
>
> Manu. SBE. XXV.p.196. Ch. v. *v.*157

But a man is told that he is free to re-marry.

Punar dārakriyām kuryāt punar ādānam eva tu.

Manu once again.

Having thus, at the funeral, given the sacred fires to his wife who dies before him, he may marry again, and again kindle [the fires].

Manu quoted above. Ch. v. *v*168

Protestant Reforms and New Thinking

But both Pārśva Nātha of Jainism [a senior of Gautama] and Gautama the Buddha, as non-Brahmanic protestant leaders, appear to have totally rejected this position. They both opened the doors of their monastic communities, of course with strict provisos at times, for the admission of women. Hundreds and hundreds of women perfected their spiritual pursuits under Gautama. One single peep into the Psalms of the Sisters [Therī Gāthā] alone will provide much more evidence of this than one needs. Widows, bereaved mothers grieving over infant mortalities, victims of sexual assaults and exploited women of many other sorts, all appear to have had solace in the religion of the Buddha. Rejoice over the restoration to glory of the vast segment of the community of India's women whom these stories bring before us.

It is around this time, the sixth century B.C. or even a little earlier, that protestant movements like Jainism and Buddhism had to appear on the Indian scene to do quite a bit of violent clean up and restore lost rights of many social groups, sex wise as well as class and caste-group [*varṇa* and *jāti*] wise.

Buddhist women, young as well as old, are emboldened through their own religious convictions and awakening to challenge the existing Indian social and religious conventions on these matters. They were absolutely retrograde and misogynous. The Bhikkhuni Somā fires back at a challenger, a doubting Thomas of pre-Christian origin, who tells her that as a woman, with only her two-finger wisdom [*dvaṅgulapaññā*], she could never aspire to get anywhere near true sainthood [*yaṃ taṃ isīhi pattabbaṃ*]. This is what she bravely tells him at Thig. v. 61.

"What does it matter our being man or woman, when our minds are perfectly under our command? Our wisdom and judgement are wholly mature and the Truth of the Norm [*dhamma*], we clearly see ".

In the Indian context of the sixth century B.C., Somā's reply indeed would be the highest point of emancipation in the ladder of the women's lib. Spiritual emancipation was one of the major hurdles to clear.

A few observations from the Buddhist angle

On the other hand, Buddhism's contribution to the liberation and uplift of the Indian woman in the social sector was equally immense. Here again the elevation of the woman in the Buddhist set up was conceptually much nobler. It was much more than a question of 'rights" or 'duties". The Buddhists have to seriously respect inter-personal relationships so much that it would be painful for them to tear away any portion of society and isolate it from the rest on any basis like duties or rights. To the Buddhist, it is an achievement in the total integration of the woman [i.e. all females in the social set-up of the home] into the social fabric of the human community, the family being the smallest unit from where one should [and could] make the start. In Buddhist thinking, the male's respect for the female had to be so high that we could say with a deep conviction that the Buddhists perhaps knew the full connotation of *apres vous,* in the presence of ladies, well before the French. Even on the occasion of the Buddha's passing away, the Buddha's steward monk Ananda is said to have given the first offer to the females who had assembled to pay their respects to the dead Buddha on this understanding that they were ladies and therefore had to be treated with courtesy and consideration.

Buddhists refuse to forget that the mother is the highest symbol of respect in the home. She is after all the progenitor, the one who begat us. Biologically, she is the one who is nearest to us. It is the increased warmth of her body [conditionally generated at child-birth for our sake], during the earliest phase of our life here, that gave us infants the sense of safety and security. So we call the mother the *Friend in the Home -- Mātā mittaṃ sake ghare* SN. I. p. 37. Along with the father [if it does not turn out to be a miserable single parent home], she takes her rightful place as our first teachers, guiding us and ushering us into the new world of ours. As she gets older, as the mother of a mother, she becomes the patron of the extended family. This being her very wholesome domestic position, she does not need as a rule to defend herself with the use of a fire-arm [privately owned and secretly kept in a handbag] against a heartless husband or cruel boy friend, as it does happen often in many parts of the world. These, we know, are very much realities round the world, in the developed and less developed countries. These are regular news items in daily papers. To-day, the degradation has fallen so low that aged mothers can even become victims of their own child-murderers. These, we feel, are areas where women's prestige, rather than rights, have to be restored.

Through years of investigation and research, we have gained the conviction that wherever a woman tends to entertain the idea that she is more the wife of a husband than a mother of children, there is evidence of a misdirection of priorities. This invariably leads to a really serious rot in the main emotional trunk of the family. This applies to the misplaced role of a father as well. Firstly this leads to frustration and discontent in the minds of growing up children, generated through a sense of neglect and inadequate care and love. This in turn leads to deep-seated bitterness, jealousies and rivalries and even violent challenges.

Next take a look at the Indian woman as the wife in the home. The Rig Veda, perhaps among our oldest literary records, places the newly-wedded young woman in a very prestigious position [Rig Veda. X. 85. 46]. She is invoked to be a queen - *Rājñī* - among the in-laws in the household. Her role as mother of children is extolled. But latterly, by the time of the Dharma Śāstras, she is stigmatized as being ritually impure. No matter from where the insult or the assault came, the woman in society in the Buddha's day was thoroughly crushed and was literally on the mat. In Buddhist literature, the Buddha's own challenging statements, clearly reveal this. If she is a wise and virtuous girl, she must know how to keep her household in proper gear, with due respects to her husband and her in-laws in her new home. She must also take good care of her children and handle the household management well, with her domestic aids happy and content. Then all the success she needs for this world and the next are all within her command. One of the best in this area of counselling comes in the Buddha's advice to King Pasenadi Kosala who is said to have turned a little sour in the very presence of the Buddha, on hearing the news of the birth of a daughter. The above observations are a brief summary of the Buddha's words of advice to the king [See Saṃyutta Nikāya I. p.86. and *Kindred Sayings* I. 110 f.].

In the light of these, let us try to understand a few modern stresses in the re-defining of the status of woman in our society. If any harsh or unsympathetic curbs are really found to be placed on her today, in this tradition or that, let us view them with a total understanding of her real place in the human community, as a part fitting into a whole, effectively contributing to the total functioning. Highly finished and polished parts are of very little avail if they are not going to be parts of a whole. However, there may still be the need to respect differences in religio-cultural traditions, as long as they do not blatantly ride roughshod over basic human values.

I wish to add a few comments here on the question of ***women's employment*** [Article 11].

Buddhist thinking unequivocally defines the vital role of the female in relation to her domestic setting as 1. the young growing up daughter, a girl to be adequately equipped, through the mediation of her parents, with wisdom and virtue [*medhāvinī sīlavatī*] to steer clear in her journey through life, in the midst of temptations, threats and trepidations which a challenging world hurls at her, and 2. a newly-wedded wife, safely and securely established in her home, with delightfully warm-hearted relationships with every member of the homestead to which she has newly arrived [including all her in-law relations: *sassu-devā*], and well secured on the foundations of conjugal fidelity [*patibbatā*]. Finally 3. she is the large-hearted loving mother who is the friend-in-the-home [*mātā mittam sake ghare* SN. I.37], a friend to everyone, including the domestic aids of the household.

With that understanding of the position of woman within the fundamental social unit of the home, it should not be difficult at least for the vast majority of people in Asia who have had a distinctly Buddhist cultural background to determine as to what should be the priorities in the determination of the day to day activities of a female in society, and to align her in relation to the male members of the community. The separatist and splitist tendency within the family unit in terms of male or female rights would be most abhorrent to such a society. It would not only be theoretically hostile, but would in practice be disruptive and destructive.

Before concluding I would take one single instance to illustrate a point. Let us take into consideration a woman's capacity to be a wage-earner and her need to do so. Anywhere in the world today money has reached a very high position. It is the most efficient basis of buying power, of anything and at any time. At the same time, the world today has not been educated with regard to regulating the buying needs. With a devastatingly competitive market economy, producers and manufacturers continually stimulate the world at large to step out and buy, unmindful of their need to do so. That is the producer's own formula for their survival.

In the world of today, what is referred to as the concept of 'delay gratification" is a thing of very recent origin. In such a set up, where needs and the choice of needs are not regulated, everybody feels it necessary to possess money, his or her own, and that in unlimited quantities. It is that unlimited buying power which is believed to get one today higher and higher in the social ladder. This is what generates the need to create more and more avenues of employment, the need being for more and more avenues for earning money, even by fair or foul means. Whether it be that of the drug-peddler, or the one who sells illicit fire-arms or the sophisticated professional who ventures to carry out unauthorized abortions. Being employed in this manner is certainly no part of occupational therapy.

That being so, we would make bold to say many people irresponsibly desert their posts in quest of more opportunities to earn more and more money. In this quest, everybody would agree, the sky is the limit. Teachers would teach less in their regular class rooms and turn up with far greater enthusiasm at their pre-planned tuition sessions. Top-ranking medical practitioners would work less at their regular clinics and be more readily available as specialist consultants at a pre-determined higher rate of consultant fees.

Mothers would leave their younger children at state-run or privately owned day-care centres and be working in all manner of places, from daily-paid labour hands to high-ranking specialists at scientific and technological jobs. Our concern is about this latter and their absence from homes where their presence, we feel, would be more primarily needed. A stubborn defence of the one or the other is not what we are interested in. We need an honest approach to an essentially human problem. The question is 'Whose cause are we serving?" Can we honestly answer this, internationally? Or have we got to be reminded of the line 'Never the twain shall meet ".

[A paper presented at the UNICEF Conference in Kathmandu - 1996].

Dignified Position of Woman in Religion and Society

as seen through Buddhism

Indian culture, from very early times, appears to recognize woman as the matrix of society. Even the Rig Veda [X. 85 . 46] recognizes her rightful place in the home as the newly-wedded wife. In the Sūrya's Bridal Hymn, a prayer is offered that she may reign supreme over all her in-laws, father, mother, sister and brother. Her role as mother of children is extolled and it is wished with eagerness that she presides over the arrival of grandchildren too. Even in India she does not appear to have been divorced from her position as progenitor. Being stigmatized as ritually impure, the woman is nevertheless drawn in to participate in sacrifices, even through humiliating concessions, for in her absence the very existence and perpetuation of mankind is threatened.

The first expression of fair play towards woman as an equally privileged member of the human community is seen in the Manusmṛti [IX. 96] where it is said that woman was created as the progenitor and man as the perpetuator of the human species and as such a common dharma has been laid down for man and woman: *Tasmād sādhāraṇo dharmah saha patnyā udīritah*. With the growth of so-called religious institutions and the build-up of priestly power, it is true that the social and religious position of woman in India has witnessed a lamentable corrosion. She has come to be ranked with the *Caṇḍāla* [i.e. the socially most despised] and the ill-omened raven. Surprisingly enough, even the Manusmṛti we quoted above, rejects a woman's right to ascend to heaven by her own religious striving. A woman has no right of religious observances, it is said, no fast, no sacrifices. The glory of heaven is only for the woman who subserves her husband [*Patiṃ suśrūyate yena tena svarge mahīyate.* Manu. 5. 153].

At the time of the appearance of Buddhism in India, these fluctuations in the fortunes of woman were a reality and the exploitation of woman had reached an irritating high water mark. A rebuking Mara, reflecting the contemporary non-Buddhist views about the social and religious standing of woman, scoffs at Bhikkhuni Somā who as a nun was striving for self-liberation [SN. I. 129]. Spiritual heights are to be attained only by sages [*isīhi pattabbaṃ*], says Māra, implying specifically a male domination in the sphere of religion. This is unmistakably indicated in the rest of the remarks which say that a woman with her two-finger wisdom cannot ever hope to reach such spiritual heights [*na tvaṃ dvaṅgulapaññāya sakkā pappotuṃ itthiyā*].

Thus, at the time of the appearance of Buddhism, the Indian woman who earlier had occupied, on her own right, a prestigious position had sunk to a lamentable low. In childhood, in marriage and even in widowhood, the female in society was under the vigil of the male, thus most often being robbed of her initiative and originality, This was unquestionably an unwarranted subordination. This attitude had swept thorough the entire Indian society, reaching as high as the social elite. Even King Pasenadi Kosala had to be reminded by the Buddha of the fallacy of this assumption. This King who was saddened on the news of the birth of a daughter was told by the Buddha that if a girl were properly groomed to play her role in society efficiently, on that skill of her alone she would outshine men.

Itthī pi hi ekacciyā seyyā posā janādhipa.
Medhāvinī sīlavatī sassudevā patibbatā. SN. I. 86

Some women would, in their perfected feminine role, even excel men. Endowed with wisdom and virtue, she is chaste in her domestic behaviour as loyal wife, observing conjugal fidelity as the highest virtue in her married life, and holds in high esteem her husband's parents as her own [*sassudevā*].

Chastity of woman, both pre-marital and within marriage is a solemnly guarded virtue in Buddhism, both in terms of lay Buddhist society and the Buddhist religion. But some students of religion and culture, apparently lacking in a basic academic discipline, turn so wild in their generalizations as to declare:

"For example, virginity and chastity in females are not associated with Buddhist ethics or doctrine. One consequence of this is that marriage is a secular affair in Buddhist Sri Lanka, whereas it is a sacrament according to Brahmanic values." [Gananath Obesekera: *The Cult of the Goddess Pattini*, Chicago, 1984. p.445]. Any Sri Lankan who is not denuded of his cultural heritage through any process of alienation, has to be aware of the fact that virginity and chastity in females, coupled with the idea of conjugal fidelity [for all of which the males in the society are equally held responsible] are all well saddled in the five basic precepts or *pañcasīla* of the Buddhists. Thus it is very much associated, or better say contained in Buddhist ethics and doctrine. One has to be adequately guarded against such situations of misdirection and misrepresentation generated by groups of neo-scientific analysts who at times appear to be playing with far too many words.

Thus according to Buddhism the woman is respected and loved as an indispensable component of society, starting from her basic role as progenitor and spreading over leadership and guidance in the bringing up of children, care of the total household including the domestic aids, and the administration of finances. One needs only glance through a text like Mātugāma Samyutta [SN. IV. 238 ff.] to appreciate the full role a woman is expected to play in religion and society, a role which is complementary to that of man.

In the service of religion, it is once again the exemplary life of those who have opted to renounce the world and take to a full-time religious career in earnest, whether they be male or female which should be held out as a model. They alone, and not the propgandists, serve the cause of religion. They teach by example, with a convincing depth of understanding. What Vaḍḍhamātā [Thig. v. 204 ff.] tells her son about the unending stresses and strains of life or what Uppalavaṇṇā tells about the ensuing foulness in the pursuit of sense pleasures [Ibid. v. 224 ff] are eternal sermons which can be repeated and reproduced without any loss of their charm and vibrancy. A few such women must emerge in society. To make the men more gentle, that is to make gentlemen of them, to wean them from such corrosive habits like proneness to drinking and gambling, the women of this country could play a marvelously efficient role. They must reaffirm the adequacy of pleasure in the home, in terms of food and drink, sex and emotional gratification as parents of growing up healthy and promising children. We consider a resetting of the approach to cooking and eating in the home, what one cooks and how one does it, how one serves it and eats it, delightfully and dexterously, would go a long way in this direction. Now is the time to re-tap and re-harness the resourcefulness of our women in its totality for the good of everyone. We need them very much today. We have to appreciate the possible leadership they could provide. Such women would be the *primus inter pares* even in a society where people speak of women's lib, not only for equality with men for women but also for the possibility to outdo the male of the species, when and wherever he nods at his desk.

These brief remarks are made with a view to introducing the true Buddhist concept of woman, what she should symbolize and what she should stand up for, with the primary awareness that everyone of these champions should first qualify themselves for the task.

> *Attānaṃ eva paṭhamaṃ patirūpe nivesaye*
> *athaññaṃ anusāseyya na kilisseyya paṇḍito.* Dhp. v. 158

Let one first establish oneself in what is proper, and then instruct others. Such a wise one will never be defiled.

We need a few more seminars on this subject, undertaken with honesty and a sincerity to serve a cause. Being aggressive and vindictive, and ill-equipped with regard to necessary information, only leads to misanthropy. Let us help each other, with gentleness and restraint to reach, with the necessary detachment, the data bank on these subjects which well deserve careful and closer scrutiny.

Woman Within the Religious Frame of Buddhism

At the time the Buddha set up his Order of Bhikkhus, there was in Indian society the widespread but groundless belief that woman is inferior to man. The position which the woman lost under the dominance of the Brahmanas had not yet been retrieved. The brahmins of the day evidently showed little sympathy for her sad lot. Altekar describes the position of woman in India at the time as follows: "The prohibition of *upanayana* amounted to spiritual disenfranchisement of women and produced a disastrous effect upon their general position in society. It reduced them to the status of Śūdras.. What, however, did infinite harm to women was the theory that they were ineligible for them [Vedic sacrifices] because they were of the status of the Śūdras. Henceforward they began to be bracketed with Śudras and other backward classes in society. This we find to be the case even in the Bhagavadgītā (IX.32) [Altekar, A.S., *The Position of Women in Hindu Civilization*, p. 204f]. In the Manusmṛti we witness the cruel infliction of domestic subservience on woman. The road to heaven is barred to her and there is hard bargaining with her for the offer of an alternative route. Matrimony and obedience to the husband are the only means whereby a woman can hope to reach heaven.

> *Nāsti strīnāṃ pṛthag yajño na vrataṃ nāpyupoṣathaṃ*
> *patiṃ suśrūyate yena tena svarge mahīyate.* Manu.V.153.
>
> Women have no sacrifices of their own to perform nor religious rites or observances to follow. Obedience to the husband alone would exalt the woman in heaven.

This hostile attitude to woman both in religion and in society was repeatedly criticised and challenged by the Buddha on numerous occasions. In the Kosala Samyutta the Buddha contradicts the belief that the birth of a daughter was not as much a cause of joy as that of a son, a belief which the ritualism of the Brahmanas had contributed to strengthen. The Buddha pointed out clearly that woman had a dignified and an important part to play in society, and he defined it with great insight, fitting her harmoniously into the social fabric. She is a lovable member of the household, held in place by numerous relationships, and respected above all, as the mother of worthy sons. The sex did not matter, he argued, and added that in character and in her role in sọciety, she may even rival men.

Itthī pi hi ekacciyā seyyā posā janādhipa
medhāvinī sīlavatī sassudevā patibbatā.
Tassā yo jāyati poso sūro hoti disampati
evaṃ subhagiyā putto rajjam pi anusāsati. SN. I .86

A woman child, O lord of men, may prove
Even a better offspring than a male.
For she may grow up wise and virtuous,
Her husband's mother rev'rencing, true wife.
The boy that she may bear may do great deeds,
And rule great realms, yea, such a son
Of noble wife becomes his country's guide.

Kindred Sayings, I.p.111

But it is not unusual to find scholars who have missed this singular virtue of Buddhism. It would be grossly unfair to say that the Buddha did not devote much attention to the duties and ideals of lay women or that he showed indifference to or contempt of women. Speaking of Buddhism and Jainism, Altekar unjustly says: 'Both these were ascetic religions, and they have not devoted much attention to the duties and ideals of lay women. The founders and leaders of both these novements showed the indifference to, or contempt of women, which is almost universal among the advocates of the ascetic ideal." [Altekar, A.S., op.cit. p.208].

The instances are numerous where the Buddha defines and describes the duties of woman in society [AN. IV. p. 265 f]. Further, the Buddha recognises the fact that these do not constitute the whole of her life. It is not with a view to limiting their life solely to the secular affairs of the household that the Buddha laid down a code of good living for women, but to serve as a complement to the good life already enjoined in his religion to all his followers, irrespective of their sex. A host of these considerations as they are addressed to women are grouped together in the Saṃyutta Nikāya in a chapter solely devoted to them [SN.IV. 328f]. A good lay woman endowed with religious devotion, moral virtue and liberality as well as wisdom and lerarning, makes a success of her life in this world. For it is said:

> *Saddhāya sīlena ca y'idha vaḍḍhati*
> *Paññāya cāgena sutena cūbhayaṃ*
> *etādisī sīlavatī upāsikā*
> *ādiyati sāram idheva attano ti.* SN. IV. 250
>
> Such a virtuous lady who possesses religious devotion, cultivates virtue, is endowed with wisdom and learning and is given to charity makes a success of her life in this very existence.

Her virtuous character gives to her life in the household poise and dignity [*Pañcahi bhikkhave dhammehi samannāgato mātugāmo visārado agāram ajjhāvasati. Katamehi pañcahi? Pāṇātipātā pativirato ca hoti.. surāmeraya-majjapa-mādaṭṭhānā paṭivirato ca hoti.* SN. IV. 250]. The following are also given as virtues by means of which she can make her life fruitful, both here and hereafter: *Saddho* (religious devotion), *hirimā ottappī* (sense of shame and fear), *akkodhano anupanāhi* (not given to anger), *anissukī* (not jealous), *amaccharī* (not niggardly), *anaticārī* (chaste in behaviour), *sīlavā* (virtuous), *bahussuto* (learned), *āraddhaviriyo* (zealous), *upaṭṭhita- ssatī* (mentally alert), *paññavā* or wise [ibid. 243–44]. We notice that all these virtues enumerated so far are within the reach of a woman living in the household. She is not rooted out of her domestic setting. The good and successful life of the laywoman, as much as of the layman, seems to have loomed large in the ethics of Buddhism. In the Anguttara Nikaya two sets of virtues are given whereby a woman is said to strive for success in this world as well as in the other: *idha-lokavijaya* and *para-lokavijaya* [*Catūhi kho Visākha dhammehi samannāgato mātugāmo idhalokavijayāya paṭi- panno hoti ayam sa loko āraddho hoti. Katamehi catūhi? Idha Visākha mātugāmo susamvihita-kammanto hoti saṅgahitaparijjano bhattu manāpaṃ carati sambhatam anurakkhati.. Catūhi kho Visākha dhammehi samannāgato mātugāmo paralokavijayāya paṭipanno hoti parassa loko āraddho hoti. Katamehi catūhi? Idha Visākha mātugāmo saddhāsampanno hoti sīlasampanno hoti cāgasampanno hoti paññāsampanno hoti.* AN. IV. 269f.].

It is also worth noting here that the Buddha accepts the reality and significance of the instituton of marriage for woman. But, unlike in Hindu society, it was not the only means for the social elevation of woman. In Hinduism, a woman is supposed to become a dvija, a truly initiated member of the religion and the society, only after her marriage [Prabhu, *Hindu Social Organisation*, p. 284].

The virtues referred to in the Aṅguttara Nikāya [AN. IV. 269f] are household duties of a woman as wife which lead to domestic peace and concord. They are also calculated to keep the family administration in gear and secure for the family economic stability. This significant part which she is called upon to play is meticulously defined and it reveals neither indifference to nor contempt of women on the part of the Buddha.

The good laywoman has also her duties for the development of her religious life. It is a course of graduated training which does not conflict with her household life. It is, in fact, smoothly woven into it. Religious devotion (*saddhā*), moral virtue (*sīla*), and a generous disposition (*cāga*), for instance, form part of it. This healthy combination of social and religious virtues of woman is further witnessed in the Aṅguttara Nikāya where it is said that the following eight virtues pave the way for her to proceed to heaven.

Susamvihitakammantā saṅgahita-parijjanā
bhattu manāpaṃ carati sambhataṃ anurakkhati.
Saddhāsīlena sampannā vadaññū vītamaccharā
niccaṃ maggaṃ visodheti sotthānaṃ samparāyikaṃ.
Iccete aṭṭhadhammā ca yassā vijjati nāriyā
taṃ pi sīlavatiṃ āhu dhammaṭṭhaṃ saccavādiniṃ.
Soḷasākārasampannā aṭṭhaṅgasusamāgatā
tādisī sīlavatī upāsikā upapajjati devalokaṃ manāpam.

AN. IV. 271

They are:

1. organises the work of the household with efficiency,
2. treats her servants with concern,
3. strives to please her husband,
4. takes good care of what he earns,
5. possesses religious devotion,
6. is virtuous in conduct,
7. is kind,
8. is liberal.

The first four items of this list are identical with the first four of the five good qualities ascribed to the virtuous wife in the Singālovāda Sutta, the fifth being general efficiency (*dakkhā*) and enterprise (*analasā sabbakiccesu*) DN. III. p. 190 .

It was also held in Indian belief that woman was intellectually inferior to man and therefore had no capacity to man and therefore had no capacity to reach higher spiritual attainments. This idea clearly echoes in the Samyutta Nikaya where Mara, as the personification of the forces of evil, strives in vain to dissuade a Bhikkhuni from her religious endeavours.

> *Yaṃ taṃ isīhi pattabbaṃ ṭhānaṃ durabhisambhavaṃ*
> *na taṃ dvaṅgulapaññāya skkā pappotuṃ itthiyā.* SN. I. 129.
>
> No woman, with the two - finger - wisdom which is hers, could ever hope to reach those heights which are attained only by the sages."

These words of Māra are undoubtedly resonant of the beliefs of the day and the Buddha was vehement in contradicting them. Bhikkhuni Somā to whom Māra addressed these words answered. Illustrating the Buddhist attitude to the spiritual potentialities of woman she said:

> *Itthibhāvo no kiṃ kayirā cittamhi susamāhite*
> *ñāṇamhi vattamānamhi sammā dhammaṃ vipassato.* SN. I. 129
>
> 'When one's mind is well concentrated and wisdom never fails does the fact of being a woman make any difference?"

However, there is evidence that this age-old scepticism about the spiritual potentialities of woman died hard. Even in the face of success achieved by Bhikkhunis in Buddhism, a groundless belief seems to have prevailed which distrusted the capacity of woman for spiritual perfection. On the eve of her final passing away, when Mahāpajāpatī Gotamī visits the Buddha to bid him farewell, he calls upon her to give proof of the religious attainments of the Bhikkhunis in order to convince the disbelieving sceptics, the men in society.

> *Thīnaṃ dhammābhisamaye ye bālā vimatiṃ gatā*
> *tesaṃ diṭṭhipahānatthaṃ iddhiṃ dassehi Gotamī.* Ap. II. 535
>
> 'O Gotami, perform a miracle in order to dispel the wrong views of those foolish men who are in doubt with regard to the spiritual potentialities of woman."

Buddhism, with its characteristic note of realism, also recognises the inherent qualities of woman which make her attractive to the opposite sex. Nothing else in the world, it is said, can delight and cheer a man so much as a woman. In her, one would find all the fivefold pleasures of the senses. The world of pleasure exists in her.

> *Pañcakāmaguṇā ete itthirūpasmiṃ dissare*
> *rūpā saddā rasā gandhā phoṭṭhabbā ca manoramā.*
>
> AN. III. 69
>
> All these five-fold pleasures of the senses which gratify the mind are centered in the feminine form.

The power which the woman derives through this may, at the same time, extend so far as to make man throw all reason to the winds and be a pawn in her hand, under the influence of her charm. Thus, it is even possible that a mother may err in relation to her son or vice versa.

> *Kin nu so bhikkhave moghapuriso maññati na mātā putte*
> *sārajjati putto vā pana mātari ti.* AN. III. 68
>
> What, O monks, does that foolish man think that a mother would not feel lustfully attached to her son or the son to his mother."
>
> See *Gradual Sayings*, III. p.55 for a different translation of this passage which we consider to be incorrect.
>
> *Nāhaṃ bhikkhave aññaṃ ekarūpaṃ pi samanupassāmi evaṃ rajanīyaṃ evaṃ kamanīyam evaṃ madanīyaṃ evaṃ bandhanīyaṃ evaṃ mucchanīyaṃ evaṃ antarāyakaraṃ anuttarassa yogakkhemassa adhigamāya yathayidaṃ bhikkhave itthirūpaṃ. Itthirūpe bhikkhave sattā rattā giddhā gadhitā mucchitā ajjhopannā te dīgharattaṃ socanti itthirupa-vasānugā.*
>
> [AN. III. 68].

Therefore a man might say without exaggeration that woman is a trap laid out on all sides by Māra [*Yaṃ hi taṃ bhikkhave sammā vadamāno vadeyya samantapāso mārassā ti mātugāmaṃ yeva sammā vadamāno vadeyya samantapāso mārassā ti.* ibid]. These observations are made, however, not as a stricture on their character but as a warning to the men, who in seeking their company, might err on the side of excess. It is true that at times they tend to be overstressed, but obviously with no malice to women. There is pointed reference to the unguarded nature of the man who falls a prey to these feminine charms.

> *Muṭṭhassatiṃ tā bandhanti pekkhitena mihitena ca*
> *atho'pi dunnivatthena mañjunā bhaṇitena ca*
> *ne'so jano svāsaddo api ugghātito mato.* AN. III. 69
>
> 'Women ensnare a man of heedless mind with their glances and smiles or with artful grooming [*dunnivattha*] and pleasing words. Women are such that one cannot approach them in safety even though they may be stricken and dead"
>
> [G.S. III. 57].

Thus it becomes clear that it is not in the spirit of Buddhism to brand woman as a source of corruption for man. Note the words 'a man of heedless mind'in the above quotation. It would be interesting to contrast here the words of Manu who says, 'It is the nature of woman to seduce men in this world": *Svabhāva eva nārīṇāṃ narāṇāṃ iha dūṣaṇaṃ*. Manu. II .213. The Jains too inspite of their admission of women into the Monastic Order, do not seem to have differed very much from the Brahmins in their attitude towards women. The Ācaranga Sutra, in the course of a religious admonition known as the Pillow of Righteousness, makes the following comment which stigmatises woman completely: 'He to whom women were known as the causes of all sinful acts, he saw the true state of the world. [Jaina Sūtras I., SBE.XXII. p.81]. The position of woman in Jainism is summed up as follows: "Right in the earliest portions of the Canon woman is looked upon as something evil that enticed innocent males into a snare of misery. They are described as 'the greatest temptation", 'the causes of all sinful acts," 'the slough", 'demons" etc. Their bad qualities are described in exaggerated terms. Their passions are said to destroy the celibacy of monks 'like a pot filled with lac near fire"." [Deo .S.B., *History of Jaina Monachism*, p. 493]. In Buddhism, on the other hand, the caution which men are called upon to exercise in their dealings with the opposite sex springs solely from the Buddhist attitude to *kāma* or the pleasures of the senses. *Kāma* are described in Buddhism as leading to grief and turbulence. *Kāmā* thwart the path to transcendental happiness. This attitude is eloquently manifest in the counsel given to Ariṭṭha in the Alagaddūpama Sutta [MN. I.130].

Of this vast field of sense experience of man, sex is only a segment but it is admittedly one with irresistible appeal and thus required a special word of warning, particularly to those who are keen on the pursuit of mental equipoise. The Buddha says that if it were left unbridled, it would, in expressing itself, shatter all bounds of propriety [*Kin nu so bhikkhave moghapuriso maññati na mātā putte sārajjati putto vā pana mātarī ti.* AN. III. 68].

Hence the desire to lead a chaste and moral life, eschewing, even completely, the gratification of sex desires, can as much be the aspiration of a woman as of a man. Besides this philosophic attitude to the pleasures of the world in which the woman admittedly plays a dominant part, there seems to be nothing in Buddhism which looks upon sex or woman as being corrupt in themselves.

Thus it becomes clear that the philosophy of early Buddhism had no reservations whatsoever regarding the spiritual emancipation of woman. In the ocean of samsāra her chances of swimming across to the further shore were as good as those of man. Emancipation of the mind through perfection of wisdom which is referred to as *cetovimutti paññāvimutti* was the goal of religious life and for this the way which had proved most effective was the life of renunciation. The woman was as much encumbered by household life as man and in her spiritual earnestness she would have equally well echoed the words of the man who chooses renunciation. She would say with him that the household life is full of impediments and contrast it with the life of *pabbajjā* [*Sambādho gharāvāso rajopatho abbhokāso pabbajjā*. MN. I. 179].

But according to the evidence of the Pali texts [AN. IV. 274 ; Vin. II.253] the admission of women into the life of *pabbajjā* in Buddhism does not seem to have been effected with as much ease as one would expect. According to these, the Buddha appears to have shown some reluctance to admit women into the Order. When Mahāpajāpatī Gotamī requested the Buddha to consent to the entry of women into his Order he is said to have put her off three times, saying: 'Do not be interested O, Gotamī, about the entry of women into my Order" [Ibid]. This does seem to imply that the presence of women in the monastic institution of *brahmacariya* was considered, for some reason or other, to be detrimental to its well-being. In an atmosphere where women were considered a danger to spiritual life, their presence in the inner circle of religious life as members of the monastic community would have naturally called for serious comment. However, there is evidence that Jainism had already broken through this barrier against women. But the vicissitudes of the Jaina monastic community, in the relations between the two orders of monks and nuns, as well as of nuns and laymen, could not apparently have been very heartening to the Buddha. Speaking of the reforms introduced by Mahāvīra with the addition of the fifth vow of chastity to the earlier *catuyāma saṃvara* of Pārśva, Jacobi says, 'The argumentation in the text presupposes a decay of morals of the monastic order to have occurred between Pārśva and Mahāvīra." [Jaina Sūtras, II, SBE. XLV. 122 n.3]. There is also evidence from another quarter of the promiscuity in the behaviour of male and female mendicants in the Buddha's day. The Buddha takes note of this in the Culladhammasamādāna Sutta.

He speaks of Samaṇas and Brahmanas who repudiating the view that sensual pleasures are detrimental to spiritual progress, mingle freely with female mendicants, vociferously enjoying their company. They are reported as saying:

> 'Whatever can be the basis for pleading for future calamity can lie in wait for us? Blissful indeed is the contact of the soft and tender hands of these young female mendicants."
>
> [MN. I.305].

However, the Buddha concedes to Ānanda that women, having taken to the life of *pabbajjā* in Buddhism, are capable of attaining the higher fruits of religious life as far as Arahantship. [*Bhabbo Ānanda mātugāmo tathāgatappavedite dhammavinaye agarasmā anagāriyaṃ pabbajitvā sotāpattiphalaṃ pi sakadāgāmiphalaṃ pi anāgāmiphalaṃ pi arahattaphalaṃ pi sacchikātun ti.* AN. IV. 276 ; Vin. II. 254]. The considerations which seem to have weighed heavy in the mind of the Buddha regarding the admission of women into the Order are concerned more with the wider problem of the monastic organization as a whole. He would have been undoubtedly most averse to stand in the way of the personal liberty of woman. But in the interests of the collective good of the institution of *brahmacariya*, which was the core of the religion, women had to make certain sacrifices, surrendering at times even what might appear to have been their legitimate rights. This is evident from the following eight conditions [*aṭṭhagarudhammā*] under which the Buddha granted them permission to enter the Order.

1. A nun who has been ordained (even) for a hundred years must greet respectfully, rise up from her seat, salute with joined palms, do proper homage to amonk ordained but that day.
2. A nun must not spend the rains in a residence where there are no monks. [See Bhikkhuni Pācittiya 56: Vin. IV .313].
3. Every halfmonth a nun should desire two things from the Order of monks: the asking the date of the Observance day, and the coming for the exhortation. [See Bhikkhuni Pāc.59: Ibid. 315.].
4. After the rains a nun must 'invite" before both Orders in respect of three matters: what was seen, what was heard, what was suspected.
   [See Bhikkhuni Pāc. 57: Ibid.314.].
5. A nun, offending against an important rule, must undergo *mānatta* discipline for half a month before both Orders.
6. When, as a probationer, she has been trained in the six dammas for two years, she should seek higher ordination from both Orders.
7. A Monk must not be abused or reviled in any way by a nun.
8. From today admonition of monks by nuns is forbidden, admonition of nuns by nonks is not forbidden.

Book of the Discipline, V.354–55

The insistence on these *aṭṭha-garudhammā* is the most vital issue, much more than the delayed consent of the Buddha, in the founding of the Bhikkhuni Sāsana. The delay, it may in fact be argued, would have proved useful to emphasise the conditions which he was going to lay down. It is these conditions alone which gave the women access to the monastic life in Buddhism [*Sace Ānanda Mahāpajāpatī Gotamī aṭṭhagarudhamme paṭigaṅhāti sā va'ssa hotu upasampadā*. Vin. II .255]. The Dharmagupta Vinaya in the Chinese version compares them to a bridge over a great river by means of which one is enabled to cross over to the further bank [*Taisho* Vol.22. p. 923 B.]. These *garudhammā* are observances which pertain to monastic propriety and procedure in the Order of Bhikkhunīs in relation to the Bhikkhus. The women are not to violate these as long as they remain in the monastic community. In the establishment of the Bhikkhunī Sāsana, these conditions seem to have engaged greater attention than even the formulation of the code of moral precepts, which incidentally is not even mentioned at this stage. There is no doubt that in maintaining the vigour and vitality of the Sangha, whether of the Bhikkhus or of the Bhikkhunis, the code of the Pātimokkha played a vital part. But it seems to be equally true to say that in bringing the newly inaugurated Bhikkhunī Sangha into a healthy relationship with the older institution of the Bhikkhu Sangha, the *aṭṭha-garudhammā* were calculated to play a greater role. They take no note of moral considerations. A perfect functioning of the latter, in the case of the Bhikkhunis too. was apparently taken for granted at this early stage of their Sāsana. That a similar state of affairs did exist even in the Bhikkhu Sangha in its early history is evident in the Kakacūpama Sutta [MN. I. 124].

On a closer examination of the *aṭṭha-garudhammā* we are led to make the following observations. According to these the Bhikkhu Sangha is looked upon as the more mature and responsible body, evidently on account of its seniority, which is capable of leading the way for the Bhikkhunī Sangha. This is clearly evident from the garudhammas 2 and 3 [Vin. II .255]. The Bhikkhunīs are expected to recognise the spiritual leadership of the Order of Bhikkhus. At least at the outset, the Bhikkhunis had to seek the assistance of the Bhikkhus in such vital monastic rituals like the *Pātimokkhuddesa* and *Bhikkhunovāda*. But it is also evident that, as circumstances necessitated and experience proved opportune, the Buddha did transfer some of these powers to the Bhikkhunis themselves [Ibid.259]. However, the recognition of the leadership of the monks over the community of nuns and this position of the Bhikkhus *in loco parentis* to the Bhikkhunis seem to have continued much longer. Even when the authority to recite the Pātimokkha by themselves was finally transferred to the Bhikkhunis, the Bhikkhus were still left with the right to instruct them on its proper performance [*Anujānāmi bhikkhave bhikkhūhi bhikkhunīnaṃ ācikkhituṃ evaṃ pātimokkhaṃ uddiseyyāthā'ti.* Vin. II. 259.].

There is slso evidence of a similar reservation of power in the transference of authority to the Bhikkhunis to impose penalties and punishments on their fellow members. The Bhikkhus who carried out these acts at the outset are latterly barred from doing so and are authorised only to explain to the Bhikkhunis the proper procedure. [*Anujānāmi bhikkhave bhikkhūhi bhikkhunīnaṃ ācikkhituṃ evaṃ kammaṃ kareyyāthā'ti.*

Vin. II. 260.]. In the matter of *bhikkhuṇovāda* too, it was a Bhikkhu who was appointed to remind the Bhikkhunis regularly of the proper observance of the *aṭṭha-garudhammā* [Vin. IV. 51.f]. Thus on account of this complete dependence of a bhikkhuni on the leadership of a bhikkhu the second of these eight *garudhammā* forbade the bhikkhunis from going into residence for the rains-retreat in a place where there were no Bhikkhus. The third garudhamma too, implies the reliance of the bhikkhunis on the functions of *uposathapucchaka* and *ovādaupasan-kamana*. Both the Bhikkhus and he Bhikkhunis seem to have been vigilant about the proper observance of these functions which they considered, no doubt, to be vital for the healthy progress of the newly established Order of nuns. At the first sign of slackness with regard to these there is a storm of protests and we notice that the authorities take immediate action to remedy it.

These considerations are brought within the legal framework of the Bhikkhunī Sāsana and the failure to observe these come to be declared punishable offences [Ibid.313, 315 .See Bhikkhunī Pācittiya 56, 59]. In other words they become part of the Bhikkhunī Pātimokkha. In the study of the sikkhāpadas of the Bhikkhu Pātimokkha we have already noted this interesting phenomenon of the change over into legal statutes of what was once observed as honoured conventions.

The *garudhammā* 4, 5 and 6 concern themselves with some of the other major items of administration in the Buddhist monastic community, viz. (i) the performance of the *pavāraṇā* at the end of the rains retreat, (ii) the imposition of necessary penalties on the commission of a grave offence, and (iii) the conferment of *upasampadā* or higher monastic status. As far as the Bhikkhunīs are concerned, they are barred under these garudhammā from performing any of these acts within their own Order of the Bhikkhuni Sangha. These acts of the Bhikkhunīs are not considered valid unless they are carried out jointly together with the monks. However, practical considerations soon necessitated amendments to these and we see in the revised version of these conditions the sanction given to the bhikkhunis to perform these acts, in the first instance, by themselves. Then they are expected to bring their decisions before the Bhikkhu Sangha for ratification. The following is the amended procedure for the conferment of *upasampadā* on a Bhikkhuni by the Bhikkhu Sangha: [*Anujānāmi bhikkhave ekato upasampannāya bhikkhunīsaṅghe visud-*

dhāya bhikkhusanghe upasampadan ti. Vin. II. 271, 274.]. It shows that the candidate had been already approved by the Bhikkhuni Sangha. The Bhikkhunis were also allowed to perform their *pavāraṇā* in two stages before the two assemblies, first among themselves and then before the Bhikkhu Sangha [*Anujānāmi bhikkhave ajjatanā pavāretvā aparajju bhikkhusaṅghe pavāretun ti.* Ibid. 275.]

Thus, from the manner in which the Buddha directed the activities of the BhikkhunĀs it becomes clear that he did realise that as the Bhikkhunis formed a part of the single body of the Sangha, their decisions would affect not only themselves, but also the rest of that vast organization. Hence the Bhikkhus were given the right to advise and assist the Bhikkhunis in their affairs, and thus regulate the destinies of the Sasana. Public opinoin must have played a considerable part in bringing Bhikkhunis under the wing of the Bhikkhu Sangha. At any rate, it appears to have been considered wise to have all the important monastic activities of the Bhikkhunis linked up with the more established and senior group of the Bhikkhu Sangha. However, when and wherever this advisory role had to be transferred from the collective organization of the Bhikkhu Sangha to a single individual, the Buddha took every necessary precaution to avoid possible abuse of privilege.

He has laid down a very comprehensive list of eight requirements which should be satisfied before a monk could be selected to the role of a *bhikkhuṇovādaka* to give counsel to the congregation of nuns. There seems to be little doubt about his anxiety and his foresight regarding the safety and well-being of the female members of his Order. A monk who is entrusted to preside over their welfare should conform to perfect standards of moral virtue. He should also possess a thorough knowledge of the teaching of the Master and know well the complete code of the Pātimokkha covering both the Bhikkhus and the Bhikkhunis. He should be of pleasant disposition, mature in years and acceptable to the Bhikkhunis, and above all, should in no way have been involved in a serious offence with a Bhikkhuni [Vin. IV.51].

The three remaining *garudhammā* 1, 7 and 8, appear to have baffled some students of Buddhism as being contrary to the Buddha's general attitude to women. However, if these are examined carefully in their context, this apparent contradiction becomes less glaring. They all strive to see that the Bhikkhunis do not, under any circumstance, assert their superiority over the Bhikkhus. We notice that even in the observance of sikkhapadas, the Bhikkhunās are to follow the lead of the Bhikkhus wherever the sikkhapadas are common to both groups. The Buddha advises the Bhikkhunās to follow the Bhikkhus in the practice of such sikkhāpada [*..yathā bhikkhū sikkhanti tathā tesu sikkhāpadesu sikkhathā " ti.* Vin. II 258.] But referring to the sikkhāpada which are peculiar to the Bhikkhunis, he suggests that they should be followed, as they are laid down, according to the letter of the law [*yathāpaññattesu sikkhāpadesu sikkhathā ti.* Ibid. 258]. What seems to follow from these words of instruction to the Bhikkhunīs is that even if there was a difference between the text of the sikkhāpada laid down for the Bhikkhus and their practice at the time, the Buddha did not think it wise, for purposes of communal harmony, to leave room for the Bhikkhunis to be critical of this discrepancy. Such a challenge would have completely undermined the prestige and the authority of the older institution of the Sangha, quite out of proportion to any degree of moral good it could bring about by the correction of Bhikkhus by the Bhikkhunis.

There is evidence to show that the Buddha was always concerned with the esteem in which the public held his monastic organization. Such a consideration was vital for its existence and prosperity. The first remarks which he made to his erring disciples as he criticised their conduct always pertains to this [*N'etaṃ mogha purisa appasannānaṃ vā pasādāya pasannānaṃ vā bhiyyobhāvāya.* Vin. I.58 ; II.2 ; III. 21, 45.]. As much as the Buddha wanted his disciples to correct their mistakes and be of faultless conduct he did not want any of them to divulge to any one other than a Bhikkhu or a Bhikkhuni the more serious offences of their fellow members. Such an intimation was allowed only with the approval of the Bhikkhus [*Yo pana bhikkhu bhikkhussa duṭṭhullaṃ āpattiṃ anupasampannassa āroceyya aññatra bhikkhusammutiyā pācittiyaṃ.* Vin. IV. 31.]. One who violates this injunction is guilty of a Pācittiya offence [Pāc.9]. This provision was undoubtedly made with the best of intentions and should not be misjudged as contributing in any way to the perpetuation of monastic offences. On the other hand, it is in fact repeatedly declared that it is irregular for a monk to conceal intentionally an offence of one member from the rest of the community. Pācittiya 64 of the monks and Pārājikā 2 and Sanghādisesa 9 of the nuns are all calculated to avoid such a possibility [Vin. IV. 127, 216, 239]. All these precautions, therefore, seem to be a part of a system of internal security set up by the Buddha in the interest of the monastic organization. They emphasise the Buddha's concern both for the public esteem and for the moral soundness of his Order.

There seems to be a general agreement about the fact that the eight *garudhammā* were laid down by the Buddha as a condition governing the establishment of the Bhikkhunī Sāsana. However, strange as it may seem, after the Bhikkhunī Sāsana was instituted under the leadership of Gotamī, she appears before Ānanda to make the request that the Buddha should remove the first *garudhamma* and allow Bhikkhus and Bhikkhunis to pay courtesies to each other according to seniority alone [ibid. 257–58]. This is hardly true to the spirit in which Gotamī accepted the *garudhamma* [Ibid. 255 -56]. We are inclined to think that she was here undoubtedly subjected to the pressure of her own group.

This dissentient note which we find recorded in the Cullavagga does not seem to have found general acceptance elsewhere. Of the Chinese Vinaya texts it is only the Mahīśāsaka who record it and that too with a different emphasis [*Taisho.* Vol. 22 p.186 A]. According to their text Gotamī, prior to her being ordained, sends Ānanda to the Buddha to request him to make this change. The Buddha refuses to do so and says that since he has now allowed women to enter the Order they should follow what has been laid down and not go against it. In the Cullavagga too. the Buddha declines to make this concession. But in trying to give a reason for this attitude of the Buddha the Theriya tradition attempts to make out that in the organization of the Sasana social considerations, as much as moral and ethical values, loomed large in the mind of the Master. In the Cullavagga he is reported as saying: ' Not even the Titthiyas who propound imperfect doctrines sanction such homage of men towards women. How could the Tathāgata do so?" [Vin. II. 258].

We should also here consider the fact that any concession for the abrogation of what had already been laid down after careful deliberation would be grossly contradictory to the ideal which the Buddha and his early disciples appear to have upheld regarding the observance of the rules and regulations laid down for the guidance of monastic life [Ibid. III. .231]. The reply which the Buddha seems to have given to Gotami in the Chinese version of the Mahīśāsaka Vinaya is definitely more in keeping with this spirit. But we should take note of the fact that this reply would run contrary to the Theriya tradition, which at some stage, seems to have accommodated the idea that the Buddha conceded the abrogation of the minor rules [DN. .II. 14 ; VIn. II. 287].

As far as we are aware there is one other Vinaya tradition which records a challenge of the *garudhammā*. The Chinese version of the Dharmagupta Vinaya has a chapter entitled Bhikkhunī Khandhaka wherein the question is asked whether the Bhikkhunis cannot accuse the Bhikkhus under any circumstances [*Taisho*. Vol. 22 p. 927 A]. The Buddha replies to say that they could not do so even if the Bhikkhus violated the rules of discipline or were guilty of offences. These two protests on the part of the Bhikkhunis seem to show that the Bhikkhuni Sangha, or at least a section of it, resisted what it considered to be harsh legislation unfavourable to them.

At the same time one has to view dispassionately the position of the Buddha, who as the head of the Bhikkhu Sangha which was already a well groomed institution, had to safeguard against its disintegration through dispute and discontent. The fifth accusation levelled against Ānanda at the First Council, that he agitated for the admission of women into the Order [Vin. II. 289], is a clear indication that even after the recognised success of the Bhikkhunī Sāsana [Apadāna II. 535 v.79] there was a section of the Bhikkhus who formed as it were a consolidated opposition against it. The motive for such an attitude could have been generated by the fear of being eclipsed by the newer Order. The Chinese version of the Mahīśāsaka Vinaya includes a statement which is ascribed to the Buddha which seems to lend support to this assumption. The Buddha says that if there were no Bhikkhunis in the Sasana, then after his death the male and female lay-devotees [*upāsaka* and *upāsikā*] would have honoured the Bhikkhus in diverse ways. But now that the Bhikkhunis had entered the Order it would not happen so [*Taisho* Vol. 22. p.186 B]. It is difficult here to decide how and why the presence of Bhikkhunis in the Sāsana brought about such a radical change in the attitude of laymen towards the Bhikkhus.

Why were the Bhikkhus deprived of the honour that would have been theirs had not the Bhikkhunis appeared on the scene? Are the Bhikkhunis to be held responsible for the loss of prestige of the Bhikkhus? At any rate, this record of the Mahiśāsakas was undoubtedly representative of the opinion of the day regarding the Bhikkhuni Sāsana.

The Pali records of the Theriya tradition which belong to an earlier phase of the history of the Sāsana give expression to a similar feeling in the chastisement of Ananda in whom ultimately lay the responsibility for the admission of women into the Order. An echo of this is felt in the Mahīśāsaka Vinaya where Ananda apologises to the Buddha for having requested him to permit women to enter the Order. But the Buddha absolves him saying that he did so unwittingly under the influence of Māra [*Taisho* Vol.22 p.186 A]. The Theriya tradition is not alone again in expressing the fact that the presence of women in the Sasana would reduce its life span by half. We find it recorded in the Chinese version of the Dharmagupta Vinaya that the Buddha told Ananda that if women did not enter the Order it would have lasted 500 years longer [Ibid. p.923 C. See also Vin. II. 256].

It becomes clear from what has been said so far that at the time of crystalization of Theriya traditions two ideas regarding the establishment of the Bhikkhunī Sāsana stood out clearly. A section of the Bhikkhu Sangha was reproachful of Ananda because he interceded with the Buddha for the sake of the bhikkhunis. The admission of women was also considered a categorical danger to the successful continuance of the Sasana. In the light of all this evidence a study of the garudhammā reveals to us the fact that the Buddha was keenly conscious of the need to steer clear of the possible rivalries of the Bhikkhus and the Bhikkhunis and maintain healthy and harmonious relations between the two groups.

For the Love and Care of the Woman

We feel we would be failing in our obligation to the lay community if we do not include in this collection of essays a special one we make on the Aṅgulimāla Sutta of the Majjhima Nikaya [MN. II. 97–105]. Long before the initiation of worldwide movements like Women's Liberation and Feminist Activists, the Buddha appears to have felt the need to pay serious respect to the role the woman plays as mother of children. This was, of course, more than twenty-five centuries ago and was introduced to mankind in the eastern theatre of the world, namely India.

To assign to the woman the diginified role of mother comes from a much more-to-be respected conservasionist attitude that the Buddha adopted regarding a total growth [i.e. physical, moral and intellectual] of humanity. The concept of mother [*mātā*], in an age of pre-test-tube babies, looms large in Buddhist thinking: *Mātā mittaṃ sake ghare,* i.e. The mother is the friend in one's own home says the Samyutta Nikaya [SN. I. 37]. The woman, as the growing up young girl in the home, is guarded with serious concern as the future wife and would-be mother. She must be fit and qualified enough to stand up to the count down before being launched into the challenging role of multi-purpose womanhood. Whichever be the century we live in or the millennium we have moved into, these roles cannot be, with any degree of sanity in our heads, be underrated or underestimated. The Buddhists are not oriented to labour too much to accommodate unmarried mothers or fatherless children. These are believed to be lapses which are to be conscientiously guarded against. They rightly visualise the dangers and deficiencies of single-parent homes.

This respect for motherhood in a civilized social set-up has directed Buddhist thinking to prepare for preliminaries of maternity care. Physical ease and comfort of a pregnant would-be mother and her clinical mental grooming for motherhood are very much part and parcel of a well-run household with generous and well-meaning in-laws. Sri Lanka of more than fifty sixty years ago knew of many miniature domestic ceremonies of the white magic type which were quietly carried out in the home for the security and well-being of expectant mothers. The morning to evening day-time ceremony of *Māṭi-ata-perīma, Atta-gaha-metirīma* or *Ambakola-atten-metirīma* were delightful rituals carried out in our village homes on the advent of the arrival into the family of new-born babies. We all rejoiced over it. Everyone of us in the home, the young and the old, made our contribution towards it by carrying messages to the master of the ritual in his own home [not through calls on the mobile telephone], by gathering from the nearby woods the fruits and leaves needed for the creation of the associated artifacts. They included ant-hill clay for moulding the sun-disc, tender coconut leaves for numerous types of decorations, creepers like *hīressa* and leaves of the *tolabo* lily plant, perhaps to be used as mock weapons of offence and defence of various divinities associated with the ritual.

Besides these, there is also maternity care coming to the Sri Lankan Buddhists via religious considerations. In the category of Buddhist *parittas,* we have the Aṅgulimāla Sutta [M.II. 97 - 105] referred to above, the use of which for this purpose appears to date back to the time of the Buddha himself. This sutta tells that Aṅgulimāla, the erstwhile bandit, after his ordination as a disciple under the Buddha, reported to him of a woman whom he had seen during his alms round, suffering severe pains owing to her pregnancy. Seeing Aṅgulimāla's anguish and concern, the Buddha admonished him to go to that woman in pain and to wish her well and pray for the safety of her unborn babe through the asseveration of his personal purity. Aṅgulimāla immediately pointed out to the Buddha his pre-ordination crimes and the Buddha promptly advised him to make the asseveration from the time of his admission to the noble order [*ariyāya jāiyā jāto*]. Aṅgulimāla acted accordingly and she is said to have been immediately relieved [*Atha kho sotthi itthiyā ahosi sotthi gabbhassa.* op. cit. p. 103]. It is undoubtedly the pre-arahant spiritual prowess of Aṅgulimāla that did it. All that happened is described as *sotthi itthiyā ahosi,* i.e." To the woman there was security and well-being". There is not a word about the delivery of the baby.

It appears that in the years that followed, this incident has been simulated in its entirety. In the manner of other *paritta* recitals where the monks in congregation emphatically assert the power of the Buddha, Dhamma and the Sangha [as in the Ratana Sutta], and thereby invoke blessings on those in need of them, in the case of Aṅgulimāla *paritta* too, the monks in congregation appear to repeat the words of Aṅgulimāla which are no more than a record of his own spiritual prowess, and invoke blessings thereby on the pregnant mother and her unborn babe. However, in the Aṅgulimāla *paritta* as recited today we discover ten additional lines as a preface to what Aṅgulimāla himself recited under the direction of the Buddha.

Stories associated with the Sutta discloses the manner in which the Aṅgulimāla *paritta* appears to have developed itself to a high-powered pregnancy [or we should say more precisely child-delivery] *paritta*. Those ten lines in translation are as follows.

> Whosoever shall recite this *paritta*, the seat on which he sits,
> The water with which it is washed shall eliminate all labour pains.
> With ease shall there be delivery, that very moment it shall be done.
> This *paritta* which the Lord-of-the-World had given unto Angulimala,
> Is one of great majesty which shall keep its efficacy for a whole eon.
> That *paritta* we shall now chant.

The growth of this legendary process is witnessed in the Commentary to the Aṅgulimāla Sutta [MA. III. 337]. The Commentary elaborates it in this manner. Aṅgulimāla learnt this asseveration procedure or *saccakiriyā* from the Buddha and went to the woman to provide her comfort and security. As males were not allowed within the labour room, the monk was accommodated behind a curtain from where he did his chant. That very moment the woman is said to have delivered her baby with perfect ease.

In recognition of the very great efficacy of this sutta, a seat is said to have been constructed at the place where the monk did the chant. This seat is believed to have acquired such a reputation for its power and potency for easy delivery of offspring, it is said that even animals with difficulty of delivery benefit by being placed on it. In the case of feeble ones who cannot make the journey there, the water with which the seat is washed is to be applied on their head. This enables easy delivery. Even other diseases are said to be cured thereby [*Yā dubbalā hoti na sakkā ānetuṃ tassā pīṭhaka-dhovana-udakaṃ netvā sīse siñcanti taṃ khaṇaṃ yeva gabbha-vuṭṭhānaṃ hoti. Aññaṃ pi rogaṃ vūpasameti. Yāvakappā tiṭṭhanaka-pāṭihāriyaṃ kir'etaṃ.* MA. III. 338]. Thus in Sri Lanka, the Aṅgulimāla *paritta* today has changed its original rightful place in being a pre-natal child-and-mother care chant, to one of easy delivery in the labour room. The role of chanted water has reached its highest ascendancy.

This same Buddhist concern for pre-natal maternity care of both the mother and the unborn child [which would be deemed a basic and fundamental humanitarian concern] in seen to exist in the Mahayana countries of the Far East like China and Japan as far back as the 8th century A.D. With the profusion and proliferation of *Boddhisattvas* in the Mahayana to serve in specialised capacities the needs of worldlings, it is not surprising to discover one like Koyasu Kwan-non [Kwan-non of Easy Deliverance], a lady-like Goddess of Mercy, holding a child on her lap. Alice Getty thinks "she was unquestionably brought to Japan from Northern India via Central Asia and China". She also further says: 'We know from reliable texts that in the eighth century there existed a Kan-non cult in Japan, and that the Kan-non was called Koyasu or the Kan-non who brings about Easy Deliverance". [Alice Getty - *Gods of Northern Buddhism*, p. 96 f.].

For purpose of comparison with the obviously earlier genesis of the mother-care concept in the Aṅgulimāla Sutta, we reproduce here a statement from Alice Getty's Gods of Northern Buddhism.

In the *Bukkyo Daiji-ten* is the following legend: The Empress Komyo (710–760), being with child, invoked the Shinto goddess Amaterasu, and prayed that she might have an easy deliverance. One night she saw in a dream the Bodhisattva Avalokiteśvara standing at her bedside, and when she awoke she found a small image of the Bodhisattva lying beside her. She kept it preciously until after her deliverance, and then ordred it to be placed inside a statue of the thousand-armed Avalokiteśvara which she had enshrined in the Taisan-ji [Temple of Easy Deliverance] in Kyoto. According to popular belief, the Empress Komyo founded the Taisan-ji and dedicated it to the Koyasu Kwan-non, and it has remained up to this day one of the most flourishing centres of devotion in Japan. [p. 97].

With due deference to the traditions of both the Theravada and the Mahayana on this subject, we therefore wish to add to this collection of essays, the text of the Aṅgulimāla, indicating what the original canonical version was and how it was used as a simple pre-natal mother-and-child protective chant [*sotthi te hotu sotthi gabbhassa*] as well as its apparently more developed easy delivery concept [*sotthinā gabbha-vuṭṭhānaṃ yañ ca sādheti taṃ khaṇe*], with its Pregnancy Care parallel in Koyasu Kwan-non of Japan. We are more inclined to popularise what we consider to be the earlier canonical tradition of pre-natal care of the mother and the child [*sotthi te hotu sotthi gabbhassa*] which can quite harmlessly begin from the earliest indications of pregnancy, thus building up confidence and comfort in the mind of the would-be-mother. That kind of religious solace, the presence of comforting religious grace of the *tisaraṇa* must necessarily come to all areas of life in society, well before the outburst of crisis situations. This would eliminate the not very honourable last minute rush to wayside-shrine-divinities for guard and protection through the local *bāra-hāra* type of supplication.

Aṅgulimāla Parittaṃ

[Paritta as recited today, with the added-on introductory preface and the original text.]

Preface:

Parittaṃ yaṃ bhaṇantassa nisinnaṭṭhāna-dhovanaṃ
udakam'pi vināsesi sabbaṃeva parissayaṃ.
sotthinā gabbha-vuṭṭhānaṃ yañ ca sādheti taṃ khaṇe
therassa'ṅgulimālassa lokanāthena bhāsitaṃ
kappaṭṭhāyi-mahātejaṃ parittaṃ taṃ bhaṇāmahe.

Translation:

Whosoever shall recite this *paritta*, the seat on which he sits,
The water with which it is washed shall eliminate all labour pains.
With ease shall there be delivery, that very moment it shall be done.
The *paritta* which the Lord-of-the World had given unto Aṅgulimāla,
That *paritta* we shall now chant.

Original Text:

Yato'haṃ bhagini ariyāya jātiyā jāto
nābhijānāmi sañcicca pāṇaṃ jīvitā voropetā.
Tena saccena sotthi te hotu
sotthi gabbhassā'ti.

Translation:

O, Sister, from the moment I entered this noble life of a recluse,
I reckon not having deprived any living thing of its life.
By the truth of this, may there be happiness and well-being
To you and to your unborn babe.

Note: The original text with which the Buddha is said to have commissioned Thera Aṅgulimāla to go to the woman in pregnancy discomfort and make an asseveration [*sacca-kiriya*] to relieve her of her agony consists only of the eighteen words given above, beginning with *Yato'ham. bhagini* and ending with *sotthi gabbhassa*.

[See MN. II. 102 and MA. III.337 f.].These alone tell us of Thera Aṅgulimāla's pre-arahant spiritual prowess whereby he was able to provide comfort [*sotthi*] to the pregnant mother in pain. The ideas expressed in the apparently later composed preface reduces the force of the directly communicated power of the *sacca-kiriya* and brings it down to the level of a mere water-powered ritual. It is time we retrieved the worth of the original.

We suggest that all those who are closely connected with a pregnant mother, like the husband, the mother and the mother-in-law, all lovingly chant this *paritta* to her whenever they can, morning and evening, no matter how early or late she is in her pregnancy. This invariably introduces even to the unborn child the feeling of love and care which is so much needed at this stage of pre-natal human growth. Let it be known by all and sundry, both medical and non-medical, that even those well learned in the field of medical science admit today that an unborn baby in the mother's womb begins to be aware of sounds outside world by the twentieth week.

May this magnanimous attitude of love, share and care towards a pregnant mother and her unborn child spread island wide in Sri Lanka.

Paṭiccasamuppāda

(Dependent Origination)

Part 2

Achieving Transcendence

by

Ron Wijewantha

The Wheel Publication No. 455/457

First published 2003

ACKNOWLEDGEMENTS

I am indeed grateful to the Buddhist Publication Society for issuing this current tract as a Wheel Publication, so that the same readers as the first, as well as a new audience, can have access to these essays. Hopefully, we may see the day when both unabridged parts are integrated and reprinted as a single volume.

My thanks to Professors Lily de Silva and Chitra Wickramasuriya, my mentor Ven. M. Seelawimala Maha Thera, and kalyana mittas Martha Craft and Sondra Jewell who took the time to read through these essays and offer constructive criticism. I am also thankful to Ven. T. Shantarakshita Maha Thera and Ven. H. Medhananda for helping me with relavent Pali sutta passages and Sinhala commentaries thereon.

I have quoted rather copiously from many authors, and I wish to acknowledge and offer my grateful thanks to them and their respective publishers, too numerous to be mentioned individually.

Thanks also to my daughters Kamini, Chinta and Niromi for much help and encouragement, and my grandsons Ashok, Avinda and Arjun for computer assistance. My brother Emil and my brother-in-law cum best friend Wickrama Atukorale helped me in many tangible and intangible ways. My sincere thanks to them.

Mr A.G.S. Kariyawasam has once again helped with the editing of this book with his usual elegant style. My thanks to him.

It is with much pleasure that I dedicate this writing to my dearest wife Sita, who has shared with me the joys and sorrows and the vicissitudes of life for almost half a century, making me, I hope, a better person each passing day.

May all of the above persons share in the merit arising from this presentation, for the gift of the Dhamma surpasses all other gifts.

I shall feel amply rewarded if I have assisted at least a few of my readers in some little way, particularly advanced *vipassanā* meditators in Sri Lanka, Asia and in the West, by guiding them in the right direction. Hopefully, they will feel encouraged to think freely and adopt a scientific approach while maintaining the integrity of the Buddha-word as another way of pressing forward on their journey to transcend the mundane and achieve the supra-mundane, thereby joining the ranks of the Ariyas - the Noble Ones.

May our journey through saṃsāra be short and free of difficulties.

Ron W.
June 2003

AUTHOR'S PREFACE

This presentation is essentially a continuation of the discussions on *Paṭiccasamuppāda* in *The Road to Liberation* (Wheel 450-452). Many readers considered it incomplete without specific instructions on how to arrive a step closer to liberation. They also wanted more information on the interconnectedness and inter-relationships of *Paṭiccasamuppāda* to the Four Noble Truths and the Four Foundations of Mindfulness, and how a study of the three together could make our understanding easier. But, most importantly, there was a demand for a list of the minimum amount of doctrinal texts and simple *vipassanā* meditation instructions that could lead a dedicated person to transcendence.

I hope this current presentation will fill this vacuum. For I believe that the achievement of awakening is made easier when we engage the original doctrine of *Paṭiccasamuppāda* and the original teaching of the Four Noble Truths together with *Satipaṭṭhāna* in our understanding of the fundamentals of the Dhamma. *Vipassanā* meditation practice only comes thereafter. Our experience shows that Western readers in particular benefit most when this method is adopted. My mentor, Ven. Seelawimala Mahathera, has quite correctly pointed out to me that in regard to explaining the essence of the Buddha Dhamma, erudite and knowledgeable members of the Sangha can play a very important part. The Buddha said that one should make the Dhamma one's island and refuge. It is therefore preferable for the earnest meditator to first acquaint himself wherever possible with this Dhamma base before proceeding to find a *vipassanā* meditation master. This will undoubtedly make the latter's guidance much easier to follow.

I have also added the relevant sections of the Bāhiya, the Anāthapiṇḍika, the Rāhulovāda, as well as the Anattalakkhaṇa Suttas, because of their importance in meditating on *anicca, dukkha* and *anatta*. I can personally vouch for the fact that repeated reading and contemplation on these suttas during one's own meditation sessions can result in insights, bringing a person closer to, or even to, transcendence, when the conditions are just right.

I would also like to explain the reasons for the inclusion of the experiences of an experienced *vipassanā* meditator whose approach towards transcendence would appear superficially to be quite different to that which had been adopted by the traditionalists. His experiences show that there are "many possible paths which lead to the top of a mountain". Any of the paths could surely be adopted provided that they are in accordance with the Dhamma. Our senior *vipassanā* meditator had used his knowledge of *Paṭiccasamuppāda,* the Four Noble Truths and the Satipaṭṭhānas to meditate deeply (with *sati-sampajañña*) to reach transcendence. His seeing the Dhamma from a modern perspective and the use of more recent scientific information only helped him to comprehend and gain insight into the Dhamma much faster. But transcendence was possible only when he finally focused on the three characteristics of human existence, namely *anicca, dukkha* and *anatta* – impermanence, distress and the absence of a continuing and permanent 'I.'

There may be some readers who may perhaps conclude from reading this book that I have been overly critical of present day *vipassanā* teachers. To the contrary, I have the deepest respect for these dedicated teachers. My submissions are only to the effect that it is vitally important that these teachers should impart to their pupils the core substance or essence contained in a number of other important suttas in addition to the Mahāsatipaṭṭhāna Sutta, and the Four Noble Truths. For they would know from their own experiences that it was only when they meditated with a broader perspective and understanding of the Buddha's teachings, that they comprehended and understood the truth of *anicca, dukkha* and *anatta* and thereby reached the threshold of liberation, or in fact, the first stage of liberation.

Ron W.
June 2003

Namo tassa bhagavato arahato sammāsambudhassa
(Homage to Him, the Exalted, the Worthy, the
Fully Enlightened One!)

CHAPTER VIII

Preliminary

Many of us meditators have been practising *vipassanā* meditation for decades, but have found that although we were able to reach a high level of serenity (*samatha*), we could not make a breakthrough to a supramundane state. We have often asked ourselves why there aren't more known cases of living *Ariyas*, and why we have failed to become enlightened in spite of following the meditation teachers conscientiously.

The follow-up questions arising therefrom would be: "Are we as meditators at fault or do we lack the *pāramitās* for liberation in this life, or, on the contrary, are the meditation methodologies of these various schools of *vipassanā* practice deficient in some aspect or another?"

Whenever these doubts are raised, teachers would often say that they are merely instructors and that we have to do the work ourselves. If we look at these teachers objectively, can we truly say that they are all 'on-the-path'? If they are not, then will it not be correct to assume that what they teach is suspect? It seems to me that if a teacher at the outset says, "I too happen to be a mere practitioner, but perhaps more experienced than you. So if you follow my instructions I shall guide you along the *vipassanā* highway, and I shall tell you when I come to areas which I have not explored before." I, for one, would respect such frankness and would be willing to practise with such a person till it was time to either find a more qualified teacher, or I felt competent to proceed on my own.

True enough, there were well-documented cases during the lifetime of the Buddha of persons like Ven. Poṭhila who had learnt the Dhamma under the Buddha, and had guided a large number of pupils to become *Ariyas*, although he was not one of them himself. It was only when the Buddha reprimanded him that he saw the light, got himself enrolled under one of his erstwhile pupils and attained to the supramundane state. (*Dhp.* 282)

We now live 2550 years later, and it is extremely difficult to assess whether our *vipassanā* teachers are in fact really enlightened or on the way to enlightenment, or whether they are unwitting instruments of "the blind leading the blind". We have heard of genuine meditation masters such as Ven. Mahasi Sayadaw, Ven. Achan Chah, Upasika Kee Nanayon, Ven. Ananda Maitriya, Ven. Sri Nanarama, Ven. Henepola Gunaratana, Ven. U. Silananda, Ven. U Pandita, S.N. Goenka, Joseph Goldstein and Jack Kornfield to name a few. But of the other thousands of current teachers, only a very few appear to be qualified in the sense that while they may personally know the Dhamma more than adequately, they perhaps may not be imparting the totality of their doctrinal knowledge to their respective students.

This means that it is necessary that we follow the instructions of these second and third generation latter-day teachers with reservation. For, it may become necessary to fortify ourselves with additional Dhamma information and better meditation methodology, including the selection of more appropriate meditation subjects, dependent on our individual needs and aptitudes, before we can advance to finality. Thus, it is a fact that even the five ascetics could not become arahants simply by listening to the Buddha's first sermon, the Dhammacakkappavattana Sutta (Sacca Saṃy. 11).

It is said that the Buddha had to teach them over a period of time before he felt that they were sufficiently versed in the Dhamma, and in proper *vipassanā* meditation techniques and were then able to comprehend what he had to say. It was then that he preached the Anattalakkhaṇa Sutta[1] (Khandha Samy. 59). The Buddhist scriptures tell us that it was on listening to this sermon that all five of them reached arahantship. There are also a number of cases where the Buddha himself had observed that the subjects for meditation adopted by certain meditators were inappropriate. By giving them alternative subjects, he had ensured their success. (Dhp. 25 and 285). But in these cases it

1. This sutta appears in the Khandha Saṃyutta as the Pañcavaggiya Sutta, but is now popularly known as the Anattalakkhaṇa Sutta.

would not be incorrect to assume that these meditators already had a comprehensive understanding of the essentials of the Buddha Dhamma.

The Buddha's final advice to Ānanda just before his *Parinibbāna* was as follows:

"Therefore Ānanda, be islands unto yourselves, refuges unto yourselves, seeking no external refuge, with the *Dhamma* as your island, the Dhamma as your refuge, seeking no other refuge." (Mahā Parinibbāna Sutta [D.16]).

Let us therefore keep this in mind when we listen to *vipassanā* meditation instructors.

As a further safeguard, when selecting a teacher we should ask ourselves the following questions:

9. What do previous students say of the teacher?
10. Is he well versed in the Dhamma?
11. Are his teachings in accord with the Dhamma?
12. Does the teacher show compassion and is he/she a good role model?
13. Are the Paṭiccasamuppāda, the Four Noble Truths and the Mahā Satipaṭṭhāna Sutta (D.22), all used in his/her instructions?

There are many books on *vipassanā* meditation. Most of them are very useful. A list of some of the important texts was provided in Wheel publication 450–452, along with brief instructions on how a person can arrive at the threshold of the supramundane path by following a well-planned course in *vipassanā* meditation.

There are, however, a number of readers who, in spite of intensive application, have so far failed to progress. Such meditators should first take the time to stop and look inwards and ask themselves whether in reality they are beyond reproach in regard to their morality and whether they have cultivated an ability to concentrate and be mindful at all times. In other words, whether in fact they are following strictly the Noble Eightfold Path of morality-concentration-wisdom (*sīla-samādhi-paññā*).

If they are lacking in morality, this is the time to fix the problem. Morality is indeed the root system that nourishes the tree of knowledge, the tree whose trunk is 'concentration' and 'mindfulness', and whose crown is *samatha* and *vipassanā* meditation. Meditators must also further develop the four sublime states of universal loving-kindness, compassion, sympathetic joy and equanimity, and, in fact, become living monuments to these states if they are to succeed in achieving transcendence.

CHAPTER IX

Experiences of a Knowledgeable Meditàtor

Before describing the methods of applied meditation, we could perhaps benefit more by first reading about the real life experiences of an experienced *vipassanā* meditator who discusses his personal voyage of discovery on the assurance of anonymity. In this account he traces his life's journey starting as a novice in meditation to the point of transcendence:

"I commenced *samatha* and *vipassanā* meditation in a rather experimental manner for a number of decades, but with little success. Since then, I have been exposed to the meditation techniques of a number of meditation masters. I have also often re-read selected tracts of the *Dhamma* relating to Awakening until I found for myself a technique of *vipassanā* meditation where the ultimate focus was on a full understanding of *Paṭiccasamuppāda*, the Four Noble Truths, the Four Foundations of Mindfulness (*Satipaṭṭhāna)* and the comprehension of their interrelationship.

"My meditation culminated eventually, without conscious effort, in an automatic paradigm shift which focused on the three universal characteristics of the human condition, namely: *anicca, dukkha* and *anatta:* impermanence, distress and non-ego or 'non-I'. This method has as its foundation the strict practice of morality in all daily activities, and the cultivation of the *Brahma-vihāras* of loving-kindness, compassion, non-envious joy and equanimity.

"At this point I realized experientially that, without practising morality and mindfulness at every moment of one's waking hour, genuine progress was impossible. As a *vipassanā* meditator, it now became possible, with proper application for me even to experience briefly the *jhānas*. For one can say that at such a time one is established in mindfulness and pinpointed focus on the subject of his choice. This is compatible with the *Paṭisambhidāmagga* where it is stated that as an insight meditator directs his mind to a particular section of formations, he goes on reflecting with perseverance, and his concentration will gather the same degree of strength as absorption concentration. Also, as the meditator equipped with this kind of concentration continues to reflect on the formations, insight knowledge will develop and this consciousness comes to be reckoned as a *jhāna* in itself.

"Now, without making the same mistake as the monk Sāti, Ican picture myself travelling in *saṃsāra* as an ever-changing stream of conditioned consciousness. It is in the form of an infinitesimally tiny bundle of ever-changing particles of energy subject to conditionality and containing within itself the totality of the *saṃsāric kammic* energy and life's experiences. In the Āneñjasappāya Sutta (M.106) this is called *samvattanikaṃ viññāṇaṃ* or the consciousness that links on. However, this does not imply that this consciousness remains unchanged and in the same state throughout the cycle of existence. Now, when I find myself in pinpointed focus on the twelve links of *Paṭiccasamuppāda* (dependent origination) in the forward direction (*anuloma*), I realize that the way to unbind or unravel this bundle has to be effected by dissipating its energy.

"An example of this conditioned stream of consciousness is seen in the descriptions given by the Buddha in the Jātaka stories, of how he fared in *saṃsāra* in previous existences. His stream of conditioned consciousness having taken 'residence' in different bodies, or *nāma-rūpas,* in accordance with the immanent law of *kamma,* would exist in this fashion until it was time for this ever-changing energy to move on to the next rebirth.

"I now realize that this opportunity to evolve spiritually will present itself only when I have an earth-life. For it is only then that a person has the opportunity to expend as much of the previous unwholesome *kammic* energy as possible, while at the same time accumulating more and more positive *kammic* energy by way of *dāna-sīla-bhāvanā*: giving-morality-meditation. This is how even the Bodhisattas, over countless rebirths, develop their *pāramitās* (see note 2, chapter 1) and thus spiritually evolve themselves to perfection.

"I could now relate this spiritual evolution to a similar scientific evolution, namely the natural evolution of all animal and plant life. There is sufficient scientific evidence for us to accept the fact that for man to evolve from a single-celled organism to what he is today has taken billions of years. Our spiritual evolution is similar though taking an enormously longer period of time. And, as the Buddha taught, we speak not of years but of *kappas* or eons. Every time we have an earth-life we get the chance to evolve a little spiritually. The extent of this spiritual development depends on the individual person's behaviour in each earth-life. If one commits wrong in this earth life, one will regress. On the other hand, if one does good consistently, then one will evolve progressively a little bit more.

"This is why the Buddhas have repeatedly advised people to, 'refrain from evil, do good deeds and cleanse the mind' (*sabbapāpassa akaraṇaṃ, kusalassa upasampadā, sacittapariyodapanaṃ).* (Dhp. 183)

"I understand that the frequency of an individual's earth-life is based on conditionality and the immanent law of *kamma*. We know from the Dhamma that everyone of us will have a manifold number of 'earth-appearances' during our journey in saṃsāra. The Buddha has said that even the tears that one has shed on the death of one's parents during one's travels in *saṃsāra* exceed the waters in all the oceans.

"It cannot then be far wrong if the conclusion is reached that all law-abiding, compassionate and kind-hearted individuals have evolved considerably. And that they now have the chance to make a break-through to 'Awakening', should they but apply themselves in accord with the Dhamma. We have developed our individual *pāramitās* to a considerable degree and this is why we have become dedicated *vipassanā* meditators in this life.

"When I picture the end of my previous life in terms of *Paṭiccasamuppāda*, I could see myself in the process of dying. When the final moment of death arrived, there was a microsecond of death-consciousness and the energy of this last consciousness got catalyzed or energized and conditioned the appearance of the first consciousness in the present life—*saṅkhāra-paccayā viññāṇaṃ* (with mental formations as a condition, arises rebirth-consciousness)—thereby ensuring the continuity of the stream of conditioned consciousness in the present life,—*viññāṇa-paccayā nāma-rūpaṃ* (with consciousness as a condition, arises mind-and-body). This conditioned consciousness then became part of the mind-body complex of the current life.

"Prof. Lily de Silva puts it in even simpler terms: 'When ultimately we are on the deathbed face to face with death and our body is no longer strong enough to flee from death, it is highly unlikely that we will mentally accept death with resignation. We will struggle hard, long for and crave for life (*taṇhā*), and reach out and grasp (*upādāna*), a viable base somewhere as the dying body can no longer sustain itself. Once such a viable base in a mother's womb has been grasped, the process of becoming *(bhava)* starts there, which in due course gives rise to birth (*jāti*). This is what is referred to in the twelve-linked *Paṭiccasamuppāda* as "craving conditions grasping, grasping conditions becoming, and becoming conditions birth". Thus a worldling dies and is reborn.'

"On our *saṃsāric* journey, our actions become habitual and these habits become part of our personality and we take these habits with us from life to life in the form of mental formations (*saṅkhāra*) or habit energy. Hence our actions in this life are influenced or conditioned by the habits we had developed over countless previous lives. (Do I see here the embryo of a developing conscience?) I now understood the reason for some of my previous erratic actions that were not consonant with my usual cultivated way of life. Here let me recall similar incidents of errant behaviour by certain monks and laypersons during the time of the Buddha.

"There was once an arahant who instead of gently stepping across tiny water channels in rice-fields when proceeding on alms-rounds with other monks to a nearby village, would simply jump across the obstructions in an undignified manner. This was brought to the notice of the Buddha, who then told the assembly of monks that this arahant had in previous births been born as a monkey and this was the reason for this otherwise unaccountable behaviour.

"In another instance, an arahant frequently addressed other bhikkhus in a disparaging manner using epithets employed at that time by the higher castes in addressing outcasts. Here too, the Buddha attributed it to force of habit from past lives as an affluent Brahmin landowner (Dhp. 408).

"There was an instance where a Brahmin and his wife greeted the Buddha as their son. The Buddha attributed this intimacy to numerous past associations (Dhp. 225).

"In the Upanisā Sutta (Nidāna Saṃy. 23) the Buddha explained how once rain starts eroding a mountain, future rains will continue the process till such time when rivulets are formed, and the rivulets gradually create a channel which next forms into streams and next into a river through a process of repeated erosion. All future rains will follow the path of the river, which had been made by repeated erosion. It is in a similar way that our actions become habitual and these habits become part of our personality. We take these habits with us from life to life in the form of mental formations (*saṅkhāra*) or habit energy in our *saṃsāric* journey. Thus, even in this life, an individual is making wholesome and unwholesome *kamma* continuously with every thought, word and deed, thereby adding to or subtracting from the inherited bundle of *kammic* energy, for the Buddha has said:

"Attanā va kataṃ pāpaṃ, attanā saṅkilissati
Attanā akataṃ pāpaṃ attanā va visujjhati
Suddhi asuddhi paccataṃ n' añño aññaṃ visodhaye.

"By committing wrong, one defiles oneself
By not doing wrong, one purifies oneself.
Purity and impurity depends on oneself, no one
purifies another. (Dhp. 165)

"I would then often reflect on the importance of taming the mind. The Buddha has pointed out that 'the mind is very hard to perceive, extremely subtle and goes wherever it wishes' (Dhp. 36), and asks us to guard it. He would often simply refer to the mind as consciousness. Both are often used as synonymous terms. Mind is frequently described as consisting of fleeting mental states which constantly arise and perish with lightning rapidity. 'With birth as its source and death as its mouth, it persistently flows on like a river receiving from its tributaries a stream of constant accretions to its flood.' Each momentary consciousness of this ever-changing life-stream, on passing away, transmits its whole energy to its successor. Each and every consciousness therefore consists of the potentialities of its predecessors and something more, and all its potentialities in the form of conditioned energy are transmitted from life to life.

"I recollect that the Abhidhamma explains the philosophy of the mind by dividing the mental process into two general categories: one as passive consciousness, and the other as active consciousness. Passive consciousness consists of a succession of momentary mental states of a uniform but conditioned nature, called the life-continuum (*bhavaṅga*). This type of consciousness is reported as running through and beneath the whole existence of an individual from birth to death, interrupted only by the occasions of active consciousness. The life-continuum is a result of *kamma* generated in the past existence, which determines the basic disposition of the present individual. This information also helped me to visualize and comprehend with insight for the first time, the *viññāṇa-paccayā nāma-rūpaṃ* (with consciousness as a condition arises mind and body), of *Paṭiccasamuppāda*.

"I can now understand how humankind is beset by greed, hatred and delusion (*loba-dosa-moha*), for we have two sets of factors in our makeup. First, we have the genetic predispositions arising from the genes that we have inherited from our parents. The other is the 'habits' that we have inherited from previous births in the form of *kammic* predispositions, common traits, which we all carry in our evolutionary journey involving the struggle for existence. This is the instinctive desire, just like in other animals, to place oneself above the rest, and to do so one develops a strong sense of individuality, of an 'I', an ego, a need for this 'I' to be selfish and greedy, if one is to survive. Hence the perpetuation of the delusion of 'I' as a separate ego-entity.

"We can then appreciate the fact that people are constantly subject to the negativities or defilements of greed, hatred and delusion. Man, during his evolution from a single-celled organism has, over billions of years struggled to adapt, to compete, to evolve and to survive by whatever possible means, and only the ones who could perpetuate the species best have survived. This has resulted ultimately in the evolving human prototype passing on from generation to generation the inherent tendency towards selfishness and greed. Similarly, over these millions of years, the evolving man has come to think of himself as unique and that each individual was a distinct personality, or 'I', who came first, then the family, next the tribe and so on. These values became part of our genetic make-up, which even today, after a prolonged period of 'civilizing influence', has a tendency to crop up unexpectedly. The only saving grace is our ability to restrain ourselves to keep in line with what society and our very own conscience dictates.

"We could perhaps accept the fact that if our parents were persons who had inherited good spiritual traits from their ancestors, we in turn would have inherited these 'good' genes. If we now live in a social environment that is conducive to good behaviour, we would generally be well-behaved persons. Second, we are also under the influence of our inherited dispositions from our previous travels in *saṃsāra,* and if we had been consistently cruel persons in previous births, this latent tendency ('habit energy') could spring into action and prevent us from behaving better in the present.

"This seems to suggest that we are in effect split personalities because of our inclinations based on our current genes on the one hand and our 'habit-energy' from previous lives, on the other. This is more apparent in some than in others. Remember the fictitious Dr Jekyll and Mr Hyde, and the actual case of Albert de Salvo, the "Boston Strangler", who turned out to be a mild-mannered family person in normal life? When we understand this and reflect on it during meditation we can come to terms with our latent tendencies (*anusaya*), hidden in the deep unconscious which will unaccountably surface and surprise us in moments when we are not mindful. With this knowledge I learnt to be equanimous (*upekkhā*), and to move onward.

"I continued repeatedly and constantly to meditate on *Paṭiccasamuppāda*. Then I saw with insight that all this time my perceptions of phenomena had been at fault for, instead of perceiving phenomena as coming into being because of 'conditioned arising' and therefore devoid or empty of self, my perception had been that phenomena were existent and real.

"Then it happened one day. I was sitting in mindful meditation with an open yet quiet mind reflecting and contemplating the Buddha's advice to Bāhiya as well as Sāriputta's advice to Anāthapiṇḍika. (ch 4). It then dawned on me that there was possibly yet another and more pertinent and deeper meaning in these instructions. This meaning had perhaps previously eluded me.

"Now by placing myself first in the position of Bāhiya and then Anāthapiṇḍika, I could see clearly with insight that, in the supramundane sense, there is no real person or 'I' involved in the seeing and what are cognized by the senses are only formations subject to causes and conditions. That 'letting go' was for the mind to let go of the very idea that the aggregates (all five of them) are substantial and permanent, and to realize that they are in fact nothing but formations which are subject to the three truths of appearing, momentarily existing and dying (*uppāda, ṭhiti, bhaṅga*).

"It was because my mind was clouded by remnants of greed, hatred and delusion that the true nature of things had been obscured and my perceptions, too, had been incorrect. Although I knew theoretically the truth about our perceptions, and in fact could discuss the subject with my fellow meditators, I had not totally accepted it. The truth was thus revealed through the progressive development of wisdom, which resulted from reading, reflecting and, finally, by insight meditation—*sutamaya*, then *cintāmaya* and finally *bhāvanāmaya paññā*.

"I now became quite excited, for it seemed to me that I had achieved something special. 'Was I now on the Path?' I asked myself. But logical and equanimous thinking intervened. Introspective meditation was what was needed now. Then I forced myself to slow down and look inwards with equanimity and with an open mind. With much reflection I realized that while I had seen phenomena in the proper perspective and come to the proper conclusions, dwelling on them with attachment would simply make them *vipassanā-upakkilesa* or one of the 'imperfections of insight' which I knew about, and which I had often explained to meditators who had been associated with me in group meditation sessions. Here, my own experience was unnecessarily exciting me! The important thing now was to free myself from being deceived and to move forward diligently.

"Now, with further contemplation, I can see that neither one nor all of the five aggregates which make up a person, and any activities (phenomena) resulting therefrom, are anything but mere formations which arise, stay awhile and disintegrate; but under the influence of delusion appear to have an individuality of their own, just as with a mirage where there is an illusion of water, which when approached turns out to be nothing. Neither a self or 'I' was involved in the process— only a continuity of conditioned phenomena occurring in a causal chain. Now I could see that even this present thought is impermanent, for it too will pass away before my very eyes, yielding place to another thought, and yet another, and so on. Hence, accepting every pain, every pleasure, every emotion, every delusion as 'mine', as a permanent 'I' was just a mirage, an illusion,—for they are simply phenomena occurring in a causal chain. The words 'mine' and 'I' therefore are only for use in the conventional sense. Thus, what previously was merely theoretical knowledge now became experiential knowledge. Mundane truths had taken on a new dimension and now become supramundane truths.

"I proceeded to return once again to my reflection and contemplation of the links of the *Paṭiccasamuppāda* both in the forward and the reverse directions with total concentration and immersion. I could see with insight wisdom what was previously mere theoretical knowledge, namely, the truth of both impermanence–*anicca,* and non-self–*anattā,* and that this continued travelling in *saṃsāra* was painful, distressing and unsatisfactory. This elusive breakthrough came in a 'flash' of intuition–of understanding with insight.

" Then felt I like some watcher of the skies
When a new planet swims into his ken."

John Keats (1795-1821)

"I commenced to experience an indescribable feeling of calm, peace and serenity. When I came out of this state much later, it was with the insight knowledge and acceptance of the reality that 'I' and 'my' are but conventional terms for mere formations. No phenomena, whether mental, or occurring in the external world, are permanent, nor is there a permanent self to be found anywhere. With the dawning of this comprehension, I am now relatively free of the assumption, the sense, and the delusion of a permanent and continuing 'self' travelling in *saṃsāra.*

"I can see that 'habit energy' or the stream of conditioned consciousness *(bhavaṅga)* can be compared to a 'house-guest' occupying this present body. Now, with *paññā* and equanimity I can distance myself from the mundane activities of the present body. It is now possible, with a proper disposition and continuous application supported by equanimity towards all formations, to find a sense of the quietness of the supramundane. When some negativity yet surfaces unexpectedly, it is recognized as one which had remained dormant and embedded in the deep unconscious as *anusaya*. I then automatically 'let go' of it with equanimity.

"In time, insight meditation took on a new dimension, for the focus now shifted to Nibbāna and the three characteristics of the human condition, namely impermanence, distress and the absence of a permanent 'I'. One now feels peaceful and relaxed when meditating.

"My understanding of the interconnectedness in the links of *Paṭiccasamuppāda* is now more meaningful because phenomena follow phenomena until the truth is seen. Now, with insight into 'non-self', I find a great reduction in clinging and craving and the mental processes of *viññāṇa-saññā-vedanā-saṅkhāra* now stop before *saṅkhāra* and are replaced by *saṅkhāra-upekkhā*. Then one's mind-processes could now be shown as:

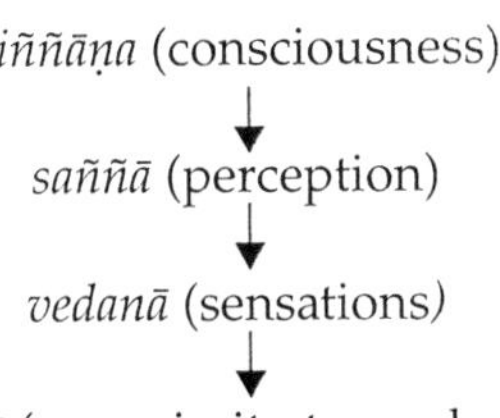

saṅkhāra-upekkhā (equanimity towards all formations).

"Consequently, one abandons craving and clinging as of no consequence. With this paradigm shift, the inclination, the energy for existence fades away and at this stage all the *kammic* energy begins to diminish automatically.

"This means that from now on, I will be constantly aware that all formations are subject to impermanence, distress and are impersonal. There is only the observation of all phenomena with equanimity. I now have much composure and feel peaceful and comfortable. There is now no occasion to react to incidents in the daily mundane life.

"That I was able to move from *vipassanā upakkilesa* finally to *saṅkhāra-upekkhā-ñāṇa*, marked for me the real break-through. But I realize that my task is not yet complete. There is more work to be done. I know that my dedicated goal will eventually be reached as a matter of course. I do not need to yearn for it, for I am confident that this will come to pass when the conditions are ripe.

"When I now focus with insight on the ten fetters (*saṃyojana*) of

1. personality view
2. doubt
3. clinging to rules and rituals as a way to liberation

4. sensual desire
5. illwill or aversion
6. passion for earthly life
7. desire for existence in the Brahma or Formless worlds
8. pride or conceit
9. self-righteousness and finally,
10. ignorance.

that bind a person to *saṃsāra,* I know which of them are not present in me and which of the rest need to be eliminated. I am aware that by continuing the practice of the Noble Eightfold Path, and by way of constant insight meditation on the three characteristics of existence, namely impermanence, distress and non-self, all of these fetters will eventually be eliminated slowly but surely.

"Now let me leave you with a riddle, which you should be able to solve with reflection and contemplation. It may in fact, perhaps, even push you from thinking of liberation to liberation itself!

"Mere suffering exists, no sufferer is found;
The deeds are, but no doer of the deeds is there;
Nirvāṇa is, but not the man who enters it;
The Path is, but no traveller on it is seen." Vism. XVI

"Thank you for listening patiently to me."

The above experiences of a knowledgeable meditator should serve as a source of inspiration to all of us. Readers will observe that he had passed through various stages of insight wisdom leading to what is called "the knowledge of equanimity towards formations"—*sankhara-upekkhā ñāṇa* (see below), and, perhaps, toeven more, which he does not divulge.

According to Srī Ñāṇārāma, "this *saṅkhāra-upekkhā* results from a conviction that all the foundational work for uprooting the defilements has been accomplished and that no further effort is required in this direction. The knowledge of this form of equanimity arises with the understanding of voidness (*suññatā*): that every thing is void of self or what belongs to self. Since the meditator sees that there is neither a self nor anything belonging to a self in relation to himself as well as others, voidness is discerned. There is equanimity at this stage because the meditator understands objects in terms of the four elements."

For further understanding of this critical stage in mental development, we find much information in the *Paṭisambhidāmagga*, which defines the knowledge of equanimity about formations in the following manner: "Wisdom consisting of desire for deliverance together with reflection and composure is the 'Knowledge of Equanimity about Formations." According to this definition, *saṅkhāra-uppekkhā* has three stages: (1) desire for deliverance, (2) reflection and (3) composure. Composure is a significant characteristic of equanimity about formations. It implies the continuity of knowledge or the occurrence of a series of knowledges as an unbroken process. For a meditator who has reached this stage, very little remains to be done."

The meditator had been contemplating the three characteristics of all formations as impermanent, suffering and devoid of self—*anicca-dukkha-anatta*. As he continues reflecting on these characteristics with insight, one of the three characteristics stands out more prominently than the others. Which one stands out depends on his dominant spiritual faculty. One is then considered to have reached insight leading to emergence. This applies to those who have a very strong background knowledge of the *Paṭiccasmuppāda* as well. They too will reach a point where, instead of the focus on all three of the characteristics, the focus automatically shifts on to a single characteristic, which stands out above the others.

One in whom faith is predominant will discern impermanence and subsequently apprehend Nibbāna as the signless (*animitta*). One in whom concentration is predominant will discern the mark of suffering and apprehend Nibbāna as the desireless (*appaṇihita*); and one in whom wisdom is predominant will discern the mark of non-self and subsequently apprehend Nibbāna as voidness (*suññatā*). The particular outstanding characteristic comes up distinctly in the most developed phase of *saṅkkhāra-upekkhā ñāṇa*.

In the previous phase the meditator's mind was focused on formations, and he was seeing formations as impermanent, suffering and non-self. His mind had then automatically let go of formations and taken Nibbāna as its object instead. This change signified the meditator's effort to ensure the occurrence of change-of-lineage-knowledge. It heralds the onset of the supramundane path, which abandons defilements permanently by cutting off their roots, and the attainment of the supramundane path is now assured.

The previously discussed knowledge-of-change-of-lineage would have taken but a few mind-moments, and would have been followed immediately thereafter by the supramundane Path-knowledge, which in turn would have been followed directly by its corresponding fruition. Both the Path-knowledge and Fruition-knowledge take Nibbāna as their object. The Path (*magga*) lasts for only a single moment of consciousness, while fruition (*phala*) occurs for two or three mind-moments.

CHAPTER X

Some Questions and Answers

Several readers of *The Road to Liberation* have written me requesting clarification on certain subjects that had surfaced during the reading of Part 1 of that book as well as during their *vipassanā* meditation practice. In this essay an effort is made to address these issues.

Q 1. In your book (Wheel Publication 450-452), you discussed Satipaṭṭhāna rather briefly, although the Buddha himself is reported to have stated that Satipaṭṭhāna is the only way to liberation. Could you please elaborate?

A. The practice of the four-fold 'foundations of mindfulness' or establishing of 'awareness of mindfulness' called Satipaṭṭhānawas highly praised by the Buddha. Mentioning its importance in the Maha Satipaṭṭhāna Sutta, he called it *ekāyano maggo*—the way pointing only[2] to the purification of beings, for overcoming sorrow, for the extinguishing of suffering, for realizing the path of truth and the experiencing of Nibbāna. This is the real meaning of the two Pali words *ekāyano maggo,—that it points the way (to no other place but) only to Nibbāna.* For the Buddha has shown us elsewhere alternate pathways to Nibbāna.

In this sutta the Buddha has presented a practical method for developing experiential knowledge of oneself by means of *kāyānupassanā* (mindful observation of the body), *vedanānupassanā* (mindful observation of sensations), *cittānupassanā* (mindful observation and awareness of the mind) and *dhammānupassanā* (mindful observation and awareness of the contents of the mind). To explore the truth about ourselves, we must examine the reality of what we are—both body and mind. We must learn to observe these within ourselves. Accordingly, we need to keep three points in mind:

---

2. Translating these words as "the only way" as traditionalists frequently do is, I think, misleading and not justified.

1. The reality of the body may be imagined by contemplation, but to experience it directly one must work with body-sensations (*vedanā*) arising within it.
2. Similarly, working with the contents of the mind one attains the actual experience of the mind.
3. Mind and matter are so closely inter-related that the contents of the mind always manifest themselves as sensations in the body.

Therefore, observation of sensations offers a means of examining the totality of our being, physical as well as mental. This strong emphasis on body sensations is because they work as a direct avenue for the attainment of fruition (Nibbāna) by means of 'strong dependence conditions'—*upanissaya-paccayena paccayā.* Thus, when sensations are experienced properly, these become the nearest dependent condition for our liberation.

We can say that there are four dimensions to our nature; the body, sensations, mind, and its contents. These are the avenues for the establishing of awareness in *satipaṭṭhāna*. In order that the observations are complete, it is necessary to experience every facet by means of *vedanā.* This experience of truth will remove the delusions we have about ourselves. In order to come out of the delusion about the world outside, we need to explore how the outside world interacts with our own mind-and-matter phenomenon i.e., our own being, for the outside world comes into contact with us only at the six sense doors: the eye, ear, nose, tongue, body, and mental base. Since all of these sense-doors are contained in the body (*rūpa*), every contact of the outside world is at the body level.

The Buddha, having learned to examine the depths of his own mind, realized that between the external objects and the mental reaction of craving is a missing link, which is feeling or sensations (*vedanā*). Thus, whenever we encounter an object through the five physical senses and the mind, a sensation arises. If the sensation is pleasant we crave to prolong it, if unpleasant, we crave to be rid of it. It is in the chain of Dependent Origination (*Paṭiccasamuppāda*) that the Buddha has expressed this profound discovery:

Salāyatana-paccayā phasso
Phassapaccayā vedanā
Vedanā-paccayā taṇhā

"Dependent on the six-sense-spheres, arises contact,
Dependent on contact arises sensation,
Dependent on sensation arises cravingr"

Thus the immediate cause for the arising of craving, and consequently of suffering (*dukkha*), is not something outside of us but rather the sensations (*vedanā*) that arise within us.

However, merely awareness of the sensations within us is not enough to remove our delusions. It is essential also to understand the three universal characteristics *(trilakkhaṇa)* of all phenomena in the world, for we must directly experience within ourselves the truth of impermanence, suffering and non-self. This is possible by meditating the *Satipaṭṭhāna* and *Paṭiccasamuppāda* way.

The Mahā Satipaṭṭhāna Sutta (D.22) begins with the observation of the body. Here, under *kāyānupassanā,* several different starting points are explained: observing the in-and-out breath, attention to body movements etc. Thereafter, we progressively develop mindful awareness of sensations, thoughts and mental objects—*vedanānupassanā, cittānupassananā* and *dhammā-nupassanā*. However, no matter from which point the journey starts, there are 'stations' which everyone must pass through on the way to the final goal. These are described in important sentences repeated at the end of each section. Namely:

Samudaya-dhammanupassī va viharati
Vaya-dhammānupassī va viharati
Samudaya-vaya-dhammānupassī va viharati

"One dwells observing the phenomenon of arising.
One dwells observing the phenomenon of passing away.
One dwells observing the phenomenon of arising and of passing away".

These sentences reveal the essence of the practice of *satipaṭṭhāna* meditation, for when these three levels of *anicca* are directly experienced, we will develop the requisite wisdom, which leads to detachment and liberation.

Q 2. In vipassanā meditation under *kāyānupassanā*, one of the subjects we are asked to reflect on is the repulsive nature of the body. Could you please elaborate?

A. In answering the previous question, I mentioned that there are four main topics for exploration and development of self-knowledge by development of insight. The first of these was *kāyānupassanā* or observation of the body, and within this body contemplation, the Buddha had recommended insight meditation on the following:

> Awareness of respiration,
> Awareness of postures of the body,
> Constant and thorough understanding of impermanence,
> and Reflection on the repulsiveness of the body.

In regard to the last of the above four subjects, the translation of the text reads as follows:

> "Again, O monks, a monk reflects on this very body, that it is covered with skin and full of impurities of all kinds from the soles of the feet upwards and from the hair of the head downwards, considering thus: 'In this body there are hairs of the head, body hairs, nails, teeth, skin, flesh, sinews, bones, bone-marrow, kidney, heart, liver, diaphragm, spleen, lungs, intestines, mesentery, stomach with its contents, faeces, bile, phlegm, pus, blood, sweat, fat, tears, lubricants, saliva, nasal mucous, synovial fluid, urine and the brain.'
>
> "Just as if there were a double-mouthed provision bag, full of various kinds of grains and seeds, such as hill-paddy rice, paddy-rice, mung-beans, cow-peas, sesame seeds and husked rice and as if there were a man with good eyesight, who, after having opened that bag would examine the contents saying: 'This is hill paddy-rice, this is paddy-rice, these are mung-beans, these are cow-peas, these are sesame seeds and this is husked rice.'
>
> "In the same way, O monks, a monk reflects on this very body, that is covered with skin and ... urine and brain.'
>
> "He thus abides observing body within body internally, or he abides observing body within body both internally and externally. Thus he abides observing the phenomenon of arising in the body, thus he observes the phenomenon of passing away in the body, and thus he abides observing the phenomenon of simultaneous arising-and-passing-away in the body. Awareness that, 'This is

body' remains present in him. Thus he develops the awareness to such an extent that there is mere understanding along with mere awareness. In this way he abides detached, without clinging, or craving towards anything in this world of mind and matter. This is how, monks, a monk abides observing body within body".

The Buddha has also described these thirty-two parts of the body and the related simile in the Kāyagatānussati Sutta (M.119) as well as in various other suttas.

The perception of bodily attractiveness lasts only as long as the body is looked at superficially and grasped in terms of selected impressions. To counter this perception, it is necessary to constantly meditate on the body by visualizing the distasteful aspects of the components of the body with comprehension and full awareness of their distastefulness. The desire, the lust, and the passion will then disappear. The meditator takes one's own body as an object and using visualization as an aid, one mentally dissects the body into its component parts and looks at them one by one, focusing on their repulsive nature. The text mentions thirty two parts: head-hairs, body-hairs, finger and toe-nails, teeth, skin, flesh, sinews, bones, bone-marrow, kidneys, heart, liver, diaphragm, spleen, lungs, large intestines, mesentery, stomach contents, excrement, bile, phlegm, pus, blood, sweat, fat, tears, lubricants, snot, phlegm, sinovial fluid, urine and the brain. The aim of this meditation must not be misunderstood. The aim is not to produce aversion and disgust, but only detachment so as to be able to extinguish the fire of lust.

This meditation is popular in South-East Asia, and is commonly referred to as asubha *bhāvanā* — "distasteful meditation subject". Alternatively, it is often referred to in the West as the meditation on a "woman or man, as a bag of bones".

A meditation teacher will often give this *asubha bhāvanā* as the subject for meditation at an early stage of a *vipassanā* meditation course to those students whom he reckons are sensually inclined.

In this context, I cannot help but relate an incident that was reported to have happened in the past. A certain conscientious meditating monk was walking one night along the road to his temple when a woman fully adorned with jewelry, earrings and anklets passed by grinning and laughing. A short while later her husband came rushing along the road and seeing the monk asked him whether he had seen a well-dressed young woman, and he then described the woman, her dress and ornaments. The monk replied that he saw no such woman, but that a skeleton with bright teeth had passed by sometime previously! The fact was that the monk had been totally immersed in the meditation on the *asubha bhāvanā* and he saw only the gleaming white teeth (the fourth of the thirty-two body parts) listed in that meditation subject!

Q 3. Can you briefly summarize contemplative meditation on *Paṭiccasamuppāda*?

A. This could be considered critically the most important part of our study, cessation or deliverance from the round of birth and rebirth. To begin our quest to understand cessation, we can practise with insight, the two-fold forward and reverse contemplation of the twelve links of dependent origination, which are: ignorance, mental formations, consciousness, mind and body, the six sense faculties, contact, feeling, craving, grasping, existence, birth, and death and decay.

Forward contemplation throws light on the existence of suffering, leading to the question, "What is the origin of suffering?". Following the causal chain of existence, we first contemplate how fundamentally does ignorance set in motion the life cycle. Ignorance then conditions action, and actions condition consciousness. From consciousness we contemplate name-and-form, and then on to the six sense-faculties and so forth until we finally see that our desire leads to grasping. Because there is grasping, there is becoming which leads to birth. Finally, we become subject to sickness, mental and physical pain, ageing and ultimately to death.

The realization of birth, existence, decay and death (*uppāda, ṭhiti, bhaṅga*) of every activity, leads to a profound understanding of the unenviable state in which we find ourselves. This is the forward contemplation of the twelve links of *Paṭiccasamuppāda*, and its purpose, as was stated previously, is to help us realize cessation.

When we practise reverse contemplation (i.e., on the absense of *dukkha*) , we can realize emptiness. Here too we begin with initial ignorance (*avijjā*), and contemplate by asking ourselves the question as to what occurs when there is no ignorance? And we see the answer, namely, that there will not be any deluded actions. Once there are no deluded actions, there is then no defilement of consciousness. We proceed in this fashion onto the six sense faculties which give rise naturally to contact, desire, grasping, existence, birth, death and so on. This is the reverse contemplation on the cessation of the twelve-linked chain of dependent origination.

However, what is most important is to understand fully the reality of the fundamental ignorance with which we enter the world. In Buddhism *avijjā* means a misconception, a misjudgement of the nature of the world. Specifically, it means not understanding the three facts of existence which are: impermanence (*anicca*), suffering *(dukkha)* and non-self (*anattā*).

We thus have forward contemplation on the cause of *dukkha*, and the reverse contemplation on the non-existence of *dukkha*. In the forward contemplation we realize how we come into being and in the reverse we realize that we have no independent self. It must be remembered that both modes of contemplation are related and it is necessary to complement one with the other. It is with this dual approach that we can truly comprehend cessation with insight, and so terminate our wandering in *saṃsāra*.

When we awaken to the true nature of things, our mind will be free of avijjā. It will be illuminated with wisdom, and by transcending ignorance we will no longer be conditioned by it. This non-conditioning will then become true for the remaining links of the chain one after another, thereby terminating birth-and-death.

Our ignorant belief that things are real is extremely powerful. But we should remember that this is nothing but an error in judgement. It is merely a delusion that we cling to, but which in fact has no foundation whatsoever. On the other hand, its opposite, the understanding that phenomena have no reality, is based on a consistent truth that stands up to investigation. If one familiarizes oneself with this understanding, it can be developed indefinitely, since it is both a true and a natural quality of the mind. It is through insight meditation that we can establish firmly the view of emptiness, and with it completely destroy the veils that obscure true knowledge.

Let us recollect that the Buddha presented the teaching on emptiness to his original band of five monks, by way of the

Anattalakkhaṇa Sutta (Khandha Samy. 59) in which he pointed out to them that every phenomenon was devoid a "self" (Ch. 4 in in Part 1, *The Road to Liberation*).

The emptiness of substantial reality is called "non-self". Those who realize the nature of emptiness also realize that their own nature is that of flux, change and impermanence. They directly experience that mind, body and environment are pervaded with a dynamic quality of emptiness. A first inkling of this emptiness comes to one who is on the threshold of awakening and is fully realized only when one "enters the stream" as an *Ariya*.

Q 4. What is the position of Satipaṭṭhāna vis-a-vis Paṭicca-samuppāda and the Four Noble Truths in our insight meditation towards Nibbāna?

A. This is a fundamental question which is quite excellent.

All our efforts in meditation are for the purpose of a gradual evolution of *paññā* or insight wisdom,— *bhāvanāmaya paññā*. Fundamentally, it is to develop experiential knowledge of *anicca, dukkha* and *anatta*—impermanence, distress and non-self. What makes this so difficult is that the human condition is beset by the three negative characteristics of greed, hatred and delusion—*lobha, dosa* and *moha*.

To understand the three factors of impermanence, distress and non-self, requires deep contemplation the *vipassanā* way. It is by focusing on the twelve links of *Paṭiccasamuppāda* that one can come to an experiential understanding of how the human condition comes to be, which with all its weaknesses, contributes to the delusion that there is a permanent entity called a "self." Once we accept this position then we see that greed and hatred become concomitant factors towards its preservation. The Noble Eightfold Path, which is the fourth Noble Truth, teaches us how to develop insight, and it is by meditating according to the directions in the Satipaṭṭhāna Sutta (M.16), that we can experientially observe impermanence and the phenomena of arising, passing away and both arising and passing away. By experiencing *anicca* at these levels, we develop *paññā*—the gateway to equanimity—based on the experience of impermanence. This in turn leads to detachment followed by liberation.

In the case of *Paṭiccasamuppāda*, our repeated contemplation of its twelve factors in both the forward and the reverse directions with *sati-sampajañña* (mindfulness with full awareness) results in detachment and the experience of all the three characteristics of existence, namely *anicca, dukkha* and *anattā*. It is here that a word of caution is merited, for it is only with a paradigm shift indicating that we are living the twelve links of dependent origination that we can come to this true understanding.

Insight meditation on the Four Noble Truths is explained as the fourth part of the Satipaṭṭhāna Sutta (M.16) under *Dhammānupassanā*, commencing with the words; *Puna ca paraṃ bhikkhave, bhikkhu dhammesu dhammānupassī viharati catusu ariyasaccesuṛ*—meaning: "Again, O monks, a monk abides observing mental contents within mental contents, concerning the Four Noble Truthsṛ"

The interconnectedness of the twelve links of the *Paṭicca-samuppāda,* the Four Noble Truths and the Four Foundations of Mindfulness (*Satipaṭṭhāna*) should thus be self-evident. They all lead to just one goal, namely, liberation – Nibbāna.

Q 5. Could you please explain the step-wise method of mettā meditation?
A. Let me explain how to practise this with meditation groups.

If the meditators are Buddhists, we start by first repeating in unison the three refuges, the five precepts and the verses in praise of the Triple Gem as follows:

> *Namo tassa Bhagavato Arahato Sammā Sambuddhassa*
> (three times)
>
> "Homage to the Blessed One, The Perfect One,
> the Fully Awakened One."

The Refuges

> *Buddhaṃ saraṇaṃ gacchāmi,*
> *Dhammaṃ saraṇaṃ gacchāmi,*
> *Saṅghaṃ saraṇaṃ gacchāmi.*
> *Dutiyampi ... gacchāmi,*
> *Tatiyampi ... gacchāmi.*
>
> "I go to the Buddha for refuge, I go to the Dhamma for refuge and I go to the Sangha for refuge." I go a second and a third time for refuge to the Buddha, the Dhamma and the Sangha."

The Precepts

Pāṇātipātā veramaṇī sikkhāpadaṃ samādiyāmi
Adinnādānā veramaṇī sikkhāpadaṃ samādiyāmi
Kāmesu michācārā veramaṇī sikkhāpadaṃ samādiyāmi
Musāvādā veramaṇī sikkhāpadaṃ samādiyāmi
Surāmerayamajjapamādaṭṭhānā veramaṇī sikkhāpadaṃ samādiyāmi.

"I volunteer to abstain from killing and hurting sentient beings;
I volunteer to abstain from stealing;
I volunteer to abstain from sexual misconduct;
I volunteer to abstain from telling lies;
I volunteer to abstain from taking drugs and intoxicants that cause intoxication and heedlessness.

Praise of the Buddha

Iti'pi so Bhagavā arahaṃ, sammā-sambuddho, vijjā-caraṇa-sampanno, sugato, lokavidū, anuttaro purisadammasārathī, satthā devamanussānaṃ, buddho bhagavā'ti.

"Such indeed is the Blessed One: perfected, fully awakened, endowed with knowledge and discipline, having walked the right path, the knower of the worlds, incomparable guide of amenable men and women, teacher of gods and humans, awakened and blessed."

Praise of the Dhamma

Svākkhāto bhagavatā dhammo, sandiṭṭhiko, akāliko, ehipassiko, opanayiko paccattaṃ veditabbo viññūhi'ti.

"Well taught is the doctrine of the Blessed One, of immediate benefit, timeless, inviting us to experience it, leading us onwards, to be comprehended individually by the wise."

Praise of the Saṅgha

Supaṭipanno bhagvato sāvakasaṅgho, ujupaṭipanno bhagavato sāvakasaṅgho, ñāyapaṭipanno bhagavato sāvakasaṅgho, sāmīcipaṭipanno bhagavato sāvakasaṅgho: yadidaṃ cattāri purisayugāni aṭṭhapurisapuggalā, esa bhgavato sāvakasaṅgho, āhuneyyo, pāhuneyyo, dakkhiṇeyyo, añjalikara-ṇīyo anuttaraṃ puññakkhettaṃ lokassā'ti

"Wholesome in conduct is the community of disciples of the Blessed One, honest in conduct is the community of disciples of the Blessed One, wise in conduct is the community of disciples of the Blessed One, proper in conduct is the community of disciples of the Blessed One. These four pairs of persons, eight individuals, this is the community of disciples of the Blessed One: Worthy of offerings and hospitality, gifts and homage, it is an incomparable field of merit for the world."

Reciting these verses while focusing on the meaning of the words helps one to calm the mind and make it pliable for meditation.

On the other hand, if I were meditating with a group of non-Buddhists, I would request all the participants to first gently close their eyes and then to start relaxing all the muscles in the body consciously: begin with the head, then the facial muscles, next those in the neck, and so on until one comes to the toes, until they are fully relaxed and devoid of tensions in body and mind. They are then asked to take one or two breaths consciously and while exhaling say to themselves that all negativities are being expelled with each exhalation.

Mettā Meditation

After a moment of silence, now that they are fully relaxed, I ask them to imagine that there is a rosebud about to bloom where our hearts are. (For Sri Lankans and South-East Asian groups it would be a lotus.) Participants are then asked to imagine that this flower bud is now slowly opening in the morning sun, and that as its petals unfold, the sweet scent of the flower spreads first to its immediate surroundings and then a gentle wind wafts its fragrance farther and farther. I then ask them to fill their hearts with universal kindness or *mettā*, and then release the scent of this goodness slowly so as to fill the entire meditation room, then to spread out to the garden outside, next to cover the entire city, then the State, then the whole country, the whole world, and finally to embrace the entire universe with all its living beings.

We then request one of the participants to lead the rest in repeating a 'wish for happiness'. This could be similar to the one in Wheel 450-452, or it could be one which the participant had himself formulated. As an alternative I give below an invocation offered by Sondra Jewell, a friend of mine (after attending a *vipassanā* retreat with Ven. Gunaratana Mahā Thera in Canada), which we find quite soothing and appropriate during group meditation sessions.

Loving-Friendliness Meditation

"May I be healthy. May I be happy. May my heart be filled with love. May I be peaceful. May I have ease of well-being. May I live in safety. May no problems come to me. May no difficulties come to me. May no harm come to me. May I always meet with success.

May I have patience, strength, courage, inner clarity and wisdom to meet and overcome inevitable difficulties, problems and failures in life.

May my whole heart be filled with loving-friendliness. May every cell of my body be filled with loving-friendliness. May every level of my consciousness be purified with loving-friendliness. May I build a healthy, happy aura of loving-friendliness all around myself, and may I be protected.

May my parents be healthy. May they be happy. May their hearts be filled with love. May they be peaceful. May they have ease of well-being. May they live in safety. May no problems come to them. May no difficulties come to them. May no harm come to them. May they always meet with success.

May they have patience, strength, courage, inner clarity and wisdom to meet and overcome inevitable difficulties, problems and failures in life.

May their whole hearts be filled with loving-friendliness. May every cell of their body be filled with loving-friendliness. May every level of their consciousness be purified with loving-friendliness. May they build a healthy, happy aura of loving-friendliness all around themselves and may they be protected.

May my teachers be healthy. Mayṛ and may they be protected.

May my loved ones be healthy. Mayṛ and may they be protected.

May my friends, co-workers and neighbours be healthy. Mayṛ and may they be protected.

May those I have harmed, or who have harmed me, be healthy. May ... and may they be protected.

May all living beings be healthy. May ... and may they be protected." – S.J.

We follow this with five to ten minutes of silent meditation on *mettā* (loving-kindness), as well as *karuṇā* (compassion), for we know that the practical application or consummation of *mettā bhāvanā* (meditation) is by acts of compassion directed towards the deserving.

At the conclusion of the *mettā bhāvanā* session, I would briefly describe the method suggested by the Buddha for developing these sublime states. (See Wheel Publication 450-452, page 100).

Q. 6. Over the last decade, a number of friends of mine and I have attended several ten-day and even monthly retreats at various vipassanā training centers. We now do individual meditation as well as regular group meditations. But, while we can reach a satisfactory level of serenity during and after these meditation sessions, a "break-through" to the Ariya life eludes us. Why is this?

A. It is not possible to generalize about this kind of situation. I appreciate your question, but there are so many possible problems, permutations and combinations of such problems that a completely satisfactory answer is impossible. It would perhaps have been easier if each of you had discussed your individual problems with your respective meditation masters.

However, I can suggest some questions, which you can ask yourself first. You can use them as a checklist and proceed onwards with confidence, correcting the deficiencies and the day will surely come when, like the "knowledgeable meditator" whose experiences are described in chapter 3 of this book, you will be able to make a break-through from the mundane to the supramundane. Please always remember that everything must be observed, discovered and experienced only in one's body, and nowhere else.

1. Do you spend a sufficient number of hours regularly each day for meditation?
2. Do you practise the five or eight precepts in thought, word and deed at all times?

3. Have you read and understood the Dhamma in such aitushion that you can unhesitatingly understand references to *kamma, kamma-vipāka, anicca-dukkha-anatta, loba-dosa-moha, vipassanā* and so on as explained in Dhamma talks and in this book?
4. Do you understand the twelve links of the *Paṭiccasamuppāda* and their interdependence and conditionality (*paccaya*)?
5. Are you earnestly following the Noble Eightfold Path?
6. Do you see the interconnectedness of *Paṭiccasamuppāda*, the Noble Eightfold Path and the four *Satipaṭṭhānas*?
7. Can you understand fully what is meant by formations, phenomena and conditionality when your meditation master mentions them during lectures?
8. Has your meditation teacher walked you through the twelve links of *Paṭiccasamuppāda* as an intensive meditation subject?
9. Do you spend some time each day meditating on the *brahma-vihāras*? Do you develop and practise them in your daily life?
10. Do you discuss your doubts, and does your meditation teacher clarify them?
11. Do you practise walking meditation in addition to seated meditation daily?

Are you equanimous and mindful at all times?

Q. 7. We often hear of "Three Turnings of the Wheel". What does it mean?

A. We come across this in the Mahāyāna tradition and it essentially is not contradicted in the Theravāda suttas. When the Buddha originally proclaimed the Four Noble Truths, which includes the Eightfold Path, to the *Pancavaggiyas* (group of five ascetics), He is supposed to have repeated the exposition of the Dhammacakkappavattana Sutta (Sacca Saṃy. 11) three times. On his first preaching, Kondañña is believed to have become an *Ariya*; with the second; Vappa and Bhaddiya; and with the third turning Assaji and Mahānāma.

According to the Theravada tradition, after his first sermon the Buddha is said to have taught the Dhamma to these five disciples for a period of time. It is said that while three of the disciples went for alms, the Buddha would teach the other two, and when these two went for alms he would teach the other three. It was only when he was fully satisfied that all five could understand and comprehend his Dhamma, that he preached his next sermon, which was the Anattalakkhaṇa Sutta, hearing which all five of them attained *arahantship*.

Q. 8. I was fascinated after listening to your description of the experiences of a knowledgeable meditator. Do you have other examples of persons who have recently achieved transcendence?

A. Upāsikā Kee Nanayon (1901-1978) was one of the foremost Dhamma teachers of modern Thailand. Her talks, concise and to the point, have provided an enormous number of people with incisive insight into meditative techniques leading to liberation.

The following is what she had to say about herself, without claiming in words that she was an *Ariya*.

> "... One night, I was sitting in meditation outside in the open air—my back straight as an arrow—firmly determined to make the mind quiet, but even after a long time it wouldn't settle down. So I thought, I've been working at this for many days now, and yet my mind won't settle down at all. It's time to stop being so determined and to simply be aware of the mind. I started to take my hands and feet out of the meditation posture, but at the moment I had unfolded one leg but had yet to unfold the other, I could see that my mind was like a pendulum swinging more and more slowly, more and more slowly—until it stopped.
>
> "Then there arose an awareness, which sustained itself. Slowly I put my legs and hands back into position. At the same time, the mind was in a state of awareness absolutely and solidly still, seeing clearly the elementary phenomena of existence as they arose and disbanded, changing in line with their nature—and also seeing, a separate condition inside, with no arising, disbanding or changing, a condition beyond birth and death: something very difficult to put clearly into words, because it was a realization of the elementary phenomena of nature, completely internal and individual.
>
> "After a while I slowly got up and lay down to rest. This state of mind remained as a stillness, which sustained itself deep down inside. Eventually the mind came out of

this state and gradually returned to normal"

In the above anecdote this meditation teacher shows us how she achieved transcendence when focusing on *Anatta*. (From B.P.S.Wheel No. 373/374)

Q. 9. Could you please summarize for us the Buddha's thinking on conditionality, which in turn leads to his doctrine of Dependent Origination or Paṭiccasamuppāda?

A. During the time of the Buddha, there were numerous speculative theories on 'Causation' such as self or internal causation, external causation, a combination of the two, and finally, that things originate due neither to internal or external causes but due to mere chance or accident.

The Buddha carefully examined these theories and found no substance in them. To the contrary, he saw some uniform causal patterns in the world, which could be summarized into four groups, namely:

1. That causation actually takes place in the world. It is an actual happening, but not the work of any person.
2. That as long as certain conditions exist, certain effects are bound to come into being, or even more simply, take place.
3. That under a certain set of conditions (and as long as they remain unchanged), they give rise to certain predictable effects.
4. That for things to come into being, there should be certain conditions (conditionality), thus emphasizing the fact that causation is neither a chance happening nor a pre-determined happening.

The Buddha used the above observations when formulating the theory of origination, cessation and causation, which he summarized as follows:

This general theory of causality explains the origin and cessation of everything in the world. The whole universe (including everything in it) comes within the operation of this principle.

The Buddha's main concern, however, was with regard to man and his experiencing of unsatisfactoriness or distress (*dukkha*), and his mission was to find an answer leading to the cessation or escape from *dukkha*. It was by applying this general theory of causality that he was able to evolve a specific formula to explain how man continues to travel in *saṃsāra* undergoing distress, and how this journey could be terminated. This formula is what we know as the Dependent Origination or *Paṭiccasamuppāda*. It is as follows:

> 'When this is present that comes to be. On the arising of this that arises. When this is absent, that does not come to be. On the cessation of this, that ceases. That is to say: On ignorance depends dispositions or mental formations; on dispositions or mental formations depends consciousness; on consciousness depends name and form or the psycho-physical personality; on name and form depend the six 'gateways' of sense perception; on the six 'gateways' depends contact; on contact depends feeling; on feelings depends desire (craving); on desire depends grasping; on grasping depends becoming; on becoming depends birth; and on birth depends ageing, sorrow, lamentation, suffering, dejection and vexation. In this manner arises a mass of suffering'.

Paṭiccasamuppāda clearly shows that things come into existence through cause and conditions and cease when these causes and conditions are absent. It should, however, be kept in mind that although ignorance is at the head of the list of the twelve factors, it does not mean that it is a *first cause,* for the twelve factors can be considered in the form of a circle or an ever-continuing repetitive chain in which *any of the twelve factors can be used as a starting point.* We also need to remember that in addition to the absence of a first cause, there is also no single cause but only causes and conditions that invariably bring related effects. In fact, *all twelve factors are inter-related, inter-connected.* They are merely causes and conditions that produce effects.

The Buddha used many simple examples to illustrate the nature of dependent origination. He said that the flame in an oil lamp burns "dependent on the oil and the wick". When both of these are present, we see a flame, but if either is absent, the flame will cease to exist. He also used the example of the sprout, which he pointed out, arises dependent on the seed, earth, water, air and light.

Our interest in the principles underlying *Paṭiccasamuppāda* lies in its relationship to the problem of impermanence, distress or unsatisfactoriness (*dukkha*), and rebirth. We are in fact interested in how dependent origination explains the situation in which we find ourselves here and now, and how to free ourselves from this suffering.

Q. 10. Could you tell us briefly the manner in which the Buddha made the greatest of his discoveries?
A. It was on the night of his enlightenment that the Buddha discovered the cause of suffering which he attributed to craving (desire), ill will and delusion (ignorance of *anatta*).

Thus in the Mūlapariyāya Sutta (M.1) he says:

> "Therefore, bhikkhus, through the complete destruction, fading away, cessation, abandoning and relinquishing of cravings, the Thathāgata has awakened to the supreme perfect enlightenment. —What is the reason? Because he has understood that delight is the root cause of suffering, and that with existence (as condition) there is birth, and that for what has come to be there is ageing and death. Therefore, bhikkhus, through the complete destruction, fading away, cessation, abandoning, and relinquishing of all cravings, the Thathāgata has awakened to the supreme perfect enlightenment, I declare".

Elsewhere too the Buddha has said the same thing, that the door to his enlightenment was opened when he saw the cause of suffering as desire, ill will and ignorance. And if we want to be rational in our examination, *we must focus upon ignorance,* because it is due to ignorance that desire and ill will arise.

Essentially, ignorance is the idea of a permanent, independent self. It is this conception of an 'I', opposed to and separate from the people and things around us, that is the root cause of suffering. Once we have the notion of 'I', we have an inclination to favour those things that sustain this 'I' and to be averse to those things that we think threaten this 'I'. It is this conception of the self that is the fundamental cause of suffering, and the root of the various negative emotions such as anger, envy, desire, ill-will, jealousy and greed. To add to the confusion is our ignorance of the fact that in reality there is no such permanent thing as 'I' and that what we label as 'I' is merely a convenient name given to a collection of ever-changing, dependently originating factors or aggregates. The 'self' then is just a convenient name for a collection of processes.

In this context the self is compared to a rope, which in the dark may be mistaken for a snake, thus causing fear. Similarly, in the darkness of ignorance, we take the impersonal processes of feelings (*vedanā)*, perception (*saññā*) and so forth to be a self. As a result we desire certain things and we are averse to others. So ignorance in this sense is the mistaken notion of a permanent ego (*atta*) as a real self.

It is only when this egotism is removed or dispelled by right understanding (which in turn is possible only with insight meditation) that greed, anger and delusion become things of the past and the end of suffering is gained.

Q. 11. We now hear a lot about emptiness and voidness. Could you please explain?

A. True cessation is the full realization of the nature of emptiness (egolessness) and the liberation of oneself from the cycle of birth-and-death. How does one fully realize the nature of emptiness (*suññatā*)? To understand emptiness we need to first understand the working of causes and conditions as was explained previously. Phenomena come into being through "conditioned arising", the coming together of causes and conditions mutually influencing one another. Everything is in a state of constant flux. Nothing remains the same one instant to the next. Through this constant transformation all phenomena arise, change and eventually cease. Since everything is in flux without a permanent nature or identity, there can be no separately identifiable "self". This condition is known as the phenomenon of "emptiness".

The Dalai Lama has explained emptiness as follows: "All phenomena are by nature empty, devoid of true existence. But what is our perception of phenomena at the moment? What we experience is just the opposite. Rather than perceiving phenomena as empty, we see everything as existent and real. It is only through study and practice that we gain some understanding and confidence that the nature of things is emptiness. Then we realize that our perceptions hitherto have not corresponded at all to the way things really are and that we ignorantly cling to our mistaken way of seeing things."

It is this ignorance, which is at the root of desire and hatred. In other words, it is the very root cause of our travels in *saṃsāra*.

There is a saying which is quite apt here:

Thirty spokes converge upon a single hub,
It is on the hole in the centre
that the use of the cart hinges:
We make a vessel from a lump of clay,
It is the empty space within the vessel
that makes it useful.
We make doors and windows for a room,
But it is these empty spaces that make the room liveable.
Thus, while the tangibles have advantages,
It is the intangible that makes it useful.

Q. 12. Why do we need to realize emptiness? And how?

A. We need to realize emptiness because we do not wish to suffer and we know that the root cause of suffering is the untamed mind. Because the mind perceives and understands things mistakenly, negative emotions arise and the mind is never at peace. To avoid this, we must develop the mind so that it perceives the true nature of phenomena. It is because of our mistaken perception that we fail to see things as they really are.

Much of what we perceive is perceived in a mistaken way, seeing things not as they truly are. This is how we become deluded. To avoid this, we should not accept our perceptions in the way we experience them. We should rather analyze and investigate whether we are seeing things as they truly are or not.

The mind's ignorant clinging to things and its subsequent way of functioning obscure our vision regarding the true nature of things. Thus, relative truth is based on the findings of the mind that examines things in a conventional way. If we analyze further and try to see the true nature of phenomena, we can find the ultimate nature of reality. Here we distinguish between the way things appear (relative truth) and the way they really are (absolute truth), which is what is perceived by the non-deluded mind. The absolute truth is revealed through the development of wisdom, which in turn is evelopedthrough skillful listening, reflecting and insight meditation. When one investigates the nature of the individual and of all phenomena, one finds that their nature is emptiness. This emptiness is an absolute truth that is apparent to the mind. One can see it with one's awareness—*sati-sampajañña*. Once it has been experienced, it is not necessary to demonstrate it again. By referring to one's experience of this nature, one can recall it. Its existence is true, and one does not have to rely on argument to prove that it exists. This absolute nature is established through the three stages of evolutionary development of wisdom—*sutamaya paññā, cintāmaya paññā*—and *bhāvanā-maya paññā* by listening, reflecting and meditation. It is something that we can experience.

The Dalai Lama explains further: "However, when one looks for this emptiness, and tries to find where it is, one cannot find it. Its nature is nonexistence, for it is not something that can be analyzed and discovered. To take an example, we can say that a vase has the nature of emptiness, but when we look for the emptiness, it is nonexistent. All we can find is the emptiness of emptiness, but we cannot find emptiness. What has been found by experiencing it through listening, reflecting and meditating cannot be found other than experientially".

This is the important point. For, the understanding and experiencing of this truth comes only by progression or development of wisdom along the path of listening (or reading), reflecting and meditating.

Q. 13. Some speak of time and space in relation to the Dhamma. What does it mean?

A. The Four Noble Truths show us two kinds of cause-and-effect principles at work. One can be called "worldly-cause-and effect", which leads to suffering, and the other "transcendent cause-and-effect", which leads to liberation.

Worldly cause-and-effect takes place in space and time and whatever exists in space and time is characterized by impermanence. Yesterday you were not listening to me; today you are doing so; and after listening you will probably not reflect on it for some time. What we experience here is impermanence. This sense of change also gives us a sense of continuity in our lives. But let us not forget that as the days go by, our lives are also coming to a close, day by day. So impermanence is essentially this progression from birth to death, from existence to non-existence.

To experience impermanence we must exist in the space-time continuum. Our sense of space can be great or small. What is different is the key to how we experience the workings of causes and conditions. The different factors coming together and dispersing give us a sense of time. The very fact that the different aspects of our lives shift, alter and transform, results from these causal relationships. The workings of cause and conditions, which take place in space, are inseparable and imbedded in time, so we experience time and space together. And this experience of constant change is impermanence.

Simply put, world transcendence is freedom from worldly cause-and-effect, freedom from suffering in time and space. The awakened or liberated ones—the arahats, are no longer fettered by time-and-space, and therefore no longer influenced by the suffering which impermanence brings. The state of world-transcendence is a state of liberation.

Q. 14. How do the worldly and world-transcending realities relate to the Four Noble Truths?
A. Worldly cause-and-effect encompasses the first two Noble Truths of suffering and the origination of suffering. Suffering is actually an effect of living in time and space, and its origin is our ignorance (first factor in *Paṭiccasamuppāda*).

World-transcending cause-and-effect relates to the third and fourth of the Four Noble Truths of the cessation of suffering and the path that leads out of suffering. Cessation is the state in which worldly cause-and-effect is abandoned, there is no more accumulation of *kamma*, and liberation is realized. Thus, when the Buddha taught the doctrines of *Paṭiccasamuppāda* and of the Four Noble Truths, he also taught that the path of liberation is the path of moving from the worldly to the world-transcending modes of acting, thinking and speaking.

CHAPTER XI

The Suttas and Transcendence

When we survey the Sutta Piṭaka, we find a number of suttas which, when comprehended with insight, have inspired many a meditator to directly achieve liberation. We are no doubt familiar with the fact that at the very first preaching of the Dhammacakkappavattana Sutta (Sacca Saṃy. 11), Koṇḍañña "saw the eye of the *dhamma*" and became a *sotāpanna*. According to legend, two more of the original five bhikkhus (*pañcavaggiya*) became *sotāpannas* when he repeated to them this sutta, and the last two similarly became stream-winners when he repeated this sutta to them for the third time. In Mahāyāna literature these are called the 'three turnings of the Wheel" of the Dhamma. As stated elsewhere in this current presentation, it is said that when the Buddha preached his second sermon, the Anattalakkhaṇa Sutta, all five of them reached liberation and became arahants. The Salāyatana Saṃyutta too is replete with examples of individual monks achieving liberation at the end of one-on-one discussions with the Buddha.

Serious advanced meditators would also be aware of the fact that comprehension of *Paṭiccasamuppāda* with insight wisdom through *vipassanā* meditation can be a direct route to transcendence, for the Buddha has said in the Satipaṭṭhāna Sutta (M.16): "He who sees dependent origination sees the dhamma, he who sees the dhamma sees dependent origination".

And at the end of the Mahā Satipaṭṭhāna Sutta (D.22), the Buddha says: "Indeed, O monks, whoever practises this fourfold establishing of awareness in exactly this manner for seven years ... let alone seven months ... let alone half a month, O monks ... for seven days, one of two results can be expected in him: highest wisdom or, aware of a substratum of aggregates remaining, the stage of non-returner."

For the convenience of advanced *vipassanā* meditators, I wish to discuss below a few of the popular suttas, an intensive study of which can provide the background material for the development of insight wisdom that will lead them, when conditions are ripe, to transcendence. In each case, I propose to briefly point out the most significant aspects from my limited comprehension. It is left to the meditator to apply himself thereafter in the appropriate fashion of contemplation and reflection to achieve his goal.

The Anattalakkhaṇa Sutta (Khandha Saṃy. 59)

On one occasion the Exalted One was dwelling at the Deer park in Isipathana, near Benares. Then the Exalted One addressed the band of five bhikkhus, saying, "O bhikkhus!" "Ven. sir," they replied. Thereupon the Exalted One spoke as follows:

"The body (*rūpa*), O bhikkhus, is soulless (*anatta*). If, O bhikkhus, there were in this a soul, then this body would not be subject to suffering. 'Let this body be thus, let this body be not thus,' such possibilities would also exist. But, inasmuch as this body is soulless, it is subject to suffering, and no possibility exists for (ordering): 'Let this be so, let this not be so.'

"In this same manner feelings (*vedanā*), perceptions (*saññā*), mental formations (*saṅkhāra*) and consciousness (*viññaṇa*) are soulless.

"What think ye, O bhikkhus, is this body permanent or impermanent?" "Impermanent, Ven. Sir."

"Is that which is impermanent happy or painful (*dukkha*)?" "It is painful, Ven. Sir."

"Is it justifiable then, to think of that which is impermanent, painful and transitory as: 'This is mine; this I am; this is my soul?'

"Certainly not Ven. Sir."

"Similarly, O bhikkhus, feelings, perceptions, mental formations and consciousness are impermanent and painful.

"Is it justifiable to think of these which are impermanent, painful and transitory as: 'This is mine; this I am; this is my permanent 'I'?

"Certainly not, Ven. Sir."

"Then, O bhikkhus, body, whether past, present or future, personal or external, coarse or subtle, low or high, far or near, should be understood by right knowledge in its real nature— 'This is not mine (n'etam mama); this I am not; (*n'eso h'amasmi*); this is not my soul (*na me so attā*).'

"All feelings, perceptions, mental formations and consciousness, whether past, present or future, personal or external, coarse or subtle, low or high, far or near, should be understood by right knowledge in their real nature as: 'These are not mine: these are not I: these are not my soul.'

"The learned Ariyan disciple who sees thus gets disenchanted with body, feelings, perceptions, mental formations, consciousness, and is detached from the abhorrent thing and is emancipated through detachment. Then dawns on him the knowledge — 'Emancipated am I'. He understands that rebirth is ended, lived is the holy life, done what should be done, there is no more of this state again."

"Thus the Exalted One said, and the delighted bhikkhus applauded the words of the Exalted One."

When the Buddha expounded this teaching the minds of the group of five bhikkhus became freed of defilements without attachment.[3]

Discussion

The Buddha explains to the original five bhikkhus (*pañca-vaggiyas*) his doctrine of non-self or absence of a permanent and continuing 'I'. He uses a form of logic which was popular at that time called *reductio-ad-absurdum* or "reduction-to-absurdity". It is a method of counter-argument.

There are three meanings to it:

1. Proof of falsity by showing absurd logical consequences.
2. Proof of truth by thus proving falsity of alternatives.
3. Carrying of the principle to unpractical lengths.

The fact that the five bhikkhus understood these arguments and attained arahantship is clear proof of the efficacy of the method. When we reflect on this sutta with insight and wisdom (*paññā*), we too should be able to comprehend what the Buddha had to say on the subject of *anattā*.

3. They all attained arahantship.

The Anāthapiṇḍikovada Sutta (M.143)[4]

There is another important sutta which we can utilize for the development of insight into the characteristic of *anattā* during intensive meditation. This is the Anāthapiṇḍikovāda Sutta.

Anāthapiṇḍika was a great benefactor of the Buddha and of the *ariya saṅgha*. When he was on his deathbed, Ven. Sāriputta and Ven. Ānanda visited him. Ven. Sāriputta had then instructed Anāthapiṇḍika as follows:

1. "Wherefore you, householder, must train yourself thus: 'I will not cling to the eye, and there will be no consciousness associated with the eye.' Thus should you train yourself.
   'I will not cling to the ear ...
   'I will not cling to the nose ...
   'I will not cling to the tongue ...
   'I will not cling to the body ...
   'I will not cling to the mind ...
   Thus you should train yourself".
2. "Householder, you should train yourself thus: 'I will not cling to visual consciousness and there will be in me no consciousness associated with forms. Thus you should train yourself.
   'I will not cling to auditory ... sounds ...
   'I will not cling to olfactory ... smells ...
   'I will not cling to gustatory ... tastes ...
   'I will not cling to tactile ... tangibles ...
   'I will not cling to mental ... thoughts ...
   Thus you should train yourself".
3. "Householder, you should train yourself thus: 'I will not cling to eye-consciousness, and there will be no consciousness in me associated with eye--consciousness. Thus you should train yourself".
   'I will not cling to ear ...
   'I will not cling to nose ...
   'I will not cling to tongue ...
   'I will not cling to body ...
   'I will not cling to mind ...
   Thus you should train yourself".

---

4. (Translated by Ven M. Seelawimala Mahā Thera)

4. "Householder, you should train yourself thus:
'I will not cling to eye-contact and there will be no consciousness in me associated with eye-contact. Thus you should train yourself".
'I will not cling to ear-contact ...
'I will not cling to nose-contact ...
'I will not cling to tongue-contact ...
'I will not cling to body-contact ...
Thus you should train yourself".

5. "Householder, you should train yourself thus: 'I will not cling to sensations born of eye-contact, and will also have no consciousness born from and in association with feeling born of eye-contact. Thus you should train yourself.
'I will not cling to feeling born of ear-contact ...
'I will not cling to feeling born of nose-contact, ...
'I will not cling to feeling born of tongue-contact ...
'I will not cling to feeling born of body-contact ...
'I will not cling to feeling born of mind-contact ...
Thus you should train yourself".

6. "Householder, you should train yourself thus:
'I will not cling to the earth-element, and there will be in me no consciousness associated with the earth-element. Thus you should train yourself".
I will not cling to the water element ...
I will not cling to the fire-element ...
I will not cling to the air-element ...
I will not cling to the space-element ...
I will not cling to the consciousness element ...
Thus should you train yourself".

7. "Householder, you should train yourself thus: 'I will not cling to material form and there will be in me no consciousness in association with material form. Thus you should train yourself".
I will not cling to feeling ...
I will not cling to perception ...
I will not cling to formations ...
I will not cling to consciousness ...
Thus should you train yourself".

8. "Householder, you should train yourself thus:
'I will not cling to the sphere of infinite space, and there

will be in me no consciousness associated with the sphere of infinite space. Thus you should train yourself".

'I will not cling to the sphere of infinite consciousness ...

'I will not cling to the sphere of nothingness ...

'I will not cling to the sphere of neither-perception-nor-non-perception ...

Thus should you train yourself".

(These refer to the four formless or immaterial absorptions –*jhānas*– namely: *ākāsānañcāyatana, viññāṇañcāyatana, ākiñcaññāyatana* and *nevasaññā-nāsaññāyatana* respectively).

9. "Householder you should train yourself thus: 'I will not cling to this world, and there will be in me no consciousness associated with this world.

I will not cling to the world beyond, and there will be in me no consciousness associated with the world beyond'.

Thus you should train yourself".

10. "Householder, you should train yourself thus: 'I will not cling to what is heard, sensed, cognized, encountered, sought after and examined by the mind, and there will be in me no consciousness associated with that'. Thus you should train yourself."

Discussion

Anāthapiṇḍika was already a *sotāpanna* and therefore understood the true meaning contained in this advice. But for us to truly comprehend this advice it is necessary for us to first remind ourselves of how the aggregates comprising the mind work.

This is explained in the Honeyball or Madhupiṇḍika Sutta (M.18) in which the Buddha states:

> "Dependent on the eye and forms, eye-consciousness arises. The meeting of the three is contact (*phassa*). With contact as condition there is feeling (*vedanā*). What one feels, that one perceives. What one perceives, that one thinks about. What one thinks about, that one proliferates. With what one has proliferated as the source, perceptions and notions tinged by mental proliferation beset a man with respect to past, future and present forms cognizable through the eye.

"Dependent on the ear, sounds... Dependent on the nose and odours... Dependent on the tongue and flavours... Dependent on the body and tangibles... Dependent on the mind and mind-objects, mind consciousness arises. The meeting of the three is contact. With contact as a condition there is feeling. What one feels, that one perceives. What one perceives, that one mentally proliferates. With what one has proliferated as the source, perceptions and notions tinged by mental proliferation beset a man with respect to the past, future and present mind-objects cognizable through the mind.

"When there is the eye, a form and eye-consciousness, it is possible to point out the manifestation of contact. When there is the manifestation of contact it is possible to point out the manifestation of feeling. When there is the manifestation of feeling, it is possible to point out the manifestation of perception. When there is the manifestation of perception, it is possible to point out the manifestation of thinking. When there is the manifestation of thinking, it is possible to point out the manifestation of being beset by perceptions and notions tinged by mental proliferation.

"When there is no eye, no form, no eye-consciousness, it is impossible to point out the manifestation of contact. When there is no manifestation of contact, it is impossible to point out the manifestation of feeling. "When there is no manifestation of thinking, it is im-possible to point out the manifestation of being beset by perceptions and notions tinged by mental proliferation."

We can visualize and then comprehend the working of the mind by looking at its primary components of contact, sensations, perception, volition and consciousness diagrammatically, along with the mental proliferations and conceiving referred to in the above sutta:

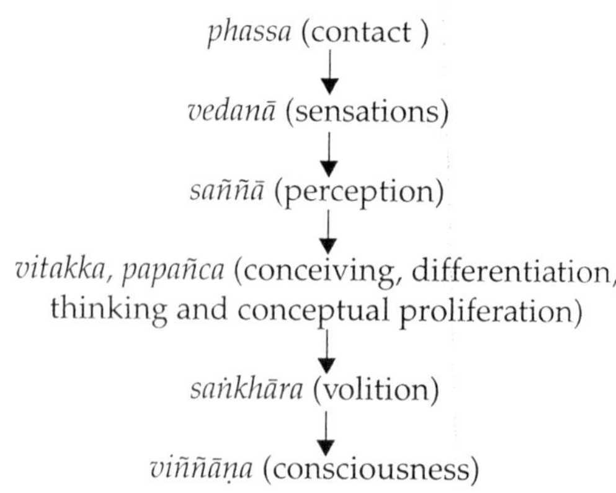

Keeping the above visualization in front of us, we can now examine with *paññā* the advice given to Anāthapiṇḍika.

In the first five stanzas of the sutta, reference is to the aggregates of the body and the aggregates of mind – *rūpa* and *nāma*.

In the sixth stanza the body (rūpa) aggregate is further reduced to its component parts and the concept of space and consciousness are added thereto.

In the seventh stanza, Anāthapiṇḍika was advised to give up clinging to the body and to the aggregates comprising the mind (*rūpa-nāma*).

And in the eighth stanza, householders are advised to focus with non-attachment on the consciousness pertaining to the four immaterial (formless) spheres.

In the ninth stanza, householders are told that by this time a meditator should have achieved sufficient progress enabling him to be devoid of all clinging, and consequently there will be no clinging in a next world as well.

The householder is told that if he were to follow the advice mentioned in this final stanza, he will achieve what was stated in the previous stanza, which is transcendence.

Discussion

When we look at the suttas in the Majjhima Nikāya, we see that Sāriputta's above advice was in fact a more detailed description of what the Buddha had said in the Mahā Saḷāyatanika Sutta (M.149).

> "Knowing and seeing the eye, monks, as it really is, knowing and seeing forms as they really are, knowing and seeing eye-consciousness as it really is, knowing and seeing eye-contact as it really is, and knowing and seeing whatever feeling—pleasant, unpleasant or neither-pleasant-nor-unpleasant—arises dependent on eye-contact as it really is, one gets not attached to the eye, gets not attached to forms, gets not attached to eye-consciousness, gets not attached to eye-contact and gets not attached even to that feeling that arises dependent on eye-contact.
>
> "And for him as he abides unattached, unfettered, not infatuated, contemplating the peril (in the eye, ear etc.), the five aggregates of grasping go on to future diminution. That craving which makes for re-becoming decreases in him".

We should now be able to see with insight that all actions of this body-mind complex are tainted by the delusion that there is what we call a person or 'I'. But at the ultimate level there is in fact no real 'I'. We have the wrong concept of 'I". Nevertheless, we think, speak and act always influenced by this characteristic. *Vipassanā* meditation on the Anathapiṇḍikovāda Sutta makes us comprehend with insight leading to *paññā* the ultimate truth of ***anatta.*** This in turn can serve as the gateway to Nibbāna for those who are intellectually inclined.

Other dedicated meditators may perhaps find it necessary to combine the knowledge of the above with the comprehension of the Anattalakkhaṇa Sutta (Khandha Samy. 59) and/or *Paṭiccasamuppāda* (explained in the previous volume) before they can come to the very threshold of Nibbāna or to the first glimpse of Nibbāna by the attainment of the first of the four *Ariya* states, namely *sotāpanna,* and thereafter progress through the next three stages, ending with arahantship.

The Bāhiya Sutta (Ud.1.100)

The full text of the Buddha's advice to Bāhiya Dārucīriya reads as follows:

> "Herein, Bāhiya, you should train yourself thus:
> 'In the seen will be merely what is seen;
> In the heard will be merely what is heard;

In the sensed will be merely what is sensed;
In the cognized will be merely what is cognized.'
In this way you should train yourself, Bāhiya.

"When, Bāhiya, in the seen is merely what is seen;
in the heard is merely what is heard,
in the sensed is merely what is sensed,
in the cognized is merely what is cognized,
then, Bāhiya, you will not be 'with that';
when Bāhiya, you are not 'with that';
then, Bāhiya, you will not be 'in that';
when Bāhiya, you are not 'in that';
then, Bāhiya, you will be neither here nor beyond
nor in between the two,
just this is the end of suffering."

The commentaries explain these cryptic statements in the following manner:

> "In the seen is merely what is seen" — see without adding one's own views, mental proliferations such as opinions and concepts, personal likes and dislikes etc. In other words, it is just seeing what is there, as it actually is.
>
> "You will not be with that," — you will not be bound by that view, by attraction or repulsion etc.
>
> "You will not be in that," — you will not be in a situation of being deluded and led astray by views and emotions.
>
> "You will be neither here nor beyond nor in between the two" — then you will neither be in this world nor in another world. This would mean the experience of transcendence, Nibbāna or enlightenment, which in effect is the stepping out of the mundane world.

Discussion

So what Bāhiya comprehended with insight was the fact that "seeing, hearing, smelling" and so on are mere conditioned phenomena, and that there was no permanent "I" behind them. He thus saw the Truth, becoming thereby a liberated *Ariya*.

In the above instructions, the Buddha tells us that the concept of a permanent 'I' should be abandoned. Instead, to see with insight *anatta:* for, if there is no permanent entity called an

'I', then there is nothing to crave for or cling to. And once we abandon craving and clinging, we have broken the vicious *saṃsāric* cycle of existence: *Taṇhānirodhā upādāna-nirodho: upadāna-nirodhā bhava-nirodho: bhava-nirodhā jāti-nirodho.*

(Through the abandoning of craving 'clinging' ceases. Through the abandoning of clinging 'becoming' ceases. Through the abandoning of becoming 'rebirth' ceases).

These are the links 9, 10 and 11 of Paṭiccasamuppāda.

Readers would perhaps have realized that the instructions given in the sutta discussed earlier to Anātapiṇḍika were in essence similar to the brief but complete advice given to the spiritually advanced Bāhiya.

As an additional bonus we can also bring to mind the Buddha's discovery of the critically important role played by craving in the perpetuation of saṃsāric existence, on the night of his enlightenment, when he joyously proclaimed:

> "Through many a birth in existence wandered I
> Seeking, but not finding, the builder of this house,
> Sorrowful is repeated birth:
>
> O house-builder, thou art seen.
> Thou shalt build no house again:
> All thy rafters are broken:
> thy ridgepole is shattered:
> Mind has attained to the unconditioned:
> achieved is the end of cravings."[5]

Dhp. 153 –154
Trans. by Nārada Mahāthera

Concluding Remarks

The way to awakening is through insight wisdom into one or more of the three characteristics of the human condition, namely, impermanence, distress and absence of a permanent non-changing self or 'I' — *anicca, dukkha* and *anatta* respectively.

At the risk of repetition, it is necessary to emphasize that true comprehension and understanding of *Paṭiccasamuppāda* have the advantage that they will lead to an understanding of all

---

5. House builder: craving (taṇhā); house: physical body; rafters: defilements (*kilesa*); ridgepole: ignorance; unconditioned: Nibbāna.

of the above three characteristics of existence. For craving, clinging and birth (*vedanā, upādāna, jāti*) are phenomena that are in a constant state of flux. They are born, exist for a while (a fraction of a micro-second) and then die. This constant change is *anicca* (impermanence). Birth, decay and death — *jāti, jarā, maraṇa*— links 11 and 12, show us the inevitableness of suffering or unsatisfactoriness - *dukkha*. Finally, consciousness, name-and-form – *viññāṇa, nāma-rūpa*, links 2 and 3, reveal *anatta*, that there is no permanent "I" or a self.

The Cūla Rāhulovāda Sutta (M.147)

This is another sutta in which the Buddha uses once again the technique of question and answer to instil into the mind of the recipient his teachings. The relevant part of this sutta reads as follows:

> "What do you think, Rāhula, is the eye permanent or impermanent?"
>
> "Impermanent, Ven. Sir".
>
> "Is that which is impermanent, painful or pleasant?"
>
> "It is painful, Ven. Sir".
>
> "Is it justifiable, then, to think of that which is impermanent, pain-laden and subject to change as 'This is mine; this I am; this is my self?'"
>
> "Certainly not, Ven. Sir".
>
> "What do you think Rāhula, are forms (visual objects) permanent or impermanent?"
>
> "Impermanent, Ven. Sir".
>
> "Is that which is impermanent, painful or pleasant?"
>
> "It is painful, Ven. Sir".
>
> "Is it justifiable, then, to think, of that which is impermanent, pain-laden and subject to change as 'This is mine; this I am; this is my self?'".[6]
>
> "Certainly not, Ven. Sir".
>
> "What do you think, Rāhula, is eye-consciousness (visual contact) permanent or impermanent?"

---

6. 'This is mine' — as motivated by craving (*taṇhā*)
'This I am' — as motivated by pride (*māna*)
'This is myself' — as motivated by wrong views (*diṭṭhi*).

"Impermanent, Ven. Sir".

"Is that which is impermanent, painful or pleasant?'

"It is painful, Ven. Sir".

"Is it justifiable, then to think of that which is impermanent, pain-laden and subject to change as 'This is mine; this is my self?'"

"Certainly not, Ven. Sir".

"What do you think, Rāhula, that which arises conditioned by visual contact, namely all that belongs to feeling, perception, mental formations and consciousness, is that permanent or impermanent?"

"Impermanent, Ven. Sir".

"Is that which is impermanent, painful or pleasant?"

"It is painful, Ven. Sir".

"Is it justifiable, then to think of that which is impermanent, pain-laden and subject to change as 'This is mine, this I am, this is my self?'".

"Certainly not, Ven. Sir".

"What do you think, Rāhula; ear and sounds, nose and smells, tongue and tastes, body and tangibles, mind and ideas and the (corresponding types of) consciousness and contact and the feelings, perceptions, mental formations and the forms of consciousness that arise conditioned by that contact are all these permanent or impermanent?"

"Impermanent, Ven. Sir".

"Is that which is impermanent, painful or pleasant?".

"It is painful, Ven. Sir".

"Is it justifiable, then to think of that which is impermanent, pain-laden and subject to change as 'This is mine; this I am; this is my self?'"

"Certainly not, Ven. Sir".

"The learned noble disciple, Rāhula, who sees thus, gets disenchanted (*nibbidā*) for the eye, gets disenchanted for forms, for visual consciousness, visual contact, and for that which arises conditioned by visual contact, namely all feelings, perceptions, mental formations and forms of consciousness.

"He turns way from ear and sounds, nose and smells, tongue and tastes, body and tangibles, mind and ideas, turns away from (the corresponding types of) consciousness and contact, and from that which arises conditioned by that contact, namely all that belongs to feelings, perceptions, mental formations and consciousness".

"In him who gets disenchanted passions fade out (*virajjati*). With the fading out of passions (*virāga*) he is liberated. Thus liberated, the knowledge arises in him: 'Liberated am I, birth is exhausted, fulfilled is the holy life, done is what should be done and nothing further remains after this' Thus he knows".

Thus spoke the Blessed One. Glad at heart, venerable Rāhula rejoiced in the words of the Blessed One.

Now, during that utterance, the mind of venerable Rāhula was freed from the corruptions through clingings and there arose the stainless, immaculate Eye of Truth[7]: "Whatever is subject to origination is subject to cessation".

Discussion

Since this is the last of the suttas which will be discussed in this book, we can make use of this opportunity to describe a methodology which an earnest meditator could perhaps adopt in his journey towards transcendence.

The Buddha preached the Cūla Rāhulovāda Sutta (M.147) to his son Rāhula when the latter had reached twenty-one years of age. According to the commentaries, the Buddha had taken constant interest in Rāhula's development and guided him wisely through the years. There are a number of suttas addressed to Rāhula. We have looked at only the last of these suttas. One earlier to this sutta is the Mahā Rāhulovāda Sutta (M.62) which was spoken to Rāhula when he was eighteen years of age. It contains a large number of meditation subjects and, *inter-alia,* detailed instructions on *ānāpāna-sati* or mindfulness of in-and-out breathing. It appears that the Buddha considered these subjects to be sufficient to bring Rāhula to intellectual and spiritual maturity by his twenty-first year. That this was so is proven by the fact that on hearing the Cūla Rāhulovāda Sutta (M.147), venerable Rāhula attained arahantship immediately.

This sutta contains a clear exposition of all the three characteristics of human existence, namely *anicca-dukkha-anatta,*

---

7. *Dhamma-cakkhu,* the vision of Dhamma; in this case, the attainment of arahantship.

which the advanced meditator should be able to see with application of deep and dedicated insight meditation.

A Suggested Methodology

An advanced meditator should, in the first instance, read the sutta at a normal reading speed and gather what the Buddha is telling Rāhula. Having grasped with *sutamaya-paññā* the essence of the advice, he should set the sutta aside, and recall or recollect what he already knows about the the five aggregates, which in the present context could be understood as the *pañcupādānakkhandha* or the five aggregates of clinging. He should then recollect how the aggregates become operative. Towards this end, he could conveniently refer to the topical information provided below. Before describing the methods of applied meditation, we could perhaps benefit more by first reading about the real life experiences of an experienced vipassanā meditator who discusses his personal voyage of discovery on the assurance of anonymity. In this account he traces his life's journey starting as a novice in meditation to the point of transcendence:

He should contemplate what he has read and develop *bhāvanāmaya-paññā*. Now, keeping the above information mentally in front of him, the advanced meditator should read the Rāhulovāda Sutta slowly and carefully, a paragraph at a time, comprehending its contents with deep insight. Next, he will review the contents of the sutta from this new perspective. On doing so, there is the possibility that he will be successful in transforming these doctrinal truths into a tangible personal experience, leading him, if all other dependent conditions at this moment are just right, to transcendence.

While a fortunate few may, in this manner, be successful at their first attempt, it may, in most cases, require repeated application. Other advanced meditators may, perhaps, need similar application to some other suttas of their choice, or other methodology for fruition of their efforts. For, as we all very well know, "there are many paths leading to the top of a mountain". Finally, as I said before, our efforts should be aimed at insight knowledge of the riddle of life, rather than transcendence itself. For the latter comes automatically with the realization of the former.

CHAPTER XII

Meditating our Way to Transcendence

A significant matter that many Western *vipassanā* meditators have raised is the unavailability of simple texts that could guide meditators to insight knowledge. They have asked for a model comprising progressive but simple step-by-step meditation instructions leading to transcendence.

However, planning a programme of *vipassanā* meditation leading to transcendence is a difficult thing to do. For we can recollect that when the Buddha attempted to teach his five original disciples (the *pañcavaggiyas*), who already knew a considerable number of meditation techniques, he realized that they could not fully comprehend his first sermon, the Dhammacakkappavattana Sutta (Sacca Saṃy. 11), in the absence of insight-wisdom or *bhāvanāmaya-paññā*. The Buddha first taught them the doctrine (Dhamma) and re-moulded their way of thinking. It was only when he knew that they were in a proper frame of mind, an open mind that could understand and absorb his Dhamma, that he expounded the Anattalakkhaṇa Sutta (SN 22:59) (see Part 1, chapter 4). On listening to this sermon, all the five disciples attained arahantship.

Instead of providing us with just twenty five to fifty suttas of doctrinal discussions, the Buddha chose to preach thousands of suttas throughout his life, all encompassing one theme: suffering and the way out of suffering. We must realize that our priority is to know and understand the basics of Buddhism as contained in *Paṭiccasamuppāda*, the Four Noble Truths, *Satipaṭṭhāna* (four-fold foundation of mindfulness), *kamma* and rebirth, the manner in which the mind works as explained in the Madhupiṇḍika Sutta (M.18), the three negative behavioural patterns of the human condition (greed, hatred and delusion), and the three characteristics of human existence (impermanence, distress and the absence of an enduring ego or self or 'I'), before embarking on a voyage of discovery along the *vipassanā* path leading to transcendence.

The Buddha explicated the Dhamma to his monks in various ways, and it was left to each monk to interpret and comprehend the universal message according to his ability. Hence, by listening regularly to the Dhamma, they had the opportunity of one day hearing a sutta that struck a resonant chord in their consciousness, which in turn would triggered them to apply themselves to intensive *vipassanā* meditation leading to transcendence. This is evident from the reported instances when the Buddha found the subjects on which monks were meditating to be inappropriate, and therefore changed the subjects to the advantage of the meditators (Dhp. 25 and 285).

It is now left to us to study and meditate on the Dhamma until we come across a sutta, or even a passage from a sutta, to which we can relate, and then proceed onwards with wisdom (*paññā*) to the point where we can relate the subject of meditation to one of the three characteristics of the human condition, namely impermanence, distress and non-self. Fortunately for us, we now have a short list of doctrinal subjects on which we can concentrate (see the third paragraph of this chapter), as well as a number of suttas in the previous chapter, which can be focused on, followed by insight meditation, reflection and contemplation till we reach transcendence.

But we must first develop our morality until it is above reproach and then our power of mindfulness too is to be developed to a suitable level. We should also develop even more the *brahma-vihāras* (devine abidings) of loving-kindness, compassion, non-envious joy and equanimity. This level of development will make us fitting receptacles for receiving perhaps just one or two significant words of the Buddha and we may be fortunate enough for such revelation to trigger us towards a transcendental state.

Take the case of Bāhiya Dārucīriya (in the previous chapter), where just a few words were sufficient for him to reach immediate transcendence. Similarly, you will recollect that our knowledgeable meditator in chapter 2 also had developed a feel for, and then studied, contemplated and meditated on the Bāhiya and the Anāthapiṇḍikovāda Suttas, which led him to transcendence. He saw the total picture, and it came to him like a flash of lightning, that the aggregates comprising a person are nothing but ever-changing conditioned phenomena, and that there is no real continuing entity or "I". He realized that his theoretical knowledge of *anattā* had actually transformed itself into experiential knowledge leading to transcendence.

In Part 1 of this book (Wheel: 450-452), the importance of *Paṭiccasamuppāda* in our progression towards liberation was emphasized, and its inter-relationship to the Four Noble Truths was shown only cursorily. But it is important at this stage to see this relationship more closely. In the Saṃyutta Nikāya the Buddha states:

> " ... the thought occurred to me, 'I have attained the path to awakening, i.e., from the cessation of name-and-form comes the cessation of consciousness, from the cessation of consciousness comes the cessation of name-and-form, from the cessation of name-and-form comes the cessation of the six sense media . . . Thus is the cessation of this entire mass of *dukkha*. Cessation, cessation.' Vision arose, clear knowing arose, discernment arose, knowledge arose, and illumination arose within me with regard to things never heard before.
>
> "It is just as if a man, travelling along a wilderness track, were to see an ancient path, an ancient road, travelled by people of former times. . . . In the same way I saw an ancient path, an ancient road, travelled by the rightly self-awakened ones in former times. What is this ... ancient path? Just this noble eightfold path: right view, right resolve, right speech, right action, right livelihood, right effort, right mindfulness, right concentration . . . I followed the path. Following it, I came to direct knowledge of the origination of ageing and death, direct knowledge of the cessation of ageing and death, direct knowledge of the path leading to the cessation of ageing and death. I followed the path. Following it, I came to direct knowledge of birth ... becoming ... clinging ... craving ... feeling ... contact ... the six sense media ... name-and-form ... consciousness ... direct knowledge of the origination of consciousness, direct knowledge of the cessation of consciousness, direct knowledge of the path leading to the cessation of consciousness. I followed that path.
>
> "Following it, I came to direct knowledge of suffering *(dukkha)*, direct knowledge of the origin of *dukkha*, direct knowledge of the path leading to the cessation of *dukkha*.

> Knowing that directly, I revealed it to monks, nuns, male lay followers, and female lay followers ... " (*S*.xii,65).

In view of the afore mentioned inter-relationship between *Paṭiccasamuppāda* and the Four Noble Truths, it is opportune to look closer at the latter, and in particular the First Noble Truth, which is distress *(dukkha)*, for it will also give us insight into what drives us forward into future rebirths. The Buddha taught that suffering should be seen from three aspects: first is the discomfort of suffering, the second, the suffering of change, and third the pervasive suffering of the five aggregates (*khandhas*), i.e., *dukkha-dukkhatā, vipariṇāma dukkha* and *saṅkhāra dukkha.*

The discomfort of suffering is ordinary suffering that we can feel in both body and mind. But, at a fundamental level, this suffering means that we are not our own masters. We are constantly under the influence and conditioning of other forces, from the external environment to the experiences and workings of our own minds and bodies. All these conditions are "other-powered" because all the causes and conditions that make up a particular moment are dependent on other things happening first, either in the environment or in our own body. This in effect is dependent origination.

The second aspect of suffering is dissatisfaction due to change. This is the dominant feature of existence *(Paṭiccasamuppāda*, link 10): that it is in constant flux. Things arise and perish (*uppāda-bhaṅga*)—for in the very midst of birth there is both creation and extinction.

The third aspect of suffering, pervasive suffering, has a two-fold meaning. First, it means that all beings experience suffering—that none can escape it. A second meaning is associated with the fourth aggregate, which is volition. For volition can work at a very subtle level. As the aggregate that leads to action, volition ensures that all living beings are constantly in a state of motion and arising. For this reason living beings cannot escape from the subtler form of pervasive suffering.

According to the Dhamma, there is another dimension of meaning to the five aggregates, namely 'grasping' (*upādāna)* — the ninth link in the chain of dependent origination. (Hence the aggregates are often called - *pañcupādānakkhandha*—'the five-aggregates-of-grasping'). Grasping arises when a sense faculty interacts with a sense object creating attachment, and, consequently, suffering. It is this grasping after sense experiences that assures the continuation of the five aggregates through life after life. Let us also remember that the objects of grasping are not just desires, but also hatred and delusion. Simply put, grasping causes suffering and in turn, suffering causes the continuation of the five aggregates through rebirths. On this basis we hold onto the negativities of greed, hatred and delusion (ignorance), which propel us into future rebirths. In summary, we could say that there is no suffering apart from the five aggregates, and that the escape from suffering lies in comprehension of this truth by insight and meditation.

Knowing the above, let us now try to set out a programme of development of wisdom (*paññā*) leading to transcendence. But first, a few words on *paññā*. In Buddhist philosophy wisdom *(paññā)* is described as an understanding of Dependent Origination, the Four Noble Truths, *kamma* and rebirth, the three universal characteristics of human existence namely, greed, hatred and delusion and the three verities of *anicca, dukkha* and *anatta*. But what it really implies is that the attainment of wisdom is a transformation of the above doctrinal truths from mere intellectual knowledge into personal experience. In other words, we have to change our knowledge from book learning into actual and tangible living truths.

This can be achieved through step-wise mental development as was explained in Part 1 of this book as *sutamaya-paññā, cintāmaya-paññā* and *bhāvanāmaya-paññā* – knowledge from reading and studying the Dhamma, a higher level of knowledge from reflecting and contemplating the Dhamma, and achieving insight knowledge by *vipassanā* meditation respectively.

There is the need to cultivate a positive attitude when attempting to understand the Dhamma. For, if a person listens or contemplates the Dhamma with an impure mind, a mind contaminated by defilements, in other words, bereft of *sīla*, then the teaching will be of little benefit. The correct attitude to be adopted when studying the Dhamma can be likened to a patient who pays careful attention to his physician's advice. Here the Buddha is the physician, the Dhamma is the medicine, and we are the patients. It is only by careful attention that we can progress in wisdom and move towards the realization of a true understanding of the Dhamma and from there to liberation.

In addition, let us take advantage of being able to see the Buddha's word in writing so that we can repeatedly read and refer to it as often as we wish, and have recordings which we can repeatedly play back so that we absorb, reflect and contemplate them.

However, as I have stated in Wheel 450-452, if we are really to gain insight, we need a paradigm shift whereby we 'live' in each and every one of the important suttas which we have selected for further development,. We also should not forget that mundane existence is also quite real, for when we cut ourselves it is painful. When we are abused we feel hurt and angered, and when we fall sick, it brings about agony and painful feelings. It is by using our body and mind that we can focus on the opposites to achieve transcendence. The use of opposites was exemplified when, to get rid of *loba, dosa* and *moha* – greed, hatred and delusion, we focused on *aloba, adosa* and *amoha* – non-greed, non-hatred and non-delusion. This is how we make the first differentiation of appreciating that this temporary abode is never permanent nor real, and this in turn leads us on to transcendence.

Instructions

In Wheel Publication 450-452, readers were provided with information and instructions on *vipassanā* meditation as a step-wise process. Thereafter, the *first two steps* were discussed in sufficient detail to obviate the necessity to repeat such instructions once again.

Nevertheless, it may be appropriate to emphasize the importance of *ānāpāna-sati* or in-out-breathing in the first two steps of *vipassanā* meditation. For, when we meditated on in-and-out breathing with mindfulness and concentration, we reduced the whole process of existence to a series of long and short breaths. The concept of "I" then gradually fell away. What remained was only the process of breathing. Then the "breather" or "I" too began to fade away. Thus the whole process of *ānāpāna-sati* reduces the process of life to a series of breaths in which no 'self' is present. With this realization the advanced meditator soon begins to experience the fading away of the concept of an enduring "I".

He then realizes that the efficacy of *ānāpāna-sati* can be achieved only by an impersonal attitude during *vipassanā* meditation. In other words, it is important to de-personalize the process of existence in one's mind. This in turn makes one's faculties exceptionally acute since one is not burdened with the thought "I am doing this," or "I am not doing this".

At this point in his mental development, the meditator should be able to begin viewing persons not as individuals but rather as mere aggregates of elements and, to develop this attitude of mind, a *vipassanā* meditator will contemplate the human body as consisting merely of the four fundamental elements of *āpo-tejo-vāyo-paṭhavi* or water, fire, air and earth. This he does only mentally, and from there it is just one more step to the realization that all forms of existence are mere processes thereby realizing the true nature of phenomena.

What is then left is to discuss the third or final step in the *vipassanā* practice that will lead the practitioner to transcendence. We should, perhaps, also understand that in addition to the *vipassanā* meditation practice, a type of consciousness or mental event called the 'supramundane path' achieves the breakthrough to the Unconditioned. This occurs in four stages, and each in turn is also called a "path".

These four supramundane paths have the special task of eradicating certain defilements, the fetters *(saṃyojana)*. These defilements are not strangers to the meditator, for they bothered him in the previous stages of concentration and preliminary insight meditation where these defilements were not totally eradicated. They were only checked and suppressed, and deep beneath the surface they continued to linger as latent negative tendencies as *anusaya*. But, when the supramundane paths are reached, the real work of eradication begins.

These defilements act as fetters or shackles (*saṃyojana*) and are ten in number:

1. Illusion of a continuing 'self', *(sakkāya-diṭṭhi)*
2. Doubts (*vicikicchā*)
3. Adherence to rites and ceremonies (*sīlabbata-parāmāsa*)
4. See desires (*kāma-rāga*)
5. Ill will (*paṭigha*)
6. Attachment to the sphere of forms (*rūparāga*)

7. Attachment to the formless-sphere (*arūpa-rāga*)
8. Conceit (*māna*)
9. Restlessness (*uddhacca*)
10. Ignorance (*avijjā*).

When the advanced vipassanā meditator begins realizing Nibbāna for the first time, he is called a *sotāpanna* – One who has entered the Path or stream that leads to Nibbāna. He is no more a worldling, but an *Ariya* – a Noble One. He eliminates the three fetters of self-illusion (*sakkāya diṭṭhi*), doubts (*vicikicchā*), and adherence to wrongful rites and ceremonies (*sīlabbata parāmāsa*). As he has not eliminated all the fetters, he is reborn a maximum of seven times. In his subsequent birth he may or may not be aware of the fact that he is a *sotāpanna*. Nevertheless, he possesses the characteristics of an *Ariya*. He is moreover absolved from birth in states of woe since he is destined for enlightenment.

Stimulated by this first glimpse of Nibbāna, the *Ariya* pilgrim can now make rapid progress, and perfecting his insight he becomes a *sakadāgāmin* or once-returner by attenuating two other fetters, namely sense-desire (*kāma-rāga*) and ill-will (*paṭigha*). A *sakadāgāmin* is reborn on earth only once. It is interesting to note that a *sakadāgāmin* can only weaken these two fetters, and may infrequently be bothered by thoughts of sensuality and repugnance to a slight extent, which he then consciously suppresses.

It is by attaining the third stage of saint-hood called *anāgāmin* (non-returner) that he completely eliminates the above two fetters of *kāma-rāga* and *paṭigha*. Thereafter he neither returns to this world nor to a celestial realm, for he is reborn in the 'Pure Abodes" reserved for them from where they attain Nibbāna.

The *anāgāmin*, encouraged by the success of his efforts now makes his final advance and, destroying the remaining five fetters of attachment to the form-spheres (*rūpa-rāga*), attachment to formless-spheres (*arūpa-rāga*), conceit (*māna*), restlessness (*uddhacca*), and ignorance (*avijjā*), attain *arahantship,* the final stage of sainthood.

Step Three in the *Vipassanā* Practice

This is the final and most important stage of *vipassanā* meditation. It is to follow the Buddha's instructions of bare and simple observation of everything happening in this body, avoiding proliferation of thoughts, with a mind free of concepts and orientated to simply seeing and then letting go. Therefore, from now onwards we would not need any more doctrinal material, for we already have instilled into our minds sufficient *dhamma* from the suttas enumerated in chapter World-transcending cause-and-effect relates to the third and fourth of the Four Noble Truths of the cessation of suffering and the path that leads out of suffering. Cessation is the state in which worldly cause-and-effect is abandoned, there is no more accumulation of kamma, and liberation is realized. Thus, when the Buddha taught the doctrines of Paṭiccasamuppāda and of the Four Noble Truths, he also taught that the path of liberation is the path of moving from the worldly to the world-transcending modes of acting, thinking and speaking..

As experienced *vipassanā* meditators, we can also consider ourselves as persons who have started to practise the Noble Eightfold Path and that we have developed the *brahma-vihāras* to a reasonable extent. Consequently, our minds have begun to acquire a certain amount of spiritual tranquillity. We are also firm observers of the five precepts at all times and in some cases the eight precepts. These bring about contentment. We have also trained ourselves to be restrained in regard to the five mental hindrances (*nīvaraṇa*) of:

kāmacchanda (lust),
vyāpāda (ill-will),
thīnamiddha (sloth and torpor),
uddhaccakukkucca (restlessness and anxiety) and
vicikicchā (doubt).

We can now, according to the Mūlapariyāya Sutta (M.1), consider ourselves as *noble worldlings,* (i.e., worldlings practising the course of training in insight meditation leading to the attainment of a supramundane path).

Being now mindful of all bodily functions, we become conscious only of a whole series of actions taking place. We do not in any way think of these actions as being performed by an

"I". In this fashion, activities such as walking, sitting, observing, thinking begin to be recognized as only a series of impersonal actions. With this kind of mind training, one's faculties become exceptionally 'fine-tuned', since one is not burdened with the thought that "I am doing this, or I am not doing this".

It is now quite easy to develop concentration supported by scrupulous morality and dedication to a desire to understand impermanence, suffering and absence of a permanent "I" *at the experiential level.* We leave all concepts aside and focus on the five aggregates comprising body and mind. It is a paradigm shift involving our total immersion in *Paṭiccasamuppāda*, the Four Noble Truths as well as the four Foundations of Mindfulness (the four *satipaṭṭhānas*).

We do not try to achieve anything. We do not use a checklist to measure our progress against it. We simply observe everything occurring in body and mind with equanimity. Doing so also contributes to our inner purification, for we are continuously developing non-greed, non-hatred and freedom from the delusion of a permanent self. As we advance in meditation, we shall see before our very eyes the appearance, existence and the passing away of all phenomena (*uppāda, ṭhithi, bhaṅga*). The resulting disenchantment leads to still more determination, and we continue insight meditation with equanimity.

Whoever has not penetrated the impersonality of all existence, and does not comprehend that in reality there exists only a continuously self-consuming process of arising and passing away of bodily and mental phenomena, and that there is no ego-entity within or outside this process, will not be able to understand the Truth. For he will think that it is his ego, his personality, which experiences the suffering, his personality that performs good and evil actions and will be reborn according to *kamma*. He also thinks that his personality will enter into Nibbāna, and that it is his personality that walks on the Noble Eightfold Path!

This is the point at which the meditator should once again revert to contemplating *Paṭiccasamuppāda* in the forward (*anuloma*) as well as the reverse direction (*paṭiloma*) with mindfulness and constant awareness (*sati-sampajañña)* of impermanence and non-self. Or in the alternative, like the knowledgeable meditator of chapter If they are lacking in morality, this is the time to fix the problem. Morality is indeed the root system that nourishes the tree of knowledge, the tree whose trunk is 'concentration' and 'mindfulness', and whose crown is samatha and vipassanā meditation. Meditators must also further develop the four sublime states of universal loving-kindness, compassion, sympathetic joy and equanimity, and, in fact, become living monuments to these states if they are to succeed in achieving transcendence., he can focus, contemplate and reflect on the inner truths contained in one or more of the suttas discussed in the previous chapter, by deep insight meditation.

It will then be just a matter of time before he realizes the truth of either *anicca* or *dukkha* or *anattā* experientially.

Let us summarize what we have been saying so far. We started by looking at the Dhamma in books, followed by intensive reflection on the teachings, which in turn led to an intellectual understanding of the Dhamma. But it was when we used the mind to contemplate the body that true wisdom arose. When there is wisdom in our minds, then, wherever we look, there is the Dhamma and we see *anicca, dukkha* and *anattā* at all times.

The Buddha has shown us that there is no higher practice than to see that 'this is not my self and this does not belong to me', and that 'me' and 'mine' are simply conventional terms. When we understand everything clearly in this way, we will be at peace. When we realize in the present moment the truth of impermanence, that things are not ourselves or do not belong to us, then, when things disintegrate, we are at peace with them, because they do not belong to anybody, anyway. They are merely the elements of earth, water, wind and fire.

Let me conclude this critically important chapter with a few excerpts from the teachings of Achan Chah, who was one of the foremost meditation masters of the twentieth century and who has been regarded as a monk who had attained the bliss of Nibbāna.

> "There is a fundamental difference between studying the Dhamma and applying it in the practice, for true Dhamma has only one purpose—to show a way out of the distress—*dukkha* in our lives. Our suffering has causes for its arising and a place to abide. Therefore the Buddha taught us to contemplate the movements of the mind. Watching the mind move, we can see its basic characteristics—endless

change, distress and emptiness. This, in fact, is the process of Dependent Origination.

"The Buddha taught us to let go, and just let them be—both the good and the bad. But for us to know how it is possible to give them up, it is necessary to study and observe our minds. This we can do only through meditation, for the only true knowledge is to see what is within ourselves. Therefore, when we develop *samādhi* and *vipassanā* — concentration and insight, and these arise in the mind, we have to use them fruitfully. Otherwise one will know only the words of Buddhism.

"Dhamma is everywhere you look. There is nothing in the world that is not Dhamma. But you must understand that happiness and unhappiness, pleasure and pain, in fact *the vicissitudes of life or worldly dhammas are always with us. When you understand their nature, the Buddha and the Dhamma are right there.* It is simple and direct once you understand. When pleasant things arise, understand them as empty. When unpleasant things arise, understand that they are not you or yours, for they pass away. If you do not relate to phenomena as being you or see yourself as their owner, the mind comes into balance. This balance is the correct path, the correct teaching of the Buddha that leads to liberation, to non-grasping, to *vimutti*.

The Buddha only sees you to the beginning of the Path: *ukkhātāro tathagata*—the Tathāgatas only point the way. It's up to you now".

—Ajahn Chah

Let us ponder what this illustrious teacher had to say. We now have the wisdom and the dedication to break through and comprehend with *bhāvanāmaya paññā*, the characteristics of *anicca, dukkha* or *anatta*. There will also come the day when we can achieve transcendence in the same manner as Achan Chah and our knowledgeable meditator has done. But our own work is not yet complete for, at best, we have only attained the first of the *Ariya* paths. We are 'learners' and have shattered only the first three of the fetters *(saṃyojana)* that bind us to *saṃsāra*. The way we need to proceed thereafter is discussed in the final chapter.

Chapter XIII

Concluding Remarks

We are all fellow-travellers in *saṃsāra*. How we entered this maze, this labyrinth, is beyond human perception. We are constantly subject to suffering, although most of the time we conceive this suffering as pleasure, because very often suffering is sugarcoated. We also have a tendency to think that any pain we experience is something we can live with by accepting the adage that "there is no pleasure without pain". This is as much an illusion as it is to scratch oneself intensively when we itch, or as in the unfortunate case of lepers who try to deaden the pain in their extremities by holding them to a flame as the lesser of the two evils. It is only when suffering is catastrophic that we sit up and take notice.

To end suffering we need to understand the fundamental cause of suffering, which is ignorance. But this truth has to be understood not intellectually but as a direct experience and this is possible only with intensive *vipassanā* meditation. We also need to recognize the difference between understanding *Paṭiccasamuppāda, Satipaṭṭhāna* and the Four Noble Truths intellectually, and seeing them directly.

The key to this understanding is to recognize that what we see are only phenomena and that all phenomena are empty of an enduring self. This in turn leads to the understanding of **emptiness** (*suññatā*) of all *dhammas* or phenomena.

With the proper understanding of the three characteristics of human existence as impermanent, unsatisfactory and empty of 'self', these delusions are removed and wisdom arises, and with this wisdom we can penetrate and experience liberation — Nibbāna.

The Buddha, in the Mūlapariyāya Sutta (M.1), has shown that human-kind could be divided spiritually into four classes of people:

1. The ordinary worldling (i.e., one who is not practising meditation),
2. The noble worldling (i.e., a worldling practising the course of training in insight meditation with a view to attaining the supramundane path),
3. The learner (the *Ariya* who is on the Path — *sotápanna, sakadágámin* and *anágámin*),
4. The non-learner (i.e. the *arahant*).

The ordinary worldling is destined to continue his journey in *saṃsāra* with no end in sight.

The noble worldling is a person who has kept the moral precepts, been generous, cultivated the *brahma-vihāras* and meditated with insight, but had not been able to make a breakthrough to enter the Path in this lifetime. He is now free from birth in disadvantaged *loka* (worlds), but will travel in *saṃsāra* perfecting his *pāramitās* and inclined towards Nibbāna until he is able to make a break-through to enlightenment.

The 'learner' is one who has successfully entered the Path in this very life. He is now an *Ariya* and is destined to have at a maximum only seven more rebirths either in the heavens or on earth until he achieves liberation. He has eliminated the three fetters of self-illusion, doubt and adherence to wrongful rites and ceremonies, and thus become a *sotāpanna*, but has not eradicated all the fetters that bind him to existence.

The *Ariyan* pilgrim now makes rapid progress, and by perfecting his insight, attenuates the two fetters of sense-desires and ill-will and thereby becomes a *sakadāgāmin*. A *sakadāgāmin* is reborn on earth only once, in case he has not attained arahatship in that life itself.

Now he totally eliminates the above two fetters of sense-desires and ill-will and thereby becomes an *anāgāmin*. If he fails to persevere and attain arahantship in this existence, he is destined to end his days in a *suddhāvāsa* Brahma-world that is reserved for them.

Finally, there is the worldling who is born in this world with his *pāramitās* fully developed. He will be a person with the highest of moral rectitude. He will either leave the lay-life or spend most of his time in meditation, contemplation and reflection on the Dhamma till he makes a breakthrough with wisdom and attains *Nibbana* in this very life as an *arahant*.

Once we are aware of the above hierarchy and know where we presently stand, it is possible for us then to decide what our aspirations should be. Only then can we apply ourselves accordingly in terms of morality, concentration and development of wisdom by insight *(vipassanā)* meditation. We should remember the inspiring way in which the Buddha described his Dhamma:

> *svākkhāto bhagavatā dhammo sandiṭṭhiko, akāliko, ehipassiko, opanayiko, paccattaṃ veditabbo viññūhi'ti.*
>
> "Well explained is the teaching of the Blessed One; of immediate benefit, timeless, inviting us to experience it, leading us onwards, and *to be comprehended individually by the wise*".

The words 'to be comprehended individually by the wise' affirm what we had previously known experientially: that it is only by developing *bhāvanāmaya paññā* or wisdom through insight-meditation that we can comprehend the Dhamma individually. Mundane truths take on a new dimension and now become supramundane truths. What was theoretical knowledge becomes experiential knowledge, and then all actions become effortless, for craving and clinging have been understood and eliminated.

But the final breakthrough to transcendence can be quite elusive, to the chagrin of many an advanced meditator. It then becomes necessary for the dedicated meditator to exercise equanimity and to look inwards with an open mind and see whether there are any defilements yet remaining within oneself and also whether one has successfully developed the seven *bojjhaṅgas* or seven factors of enlightenment, namely: mindfulness, investigation, effort, rapture, calm, concentration and equanimity (*sati, dhamma-vicaya, viriya, pīti, passaddhi, samādhi* and *upekkhā*).

It is assumed that by now these factors are developed and present in all of our advanced meditators. If, however, the serious meditator finds himself wanting in this regard, he should quickly resort to developing these factors by means of *vipassanā* meditation, for in the Ānāpānasati Sutta the Buddha states: "Bhikkhus, ... the seven enlightenment factors, developed and cultivated, fulfill true knowledge and deliverance".

It is also interesting to note that these factors of enlightenment which bring the advanced meditator to transcendence, can bring healing to sicknesses as evinced in the Bojjhaṅga (Gilāna) Suttas (Bojjhaṅga Saṃy. 14, 15, and 16).

Summary of the Final Practical Steps Leading to Transcendence

5. Achieve concentration and one-pointedness
6. Live experiencing *Paṭiccasamuppāda* and the Four Noble Truths.
7. Experience the fading away of the concept of "I" during *ānāpāna* meditation.
8. Similarly, experience *uppāda, ṭhithi* and *bhaṅga.*
9. Develop equanimity even more.
10. Experiential realization of conditionality and emptiness.
11. Letting go of all experiences in body and mind, and recognizing them as mere phenomena and formations.

By travelling together along the *vipassanā* path we have come to the threshold of Awakening. We are just a step away. Only a bit more sustained *vipassanā* meditation is now required. This is in the form of intensive insight contemplation by picturing oneself in the cycle of conditioned existence—*Paṭiccasamuppāda,* or by total immersion in one or more of the afore-mentioned suttas, Anāthapiṇḍikovāda, Anattalakkhaṇa (Khandha Samy. 59), Bāhiya (Ud.1.10) and Rāhulovāda (M.143) Suttas, or by intensive application to the meditation subjects mentioned in the Mahā Satipaṭṭhāna Sutta (D.22).

The above paragraph does not mean that the suttas which can trigger the earnest meditator to transcendence are limited to the ones mentioned in the previous paragraph. On the contrary, most of the suttas of the Buddha have this potential. But, if we are asked for a short list, we would, in addition to the above, recommend (with our limited knowledge of the suttas), the Ānāpānasati Sutta, the Girimānanda Sutta (A.X.60), the Mahā Kassapa Thera Bojjhaṅga Sutta (Bojjhaṅga Saṃy. 14), the Upanisā Sutta (Nidāna Saṃy. 23) and the Māluṅkyaputta Sutta (Salāyatana Saṃy. 95), as ones which, when read with *sati-sampajañña* (mindfulness and awareness), may catalyze the fruition of insight wisdom *(sutamaya-paññā)* leading to transcendence.

It is important to remember that we must strive for wisdom (*paññā*) regarding the truth of existence, namely *anicca, dukkha* and *anatta* (impermanence, distress and non-self) and not to strive for awakening or liberation.

Once we have passed through the above stages and achieved insight wisdom, enabling us to "enter the path" and thus making us *Ariyas,* there is very little more to be done. All that remains is for us to observe everything happening in this fathom-long body and then to let go. By doing so, we should be able gradually to eliminate the rest of the *saṃyojanas* (fetters) that hold us back from total liberation.

Awakening will come naturally once the mind is pure and open, when our *pāramitās* are appropriately developed and we have penetrated the cause and conditions of existence and also we have sufficient supporting conditions to realize the bliss of liberation.

We should, and only then, be able to boldly say:

"This is the Fourfold Truth.
It must be comprehended with wisdom.
It has been comprehended with wisdom.

"This is the Doctrine of Dependent Origination.
It must be comprehended with wisdom.
It has been comprehended with wisdom.

These are the *Satipaṭṭhānas.*
They have to be meditated upon.
They have been meditated upon,
and comprehended with wisdom.

Paṭiccasamuppāda

(Dependent Origination)

Part 3

Attaining Nibbāna

by

Ron Wijewantha

THE WHEEL PUBLICATION NO. 458/460

First published 2004

AUTHOR'S PREFACE

This presentation marks the completion of my efforts at providing seekers of the Truth with a single book incorporating all the necessary doctrinal information as well as detailed instructions on the *vipassanā* practice. It is my belief that it can in many ways act as a catalyst leading the dedicated *vipassanā* practitioner to at least the threshhold of liberation, if not to liberation itself, which latter is of course subject also to 'conditions'.

My essays are in three parts, entitled, "The Road to Liberation", "Achieving Transcendence" and "Attaining Nibbāna" respectively. All were written under the umbrella title "*Paṭiccasamuppāda* — Dependent Origination". Readers should understand that in the end, everything comes back to the need for a person to comprehend with experiential wisdom the *paṭiccasamuppāda*. For the Buddha unequivocably said that by understanding the *paṭiccasamuppāda* one would see the Dhamma.

The discerning reader would appreciate that this trilogy takes him or her from the simplest meditation practice through the intermediate level of understanding to the most advanced forms of *vipassanā* meditation resulting in the deep comprehension with experiential wisdom of the Buddha's message of deliverance from *saṃsāra*.

May all readers find these essays useful and profitable. And may we all attain Nibbāna.

Ron Wijewantha

Namo tassa bhagavato arahato sammāsambuddhassa
(Homage to Him, the Exalted, the Worthy, the Fully Enlightened One!)

CHAPTER XIV

An Overview of the Vipassanā Practice

Readers who have had the opportunity to study the contents of the previous two presentations on *vipassanā* meditation in Wheel Nos. 450-452 and 455-457 would be familiar with the general practice of *vipassanā* meditation. This chapter is therefore for the benefit of new readers, although the experienced meditators too could perhaps use the opportunity to recollect their own previous practices and so use the current information as a stepping stone to further development of their respective practices.

When a novice meditator has studied and compre-hended the fundamentals of the Buddha Dhamma while leading a life of moral rectitude, he could then proceed to first learn how to concentrate on the breath, or any other subject of meditation of his choice for a reasonable period of time continuously and then to stay focused thereon. He is now a suitable candidate to be introduced to insight or *vipassanā* meditation proper.

Vipassanā or insight is the experiential understanding of the true nature of all corporeal and mental phenomena within the frame-work of one's own mind and body. It was this very same model that the Buddha adopted on the day of his Enlightenment. It is to observe each and every thing happening in this fathom-long body with a clear unclouded and non-judgmental mind.

We need to follow this same method by observing and developing insight within ourselves experientially. The universal method of insight meditation consists of a progressive development of one's own *vipassanā* meditation techniques. This comes from *sati-sampajañña* — 'mindfulness with full awareness and comprehension' of one's own experiential practice.

The meditator could also perhaps evaluate his progress by checking his experiences against the 'stages' of progressive development as stated in pages 77-79 of vol. 1, or against the sign-posts enumerated in the *Upanisā sutta* (pages 73-74 of vol. 1), but should not at any time think that this is a *sine-qua-non* to advancement in *vipassanā* insight.

The meditator will now choose a subject such as the breath, to discern mentally and recognize the subtle differences in the ultimate constituents of actuality *via* the chosen subject of meditation. However, for the benefit and encouragement of readers who are perhaps hesitant, a short over-view of what we now finally need do is outlined below.

The accepted method of insight (*vipassanā*) meditation is initially to cultivate progressively the virtues of moral conduct (*sīla*), concentration (*samādhi*) and wisdom (*paññā*). These, incidentally, coincide with the groupings given in the Noble Eightfold Path.

For laypersons the minimal measure of moral conduct is the observance of the five precepts daily and on retreat days the eight precepts. However, this ordinary form of mundane morality is not quite adequate for mental development to the highest level. It is therefore desirable to cultivate the higher form of supra-mundane morality (*lokuttara-sīla*). When one has fully acquired the virtue of this morality, one will be safeguarded against moral decline.

However, moral conduct alone is not sufficient. It is also necessary to learn to practise *samādhi* or concentration as well. *Samādhi* brings about a permanent tranquil state of mind. Such a mind is under control, whereby the mind is prevented from wandering enabling one to stay continuously on selected subjects of concentration. When one advances in this practice, the mind abandons its distractions and remains fixed on the object to which it is directed. This, in effect, is *samādhi*.

There are two kinds of concentration: mundane (*lokiya)* and supramundane (*lokuttara*). Of these the former consists of mundane absorptions, called *jhānas*. These can be attained by such methods as mindfulness of breathing, and *mettā* or loving-kindness meditation.

But for those whose aim is to realize Liberation, it is desirable to work for supra-mundane concentration — the concentration that leads to the path (*magga*) and fruit (*phala*). To acquire this concentration it is essential to cultivate wisdom (*paññā*).

There are two forms of wisdom: mundane and supra-mundane. True mundane wisdom comprises the knowledge used in welfare and relief work, which causes no harm; learning to acquire knowledge about the true meaning and true nature of the Buddha Dhamma, and the three classes of knowledge of mental development leading to insight, which are, knowledge from learning (*sutamaya-paññā*), knowledge from reflection (*cintāmaya-paññā*), and wisdom arising from meditative absorption (*bhāvanāmaya-paññā*).

On the other hand, supra-mundane wisdom is the wisdom of the Path and the Fruit. In order to develop this form of wisdom it is necessary to continue practising insight meditation (*vipassanā-bhāvanā*) by way of morality, concentration and wisdom. When wisdom is fully developed, the necessary qualities of morality and concentration will follow.

The methodology for this is to perceive materiality (*rūpa*) and mentality (*nāma*), which are the two elements comprising a living being, with a view to comprehending their true nature. The method adopted by the Buddha to deal successfully with materiality and mentality was to view one's own mind analytically by fixing bare attention on the activities of both body and mind as they occur within oneself.

By continuously repeating this exercise, the necessary concentration can be gained, and when this concentration is acute enough, the ceaseless course of arising and passing away of both materiality and mentality will become manifest because living beings comprise solely of this dichotomy of materiality and mentality. The solid substance of the body in its general form belongs to the materiality group. It changes its form (*ruppati*) under the physical conditions of heat, cold, etc. and because of its ability to change under different physical conditions, it is called *rūpa*. But significantly, it does not possess the faculty of conceiving an object.

In the *Abhidhamma*, the elements of materiality and mentality are classified as "states with objects" (*sārammaṇa-dhamma*), and "states without objects" (*anārammaṇa-dhamma*) respectively. The element of mentality has an object, while that of materiality has not as it does not hold or knows an object. A meditator also perceives in like manner that "materiality has no faculty of knowing".

Thus, bricks and stones, logs and pillars and baskets of earth are masses of materiality. They do not have the faculty of knowing. It is the same with the materiality which makes up a living body, — it does not possess any faculty of knowing. However, people generally believe that the materiality of a living body possesses the faculty of knowing an object and that it loses this faculty only at death. This of course is not so. In actual fact, materiality does not possess the faculty of knowing an object whether the body is dead or alive.

What is it then that does know objects? It is mentality, which comes into being depending on materiality. It is called *nāma* because it 'inclines' (*namati*) towards an object. Mentality is also spoken of as thought or consciousness. Mentality arises depending on materiality. Depending on the eye, eye-consciousness (seeing) arises; depending on the ear, ear-consciousness (hearing) arises; depending on the nose, nose-consciousness (smelling) arises; depending on the tongue, tongue-consciousness (tasting) arises; depending on the body, body-consciou-sness (sense of touch) arises. There also comes into being mind-consciousnesses such as thoughts, ideas, emotions, imaginings etc., dependent on the mind base. All these are elements of the mind.

People who are without experience in insight meditation hold the view that seeing belongs to a "self", "ego", "living entity" or "person". They believe that "seeing is I" or "I am seeing" or "I am knowing". This kind of view or belief is called *sakkāya-diṭṭhi* or personality belief. *Sakkāya* means the group of materiality (*rūpa*) and mentality (*nāma*) treated together as a separate entity. *Diṭṭhi* means a wrong view or belief. Therefore *sakkāya-diṭṭhi* means a wrong view or belief in a self with regard to *nāma* and *rūpa*, both of which exist only in actuality.

For better understanding, the manner of holding the wrong views or beliefs needs further elaboration. At the moment of seeing, the things which actually exist are the eyes, the visual objects (both materiality) and the seeing (mentality). *Nāma* and *rūpa* are actuality, yet people hold the view that this group of elements is self, or ego, or a living entity. They tend to consider that "seeing is I" or "that which is seen is by I", or "I see my body". Thereby, the simple act of seeing is accepted as self. This is *sakkāya-diṭṭhi* or the wrong view of self.

As long as one is not free from the wrong view of self, one cannot move forward in one's quest for liberation. For this reason, the Buddha has pointed out on many an occasion that it is essential to work for the total eradication of the wrong view of self. For, the Buddha had said that a monk should go forth mindfully to abandon the wrong view of self.

But we must remember that *sakkāya-diṭṭhi* can only be abandoned completely by insight knowledge of the *paṭiccasamuppāda* as well as of the Noble Path, the latter of which contains within itself the three supramundane virtues of morality, concentration and wisdom. It is therefore imperative that one works to develop these virtues. The way to do so is by noting or observing every act of seeing, hearing etc. in an undeluded fashion until one is freed from the wrong view of self.

Seeing

In this respect, the exercise is simply to note or observe the existing elements in every act of seeing. It should be noted as "seeing, seeing" on every occasion of seeing. By the term "note" or "observe" or "contemplate" is meant the act of keeping the mind fixed on the object with a view to knowing it clearly.

When this is done, and the act of seeing is noted as "seeing, seeing", at times the visual object is noticed, at times the consciousness of seeing is noticed, and at times the eye-base — the place from which one sees — is noticed. It will serve the purpose of the meditator if he can distinctly see any one of the three. Otherwise, based on the act of seeing, there will arise *sakkāya-diṭṭhi*, which will view it in the form of a person or as belonging to a person, and as being permanent, pleasurable, and self. Therefore, the meditator should constantly note or observe the existing elements in every act of seeing. Otherwise the defilements of craving and attachment will arise, which in turn will lead to negative results causing a regression of one's efforts.

Hearing, smell, tasting and touch, etc.

Similarly, in the case of hearing, there are only two distinct elements of materiality and mentality. The sense of hearing arises depending on the ear. While the ear and sound are two elements of materiality, the sense of hearing is the element of mentality. In order to know clearly any one of these kinds of materiality and mentality, every occasion of hearing should be noted as "hearing, hearing." So also, "smelling, smelling" should be noted on every occasion of smelling, and "tasting, tasting" on every occasion of tasting.

The sensation of touch in the body should be noted in the very same way. There is a kind of material element known as bodily sensitivity throughout the body, which receives every impression of touch. When any kind of touch, either agreeable or disagreeable, comes into contact with body sensitivity, there arises body-consciousness, which feels or knows the touch on each occasion. This shows that at every moment of touching there are two elements of materiality — body sensitivity and the tangible object,—and one element of mentality involved.

In order to know these things distinctly at every moment of touching, the practice of noting as "touching, touching" has to be carried out. This merely refers to the common form of sensation arising from touch. There are, however, special forms which accompany painful and disagreeable sensations, such as feeling of stiffness or tiredness in the body or limbs, feeling hot, pain, numbness, aches etc. Because feeling (*vedanā*) predominates in these cases, they should be noted appropriately as "feeling hot", "feeling tired", "feeling pain" etc., as the case may be.

It may be mentioned that there occur many sensations of touch in the hands, legs, and so on, during each occasion of bending, stretching, moving, walking etc. Because of the mentality wanting to move, stretch or bend, the material activities of moving, stretching and bending etc., occur in a series. It may then not be possible to notice all of them at the outset. They can all be noticed after some time on gaining experience by practice. All the aforementioned activities relating to movement are done by mentality. It is only when mentality wills that there arises a series of movements of the hands or legs. They fall away soon after they occur, (as one will realize with advanced meditation), at the very point of occurrence.

In every case of bending, stretching, or other related activities, there arises first a series of intentions which are moments of mentality inducing or causing in the hands or legs a series of material activities such as stiffening, bending, stretching or moving. These activities come up against other material elements, the body sensitivity, and on every occasion of contact between material activities and sensitive qualities there arises body-consciousness, which feels or knows the sensation of touch. It is therefore clear that material activities are predominant factors in these instances. It is important to note these factors as such. If not, there will arise the wrong view that these activities as the doings of an "I", — "I am bending", "I am stretching", "my hands" or "my legs". This practice of noting each activity as "bending", "stretching", "moving" is for the purpose of ensuring *right views* regarding all these activities.

Mind

Depending on the mind-base there arises a series of mental activities such as thinking, imagining, or generally speaking, a series of mental activities arising depending on the body. In reality, every case is a combination of mentality and materiality as they are mutually dependent, the mind-base being materiality and the thinking, imagining and so forth being mentality. Therefore, in order to be able to clearly distinguish between materiality and mentality, one should note them appropriately as "thinking", "imagining" and so forth in every case.

After having carried out the practice in the manner indicated above for some time, the meditator may notice an improvement in concentration. He will notice that the mind no longer wanders about but remains fixed on the object to which it is directed. At the same time, the power of noticing too would have considerably developed. Thus on every occasion of noting, he notices only the two processes of materiality and mentality.

Again, on proceeding further with the practice of contemplation, one commences to realize that nothing remains permanent, but that everything is in a state of flux. New things arise momentarily and each of them is noted as it arises. Whatever arises is then observed to pass away immediately, and another arises immediately hereafter, which too stays momentarily and when noted also passes away — *uppāda, ṭhiti, bhaṅga*. Thus the process of arising and passing away goes on and on, which clearly shows that nothing is permanent. One therefore realizes that "things are not permanent" because one now has seen experientially that they arise and pass away immediately. One will also then realize that they are at the fundamental level void or empty of a permanent core or self. This is insight into impermanence *(aniccānu-passanā-ñāṇa).*

The meditator follows this with the thought that "arising and passing away are not desirable". This is insight into suffering *(dukkhānupassanā-ñāṇa).* For, he usually experiences many painful sensations in the body such as tiredness, heat, aches, and so on and at the time of noting these sensations, the meditator feels that this body is nothing but a collection of suffering.

Finally, at every instance of noting, it is found that the elements of materiality and mentality occur according to their respective natures and conditioning, and not according to one's wishes. The meditator then realizes that "these are nothing but elements that are not governable or controllable; they are not a person or living entity". This is insight into non-self *(anattānupassanā-ñāṇa).*

On having fully acquired these insights into impermanence, suffering, and non-self — *anicca, dukkha-anatta*, the maturity of knowledge of the path (*magga-ñāṇa*) and knowledge of fruition (*phala-ñāṇa*) take place on the way to the realization of Nibbāna.

With the taste of Nibbāna in the first stage, as a *sotāpanna*, the meditator is freed from the round of rebirth in the realms of miserable existence. He is destined to have a maximum of seven rebirths before attaining Arahatship. Every one should therefore endeavour to reach at least this first stage of the *Noble Ariya Path* and fruit of *Stream-entry*, and thereafter strive to progress further.

CHAPTER XV

Meditating to Transcendence *Via* the *Ānāpānasati Sutta*

The Buddha has explained in several suttas how a person could practise meditation on the in-and-out breath. When doing so, the meditator would be practising *kāyānupassanā* or contemplation of the body *via* the breath. We have selected for discussion the *Ānāpānasati sutta* (*Mn.* 118), for the Buddha says in this *sutta* that contemplating in the manner described in this *sutta* alone could lead the dedicated meditator to liberation, which is Nibbāna.

In order to arrive at a practical understanding of the contents of this *sutta*, the method adopted here is to present the Buddha's instructions, one or two paragraphs at a time, followed by a detailed explanation or commentary thereon. The English translation of the *Ānāpānasati sutta* will be reproduced in *bold italics*, while supporting texts from other *suttas* will be printed in *italics*. The explanations will be in regular type.

We shall start at paragraph 16 of this *sutta*, where the Buddha's discussions commence.

16: And how, bhikkhus, is mindfulness of breathing developed and cultivated, so that it is of great fruit and great benefit?

17: Here a bhikkhu, gone to the forest or to the root of a tree or to an empty hut, sits down: having folded his legs crosswise, set his body erect, and established mindfulness in front of him, ever mindful he breathes in, mindful he breathes out.

In the present world, a suitable location will be one's own bedroom or a secluded spot in one's own home that is away from noise, from loud and persistent music or sounds of people as well as of animals.

During the time of the Buddha most people sat on the floor. Hence the phrase "sit down, having folded his legs crosswise, set his body erect". But presently, sitting on the floor can be a very trying and painful experience as people mostly sit on chairs, stools, or couches. If one prefers to sit on the floor, it may help if one sits on a cushion. In fact, it is far more important to observe what is happening in the mind than to sit experiencing uncomfortable or painful sensations. Remember that there is no magic in sitting on the floor. The magic comes from a clear, calm mind that is at ease. Thus, if sitting on the floor is a very painful experience, then it is acceptable to sit on a stool or a chair. There is, however, an extremely important factor which a meditator who sits on a chair should not forget. He must sit without leaning against the back of the chair. For, leaning can induce sleep. "Set the body erect" means to sit with a straight back which is not rigid and uncomfortable. This will ensure a flow of energy up and down the back without interruption. When one first starts, since one's back is not used to remaining straight and erect, some of the muscles can rebel and complain. However, with patience and perseverance, these unused muscles will gradually become adjusted and strengthened.

The phrase *"establishing mindfulness in front of him"* means that one puts aside all other worldly affairs and involvements with sensual pleasures. One now gently closes the eyes and whenever there is a distracting sound, smell, taste, sensation or thought, one is aware of that and simply lets it go. One then relaxes and redirects the attention back to the object of meditation.

The sentence *"ever mindful he breathes in, mindful he breathes out,"* tells us the way to practise mindfulness of breathing. He may watch his inhalation and exhalation at the start, but by no means should he force the breath in either direction. He should just be aware of the breath as it passes in and out while letting the breath go in and out automatically in its own way. He has only to be watchful, mindful, and attentive to it. If he is a long-nosed person, the breath will touch the tip of the nose first, and if his nose is short, the breath will touch his upper lip first. He should fix his mind and attention on the spot the breath first touches, the tip of the nose or the upper lip, as the case may be. It simply means to open one's awareness and to be attentive to the breath as much as possible and at the same time, to calm the mind.

18. Breathing in long, he understands: 'I breathe in long'; or breathing out long, he understands: 'I breathe out long.' Breathing in short, he understands: 'I breathe in short'; or breathing out short he understands 'I breathe out short'.

In this practice, while inhaling long, he should notice and be aware of it: "I inhale long". While inhaling short, he should notice and be aware of it: "I am inhaling short." While exhaling long he should notice it, and while exhaling short he should notice that, too. He must be careful not to allow any breath to pass unnoticed.

The words *"he understands"* are emphasized to show that one does not focus with strong attention on the breath to the exclusion of everything else. One merely understands what the breath is doing *in the present moment*. One simply knows when one breathes in long or short. There is no controlling of the breath at any time. Instead, there is only the understanding of what one is doing *at the present moment*. If one tries to over-focus or concentrate on the breath to the exclusion of everything else, one will have difficulty in progressing with the task in hand due to wrong 'concentration'.

The method taught by the Buddha was never to suppress anything. His method was to open and expand the mind and to allow everything currently arising to have its way. Thus, when a pain has arisen in the body, and the mind has gone to that sensation, the meditator then lets go of any thoughts about that sensation and opens the mind and lets it go, or in the alternative, he will let that sensation to be there by itself without any mental resistance or aversion to it. The meditator can, if necessary, mentally verbalize "never mind, it is alright for the pain to be there" and then relax, feel the mind expand and become calm, and only then re-direct the attention back to the breath.

He trains thus: 'I shall breathe in experiencing the whole body (of the breath)'; he trains thus 'I shall breathe out experiencing the whole body (of the breath)'.

The meditator should now train himself to experience the whole structure of the breath. While fixing his attention on the spot of his breath's first touch, he should be aware of the beginning, middle and end of his inhalation as well as of his exhalation. When he inhales, he should mentally follow the inhalation right from the spot his breath first touches until it reaches its end. When he exhales, he should follow the exhalation from the beginning until it reaches its end at the spot of its first touch (i.e. at the tip of the nose or the upper lip, as the case may be). One should never follow the breath inside the body.

This means that the meditator knows when the breath starts and stops on the in-breath. He also knows when the breath is starting and stopping on the out-breath. He simply knows what the breath is doing at the present moment. One just lets the breath and the awareness of the breath to be a natural process.

He trains thus: 'I shall breathe in tranquillizing the bodily formation'; he trains thus: 'I shall breath out tranquillizing the bodily formation'.

By now the meditator would feel that his breath has calmed down. If he does not feel so, he should carry out the previous practice with special effort to make his course of breath subtle, gentle and calm. After a short time, he will be successful and his breath will become calm and allayed. When he is successful in this effort, both his body and mind will feel light — in fact as light as a feather.

It is thus a **crucial point** in this entire exercise on meditation. For, it instructs the meditator to notice any tension or stress arising in the head with every arising of a consciousness, and to let that tension or stress go, while maintaining attention on the in-breath as well as on the out-breath. This is what is meant by tranquillizing. The meditator will then feel his mind opening out, expanding, relaxing and becoming tranquil. Every time he sees that the mind is distracted away from the breath, he simply lets go of the distraction, relaxes and lets go of tension, he feels the mind relax, open, expand and become calm and clear. He now gently re-directs the mind back to the breath. If and when a thought now arises, the meditator would gently let go of the thought. If the distraction is a sensation, then he would open and expand his mind and let go of the aversion or attachment to that sensation. One then opens and relaxes the mind before re-directing the attention back to the breath.

When these meditation instructions are followed closely, there will be no 'sign' or *nimitta* arising in the mind. The mind, on the contrary, becomes naturally calm and tranquil. One need not try to force the mind to stay on the breath through strong 'concentration' that causes tension in the head. Instead, the meditator begins to realize the true nature of all phenomena as impermanent (*anicca*), unsatisfactory (*dukkha*) and non-self (*anattā*), and this gives him encouragement that he is doing well.

When one practises this form of meditation, one does not have to push, force, or 'concentrate' with a fixed mind. This is a very natural form of meditation that works for every type of personality.

As regards his future practice, in order to progress steadily onwards, the meditator should improve his proficiency in concentration by fulfilling the following conditions:

1. Keeping his body, dress and place clean;
2. Bringing about evenness of the five mental faculties of: confidence, energy or effort, mindfulness, concentration and the faculty of reasoning;
3. Exerting his mind when it should be exerted;
4. Restraining the mind when it should be restrained;
5. Encouraging the mind when it is dejected;
6. Controlling the mind when it is overly exuberant;
7. Avoiding (during the meditation practice) persons who have not developed concentration;
8. Associating with persons who have developed concentration; and
9. Being resolute about the development of concentration.

The *Jhānic* experience

The meditator is now close to experiencing the *jhānas*. It is therefore perhaps useful to explain briefly what they really are. *Jhāna* or meditative 'absorptions' are achieved through the attainment of full concentration (*samādhi*), during which there is a complete, though temporary, suspension of the fivefold sense-activity and of the five hindrances *(nīvaraṇa).* This state of consciousness, however, is one of full alertness and lucidity.

Vipassanā jhāna is considered as the focusing of the mind on *paramattha-dhammā,* or "ultimate realities," but actually they are just the things we can experience directly through the six sense doors without conceptualization. Most of them are also *saṅkhāra- paramattha-dhammā,* or conditioned ultimate realities, mental and physical phenomena changing all the time.

Breathing is a good example of a conditioned process. The sensations one feels at the abdomen or tip of the nose are conditioned ultimate realities, caused by the intention to breathe. The whole purpose of concentrating one's attention on the breath is to penetrate the actual quality and nature of what is happening there. When one is aware of the movement, tension, heat or cold, then one has begun to develop *vipassanā jhāna*.

Mindfulness at the respective sense doors follows the same principle. If there is diligent effort and penetrative awareness, focusing on what is happening in any particular sense process, the mind will understand the true nature of what is happening. The sensing processes will be understood in individual characteristics as well as common ones.

According to the four-fold levels of *jhāna*, the first *jhāna* possesses five factors, all of which are important in the *vipassanā* practice. They are: *vitakka, vicāra, pīti, sukha* and *ekkagatā*, and are described below.

The first of the above, *vitakka*, is the factor of aiming or accurately directing the mind towards an object. It also has the aspect of establishing the mind on the object, so that the mind stays there.

The second factor, *vicāra*, is generally translated as 'investigation' or 'reflection'. After *vitakka* has brought the mind to bear on the object and placed it firmly there, *vicāra* continues to 'rub' the mind onto the object. This can be experienced by the meditator personally when observing the rise and fall of the abdomen when breathing in and out.

As one is mindful in an intuitive and accurate way from moment to moment, the mind becomes purer and purer. The hindrances (*nīvaraṇa*) of desire, aversion, sloth, restlessness and doubt weaken and disappear. The mind now is crystal clear and calm. This state of clarity results from the presence of the two *jhānic* factors discussed above. It is called *viveka*, which means seclusion, for the consciousness is now secluded from the hindrances. This *viveka* is by itself not a *jhānic* factor but is merely a descriptive term for this secluded state of consciousness.

The third *jhānic* factor is *pīti* or rapture which occurs when the meditator takes a delightful interest in what is occurring. This factor may manifest physically as gooseflesh, as feelings of being dropped suddenly in an elevator, or as feelings of rising off the ground. The fourth *jhānic* factor *sukha* or happiness or comfort, comes on the heels of the third, for the meditator now feels very satisfied with the practice. Because both the third and the fourth *jhānic* factors come about as a result of seclusion from the hindrances, they are called *vivekha-pīti-sukha*, meaning the rapture, joy and happiness born of seclusion.

It is profitable to think of the above sequence as a causal chain. Seclusion of mind comes about because of the presence of the first two *jhānic* factors. If the mind is accurately aimed at the object, if it hits it and 'rubs' it, after some time the mind will feel secluded. Because the mind is secluded from the hindrances, one becomes happy, joyous and comfortable.

When these four *jhānic* factors are present, the mind automatically becomes calm and peaceful, and able to concentrate on what is happening without getting scattered and dispersed. This *ekkaggatā* or one-pointedness of mind is the fifth *jhāni*c factor of *samādhi* or concentration.

It is, however, not sufficient to merely have all five factors present for one to say that one has attained the first *vipassanā jhāna*. For, the mind must also penetrate into the Dhamma sufficiently to see the inter-relationship of mind and matter. It is at this time that one could say that the meditator has achieved access to the first *jhāna*.

A meditator whose mind contains these five *jhānic* factors will experience a new accuracy of mindfulness and a new level of success in staying with the object. Intense rapture, happiness and comfort in the body may also arise. This could then become an occasion for the meditator to gloat over the wondrousness of the meditation practice. But the wise meditator will see such attachment equanimously for what it is.

The first *vipassanā jhāna* operates up to the point where a meditator attains insight into the rapid arising and passing away of phenomena. Experiencing this insight marks the stage where a meditator is said to 'grow up'.

He now leaves reflective thinking behind and enters the maturity of *simple, bare attention*. Now the meditator's mind becomes lucid and sharp. He is able to follow the very fast rate at which phenomena appear and disappear from moment to moment. Because of the continuity and sharpness of mindfulness, there is little discursive thinking. Nor is there doubt about the impermanent, momentary nature of mind and matter. At this time, the practice seems effortless. In the absence of effortful application and reflective thought, there is space for joy and rapture. This non-thinking, bare attention heralds the dawn of the second *vipassanā jhāna*.

In the first *jhāna,* then, the mind is congested with effort and discursive thinking. It is only when the second *vipassanā jhāna* arises at the beginning of insight into the arising and passing away of phenomena that clarity, rapture, faith and great comfort begin to predominate.

The mind is now able to become more precise, and concentration becomes deeper. This deepened concentration leads to clear, verified faith that arises from personal experience. It also brings about the belief that if one continues with the practice, one will gain the benefits assured by the Buddha. Rapture and mental-physical comfort also become strong at this stage. When meditators attain this second *jhāna*, there is strong likelihood that they will become attached to these extraordinary pleasant states of mind. They experience the deepest happiness of their lives. Some may even believe that they have become enlightened! But the wise meditator will identify and label them for what they are, as no more than mental states, and then cut off his attachments immediately. He will then return his attention to the primary object of meditation which is the in-and-out breath. Only then will progress continue and bring even sweeter fruit.

Arising of the third *vipassanā jhāna*: Here rapture will gradually fade, mindfulness and concentration will continue to deepen. Then insight into the nature of what is happening will become very strong. At this point, the enlightenment factor of equanimity (*upekkhā-bojjhaṅga*) becomes predominant. The mind remains unshaken by pleasant objects as well as by unpleasant ones, and a deeper sense of comfort arises in the body and mind. Meditators can now sit for long hours without pain, and their bodies become pure, light and robust. This is the third *jhāna*, of which the two *jhānic* factors are comfort and one-pointedness of mind. It will be observed that the third *jhāna* arises at a more mature stage of insight into arising and passing away.

The transition from the second to the third *jhāna* is a critical turning point in the practice. Human beings have a natural attachment to thrills and excitement which agitate the mind. Rapture is one of these agitating pleasures as it creates ripples or waves in the mind. Therefore when a meditator experiences them, he should increase his vigilance and note them as meticulously as he can. As long as a meditator remains attached to rapture, he will not be able to move forward into the more mature, subtle happiness that comes with peace and comfort.

The happiness or comfort that can be tasted in the third *jhāna* is said in the scriptures to be the peak or climax of happiness that can be experienced in the *vipassanā* practice. It is the sweetest. Nevertheless, the meditator should dwell in it only with equanimity and without attachment.

For further progress, the meditator needs to continue noting precisely. This is crucial, lest the sharpness and clarity of insight give rise to subtle attachment. But with the dedicated meditator this is unlikely to happen for he, by now, sees with mindfulness the complete picture.

Appearance of the fourth ***jhāna***: During the maturation of insight into the arising and passing away of phenomena, the rapture of the second *jhāna* gave way to the third *jhāna* factor of comfort. The unimaginable pleasure of rapture was replaced by milder and subtler feelings of comfort and peace. As comfort disappears in the dissolution stage of insight, it still does not result in mental displeasure. The third *jhāna* now gives way to the fourth, of which the characteristic *jhānic* factors are equanimity and one-pointedness of the mind.

Now, with a mind that is neither pleased or displeased, comfortable or uncomfortable, *upekkhā* or equanimity arises. Equanimity has a tremendous power to balance the mind. In this environment of balance, mindfulness can become pure, keen and sharp. Subtle aspects of phenomena can be seen with incredible and uninterrupted clarity as particles and tiny vibrations. In fact, these phenomena are present in each of the *jhānas* from the very beginning. But in the first three *jhānas* they are hidden by more assertive qualities.

With this overview of the four *vipassanā jhānas,* we can now revert to and continue our study of the *Ānāpāna-sati sutta.*

19. He trains thus: 'I shall breathe in experiencing joy' (rapture); He trains thus: 'I shall breathe out experiencing joy' (rapture).

The meditator, who has energetically followed the instructions given so far in this *sutta,* will be in a position to attain the first *jhāna,* which is a state of mind, fully open and fixed on the point of concentration. There are, however, two common obstacles at the door into *jhāna:* exhilaration and fear.

Exhilaration is to become excited. If, at this point, the mind becomes exhilarated the *jhāna* is most unlikely to happen.

Instead, the response needs to be subdued in favour of absolute passivity or equanimity. The meditator should reserve all the excitement until after he emerges from the *jhāna*. The more likely obstacle, though, is fear. Fear arises at the recognition of the sheer power and bliss of the *jhāna*, or else the recognition that to go fully inside the *jhāna*, something must be left behind — you! The 'doer' is silent before entering the *jhāna* but is still there. Inside *jhāna*, the 'doer' is completely gone. The 'knower' is still functioning, as you are fully aware, but all the controls are now beyond reach. You cannot even form a single thought, let alone making a decision. The will is frozen, and this can appear scary to the beginner. Never before in his whole life has he had the experience of being so stripped of all control, yet so fully awake. The fear is the fear of surrendering something so essentially personal as the will to do.

This fear can be overcome through confidence in the Dhamma together with the enticing bliss just ahead that one can see as the reward. The Buddha often has said that this bliss of *jhāna* 'should not be feared but should be followed, developed and practised often:

> "Here, Udāyin, quite secluded from sensual pleasures, secluded from unwholesome states, a bhikkhu enters upon and abides in the first jhāna . . . With the stilling of applied and sustained thought, he enters upon and abides in the second jhāna . . . with the fading away as well as of rapture . . . he enters upon and abides in the third jhāna . . . With the abandoning of pleasure and pain . . . he enters upon and abides in the fourth jhāna . . . This is called the bliss of renunciation, the bliss of seclusion, the bliss of peace, the bliss of enlightenment. I say of this kind of pleasure that it should be pursued, that it should be developed, that it should be cultivated, that it should not be feared" (Laṭukikopama sutta — Mn. 66).

So, before fear arises, place your full confidence in that bliss and maintain faith in the Dhamma and the examples of noble *ariyas*. Trust the Dhamma and let the *jhāna* warmly embrace you for an effortless, body-less and ego-less, blissful experience that will be the most profound of your life. Have the courage to fully relinquish control for a while and experience all of this yourself.

The meditator should remember that if he is experiencing a *jhāna* it will last a long time. It does not deserve to be called a *jhāna* if it lasts only for a few minutes. Usually, the higher *jhānas* may persist for many hours. Once inside, the meditator will emerge from the *jhāna* only when the mind is ready to come out. These are such still and satisfying states of consciousness that their very nature is to persist for a considerable length of time. Furthermore, the meditator should understand that while in any *jhāna* it is impossible to experience the body (eg. physical pain), hear a sound from outside or produce any thought, not even 'good' thoughts. There is just a clear singleness of perception, an experience of non-dualistic bliss, which continues unchanging for a very long time. It is necessary to emphasize that this is not a trance. To the contrary, it is a state of heightened awareness. This is said, so that the meditator may know for himself whether what he takes to be a *jhāna* is real or imaginary.

Perhaps it is also opportune to presently provide a description of the first two *jhānas* as given in other suttas *(Mahāsakuludāyi sutta -Mn. 77* and *Anupadā sutta -Mn. 111*):

> "Here quite secluded from sensual pleasures, secluded from unwholesome states, the bhikkhu enters upon and abides in the first jhāna, (meditation stage), which is accompanied by applied and sustained thought, with joy and pleasure born of seclusion.
>
> "Again, with the stilling of applied and sustained thought, the bhikkhu enters and abides in the second jhāna, which has self-confidence and singleness of mind without applied and sustained thought, with joy and happiness born of stillness of mind."

This means that as one starts one's meditation session, one would first gently close one's eyes. This is tantamount to being secluded from the sensual pleasures of seeing. When a sound distracts the mind, the instructions are to let the sound be there by itself, without discursive thinking about it such as whether one likes it or not. It is simply to let go of it mentally. One does the same with smelling, tasting, bodily sensations and thoughts (of any kind of sensual pleasure), which distracts the mind away from the breath. But, whenever there is a distraction *via* a sense door, one must let go, relax, loosen the tension in the head, open and allow the mind to expand from its tightness and gently redirect the attention back to the breath. It does not matter how many times sensual pleasures would arise. One has just to allow it to be there every time it arises and to treat every such experience with equanimity and to simply remember *to just let go.*

'Secluded from unwholesome states' means that when the mind is distracted from the breath and begins to think about feelings and sensations that arise, there is a tendency for the mind to evaluate such feelings as to whether the mind dislikes or likes them. This thinking and trying to control feelings cause them to become bigger and more intense. Thus more pain arises and one commences to stray away from one's meditation. But by seeing that what we normally recognize as 'one-self' is made up of only five different processes of — materiality, feeling or sensation (*vedanā*), perception, volition and consciousness —, makes one clearly comprehend that feelings are one thing and thoughts are another. Therefore, whenever a feeling or a sensation arises, no matter whether it is physical or emotional, the meditator needs to first let it go, become calm and tranquil and only then to re-direct the attention back to the breath.

When one does this, one is seeing the true nature of feelings — *vedanā*: it was not there, now it has arisen by itself. In other words we see directly impermanence. For, these feelings arise by themselves and if we watch them for a while, they go away by themselves. Therefore whenever a feeling arises, one opens the mind and *lets go of wanting to control* one's feelings. We do not resist or push, but only soften our attitudes by just letting go with an open mind. There is no ego-identification.

As one continues to free the mind from tensions and lets go any distraction, attachment becomes weaker. Finally, attachments do not have enough strength to arise any more. When this happens, the mind becomes filled with joy and relief. *This letting go of attachment* means being secluded from unwholesome states. When one lets go and joy arises, it lasts for a certain period of time. As a result the mind becomes very tranquil and peaceful. The meditator now experiences a mind that stays on the object of meditation very easily. When this occurs repeatedly, the mind will naturally become calm and composed by itself. At that time, one begins to develop equanimity(*upekkhā*) and balance of mind.

When he comes to this concentrated state of mind, he experiences the five constituents of the first *jhāna*; applied thought (*vitakka*), sustained thought (*vicāra*), joy (*pīti*), ease (*sukha*), and one-pointedness (*ekaggatā*). These five factors of the first *jhānic* consciousness make the mind's ability to remain fixed on the object stronger and also to suppress or inhibit strongly the five impediments (*nīvaraṇa*). Applied thought inhibits sluggishness and lethargy; sustained thought inhibits uncertainty; joy inhibits ill-will; comfort inhibits restlessness and worry; and one-pointedness inhibits sensuality. The meditator who has attained to this *jhāna,* experiences a feeling of ease and happiness full of ecstasy and *a peace never even dreamed of by him before.*

The above experiences make up what is commonly called the first *jhāna.* At such time, there still exists some very little wandering thoughts. But when this happens, the meditator relaxes the mind and simply lets go of the wandering thought and comes back to the breath.

When the mind begins to stay on the breath for longer and longer periods of time, the relief and joy will become quite strong. One will naturally feel pleased in both mind and body. At times the body and the mind feel quite buoyant until it is almost as if one is floating. Without getting attached to them one should then be equanimous about such feelings by returning once more to the breath. After the initial joy fades away, the mind will once again be calm, peaceful, comfortable and tranquil. It is this comfortable and tranquil feeling that is called *happiness born of seclusion.* At first, one can stay in this stage of meditation for about fifteen to twenty minutes, and longer with practice. This is the first *jhāna* and it will arise when one has let go of sensual pleasures for a period of time, and has also let go of unwholesome habits and states of mind.

The meditator who has achieved the first *jhāna* should master it in five ways for otherwise, he will not be able to rise to higher levels in the practice. He must master it by referring to it (*āvajjana*), by entering it (*sampajāna*), by steadying it (*adhiṭṭhāna*), by emerging from it (*vuṭṭhāna*) and by reviewing it (*paccavekkhana*).

To master it by *referring* to it is to turn his thoughts towards the *jhāna* at any place and at any time with no difficulty. To master it by *entering* it, is to be able to enter the *jhāna* at any place and at any time. To master it by *steadying* it, is to remain in the trance as long as one likes. To master it by *emerging* from it, is the ability to emerge from the trance at any place and at any time. Finally, to master it by *reviewing* it, is the ability to remember and examine the nature of the *jhāna* and the nature of its factors, and the like.

When he has thus achieved mastery over the first *jhāna*, he will be successful in attaining to the next higher one, the second *jhāna*. When he does so, he will experience its three constituents of joy (*pīti*), comfort or ease (*sukha*) and one-pointedness (*ekaggatā*). He must then master this second *jhāna* too, in the same way as the first.

He will then realize that this joy (*pīti*) too is a gross state of mind, and that he must progress further.

As one continues to open and calm the mind on the in-and-out breath, eventually the meditator will arrive at a stage where there is no more wandering thoughts. Then the joy is a little stronger, and also it lasts a little longer. When it fades away, the comfortable feeling of happiness is stronger and the calm mind goes deeper into the breath.

This is the state described as: "*. . . with the stilling of applied and sustained thought the bhikkhu enters and abides in the second jhāna . . . born of stillness of mind*".

This means that at this time the mind becomes very still and stays on the breath very comfortably. There is no discursive thinking about the past or the future. However, there is still open observation and feeling in the body as all sense doors are operative. For example, if there is a sound, it is heard, but the sound does not disturb the mind. The meditator knows what it is, but remains equanimous. This self-confidence is gained by seeing clearly for oneself how well the meditation works.

After entering the second *jhāna* frequently, he will be able to enter the third *jhāna*, which has no 'joy' component but is accompanied by comfort, ease (*sukha*) and one-pointedness (*ekaggatā*). He must master this trance too, in the same five ways as described previously.

We now return to the *Ānāpānasati sutta*.

He trains thus: 'I shall breathe in experiencing pleasure (happiness)' ; He trains thus: 'I shall breathe out experiencing pleasure (happiness)'.

As one continues onwards with the practice maintaining a calm and open mind, eventually a stage will be reached where the feeling of joy becomes too coarse and thereafter ceases to arise anymore. As joy fades away by itself, a very strong sense of balance and calm becomes quite apparent. One can still hear sounds but they make no impact on the hearing, and even though one may have lost the feeling of the presence of the body, one would yet know if someone were to touch him during the sitting. However, the mind does not get distracted by it. This is the experience of full awareness, which is described in the suttas as:

> "Again, with the fading away as well of joy, the bhikkhu abides in equanimity, and mindful and fully aware, still feeling happiness with the body, he enters upon and abides in the third jhāna, on account of which the noble ones announce: 'He has a pleasant abiding who has equanimity and is mindful.'"

With the above description, one can plainly see that when one has arrived at the third *jhāna,* the mind is very clear, alert and balanced. Becoming alert (and mindful), and equanimous is an unusual experience because by now, this state of meditation is the highest and best feeling that the meditator has ever experienced in his whole life. Furthermore, one is not attached to this feeling due to equanimity.

At the same time the body and the mind are exceptionally relaxed and at ease, which is the reason why this state is praised by the Noble Ones. Furthermore, now that the mind is in a buffered state, it is comfortable and tension-free, so also the body. This is the meaning of being mindful and fully aware (*sati-sampajañña*). For, the mind knows what is happening around, but does not shake or be disturbed by such phenomena.

This is *experiencing happiness on the in-and-out-breath.*

He trains thus: 'I shall breathe in experiencing the mental formations'; he trains thus: 'I shall breathe out experiencing the mental formation'; He trains thus: 'I shall breathe in tranquillizing the mental formations.' He trains thus: 'I shall breathe out tranquillizing the mental formations.' He trains thus: 'I shall breathe out tranquillizing the mental formations.'

As one continues calming and relaxing the mind, it naturally begins to delve deeper. Finally, the feeling of pleasure in the body-and-mind becomes too coarse and the mind experiences exceptional equanimity and balance. It is described thus in the suttas:

"With the abandoning of pleasure and pain, and with the previous disappearance of joy and grief, a bhikkhu enters upon and abides in the fourth jhāna, which has neither pain nor pleasure but purity of mindfulness due to equanimity".

Thus when the mind becomes very calm and still, one experiences deep tranquillity and equanimity. One can still hear sounds and feel sensations, but these do not shake or move the mind.

The above account gives the serious meditator an idea of what he could expect when he attains this stage. For, the mind is exceptionally clear, bright and alert with the ability to see instantaneously when a distraction begins to arise, then to let go and open up, expand and calm down again before coming back to the breath. At this time, the mind is very much aware when pain or pleasure arises, but the equanimity and mindfulness are so strong that it is not shaken nor overly concerned with such experiences. At this time, it can be said that there is equanimity about formations (*sankhār'upekkhā*), happiness, mindfulness and full awareness in the mind. This is how one experiences and tranquillizes the mental formations.

When the meditator reviews and examines the nature of the **fourth *jhāna*** and its factors, he may now see many of its shortcomings. For, it is still near the gross sensual states. He will see that the life after his death will be one in which he possesses a subtle material body —a body that, even though subtle, — will be subject to death and decay. Seeing so many disadvantages in the fourth *jhāna,* he will strive to attain to a state rid of any materiality.

20. "He trains thus: 'I shall breathe in experiencing the mind'. He trains thus 'I shall breathe out experiencing the mind.'

At this time, one's mind becomes very calm and alert so that the slightest disturbance is noticed and is let go of equally quickly and easily.

"He trains thus: 'I shall breathe in gladdening the mind'. He trains thus: 'I shall breathe out gladdening the mind'.

When a meditator reaches this stage of meditation, he begins to experience a finer and more exalted state of joy, which is described as 'The Joy Enlightenment Factor' (*pharaṇa pīti).* For, the mind is now very peaceful, happy and at ease, like never before.

This is called 'gladdening the mind' because it is an unalloyed pleasurable state. For, the mind is exceptionally uplifted, very clear, and mindfulness is sharper than ever before, and equanimity is even more balanced, stable and composed.

"He trains thus: 'I shall breathe in concentrating (stilling) the mind'; he trains thus: 'I shall breathe out concentrating (stilling) the mind'.

Now the mind becomes more subtle and calm, with very few distractions. But when distractions arise, they are instantly noticed, let go of, and the calm mind returns to the breath. This comes naturally, almost like a reflex action, and the calming of the mind becomes easier, making it more serene.

"He trains thus: 'I shall breathe in liberating the mind'; he trains thus: 'I shall breathe out liberating the mind.'

Liberating the mind means that one stays on the breath with sufficient joyful interest so that when the mind begins to move away from the breath, it is aware and lets the distractions go without any identification. One then relaxes the mind before coming back to the breath. When a hindrance arises, one sees it instantly and lets go of it equally fast. At this point sloth and torpor *(thīna-middha)* or restlessness and anxiety are the biggest obstacles in one's practice. These *nīvaraṇas* or hindrances can even cause a meditator to be pushed out of the *jhāna* unless they are promptly identified by the mind. Identification alone can often prevent their occurrence. Liberating the mind also means to let go of the lower *jhānas* and all of the *jhānic* factors, by not becoming attached to them or in other words, by not thinking about and identifying with them in any way.

21. "He trains thus: 'I shall breathe in contemplating impermanence'; he trains thus: 'I shall breathe out contemplating impermanence.'

As one continues with the practice of meditation on the breath, one is at the same time calming and expanding the mind, so that one now begins to notice that it is in fact expanding and becoming bigger and deeper. Silence and spaciousness of the mind goes together. The immensity of silence is the immensity of the mind in which a centre does not exist; actually speaking, at this time there is no centre and there are no outer edges. It continuous — grows and expands. One begins to see that there are no boundaries, and space and time are infinite. The Anupadā sutta (Mn. 111) describes this as follows:

> *"Again, by passing beyond perceptions of form, with the disappearance of all sense of resistance and by non-attraction to the perceptions of change, aware that space is infinite, the bhikkhu enters into and abides in the base of infinite space. And the states in the base of infinite space — the perception of the base of infinite space and the unification of the mind. One still has the five aggregates affected by clinging, the form, feelings, perceptions, volition and mind."*

Passing beyond perception of form means that even though one knows that one has a body at that time, this awareness would not readily pull the mind towards it. In this state of *jhāna*, one is quite aware of the mind and its doings. The disappearance of all sense resistance and non-attraction to the perceptions of change means that even though a pain arises in the body, the meditator knows about it but does not get involved with that sensation. He feels the mind growing and expanding but, he is not distracted from the breath. Seeing impermanence and how one's mind continuously changes and expands makes one realize that these phenomena are part of an impersonal process over which he has no control. As the meditator continues with the practice, he will eventually see consciousness arising and passing away. It is a continuous process of arising and passing away without a break or interruption. The consciousness keeps coming into being, then vanishes at all sense doors.

The classical interpretation of the above too is found in the *Anupadā sutta* as follows:

> *"Again, by completely surmounting the base of infinite space, aware that consciousness is infinite, a bhikkhu, enters upon and abides in the realm of infinite consciousness, and the states in the base of infinite consciousness — the perception of the base of infinite consciousness and the unification of the mind. (But), one still has the five aggregates affected by clinging. . .".*

When one is in this state of infinite consciousness, there can still arise the same hindrances as before. These hindrances arise because the applied energy is not quite balanced. When one is in this state, one sees changes that happen so rapidly and continuously that they become very tiresome. One begins to see just how much unsatisfactoriness arises with each consciousness.

The meditator sees impermanence (*anicca*), suffering (*dukkha*) experientially, and sees that he has no control over these phenomena, for they happen by themselves. As a result, one sees the non-self nature (*anatta*), not by thinking about it, but by direct realization.

Let us get back to the *Ānāpānasati sutta*:

"He trains thus: 'I shall breathe in contemplating fading away'; he trains thus: 'I shall breathe out contemplating fading away.'

As one proceeds with one's practice on the in-and-out-breath, letting go and calming the mind, the mind naturally lets go of all forms of consciousness that were so readily seen before. The mind then gets into the realm of nothingness. This is when there is nothing external for the mind to see and is looking at nothing outside of itself.

The *Anupadā sutta* (MN. 111) states:

> *"Again, by completely surmounting the base of infinite consciousness, aware that there is 'nothing', the bhikkhu enters upon and abides in the base of nothingness."*

This too is an exceptionally advanced state to be experienced. There are still many things to watch and observe although there is nothing to see outside of the mind and mental factors. It is here that the Seven Enlightenment Factors become very important. They can be seen one by one as they occur, and since mindfulness is quite strong, distractions are kept at bay.

They are:

Mindfulness
Investigation (of experiences)
Energy
Joy
Tranquillity
Stillness and
Equanimity.

He trains thus: 'I shall breathe in contemplating cessation'; he trains thus: 'I shall breathe out contemplating cessation'.

One still continues calming the mind on the in-and-out breath. At the same time, the mind appears to be quiet and feels as if it is in the process of actually shrinking, eventually becoming very subtle and still.

The *Anupadā sutta* describes this as follows:

'Again, by completely surmounting the base of nothingness, the bhikkhu enters upon and abides in the base of 'neither-perception nor non-perception.'

The mind has so little movement that it is sometimes difficult to know whether it is there at all. It is also difficult to know if there is any perception of a mind. This extremely subtle state of mind is not easy to attain, yet it is attainable if one continues with the practice. At this time, one cannot see the breath any longer, but there are still some feelings that arise. This is when one begins to sit for long periods of time for, the meditation is the total tranquillizing and release of all energy. As one continues with one's practice and keeps opening, expanding and calming the mind, it becomes subtle and very refined, and does not move at all. Eventually one will experience the state of *nirodha samāpatti* (i.e., the cessation of both perception and feeling).

"He trains thus: 'I shall breathe in contemplating relinquishment'; he trains thus: 'I shall breathe out contemplating relinquishment.'

This state of meditation is not the experience of the supramundane state as yet, but it is very close to it. The meditator must exercise diligence and patience now, until the perceptions and feelings come back and are noticed.

The meditator can now enter any one of the four ecstatic *jhānas* and emerge therefrom after a short time. He then reviews the nature of the *jhānic* consciousness, its constituents and the object upon which these forms of consciousness depend, which he has valued so long and attained to with much difficulty. He realizes that all of them are impermanent, unsatisfactory and lacking in a 'self' or 'entity'. He goes further in examining his breath, the spot of the breath's first touch, the nature of his physical body which supports the breath, feelings that arise when breaths touch the "spot of their first touch", consciousness that arises together with feelings, and how they are conditioned.

When he goes on carrying out this inward search with diligence, he will perceive that all those states, both mental and physical, are conditioned, phenomenal, transient, restless, unsatisfactory and insubstantial (without self). Thus, perceiving the unsteadiness, unsatisfactoriness and egolessness of this mind-body process, he erases all mistaken ideas and inferences, thereby achieving purity of views (*diṭṭhi-visuddhi*). At this stage, he sees no particular thing called the breath, but an ever-changing flow of very minute units of matter composed of the four primary qualities: hardness or softness, cohesion, caloricity and vibration, indivisibly united.

The meditator must exercise alertness and patience now, until the perceptions and feelings come back and are noticed. *When this happens, the meditator sees experientially all the twelve links of the paṭiccasamuppāda both in the forward and the reverse direction*. The meditator now examines once again how these material and mental states arise. He goes in search of their causes and finds therein the operation of the law of conditioned genesis — *paṭiccasamuppāda.*

He understands that the continuity of material and mental states that he has mistaken so long for "I" has been caused and conditioned by attachment or craving (*taṇhā*) for such an existence. He sees the past ignorance as to the nature of such an existence. He sees that the past ignorance, craving, clinging and volitional formations conditioned by the same two, have brought about the present phenomenal existence and that the same causes and conditions, if not rooted out, will build future phenomenal existences as well. When he examines thus keenly, he sees clearly and still more clearly and in detail this law of conditioned genesis and clears his uncertainty as to the nature of his own existence, and by inference that of other living beings as well. He sees more clearly than ever before the three characteristics of human existence, namely, impermanence, unsatisfactoriness and the absence of an abiding permanent self in this whole existence.

He now feels joyful and extremely blissful, serene, energetic, even-minded, more self-confident, more mindful and of keener awareness. He feels much attached to these new gains. Some meditators even mistake these new gains for "attainment to arahatship" and may stop further practice. Such ones may soon fall away even from that state and remain at the previous level.

But the wise meditator, on the other hand, discreetly examines and scrutinizes his new gains and finds out that he has still not removed his attachment to worldliness. He clearly sees that these new gains are but obstacles to his further progress. He examines these new gains and perceives their transience, unsatisfactoriness and insubstantiality. The mind now becomes dispassionate and completely lets go of the belief in a permanent and unchanging self.

The *Anupadā sutta* explains this as follows:

> *'Again, by completely surmounting the base of neither perception nor non-perception, the bhikkhu enters upon and abides in the cessation of perception and feeling. And his taints are destroyed by his seeing with wisdom.'*

When one comes out of the state of the cessation of perception and feeling with one's mindfulness suffici-ently sharp, the meditator will see directly the Second Noble Truth of the *Cause of Suffering*. i.e., the cause-effect relationship in the *paṭiccasamuppāda*.

At this stage the Third Noble Truth of the *Cessation of Suffering also reveals itself to the meditator* (i.e., how all of the links in the *paṭiccasamuppāda* cease to be and how letting go of one link directly leads to the letting go of the next and so on.) When one comes to this state of experiential knowledge, it can be said *that 'His taints are destroyed by seeing with wisdom'* meaning the seeing and realizing of all of the Noble Truths directly and achieving total comprehension and insight into the *paṭiccasa-muppāda*. This is how one contemplates relinquishment.

22. ***"Bhikkhus that is how mindfulness of breathing is developed and cultivated, so that it is of great fruit and great benefit."***

The Buddha concludes his instructions on the breath with the above self-explanatory statement. The 'great fruit and benefit' from meditating on the breath *(ānāpāna-sati)* with mindfulness and awareness *(sati-sampajañña)* of impermanence, is of course the attainment of the state of Nibbāna.

The rest of the contents of this sutta relates to an explanation of how meditating in the above manner in addition to leading to final liberation, also fulfils at the same time the Four Foundations of Mindfulness and the Seven Factors of Enlightenment.

23. "And how, bhikkhus, does mindfulness of breathing, developed and cultivated, fulfils the Four Foundations of Mindfulness?

24. "Bhikkhus, on whatever occasion a bhikkhu, breathing in long, understands: 'I breathe in long,' or breathing out long understands: 'I breathe out long'; breathing in short, understands: 'I breathe in short, or breathing out short, understands: 'I breathe out short'; trains thus: 'I shall breathe in experiencing the whole body (of breath)'; 'I shall breathe out experiencing the whole body (of breath); 'I shall breathe in tranquillizing the bodily formations'; 'I shall breathe out tranquillizing the bodily formations' — on that occasion, a bhikkhu abides contemplating the body as a body, ardent, fully aware, and mindful, having put away covetousness and grief for the world. I say that this is a certain body among the bodies, namely, in-breathing and out-breathing. That is why on that occasion a bhikkhu abides contemplating the body as a body, ardent, fully aware, and mindful, having put away covetousness and grief for the world."

'On whatever occasion' has far-reaching implications. It means not only when sitting in meditation, but all the time, during one's daily activities. It means to simply let go when the mind is full of extraneous thoughts, to calm and relax the mind, and to feel the mind becoming tranquil. This is a practical way of practising one's daily activities and improving the awareness of the states of conscious-ness.

This extends to one's walking meditation as well. Instead of focusing on one's feet, one would now keep one's attention on the mind, relaxing on the in- and- out breath while walking. This is mindfulness of body (the breath body) and can be also extended to other activities as well.

25. "Bhikkhus, on whatever occasion, a bhikkhu trains thus: 'I shall breathe in experiencing rapture (joy)'; 'I shall breathe out experiencing rapture (joy)'; 'I shall breathe in experiencing pleasure (happiness)'; 'I shall breathe out experiencing pleasure (happiness)'; 'I shall breathe in experiencing the mental formations'; he trains thus: 'I shall breathe out experiencing the mental formations'; trains thus: 'I shall breathe in tranquillizing the mental formations'; 'I shall breathe out tranquillizing the mental formations'.

"On that occasion a bhikkhu abides contemplating feelings as feelings, ardent, fully aware, and mindful, having put away covetousness and grief for the world. I say that this is a certain feeling among the feelings, namely, giving close attention to in-breathing and out-breathing. That is why on that occasion a bhikkhu abides contemplating feelings as feelings, ardent, fully aware and mindful, having put away covetousness and grief for the world."

This describes the various kinds of feelings that occur when one is in the meditative stages of the first four *jhānas*. It also emphasizes the fact that the most important feeling among these feelings is the in-and-out-breath. The importance of staying with the feeling of the breath cannot be overstated. This is how the Second Foundation of Mindfulness is fulfilled.

26. *"Bhikkhus, on whatever occasion a bhikkhu trains thus: 'I shall breathe in experiencing the mind'; 'I shall breathe out experiencing the mind'; 'I shall breathe in gladdening the mind'; 'I shall breathe out gladdening the mind'; 'I shall breathe in concentrating (stilling) the mind' 'I shall breathe out concentrating (stilling) the mind 'I shall breathe in liberating the mind'; 'I shall breathe out liberating the mind'.*

"On that occasion a bhikkhu abides contemplating mind as mind, ardent, fully aware, and mindful, having put away covetousness and grief for the world. I do not say that there is development of mindfulness of breathing for one who is forgetful, one who is not fully aware. That is why on that occasion a bhikkhu abides contemplating mind as mind, ardent, fully aware, and mindful, having put away covetousness and grief for the world."

This is more or less a repetition and needs no further discussion, except to remind ourselves that we must always remember to stay with the meditation subject with joyful interest and clear comprehension (of impermanency)— *sati-sampajañña* all the time. One's attention is then unwavering and the mind develops more composure than ever before. This is how the third Foundation of Mindfulness is fulfilled.

27, *"Bhikkhus, on whatever occasion a bhikkhu trains thus: 'I shall breathe in contemplating impermanence'; 'I shall breathe out contemplating impermanence'; 'I shall breathe in contemplating fading away'; 'I shall breathe out contemplating fading away'; 'I shall breathe in contemplating cessation'; 'I shall breathe out contemplating cessation'; 'I shall breathe in contemplating relinquishment'; 'I shall breathe out contemplating relinquishment'.*

"On that occasion a bhikkhu abides contemplating mind-objects as mind-objects, ardent, fully aware, and mindful, having put away covetousness and grief for the world. Having seen with wisdom the abandoning of covetousness and grief, he closely looks on with equanimity. That is why on that occasion a bhikkhu abides contemplating mind-objects as mind-objects, ardent, fully aware, and mindful, having put away covetousness and grief for the world.

This refers to the experiences in the higher *jhānas* where the mind develops a finer and still finer balance. One then experiences a high level of equanimity *(saṅkkhār'upekkhā)* even when one sees how tricky the mind could be when unpleasant things arise. The mind accepts such situations without becoming ruffled. This is how the Fourth Foundation of Mindfulness of mind-objects is fulfilled.

28. *"Bhikkhus, that is how mindfulness of breathing developed and cultivated, fulfils the Four Foundations of Mindfulness.*

29. *"And how, bhikkhus, do the Four Foundations of Mindfulness, developed and cultivated, fulfil the Seven Enlightenment Factors?*

The seven enlightenment factors were listed above.

30. *"Bhikkhus, on whatever occasion a bhikkhu abides contemplating the body as a body, ardent, fully aware, and mindful, having put away covetousness and grief for the world — on that occasion unremitting mindfulness is established in him. On whatever occasion unremitting mindfulness is established in a bhikkhu — on that occasion the enlightenment-factor of mindfulness is aroused in him, and he develops it, and by development, it comes to fulfilment in him."*

For clarification, we can turn to the *Satipaṭṭhāna sutta* (Dn.22), where this is explained as follows:

> *"Here, there being the enlightenment-factor of mindfulness in him, a bhikkhu understands: 'There is the enlightenment-factor of*

> *mindfulness in me'; or there being no mindfulness enlightenment-factor in him, he understands: 'There is no enlightenment-factor of mindfulness in me'; and he also understands how there comes to be the arising of the un-arisen enlightenment- factor of mindfulness, and how the arisen enlightenment- factor of mindfulness comes to fulfilment by development.*

Briefly, this means that one knows when one's mind is silent, acuity is sharp and clear and the mind is joyfully interested and focused on the breath as well as on everything else that arise. One is also now aware whenever the mind is dull or lethargic or disinterested and that it is now necessary to summon interest once more. One can then see that every breath is somewhat different and never the same. This is how the enlightenment-factor of mindfulness comes to fulfilment by development.

31. "Abiding thus mindful, he investigates and examines that state with wisdom and embarks upon a full inquiry into it. On whatever occasion, abiding thus mindfully, a bhikkhu investigates and examines that state with wisdom and embarks upon a full inquiry into it, on that occasion the investigation-of-states enlightenment-factor is aroused in him, and he develops it, and by development it comes to fulfilment in him."

This means that whatever arises in the mind, whether it is any of the five hindrances or whether it be emotional states or physical feelings, they should be examined impersonally and let go off, before relaxing the mind and getting back to the breath.

32. **"In one who investigates and examines that state with wisdom and embarks upon a full inquiry into it, tireless energy is aroused. On whatever occasion tireless energy is aroused in a bhikkhu who investigates and examines that state with wisdom and embarks upon a full inquiry into it, on that occasion the enlightenment- factor of energy is aroused in him, and he develops it, and by development it comes to fulfilment in him."**

An appropriate explanation of the above is contained in the Satipaṭṭhāna sutta as follows:

"Here, there being the energy-enlightenment factor in him, a bhikkhu understands: 'there is the energy-enlightenment factor in me'; or there being no energy- enlightenment factor in him, he understands: 'There is no energy-enlightenment factor in me';

and he also understands how there comes to be the arising of the un-arisen energy-enlightenment factor, and how the arisen energy-enlightenment factor comes to fulfilment by development.

33. ***"In one who has aroused energy, non-worldly rapture (joy) arises. On whatever occasion non-worldly rapture (joy) arises in a bhikkhu who has aroused energy, on that occasion the enlightenment-factor of rapture is aroused in him, and he develops it, and by development it comes to fulfilment in him."***

Non-worldly joy refers to joy that is experienced while in either of the first two *jhānas*. It is called *ubbhega-pīti*. (The similar forms of joy at higher stages of *jhāna* are called 'all-pervading joy' or *pharaṇa pīti*).

The most important key to success in meditation is the first enlightenment-factor of mindfulness. It is this factor, which will prevent a person who has experienced 'non-worldly' joy from losing interest thereafter experiencing sloth and torpor. For, joy can often go away very quickly, unless one takes quick and appropriate action.

34. ***"In one who is rapturous (joyful), the body and the mind become tranquil. On whatever occasion the body and mind become tranquil in a bhikkhu who is rapturous (joyful), on that occasion the tranquillity-enlightenment factor is aroused in him, and he develops it, and by development it comes to fulfilment in him."***

When joy arises in the mind, there is a very pleasant feeling in both body and mind. After a while, the joy fades away a little, but with mindfulness one's mind becomes exceptionally calm and peaceful. This is the state, which can be described as the 'enlightenment-factor of tranquillity'. At this time, one's body and mind become extraordinarily relaxed, peaceful and calm.

35. ***"In one whose body is tranquil and who feels pleasure, the mind becomes concentrated (still) and composed. On whatever occasion the mind becomes concentrated (still) and composed in a bhikkhu whose body is tranquil and who feels pleasure, on that occasion the concentration-enlightenment factor (stillness- samādhi) is aroused in him, and he develops it, and by development it comes to fulfilment in him."***

When one's mind and body have become more tranquil and at ease, the mind can then stay on the breath naturally and without distractions. There is also full awareness and mindfulness. Since the mind is still, it can observe things quite clearly. *This quiet and silent mind is the blessing that is sought by every earnest meditator.*

36. "He closely looks on with equanimity at the mind thus concentrated (stilled and composed). On whatever occasion a bhikkhu closely looks on with equanimity at the mind thus concentrated (stilled and composed), on that occasion the equanimity-enlightenment factor is aroused in him, and he develops it, and by development it comes to fulfilment in him."

The importance of developing the equanimity-enlightenment factor needs to be repeatedly emphasized. It balances the mind when it is unsettled, and it is equanimity that can gently persuade the mind to lovingly accept whatever arises in the present moment without any kind of discrimination. It is the factor that allows one to rapidly progress along the Path. At the same time one must ensure that one does not mistake indifference for equanimity, for the latter is the essential trait worth cultivating assiduously if one is to progress to fruition and emancipation.

37. "Bhikkhus, on whatever occasion a bhikkhu abides contemplating feelings as feelings, ardent, fully aware, and mindful, having put away covetousness and grief for the world . . . (rpt. same formula as in sections 30 thru 36) the equanimity-enlightenment factor is aroused in him, and he develops it, and by development it comes to fulfilment in him.

The meditator must understand that he must use these enlightenment-factors whenever any hindrance or distraction arises, no matter whether it is during one's sitting meditation or during daily activities. These factors keep one's mind in balance.

38. "Bhikkhus, on whatever occasion a bhikkhu contemplates mind as mind, . . .

39 " . . . mind-objects as mind-objects, . . . (repeat as in 30 thru 36), the equanimity-enlightenment factor is aroused in him, and he develops it, and by development it comes to fulfilment in him.

40. "Bhikkhus that is how the four Foundations of Mindfulness, developed and cultivated, fulfil the Seven Enlightenment Factors."

The possibility of attaining to the supramundane state of Nibbāna becomes possible when the seven enlightenment-factors are in perfect balance during one's meditation practice. As one goes higher and higher in the meditation practice and the achieving of the *jhānic* condition, the balancing of the enlightenment-factors become more and more refined and subtle. Meditation then turns out to be most gratifying, and an indescribable experience.

Fulfilment of true knowledge and deliverance

41. "And how, bhikkhus, do the seven Enlightenment-Factors, developed and cultivated, fulfil true knowledge and deliverance?

42. "Here, bhikkhus, a bhikkhu develops the mindfulness-enlightenment factor, which is supported by seclusion, dispassion, and cessation, and ripens in relinquishment.

"He develops the investigation-of-state-enlightenment factor . . . the energy-enlightenment-factor . . . the rapture (joy) enlightenment-factor . . . the tranquillity enlightenment-factor . . . . the concentration (stillness) enlightenment-factor . . . the equanimity enlightenment factor, which is supported by seclusion, dispassion and cessation, and ripens in relinquishment."

43. "Bhikkhus, that is how the seven Enlightenment-Factors, developed and cultivated, fulfil true knowledge and deliverance.

"Supported by seclusion," means that one must gain the lowest *jhāna*, and for this purpose the meditator must be "secluded from sensual pleasure, and free from unwholesome states". For, at that time, the mind is alert and stays with the subject of meditation, which is the breath, without distraction. "Dispassion" means that the mind is free from attachments, clinging and craving. In other words it is free from thinking or analyzing. "Cessation" means the ceasing of defilements and ego-identification with whatever arises. "Being mindful" is the most important of them all. "Being truly mindful" is to see what the mind is doing at all times, and then letting go. It also means to lovingly open the mind and to let go of all identifications with distractions and to relax and move back to the present moment."

To summarize: A meditator, who has attained to the first and second *jhāna*, enters the *jhāna*, remains for a short time experiencing and then emerges from it. Then he contemplates and examines the joy (the prominent factor thereof), perceives its impermanence, unsatisfactoriness and egolessness, and goes on developing his insight, completes his spiritual pilgrimage in the aforementioned way, and reaches its culmination by attaining to perfect sainthood.

Another meditator, who has attained to the third *jhāna*, enters that *jhāna*, remains in it for a short time, emerges from it and contemplates its prominent factor, which is the ease he felt therein, the nature of the *jhānic*-consciousness and its object, and sees that all of them are impermanent, unsatisfactory and egoless. The meditator, developing his insight as mentioned before and completing the path, attains perfect sainthood, which is arahatship.

Still another meditator, who has attained to the fourth *jhāna* in which equanimity is the prominent factor, enters the *jhāna*, experiences it, emerges from it and reviews the nature of the *jhāna,* its factors and its object, and sees that they are all impermanent, unsatisfactory and egoless. Developing *vipassanā*, he completes the holy pilgrimage and attains to perfect sainthood, which is arahatship.

This brings us to the end of the discussion of the *Ānāpānasati sutta*. It is hoped that the advanced *vipassanā* meditators find the explanations contained herein useful in their onward journey of self-realization. *For, it should by now be self-evident that meditation on this subject alone could bring a dedicated person to Transcendence.*

The *non-jhānic* practitioners: Certain meditators practise *vipassanā* (insight-development) from the beginning. They do not try to attain the *jhānas*. Instead they start with mindfulness of inhalation and exhalation. Then, by focusing on the breaths, they develop concentra-tion and mindfulness. Next they develop mindfulness over extension of breaths, both long and short, and then contemplate over the start, the middle and the end of all inhalations and exhalations. They examine the feelings that arise at the breath's first point of contact on the tip of the nose or the upper lip and see impermanence, unsatisfactoriness and egolessness of feelings. They then examine the consciousness (mind-unit), perception (*saññā)* and other mental factors (*saṅkhāra*) that arise together with the feeling and see that all of them are impermanent, unsatisfactory, and insubstantial (egoless: *anatta*).

In this way, they develop insight and pass through the stages of:

Purity of view,
Purity by overcoming uncertainty,
Purity by discriminating between right and wrong paths,
Nine stages of insight, or purity of thoughts through the course of development of insight,

When the seven factors of realization (*bojjhaṅga)* arise, (see appendix), they examine them and see impermanence in them. Thus, completing the practice, they attain to the holy stages of *sotāpanna, sakadāgāmin, anāgāmin,* and finally attain to arahatship, when their *pāramitās* are completed under the right conditions.

CHAPTER XVI

The Mahāyāna Path to Transcendence

In the two previous presentations (Wheel 450-452 and 455-457), we proceeded on a voyage of discovery within our own bodies and minds leading ultimately to a true understanding of the human condition as impermanent, unsatisfactory and bereft of self. The theoretical understanding was then raised to the level of experiential knowledge when we practised *vipassanā* meditation. This fruition of our efforts was made possible by following the Buddha Dhamma as contained in various Theravāda suttas in the Buddhist Canon, and supported by practical instructions of current meditation masters.

Nevertheless, when other meditators refer to insight and liberation based on their respective Mahāyāna practices, we sometimes wonder whether as followers of the Theravāda tradition, we are indeed seeing the complete picture on possible paths to transcendence.

Regardless of our personal inclinations towards or commitments to one particular Buddhist tradition, we must recognize the fact that the Mahāyāna has contributed a great deal to Buddhist thought. The Mahāyāna teachings as well as those of the Theravāda began to appear in written form more than five hundred years after the time of the Buddha. We know with certainty that the Theravāda canon was completed in the middle of the first century BCE. The earliest Mahāyāna sūtras[1], such as the *Lotus Sūtra* and the *Prajñāpāramitā sūtra,* are usually dated not later than the first century CE. Therefore, the written canons of the Theravāda and Mahāyāna traditions date roughly to the same period.

And, we are well aware that there is a vast and enormous reservoir of Mahāyāna information, which over these many centuries have helped earnest meditators to achieve transcendence. The Mahāyāna Tripiṭaka has many stimulating

---

1. *Sūtras*: To differentiate between the Mahāyāna doctrinal material from that of the Theravāda, the word *sūtra* is used in place of *sutta.*

and useful sūtras, which the discerning *vipassanā* meditator could peruse profitably. Such information, when mentally evaluated with mindfulness and total awareness, can be a very rewarding experience, and help fortify our own realizations so that we can arrive at the ultimate blissful unconditioned state of Nibbāna.

The followers of the Buddha consequently were presented with what appeared to be a choice between two different ideals of religious life — Arahatship (according to Theravāda tradition) or Buddhahood (according to Mahāyāna tradition). Thus, while the aspiring Arahat is interested in gaining freedom for him or herself, the Bodhisatva or the Buddha-to-be is committed to achieving Enlightenment for the sake of all living beings.

This current presentation thus, is not for the purpose of discussing the pros and cons of these two great schools of Buddhism, but to rather bring to light aspects of the Mahāyāna practice which can stimulate or provide insight thus helping the Theravāda follower to achieve transcendence.

A good simile in this regard can be drawn from what the Buddha has said in regard to arriving at the farther shore by using a raft. The farther shore being Nibbāna, the river is *saṃsāra* and the self is the passenger guiding the raft, which would be the Buddha Dhamma. In the Theravāda tradition it would be the Dhamma as contained in the Pali canon. But I would personally like to think of the raft being held secure by the Dhamma as explicated in the combined Theravāda and Mahāyāna canons. In such circumstances the onerous task of spiritual and mental development for the dedicated *vipassanā* meditator will perhaps be made that much easier.

Furthermore, it is often forgotten that not only are there many virtually identical discourses belonging to both canons, but that there are also traces in the Theravāda canon of some of the characteristic themes of the Mahāyāna — such as the supramundane nature of the Buddha, the doctrines of emptiness and the creative and luminous nature of the mind. Thus for example, in the Theravāda canon, the Buddha extolled emptiness in the highest terms, calling it profound and going beyond the world. He said that form, feeling and the like were illusory, mere bubbles. Phenomena are nothing in themselves. They are unreal deceptions. This is a theme taken up and elaborated in the Mahāyāna 'Perfection of Wisdom' (*Prajñāpāramitā*) literature.

The Buddha, we should remember, never preached a particular brand of *yāna,* be it *Hīnayāna* or *Mahāyāna* or, as a matter of fact, any other *yāna*. All he proclaimed was Dhamma or the Truth. The manner in which his Dhamma was later recorded and practised and how it came to be divisive are of recent origin. Hence, although we are more familiar with the Theravāda experience, it would be unreasonable to close our eyes to information from other sources, provided they *accord with the Dhamma*. The Buddha was quite explicit in this regard, for he constantly urged people to always have an open mind. This is very evident in his many exhortations.

Thus, on one occasion when addressing a great assembly of the Kālāmas, he said:

"Now, look you Kālāmas, do not be lead by reports, or tradition, or hearsay. Be not led by the authority of religious texts, nor by mere logic or inference, nor by considering appearances, nor by the delight in speculative opinions, nor by seeming possibilities, nor by the idea: 'this is our teacher'. But, O Kālāmas, when you know for yourselves that certain things are unwholesome (*akusala*), and wrong, and bad, then give them up . . . And when you know for yourselves that certain things are wholesome (*kusala*) and good, then accept them and follow them[2].

The Buddha went even further, for on another occasion he had told an assembly of bhikkhus that a disciple should examine even the Thathāgata, so that he (the disciple) might be fully convinced of the true value of the teacher whom he followed.

He also has stated in the sutta No.16 of the *Dīgha Nikāya*, that such (unfamiliar or new) information should neither be approved or disapproved, but the words and expressions should be carefully noted and compared with the suttas and reviewed in the light of the discipline, and only after review and comparison should they be either approved and accepted or disapproved and rejected 'as assuredly the word or not the word of the Buddha'.

---

2. See Kālāma sutta,

In the current presentation I propose to discuss a Mahāyāna sūtra which has a direct bearing on the *vipassanā* meditation practice leading to transcendence. This is the *Shūraṅgama sūtra*, which is essentially based on the monumental works known as the Perfection of Wisdom Sūtra in Eight Thousand Lines *(Aṣhṭasāhasrikā Prajñāpāramitā sūtra)* and the Perfection of Wisdom Sūtra in Twenty-five Thousand Lines *(Pañcaviṃśatisāhasrikā Prajñāpāramitā sūtra).*

Before we discuss the *sūtras*, a few words of explanation on emptiness, the void and luminosity would be necessary. In the *Prajñāpāramitā Hṛdaya* or Heart *sūtra*, the Buddha states that the Bodhisattva Avalokiteśvara found that form, feeling, perception, volition and consciousness are, in their own being, void — meaning that the nature of the aggregates is empty of independent existence. And just as the five aggregates are empty, so are the eighteen elements that comprise personal experience.

What are these eighteen elements? Analysis reveals that three elements are involved in each of the six avenues of personal experience (the five senses plus the mind). For example, the activity of seeing can be analyzed into (i) the element of form, which is the visible object: (ii) the element of the eye, which is the sense faculty of vision and (iii) the element of visual consciousness, which is the mental element.

Similarly, in each of the activities of hearing, smelling, tasting, touching and thinking, there is (a) an external or objective element, (b) an internal, subjective sense faculty and (c) the consciousness that arises in conjunction with the external object and the sense faculty.

Hence, there are three components for each of the six activities, for a total of eighteen elements that result from the analytical investigation of personal experience. According to the insight wisdom realized by Avalokiteśvara, these eighteen elements do not exist in reality; like the first aggregate, they all are empty or void.

Emptiness is, in fact, a therapeutic device. It is a corrective for the exclusively analytical view, which leaves us a residual belief in the real existence of the element of experience. Emptiness is a device that enables us to transcend this pluralistic belief in the independent existence of things. It is for this reason that emptiness is likened to a medicine that cures residual belief in the independent existence of elements. But like medicine, emptiness taken in excess, or at the wrong place or time, can be dangerous. This is why one ought not to abide in or cling to emptiness. Like a medicine, emptiness is designed *only to cure the illness of perceiving the independent existence of things.*

It is because emptiness reveals and expresses the relativity of all phenomena that it becomes the key to understanding non-duality. It can now be seen how recognition of this relativity — and subsequent transcendence — of opposites is tantamount to the perception of non-duality or non-differentiation.

Reverting to the discussion of analytical and relational investigations of object and subject, it could be said that they lead to an understanding of reality as ineffable, as beyond both existence and non-existence, as empty and luminous. *In the Mahāyāna tradition, this is the ultimate realization*: Reality cannot be described in terms of existence and non-existence. It is empty, luminous and pure. Reality is beyond existence because all existence is relative and dependent. It is beyond non-existence because, despite its emptiness and transience, reality does appear and is experienced. *Therefore, reality is not altogether non-existent.*

It may be recalled that the word *pure* was used as a synonym for 'empty'. There was then the word *luminous*. This need not confuse us. It is simply a restatement of the equivalence set forth in the Heart-sūtra's assertion that "Emptiness is form, and form is emptiness." Reality is not only empty, but it is also form and it is also luminous, bright with the potential for appearance. This luminosity — this potential inherent in the real state of things — manifests itself to the impure, afflicted consciousness as *saṃsāra*, but it manifests itself to the purified consciousness as Nibbāna — the unconditioned. Thus *emptiness and luminosity* are the characteristics of reality that emerge from the Mahāyānic investigation of the subject-object experience.

The Shūraṅgama Sūtra

According to the Mahāyāna tradition, the Buddha is reported to have recited the *Shūraṅgama sūtra* particularly for the benefit of Ānanda who was already a *sotāpanna*. Ānanda was the living repository of the Dhamma. When listening to the Buddha, he would store all the discourses in his memory and his insight wisdom was not complete because he had been concentrating mainly on the former. We shall mention here only a few passages from this *sūtra*.

The first relates to an incident when Shākyamuni Buddha had requested twenty-five enlightened persons to explain their respective methods of meditation and spiritual attainments culminating in liberation. These had then been evaluated. The Buddha thereupon had confirmed that Kuan-yin's[3] method was best suited for Ānanda as well as for the rest of the people of this world. It is therefore appropriate to discuss in his own words Kuan yin's meditation subject and methodology, for they are in many ways similar to the methods used by advanced meditators in the Theravāda tradition.

But, before we discuss Kuan-yin's method, it is important that we recall some of the fundamental teachings of the Buddha. The aim of the Buddha's teachings is the release of all sentient beings from *saṃsāra* or the round of suffering. The essential postulate is that all human suffering results from deluded craving and attachment (*taṇhā-upādāna*), which in turn is the product of our object-clinging mind *(nāma)*.

In this presentation, 'object' refers to all the objects of consciousness (*viññāṇa*), whether they be formations and phenomena in the outside world as perceived by the sense organs, or in the inside world of our thoughts, ideas etc. 'Clinging' means becoming attached through craving. Hence the object-clinging mind is the state of mind through which we become attached to objects which we encounter, and come to believe that these objects are in fact real. Such attachment is deluded and therefore our judgement becomes faulty. Ignorance, greed, hatred, and suffering are its result. In short, much of our experiences in life are based on these negative assumptions and experiences which are actually contrary to reality. The Buddha has taught various methods to reverse this process of clinging to objects and to contemplate reality with a one-pointed mind. This is the key concept involved in *vipassanā* meditation which is the act of learning to concentrate one's mental energies in a state of absorption.

---

3. Kuan-yin is a synonym for Avalokiteśvara

In order to discuss Kuan-yin's method of meditation, it is useful to re-state the relevant passages from the *Shūraṅgama sūtra*:

It reads as follows:

> *"First I concentrated on the audio-consciousness, and allowed the sounds that were contacting the ear to flow off, and thus audio-objects subsided and were lost. Then, since ear-contact and audio-objects produced no effect, the mind remained in a state of clarity and the phenomenon of motion and stillness no longer occurred.*
>
> *"Meditative absorption gradually deepened and ultimately the distinction between audio-consciousness and the objects of audio-consciousness (i.e., both subject and object) were no longer in existence — they got merged into the void. Although there was no experience of audio-consciousness, meditative absorption continued to deepen. Then, all awareness and objects of awareness became empty.*
>
> *"The awareness of emptiness expanded without boundary; then emptiness and that which is empty became extinct. Since all arising and subsiding had ceased, equanimity became manifest. Suddenly, transcending both the mundane and the supramundane, there was an all-embracing luminosity in all the ten directions. . .."*

We can now proceed to discuss the above.

As is evident, Kuan-yin's meditation method is based on the process of hearing. There should, however, be a clear understandings of the following five terms: 'I', 'the nature to hear', 'audio-consciousness', 'hearing', and 'sound'. When one gives these some thought, one will realize that these five terms correspond to five degrees of deluded attachment, the coarsest and the weakest of which is sound, and the subtlest and strongest of which is 'I'. The latter is of course the most difficult concept to eradicate. Ordinarily we tend to confuse sound, hearing, audio-consciousness, and the nature to hear. But, in reality, there are some important fundamental differences.

Kuan-yin began his cultivation of realization by recognizing these differences. He practised meditation by the sea. Every morning, when he woke up and everything was quiet around him, he would hear the sound of the tide coming in from afar, breaking the silence. After a while the sound of the tide receded and he would hear the silence restored. Then, the sound of the tide came again, and again the silence was gone. Kuan-yin studied the coming and going of the sound of the tide and discovered that there were two objects. There was the sound of the tide and there was the silence. They were mutually exclusive, for, he could not hear them both simultaneously. When the sound of the tide arose, silence ceased. When the sound of the tide ceased, silence arose. Nonetheless, he perceived that they both had something in common: both arose and then both ceased — both were impermanent. But not so his innate nature to hear. It was always present. It was this nature to hear that enabled him to hear the sound of the incoming tide, but it did not go away when the tide went back, for then he heard the silence. Indeed if it were otherwise, and his nature to hear were to have departed with the tide, then he would not only have not heard the silence, but he would not have heard the next tide advancing either. Thus, although the sound of the tide came and went, the nature to hear *per se* was not subject to those changes.

It is important to realize that while sound just comes and goes, arises and subsides, we ordinarily "pursue" sound's transient pattern of arising and cessation. For, we seize upon it as being entirely real, and therefore develop deluded attachment. The Buddha wanted listeners to understand deeply this crucial point. Let me interrupt the current discussion to quote from another section of the *Shūraṅgama sūtra*.

"The Buddha said: 'I will now do something to clear away your doubts and suspicion"

He then ordered Rāhula to ring the bell and asked Ānanda: *'Do you hear it?'* Ānanda and the others in the assembly replied that they did. When the bell was no more heard, the Buddha asked them once again: *'Do you still hear it?'* They all replied that they did not.

Rāhula again rang the bell and the Buddha asked: *'Do you hear it?'* They replied that they did. The Buddha then asked Ānanda: *'What do you mean by hearing and not hearing?'* Ānanda and the others replied: *'If the bell is rung, we call it hearing and when the sound and its echo stop, we call it not hearing'*.

The Buddha once again ordered Rāhula to ring the bell and asked Ānanda: *'Is there any sound?'* Ānanda and the others replied that there was the sound of the bell. A little later, when it could no longer be heard, the Buddha asked again: *'Is there any sound?'* They all replied that there was none. Then Rāhula rang the bell once more, and the Buddha asked again: *'Is there any sound?'* They all replied in the affirmative. The Buddha then asked Ānanda: *'What do you mean by 'sound' and 'no sound?'* Ānanda and the others replied that if the bell was rung, there was sound and when both the 'sound' and its echo stopped, this was called 'no sound.'

The Buddha then said: *'Ānanda, when both the sound and its echo ceased, you said there was no hearing: if there really were no hearing, its nature would have died. But when the bell was rung again, how then did you hear it? Existence and non-existence concern only the sound, which may be present or not present, . . . not the nature of your hearing. If it really ceased who then knew there was no sound?'*

It should thus be clear that even if one is aware of no sound at all, it is precisely by using the sense of hearing that one is aware of silence. So it is clear that while sound just comes and goes, the same is not true of our innate nature to hear. This aspect of hearing, which hears transient sounds, but does not itself change, is what is called "the innate nature to hear".

Let us now get back to the *Shūraṅgama sūtra*.

Kuan-yin begins his discourse by saying; *"First I concentrated on the audio- consciousness"* which means, "during the first stage of meditation, using my hearing". Here, special attention should be paid to the fact that Kuan-yin began his *vipassanā* practice at the level of an ordinary human being. He had a strong sense of 'self', and of an 'I'. Second, he possessed the innate nature to hear. Third, both his audio-consciousness and hearing were unimpaired. Fourth, he heard sounds, such as the sound of the tide mentioned above. We all possess these faculties and the delusions associated with them. This is significant, because we shall see how Kuan-yin progressed from this ordinary state to eradicate his deluded attachments one by one.

As mentioned above, Kuan-yin practised meditation by the sea. By listening to the coming and going of the sound of the tide, he realized that sound is neither permanent nor substantial, but arises and ceases momentarily within the field created by one's innate nature to hear. Nonetheless, one becomes attached to sounds, and as a result, delusion arises. Therefore, by allowing the sounds that contacted the ear to flow off, and thereby being detached from the object sound, Kuan-yin was able to eliminate the delusion that has its origin in sound.

The statement, "*Allowed the sounds that were contacting the ear to flow off, and thus audio-objects subsided and were lost*" has two aspects that require study. First, we should examine "allowed the sounds that contacted the ear to flow off". This refers to 'contact' (*phassa*), a technical term which we saw as the sixth link of the *paṭiccasamuppāda* and denotes the contact between a sense organ and its object in the external environment. The '*phassa*' we are considering here is that of the ear, and the contact in this case is the arising of the sensation of sound.

The meaning of "flow off" is not grasping, not abiding, but letting go. This means, that one does not linger on the sensation but rather allows the stream of consciousness to continue freely even after contact is made with the subject.

To be precise, 'allowing to flow' means that one does not cling to every single sound heard by the ear in contact with the external world. One should allow each sound to pass away, like the water flowing in a stream. This is precisely the very advice that the Buddha gave Bāhiya[4].

It is easy enough to say 'allowing to flow', but quite a feat to accomplish, for it entails our 'swimming against the current'. Our difficulty lies in the fact that we have an established habit whereby we catch hold of single sounds, string them together to form words and sentences, and then impart meanings to them. It is from this process that deluded attachments, turbulent emotions and sufferings arise.

At this point one might object to all this with the suggestion that it is just not possible for us to allow sounds to flow off without abiding. For, it seems that the consciousness is attuned in such a way as to make one string sounds together involuntarily. On reflection however, this is not entirely true. For, if one considers carefully what happens when one is in deep one-pointed meditation, one would find that allowing sounds to flow is not at all impossible. Leaving aside *vipassanā* meditation, even in normal circumstances people are in the habit of 'filtering off' external sounds. Take for example the case of a person walking in intense discussion with a companion in a

---

4. *Bāhiya sutta*. See Wheel 455-457.

park. They will not hear the sounds of passing vehicles, children calling to one another, the barking of dogs or the sound of the ice-cream van's music as it moves along. It should therefore be realized that cultivating the practice of 'allowing-to-flow method' can lead to some profound realizations.

To proceed with Kuan-yin's account, consideration should next be given to the word 'lost' in the phrase *"the audio-object subsided and was lost"*. This refers to the elimination of any consciousness relating to the object. Therefore, becoming detached from the object is to become detached from the object of hearing and all other objects that arise in connection with the object of hearing.

This was the method employed by Kuan-yin during the first stage of his cultivation of realization. By not allowing sounds, which enter through the ear to abide in the audio-consciousness, one becomes detached from the object of hearing. Therefore audio-objects subside and get lost.

Kuan-yin continued: *"Then, since ear-contact and audio-objects produced no effect, the mind remained in a state of clarity, and the phenomena of motion and stillness no longer occurred"*.

These words indicate that through ceaseless training in allowing the sounds to flow off and letting the objects disappear, one gradually attains to a state in which the innate nature to hear becomes free from the object of hearing and the contact of the ear with the external world. At this point, the nature to hear becomes thoroughly quiet and clear, and the mind is thus not torpid, but remains lucid. When this occurs, one feels neither the sensation of motion, for sound is the result of motion or vibrations, nor does one feel the sensation of stillness, for stillness is perceived in relation to motion. At this stage, *samādhi* or *jhāna* has been attained. This stage may therefore be called *the initial stage of meditative absorption.* For, deluded attachment to sound and to hearing have both been removed. In practical terms it means that at this stage we will enjoy the happiness and freedom arising there-from. And at this point the Buddha's teaching to "stop clinging to objects" is achieved. Readers would have observed the similarity with the Theravāda *jhānic* experiences as were described in the discussion of the *Ānāpānasati sutta* in the previous chapter.

The next step is to contemplate reality with a one-pointed mind. Kuan-yin now made great efforts and pushed on in his practice, deepening his *samādhi* day by day. Thus he said, "*Meditative absorption gradually deepened ...*" Many advanced *vipassanā* meditators would, no doubt, have already attained to the level of realization here described.

Kuan-yin continued: "*... ultimately the distinction between audio-consciousness and the objects of audio-consciousness was no longer in existence.*" Kuan-yin, in meditative absorption, continued to investigate the difference between the concept of the "I", who is hearing and the object of hearing, because at the stage he had attained so far, both audio-consciousness and the nature to hear were still present. In this case, the word 'audio-consciousness' is used to mean the "I" who is hearing or (having) the nature to hear. The object is the object of the audio-consciousness. In the final analysis, he realized, that there is no difference between the two. Therefore, both (the individual engaged in) hearing and his object ceased completely. In other words, they merged into one. At this time, because the concept of hearing and the nature to hear were no longer present, his mind was filled with freedom and pure happiness. All suffering had been eradicated.

Nonetheless, Kuan-yin did not stop meditating, but continued his one-pointed contemplation and found that "*all awareness and the object of awareness became empty. Then the awareness of emptiness expanded without boundary*". This is a higher level of meditative absorption wherein there is nothing but awareness left. But who is it that is aware? It is the 'I'. Thus as long as there is awareness, there remains the 'I'.

Kuan-yin proceeded to investigate further to find the difference between the 'I' who is aware and the object of awareness. In the end he found that there was no difference between the two, because they were both empty (of self), intangibly empty. This is why he said, "*awareness of this state and this state itself were realized as empty.*"

In this state of meditative absorption he no longer felt the presence of his physical body, and he was liberated from the pains of birth and death. The sensation of emptiness was so pervasive that it was felt to reach the outermost boundaries of the three realms and into the infinite past and the future. It was everywhere, and it had no temporal or spatial limits. Therefore, Kuan-yin described the stage he had reached as being without boundary. Still, this was not the stage of perfection he sought, so he cultivated his realization further.

"Then emptiness and that which is empty became extinct." This level of meditative absorption was higher than the previous one, but even at this stage there remained a sensation of emptiness. Who was it that felt the sensation of emptiness when emptiness was attained? Although he had lost the sensation of a physical 'I', there was still a vague sensation of an 'I' present in his consciousness. In other words, there were still the remnants of deluded attachment left. This stage could easily be mistaken for the highest degree to which realization could be cultivated, but there was still one more important step to be taken. Therefore, instead of stopping here, he took a further step and doubled his efforts in order to investigate the difference between the 'I' who was empty and the emptiness itself, which was its object. At last he came to realize that there was no difference between the two, but that even the sensation of emptiness was non-existent. Therefore, Kuan-yin said, that emptiness and its object were both eliminated.

Now, everything that was subject to arising and subsiding, everything that might appear and then cease, such as thoughts, sensations, mental reflections, hearing, awareness, emptiness and ego, had completely ceased. Not an iota of deluded attachment remained. All the sufferings of existence had come to an end. Darkness was dispelled and nothing was left, *the state of Nibbāna had been realized.*

Advanced *vipassanā* meditators would have realized by now that Kuan-yin was a person who had independently meditated his way to Enlightenment without the aid of a supremely enlightened Buddha. His *pāramitās* had ripened by this time and self-enlightenment had become possible. Readers would also have realized that the meditation techniques he adopted were in no way different from those taught and practised in the Theravāda tradition, except that the methodology is crafted in simpler language.

CHAPTER XVII

Reflections
Conditionality and the Paṭiccasamuppāda

We are presently in the midst of great fundamental and significant scientific discoveries. Most of them will no doubt contribute, when properly harnessed, to the physical well-being of humankind. But, none of these can be comparable to the greatest spiritual discovery of all time. It took place on that memorable full-moon day in the month of Vesak over two thousand five hundred years ago in Northern India in the little known village of Gayā, when the ascetic Siddhatta Gotama, now the Fully Enlightened Buddha, announced his discovery of the Truth or Dhamma.

Why then does this discovery stand out above the rest? The answer is easy. While even the most significant scientific discoveries have often had to be modified or replaced by further discoveries, the Truth (as discovered and taught by the Buddha) remains intact, *inviolable* and in its pristine glory. And so it will be forever. For, we can say with confidence that, despite over two thousand five hundred years of debate and discussion, as well as successful practice, it still remains acceptable in its original form. It has stood the test of time.

What then was this Discovery? It was simply an understanding of what came to be universally known as the 'Wheel of Life' or *paṭiccasamuppāda*. It was an explanation of what causes the human condition of distress or suffering, and what causes sentient beings to wander in *saṃsāra*. As a supplement to this discovery, the Buddha provided us with a remedy: the Noble Eightfold path which, when followed conscientiously, will lead a person to release from the round of recurring births and deaths.

It is inspirational to picture the ascetic Gotama sitting under a ficus tree in deep *samādhi* (absorption), bringing together in his mind's eye all relevant facets of information, observations, and their possible interpretations, like pieces of a jigsaw puzzle. He was assisted by what he had seen with his unclouded 'divine eye' in the first and second watches of the night, which was the manner in which sentient beings were drifting in *saṃsāra,* and how the immanent law of kamma operates within this process. Further, in tracing the rebirths of individual beings he saw that the human condition is invariably influenced by the three universal characteristics of greed, hatred (aversion) and delusion, and that it was delusion or *moha* that plays a pivotal role in this process. He also identified three more pieces of the jigsaw puzzle as impermanence (*anicca*), suffering (*dukkha*) and non-self (*anatta*).

All the pieces of the jigsaw puzzle were then in his mind, and by insight he was able to put the pieces together. He had thus discovered the Dhamma, which is the *paṭiccasamuppāda* — or the causal genesis, and with it he had become the Buddha, the Enlightened One.

When one sees the above causal theory unfolding in one's mind in the above fashion, it gives one the greatest of thrills. It is similar to the euphoria which an intrepid explorer feels when he has successfully traced a river to its origin. There would have been many errors when the explorer took many a wrong turn while following tributaries instead of the main stream, until he eventually came to the genuine fountainhead.

As 'noble worldlings' (fn.3 of Epilogue), we can see experientially that everything we have so far understood is centered around the *paṭiccasamuppāda.* We can now appreciate the fact that what we, as dedicated meditators, had done all this time, was to engage in a serious and systematic study of the Dhamma, followed by the intensive practice of *vipassanā* meditation with mindfulness and awareness of the underlying impermanence of all conditioned formations and phenomena. This has led us very close to true realization of the Truth, and with the latter, our entry into the Ariya clan is assured.

The Wheel of Life as depicted in the above figure, is an attempt to present vividly a person's world experience. In Tibetian monasteries in particular, it is often conspicuously painted in various vestibules or on hanging scrolls for meditation, showing graphically how the individual is bound to *saṃsāra*, the endless turning of the wheel of life.

The perimeter of the wheel is ringed with the twelve pre-conditions. In the nave are three animals: the cock, symbolizing desire, the snake, hatred and the pig, delusion. They are the propelling forces of the cycle of existence, in which kammic retribution determines or conditions where each individual will be re-born, as shown on the wheel.

There are the five rebirth realms or destinies within the wheel. Entry into the three lower destinies, which are purgatory or hells, the realms of hungry ghosts and the realm of animals, results from negative acts; the two upper realms are considered fortunate destinies rewarding positive kammic acts. Of these latter two, the human destiny is considered the lower, but the most important, since only there can virtue and wisdom be increased. The others are the celestial realms the birth wherein is a reward for choices and actions taken in the human realm. Even when someone attains Nibbāna while sojourning in a celestial realm, it is due to the ripening of merit earned as a human being. The rest of the *devas*[5] would be those not spiritually inclined, and they will be forced to leave the celestial realms when the energy from their positive acts has run out. Their loss of pleasure is painful. Some would be reborn in the human realm, but others, lacking sufficient merit and having unexpended negative energies, may be reborn even in lower realms than the human.

What is striking about the Wheel of Life is the central place human volition holds in it. No one but the individual is the author of his rebirth in a lower or higher realm, and no one else can bring about the individual's ultimate salvation. The human being stands with the assurance that whatever destiny is suffered or enjoyed is a case of obtaining one's just deserts.

The importance of comprehending with insight the *paṭiccasamuppāda* needs emphasis, for it is undoubtedly with this insight that one is able to develop meditative wisdom or *bhāvanāmaya paññā*.

Thus Bāhiya, the experienced and dedicated meditator, could not attain liberation in spite of all his efforts. It was when he met the Buddha that conditions became right and favoured his absorbing and comprehending the *paṭiccasamuppāda* by just a few words from the Buddha. This led Bāhiya to *vipassanā* meditation, which made him instantly realize with insight that

---

5. *Devas* : Celestial beings.

craving and clinging were caused by ignorance or confusion (*moha*) of the fact that the five aggregates were bereft of a self. [6]

When we are contemplating and reflecting on the doctrine of the *paṭiccasamuppāda*, there will come the day when we shall see with insight the operation of this *dhamma* in all our activities. Eventually we will really see that all our thoughts have birth followed in a millisecond by the death of such thoughts. This process takes place every second, every millisecond, whenever a thought occurs. It is a continuous process subject to conditions. This is how we are permanent! Then it will suddenly dawn on us with insight that the *paṭiccasamuppāda* is in operation all the time.

We therefore need not despair as there is hope for all of us. When our *pāramitās* become fully developed and we have followed the Noble Eightfold Path and seen with insight the continuous operation of the *paṭiccasamuppāda,* we are ready when conditions are ripe to achieve its realization. It will come naturally, suddenly and unawares. On the other hand, simply striving and focusing on final attainment without developing one's experiential wisdom is not the way to achieve liberation.

Perseverance

During our journey of discovery we have read in the suttas about numerous instances of lay-persons as well as members of the Sangha achieving what appeared to be the 'instant' entry into the Ariya clan. This could be quite misleading and could make the unwary believe that they had simply to apply themselves in a dedicated fashion to *vipassanā* meditation for a mere few months or years before they automatically attain sainthood.

It is useful to remember that *bhāvanāmaya paññā* or wisdom by insight through *vipassanā* meditation can take a very long period of time for its achievement. We can recollect that even the original band of five ascetics had to re-learn under the Buddha's guidance before they could attain Arahatship[7]. In this regard, there is an interesting section in the *Ānāpānasati sutta,* which reads as follows:

---

6. *Bāhiya sutta*: See Wheel 455-457.
7. See Wheel 455-457.

> *"Now on that occasion elder bhikkhus had been teaching and instructing new bhikkhus; some elder bhikkhus had been teaching and instructing ten new bhikkhus, some elder bhikkhus had been teaching and instructing twenty . . . thirty . . . forty new bhikkhus. And the new bhikkhus, taught and instructed by the elder bhikkhus, had achieved successive stages of higher distinction."*

The above passage clearly indicates that 'instant Nibbāna' is just a dream. Dedicated *vipassanā* practice, patience, persistence, and still more practice are necessary if we are to achieve transcendence.

THE ARIYAN PATH

It is very satisfying when one has 'travelled' according to one's best ability in the realm of the Tripiṭaka[8] and discovered therein several 'gems of purest ray serene'.[9] Erudite Buddhist writers have often quoted from these. One such quotation is the reference to what are called the ten fetters or shackles that bind persons to *saṃsāra*. However, we have often wondered whether these fetters were in fact stated and discussed by the Buddha himself, or by someone else at a much later date. When we discover that it was in fact the Buddha himself who had provided these details, it gives us a feeling of satisfaction and happiness. This is what he has said in the *Ānāpānasati sutta* (MN. 118):

> *" . . . In this Saṅgha of bhikkhus there are bhikkhus who are arahats with taints destroyed, who have lived the holy life, done what had to be done, laid down the burden, reached the true goal, destroyed the fetters of being, and are completely liberated through final knowledge — such bhikkhus are there in this Saṅgha of bhikkhus."*

This is the stage where all the fetters (*saṃyojana*) are destroyed so that they will not arise anymore. It is the state of Arahathood.

---

8. I have quoted from Keats' "On first looking into Chapman's Homer" : *"Much have I travelled in the realms of gold..."* (1795-1821)
9. I have quoted from the line: *"full many a gem of purest ray serene. . ."* in Thomas Gray's "Elegy written in a country churchyard", (1716-1771.)

"In this Saṅgha of bhikkhus there are bhikkhus who, with the destruction of the five lower fetters, are due to reappear spontaneously (in the Pure Abodes) and there attain final Nibbāna, without ever returning from that world — such bhikkhus are there in this Saṅgha of bhikkhus."

This is the stage of sainthood called *Anāgamī or non-returner,* where lust and hate no longer arise in one's mind. The five lower fetters have been destroyed but there is still more work to be done.

"In this Saṅgha of bhikkhus there are bhikkhus who, with the destruction of three fetters and with the attenuation of lust, hate and delusion (confusion), are once-returners, returning once to this world to make an end of suffering — such bhikkhus are there in this Saṅgha."

This is the stage of sainthood called Sakadāgamī or non-returner. These are the worthy ones who have given up the belief in a permanent self, belief that rituals alone could lead a person to enlightenment and have abandoned all doubts regarding the efficacy of the Noble Path. They have, in addition, weakened tremendously lust and hatred as well as the other fetters.

"In this Saṅgha of bhikkhus there are bhikkhus who, with the destruction of the three fetters, are stream-enterers, no longer subject to perdition, bound (for deliverance), headed for enlightenment . . ."

The *Ariya* who has attained to this stage of enlightenment is called a *Sotāpanna* or stream-enterer or stream-winner. Such a person has given up the three lower fetters of belief in a permanent non-changing self or soul, doubts regarding the Dhamma and the dependence on chantings, rituals and rites— *sakkāyadiṭṭhi, vicikicchā* and *sīlabbataparāmāsa* respectively— would lead him to transcendence. He is never going to be born in a lower existence again. His lowest rebirth will be as a human being, and the maximum number of lives that he will experience before attaining Nibbāna is seven.

The Buddha's Discovery

I had much difficulty in my formative years to accept what was written in religious books as well as what was preached by

Theravāda monks to the effect that what the Buddha originally discovered leading him to Buddha-hood was the insight knowledge and realization of the Four Noble Truths. It bothered me because such preachings and texts did not create any excitement or thrills, nor did they immediately inspire me. True enough, the Four Noble Truths are the fundamental and original *teachings* of the Buddha. But were they his very first *discoveries* that led him to enlightenment?

It was only when I had searched in the voluminous *Sutta Piṭaka* that I came across *suttas*, which unequivocably stated that the Buddha's original discovery in the third watch of that fateful glorious full-moon night of Vesak was none other than the theory of the conditioned genesis or *paṭiccasamuppāda*.

It is then no surprise that it gave me a thrill when I made this 'discovery'. But then, I am not the only person who had found this. For, I have recently had the opportunity of reading the Buddhist writings of several Western scholars of this decade who too have observed the same thing. Perhaps the traditionalists should now think of re-writing this fact.

A Paean of Joy

When we continue reading the Dhammapada of the Sutta Pitaka, where there are numerous oft-quoted verses, a reader cannot but be excited when reading the verses 153 and 154 comprising the Buddha's first paean of joy (*udāna*) which he gave vent to immediately after his enlightenment:

> "Through many a birth I wandered in saṃsāra,
> seeking, but not finding, the builder of this house.
> Sorrowful is it to be born again and again:
> O house-builder! thou art seen. Thou shall build no house again.
> All thy rafters are broken. Thy ridgepole is shattered:
> Mind has attained the unconditioned: achieved is the end of cravings".

The above verses are explained by Ven. Nārada in his translations from the Dhammapada as follows: "The architect here is craving *(taṇhā)*, a self-created energy, a mental element latent in us all. The rafters are the defilements *(kilesa)*. The ridgepole is ignorance (*avijjā*), which is the root cause of all defilements. Shattering the ridgepole of ignorance by wisdom (*bhāvanāmaya paññā*) results in the complete demolition of the house. With the demolition of the house, the mind (*citta*) attains the unconditioned, which is Nibbāna."

As we contemplate the above paean with wisdom, we get the feeling that in addition to the superficial meaning, there could be a deeper message which could unravel itself with our gaining of insight. This applies to the last line of this *udānā*, where the Buddha identifies the mind (*citta*) as that component of the body-mind combination which attains to the Nibbanic unconditioned state. We are told in the Abhidhamma that *bhavaṅga-sota* and *bhavaṅga citta* are the elements of consciousness which, 'like an ever-changing stream', move from birth to birth in a person's sojourns in *saṃsāra*. Is he referring to this element of the consciousness when he says 'the mind attains the unconditioned'?

"Myself, "I", "Mine"—The Ego-consciousness

Of all the tools of reference a person may use, those of greatest importance to his ego, to himself, are the ones that enable him to establish and confirm the sense of his own identity. These are the designations "mine" "I am," and "myself". In the Buddha's teachings such ideas and all the related notions are regarded as conceptual outcroppings of the ego-consciousness. They are fabrica-tions of the mind, subjective conceivings, conceptual proliferations grounded in ignorance, craving and clinging. But the individual, unlearned and untrained as he is in the Buddha's teaching, does not even suspect their falsity. He assumes simply what exists as concrete fact. Thus he takes them to possess objectively the meanings he ascribes to them, as standing for self and its belongings. Caught up in his own deception, he then makes use of the notions as instruments of appropriation and identification. Through the designation "mine" he establishes territorial claim, through the designations "I am" and "myself" he establishes an identity upon which he builds his conceits and views, his so-called personality.

The objects of these conceptual and verbal manipulations are the five aggregates, which are his referents. The uninstructed worldling's cognitive processes, being under the dominance of ignorance, do not present things as they are in themselves. They present them in distorted forms fashioned by the defilements. Therefore, when he refers to these referents in thought and speech, his references are loaded with a charge of meaning derived from their subjective roots. He would thus say: "Material form which is mine, which I am. Feeling is mine, which I am . . . Consciousness, which is mine, which I am" — (S.xxii). Since the worldling already sees a self when he considers his experiences analytically, when he encounters the *paṭiccasamuppāda* — which describes experiences dynamically — he inevitably views it through the same distorted lens.

With this we come upon the reason why the Buddha declares the *paṭiccasamuppāda* to be so deep and difficult to understand. It is deep and difficult not simply because it describes the causal pattern governing the round of existence, but because it describes that pattern in terms of bare conditions and conditioned phenomena without reference to a self. The challenge is to see that whatever that happens in the course of existence is merely a conditioned event happening through conditions in a continuum of dependently arisen phenomena. It is, in fact, not happening to anyone. For, there is no agent behind the actions, no knower behind the knowing, nor any continuing self passing through the round. What binds the factors of experience together, at any given moment and from moment to moment, is the principle of dependent arising itself — "when there is this, that comes to be; with the arising of this, that arises"[10]. This is sufficient because *'this'* by itself is adequate and complete.

Equanimity

The quintessence of equanimity in daily life is summed up beautifully in a few lines in the poem "If":

---

10. "This, that": See, AN. X. *Mahātaṇhāsaṅkhaya sutta*, 92. " . . . *And what is the noble method that is rightly seen and rightly ferreted out by discernment (paññā)? There is the case where a noble disciple notices:*

"When this is, that is,
From the arising of this comes the arising of that:
When this isn't, that isn't,
From the cessation of this comes the cessation of that. . . ."

" . . . If you can keep your head while all about you
Are losing theirs and blaming it on you,
If you can trust yourself when all men doubt you,
But make allowance for their doubting too:

If you can talk with crowds and keep your virtue,
Or walk with kings nor lose the common touch,
If neither foes nor loving friends can hurt you, . . ."

Rudyard Kipling, 1865-1936.

The dedicated *vipassanā* meditator would have already realized the importance of equanimity at all levels of his meditation experiences. Thus, during meditation, various states of mind start competing. For instance, 'faith' (*saddhā)* in the Buddha and the Dhamma tries to overwhelm intelligence or wisdom. It is the same with effort and concentration. It is common knowledge among meditators that a balance in each of these two pairs of mental states is essential to maintain progress in the meditation practice.

Novice meditators are frequently found to be very enthusiastic and ambitious and owing to this excessive effort, the meditator's mind is likely to overshoot the object of meditation or to even slip off it. It is day-to-day equanimity when cultivated that comes to one's rescue and helps one to slow down and thereafter to slip into a steady productive rhythm.

A meditator could consider that he is endowed with the necessary state of equanimity when he is able to balance the two pairs of factors faith and wisdom, and energy and concentration successfully. When this happens it may seem that mindfulness is then effortless and seems to be on cruise control. The mind that is equanimous is often compared to a carriage being pulled by two horses of equal strength and stamina. When both are running driving the carriage is easy for, the driver just lets the horses do the work.

Similarly, in meditation practice, at the early stages there is no equilibrium among the mental states. Consequently the meditator is constantly careering from enthusiasm to doubt, from over-exertion to lethargy and laziness. But as the practice continues with patience and equanimity arises, mindfulness seems to go along by itself. At this stage the meditator experiences a great amount of relief and comfort.

In conclusion, the texts tell us that equanimity is the cause for the cleansing and purification of one who has deep tendencies towards desire, which is the opposite of equanimity. For, with the presence of equanimity as an enlightenment factor, one abandons both attachment and dislike of every type. This is very important, particularly when a meditator has arrived at the threshold of the supramundane state.

Reaching For The Truth

Our search for the ultimate truth has stretched the mind and enriched the spirit. We are all, each in his own way, seekers of the Truth and we each long for an answer as to why we are here and how we could finally escape from the round of *saṃsāra*. We have come a long way, thanks to the Dhamma and our own advanced *vipassanā* practice leading to experiential wisdom. Continued application, fortified with patience and the firm belief in the *Dhamma* will undoubtedly serve as catalyst for us hopefully to be able to soon join the ranks of the Noble Ones, the *Ariyas.*

EPILOGUE

It has indeed been a pleasure to have you joined me in this voyage of discovery within the framework of our very own bodies and minds.

The contemplations and reflections entailed in writing the three volumes comprising this book and explaining the *Dhamma* as I understand and comprehend it, have helped me in my attempts to fit together the pieces of the jigsaw puzzle of life as part of my onward journey.

My life of 80 years is now slowly winding down, and it is opportune to look back, reflect and then assess what has been achieved, and what else needs to be done in the little time left.

It is only now that many of the happenings in my daily life through these many years take on any significance. They seem to fall into a pattern. This brings to my mind the proverbial story of the blind men and the elephant.

Once there was a king who, wishing to amuse himself, ordered the royal elephant to be brought before him. He also ordered some blind men, blind from birth, to be brought near the elephant. He then asked these blind persons to touch the elephant and give him a description of the elephant.

The man who touched the tail said that the elephant was like a broom. The one who touched its body said it was like a wall. The one who touched its ear said it was like a winnowing fan. Thus, each described the elephant differently, but each was sure that his own version was the true description of the elephant. They did not realize that each one had touched only a part of the elephant and thus had only a one-sided truth. They started arguing with one another, each sticking to his point of view. The argument ended up in quarrelling and fighting. The king and his ministers rolled with laughter as the blind men continued to quarrel and fight one another.

One also realizes that there is an ultimate meaning to whatever has so far appeared to be isolated incidents in one's life. It is only when we have an open and reflective mind that we can see that there always was a message, but we did not or were not inclined to step back and find out what it was. I already see more than a mere glimmer of light at the end of the tunnel.

Our progress, of necessity, has been often slow, sometimes fast, but nevertheless purposeful and determined and dedicated. Each and every step has in turn served as a stepping-stone to the next. This is how it should be, for it is equanimity which helps us when we are down, and 'cools' us when we become excited with insights as they happen and also when the Dhamma is first revealed.

This is the way we can progress in this present age. There is no instant 'revelation'. For, we do not have the luxury of *Ariya* teachers, unlike during the time of the Buddha. But with more and more confidence as we advance forward, there is no doubt in our minds that if we have not yet reached fruition, we have at least approached the very threshold of final liberation.

The year 1988 marked the commencement of my final spiritual journey, for this was the year that my wife and I immigrated to the U.S.A. and settled down in Davis, California where my youngest daughter and her husband were living. We also had a host of friends dating back to 1960 when we first came here for my graduate studies.

As a retired person, I now have the time to concentrate on learning and comprehending the Dhamma. Coincidentally, this was the period when I had the opportunity to practise serious *vipassanā* meditation. Here too, it was a request by some non-Buddhist friends living here to introduce to them the practice of *vipassanā* meditation that helped me in developing a suitable methodology, which could benefit both the participants and myself. Some of these meditation groups, I am happy to say, are still doing well.

In regard to my experiences, there is not much to tell. It has been an on-going practice, with the experiencing of more and more insights as we move along in our meditation, combined with deep contemplation of the *paṭiccasamuppāda* and a number of discourses like the *Bāhiya*, *Anāthapiṇḍika*, and the *Ānāpānasati* suttas. For, when reflecting in this manner, the mind would often dig out from memory passages from the suttas explaining the phenomena that I was experiencing. A clear example of this is seen in the *Madhupiṇḍika sutta* where the manner in which the components of the mind operate is expounded by the Buddha. Understanding the processes as described by the Buddha, at the experiential level with direct vision into the whole perceptual process, contributes deeply to our comprehension of the activities of the mind.

Thus, the more we contemplate the suttas and practise deep *vipassanā* meditation, the closer we get to our goal. Everything is governed by conditions. When all the *pāramitās* are fulfilled, and the conditions are ripe, transcendence is possible as in the case of Bāhiya. The Buddha saw that Bāhiya had perfected his *pāramitās* and had removed most of the fetters which bound him to *saṃsāra*, and that becoming an Arahat was within his reach, provided he was appropriately nudged. A few cryptic words of advice from the Buddha was all that was necessary for Bāhiya to achieve his objective.

We should now endeavour to live in the present moment. Whenever we even slightly digress, our *sati-sampajañña* and equanimity should help us to get back to the present moment.

Each one of us in this important journey will undoubtedly experience various insights. How we interpret them and progress depends on the individual. Readers may perhaps find some benefit from reading about some of my personal experiences. However, since these do not have any textual support, but only my personal insights and conclusions, this particular portion, (keeping in mind the comments of the Buddha as contained in the *Pāsādika sutta*[11], is written in *italics* so as to differentiate it from the rest of this presentation which is based on texts and commentaries.

"When persons achieve advanced states and experience the indescribable beauty and bliss built into these experiences, they would realize that these blissful states are completely separate from the physical and mental experiences of the day-to-day life which are governed by the six senses of eye, ear, nose, tongue, body and mental base. These latter activities are now placed 'on hold'. The persons are now on 'auto-pilot' for, their

---

11. *Pāsādika sutta.* DN. 29. para 16. . . . "But if one were to use that expression properly: 'he sees, but does not see', it would be like this: what he sees is a holy way of life which is successful and perfect, with nothing lacking and nothing superfluous, well-proclaimed in the perfection of its purity. If he were to deduct anything from it, thinking: "In this way it will be purer", he does not see it. And if he were to add anything to it, thinking : "In this way it will be more complete", then he does not see it."

respective bhavaṅga-sotas[12], have taken over, and during every moment in this transcendental state the bhavaṅga-citta is operative. It is like the auto-pilot in an airline sensing everything which is happening and making automatic adjustments to stay on a steady course, but not interfering otherwise with the flight.

"Once we comprehend the above with an open non-discriminating mind, true insight and wisdom occurs, leading us to a condition of dispassion. We then see the reality of the human condition unfolding before our very eyes. For, we realize the Truth,—that all aggregates are coreless, and momentary, phenomena, arising, momentarily, vibrating and then passing away—uppāda-ṭhiti-bhaṅga. Consequently comes the transcendental conclusion that the concept of aggregates is but the mind's imagination or perception of what is in fact the unreal, the void, and that it is possible by exercising insight wisdom to be mindful and thereby remain uninfluenced by the 'object-clinging' mind.

"We could perhaps state the above in even simpler form as follows: The 'self' or 'I', to which we are so firmly and dearly attached, is not our real 'I'. Rather, it is simply a 'construction' of the self-clinging mind which at the same time is also continuously clinging to various objects. Such objects, whether they be form, sound, smell, taste, idea, or something else, keep on changing from moment to moment. Hence the self-grasping, object-clinging mind perceiving that object also changes from moment to moment. Because it changes, it is impermanent, it is superficial, and it is not real. It is the 'slave' usurping the role of the real master and then proceeding to 'mimic' the master.

---

12. The *Abhidhamma Piṭaka* discusses the continuing mind or consciousness called the *'bhavaṅga-sota'* and *'bhavaṅga-citta'* . They are described as the stream of ever-changing consciousness which moves from one life to another in every existence in *saṃsāra*. The role of the *'cittas'* is best explained in the *Abhidhamma Piṭaka* in the following statement "... It also reveals the fact that the mind itself dissolves into a stream of *cittas* flashing in and out of being, moment to moment, coming from nowhere, yet continuing in sequence without pause". These *bhavaṅga cittas* are different to the *citta* relating to the six senses, which though as impermanent as the senses themselves, and conditioned by greed, hatred, delusion and clinging, are considered by unenlightened persons as real. For a fuller description see *Comprehensive Manual of Abhidhamma*, 1999, Editor, Bhikkhu Bodhi.

"It is in this fashion that we gain insight into the bright and accomplished nature of the seventh consciousness or mind. Our mind accords with whatever we observe: if we observe birth and death, there is birth and death. If on the other hand we observe no-birth and no-death, there is non-birth and non-death. All things are produced in the mind, which fact can be realized by contemplation and insight.

'Manopubbaṅgamā dhammā
manoseṭṭhā manomayā ...'

'Mind is the forerunner of all (good) states
Mind is chief, mind-made are they ...'
said the Buddha. (*Dhp*1&2).

"Everyone has a mind and consequently the potential to formulate the world according to one's own intentions. Nature is the substance, mind the function. The function can never be separate from the substance, nor the substance from the function. Function and substance, though separate, are causally linked. Although both retain their individual characteristics, they are inseparables. Dhamma practice can start right at this point. For, one needs to understand one's mind, see one's true nature and follow it to fruition, thereby attaining enlightenment.

"The above realizations and understanding came a moment after coming out of a jhānic state. A long period of time seemed to have elapsed before I realized that there was now a break-through in my understanding of the true Dhamma, with experiential wisdom (*bhāvanāmaya-paññā*). This was an experience which I had been subconsciously looking forward to for a long, long time. I next found that I was automatically seeing the operative mechanism of the 'wheel of life' or the paṭiccasamuppāda from moment to moment in this very day-to-day life, with special focus on the ninth and tenth links, namely 'taṇhā' and 'upādāna'. I thereafter saw all of the links in both the ascending and the descending order. The day that this happened is etched in my memory, for I had effortlessly spent several hours thereafter experiencing and savouring the indescribable joy of a glimpse of luminosity and emptiness.

"Realization of the nature of the mind is the truth which we all search for. If all we know of the mind is its aspect that dissolves when we die, we will be left with no idea of what continues, no idea of the new dimension of the deeper reality of the mind. So it is vital for us to familiarize ourselves with the nature of the mind whilst we are alive. This is accomplished by deep insight comprehension immediately after we come out of samādhi. We then see that our true nature is no different from the true nature of all existence. It is like the space inside a vase. There is no difference between the space inside and the space outside. They are the same. The vase, can then be compared to our ordinary mind, delimited and encircling the space inside it. But when the vase shatters — like when our ordinary mind dies, our true nature or true mind, is now freed, released. If by now it is free of defilements, it can now become one with the unconditioned state of Nibbana. For, ". . .mind has attained the unconditioned" said the Buddha in his Paean of Joy (page 43).

"Fortunate are the persons who when they come out of the *jhānic* states realize with insight and experiential wisdom, what really occurs during and immediately after coming out of a *jhāna.* This is something over and above the indescribable joy and serenity of that experience. For, one will then realize that if a person could shut out the self-grasping and object-clinging mind, and thus not be influenced by such a mind, then all actions by thought, word and deed will not be influenced by the three disadvantageous characteristics or defilements of greed, hatred and delusion (*lobha, dosa* and *moha*).

"With this realization, they should in future, attempt to emulate, in daily life, what they had realized immediately after coming out of the *jhānic* experience, which is not to react (*saṅkhāra)* but instead to act with equanimity (*saṅkhār'upekkhā*) in all the day-to-day activities. The knowledge resulting from the decision to cultivate this latter practice is called the development of *saṅkhārupekkhā-ñāṇa* or the 'equanimity-knowledge of formations'.

The experienced meditators would now realize that this is perhaps the manner in which the Arahats would have conducted themselves for the remainder of their earthly lives. The Arahats would have been living, facing every situation in daily life with *saṅkhārupekkhā-ñāṇa,* instead of reacting to each and every situation. They have permanently forsaken dependence on the object-clinging mind, thereby allowing the activities of the four aggregates comprising this impermanent mind to simply to flow without influencing their mundane activities. They would do so until the end of this mundane life.

In effect they would, in their day-to-day activities, have stopped at sensations or feelings in the following process:

Worldling: Consciousness → perception → sensation → reaction
Viññāṇa → saññā → vedanā → saṅkhāra

The 'noble worldling's, 'learners' and the Arhats:[13]
Consciousness → perception → sensation → wisdom → equanimity → *Viññāṇa → saññā → vedanā → paññā → saṅkkhār'upekkhā*

"If 'noble worldings' and 'learners' were to once again bring to mind the *Bāhiya sutta,* they would realize that there was an even still deeper meaning in the Buddha's advice. It will be recollected that Bāhiya saw with insight that seeing, hearing and so on were influenced by the 'object-clinging' mind, and that he should not allow the negative factors of *loba-dosa-moha* to have anything to do with himself. Bāhiya, then entering into deep *samādhi* (*jhāna*), would have noted that all the six of his day-to-day operative senses were now automatically placed 'on hold', and that the *bhavaṅga-sota* and *bhavaṅga-citta* have taken over as the 'auto-pilot'. This was blissful. When he now came out of *samādhi* he would have immediately seen the innermost truths and become enlightened."

The experiences of Kuan-yin, (see previous chapter) would not have been very different from the over-all experiences of Bāhiya. For, Kuan-yin's practice was to listen to, and be mindful of one's own nature and by means of listening attain to the supramundane state. Listening to a person's own nature has no boundaries and it can accommodate all sentient beings. As 'worldlings' we only react or become concerned about what we construe as external or outside sound. Negligent of our *bhavaṅga-sota,* we hardly ever try to listen to it.

During his practice of contemplation Kuan-yin attained the Truth, for, by means of his minutely subtle *vipassanā* practice he

---

13. In the *Mūlapariyāya sutta,* (*Mn.*1.) the Buddha has shown that human-kind could be divided into four spiritual classes. They are the ordinary worldling, the noble worldling, the learner and the non-learner. For a fuller description see pages 94-95 of vol. 2 of this presentation (Wheel Nos. 455-457).

penetrated the five aggregates (*khandha*), perceiving them as empty or void of a 'self'. As, "he perceived that all the five *khandhas* (aggregates) are empty", we can conclude that Kuan-yin had realized by insight that the *bhavaṅga-sota* was the real self; that it depended on the body temporarily, and the body as such, was not different from a house. As a house, once completed gradually deteriorates, the body also has birth and death and the period in between. On the other hand, the *bhavaṅga-sota,* enduring though changing all the time and dependent on conditions, has neither birth nor death whilst one is travelling in *saṃsāra.* With this under-standing clinging is automatically eliminated.

I now appreciate that the concept of self at the mundane level was the biggest hindrance to mere 'worldlings' like me achieving transcendence leading to enlightenment. To put it in another way, one cannot achieve enlightenment without first achieving the realization that the concept of self is an illusory and an invalid concept, as also a dangerous one. For, with the concept of an *atta* or self, the concept of 'this is mine' is also established and thus attachments of both self and 'that which is mine' become firmly entrenched in one's mind. In this way one can never achieve harmony and cannot attain enlightenment and realease from *saṃsāra*—the recurring cycle of birth and death.

It is now clear that the unenlightened human mind is basically a linear operator, it is finite and exclusive, and as it always thinks in terms of subject and object it is dualistic. On the other hand, the enlightened mind is all-inclusive, completely spontaneous, non-discriminating, and all-encompassing and non-dualistic. The scope of the ordinary human mind is similar to the view one gets by peering through a pair of binoculars focused only directly ahead; one is unable to see the whole horizon. Similarly, one cannot reach enlightenment by the intellect alone. Therefore, what is learnt at the intellectual level needs to be comprehended at the experiential level of *vipassanā* meditation. Only then do we comprehend personally the state of the void or emptiness wherein there is not even a shadow or pre-supposition of an ego or a non-ego.

One then realizes that there are in fact two 'I's in the consciousness, somewhat like the mythical two-faced Roman god Janus or simply put, the two sides of a coin. One side is the 'I'-consciousness containing the *bhavaṅga-citta* or *bhavaṅga-sota,* and on the other side is the 'I'- consciousness of the object-cum-self-clinging 'I', which we usually mistake for the former, because of the defilements of greed, hatred and delusion. If these defilements can be totally eradicated, then the stream of consciousnes that will be left is the undefiled *bhavaṅga-sota.*

It is therefore only deep and sustained *vipassanā* meditation which can help us to shed our attachment to this superficial body and mind (*nāma-rūpa*) and arrive at final liberation.

Readers would now appreciate the fact that the Buddha has used expedient means to deliver his message. He did no spoon-feeding but showed the way. It was and is left to the discerning individual to see the inner truths by understanding the *paṭiccasamuppāda* and following the Noble Eightfold Path. In respect of his Dhamma he has said that 'it has to be realized individually by the wise', meaning 'with experiential wisdom or personal realization'. Let us now follow this Dhamma practice with joy, confidence and determination to its final fruition.

It took me a considerable length of time and striving to reach the water-shed between ignorance and experiential wisdom. I now know that although I am perhaps not yet on the Path, I am close to the ultimate break-through, and firmly believe that when conditions are right, the fetters destroyed and the *pāramitās* matured, the attaining of the objective will eventually occur.

This means that mortals like me need to be patient, persistent, dedicated and willing to cultivate an open non-discriminating mind if we are to succeed, for:

> "A little learning is a dangerous thing:
> Drink deep or taste not the Pierian spring,
> Their shallow draughts intoxicate the brain,
> And drinking largely sobers us again."

Alexander Pope, 1688-1744.

May my humble experiences in *vipassanā* meditation help you in your effort at comprehending the supramundane meaning of the *paṭiccasamuppāda,* the path and the message of the Buddha, leading you to the saving knowledge as taught by the Buddha.

May all beings be happy and well

Appendix

1. The Seven Factors of Enlightenment — the *Bojjhaṅgas*

These are :
Mindfulness (*sati-sambojjhaṅga*),
Investigation of the Law (*dhammavicaya*)
Energy (*viriya*)
Rapture (*pīti*)
Tranquillity (*passaddhi*)
Concentration (*samādhi*) and
Equanimity (*upekkhā*)

Comments: The above qualities of the mind are actually the factors which can help to bring about enlightenment. When they are present and alive in one's mind, in that very moment, enlightenment gets facilitated and may be said to be drawing nearer. Furthermore, these seven factors belong to what is known as the 'noble path and fruition consciousness'. In Buddhism, we speak of "consciousness" when we mean specific, momentary types of consciousness, in effect, particular mental events with recognizable characteristics. Path and fruition consciou-snesses are the interconnected mental events that constitute the experience of enlightenment. They are what is occurring when the mind shifts its attention from the conditioned realm to the unconditioned reality which is Nibbāna. The result of such a paradigm shift is that certain defilements are uprooted, so that the mind is never the same again.

While working to create conditions for path and fruition consciousness, a serious mediator who understands the factors of enlightenment can use them to balance his meditation practice. Thus, the enlightenment factors of *joy and investigation* uplift the mind when it becomes depressed, while the factors of *tranquillity, concentration and equanimity* calm the mind when it is hyperactive.

Many a time a dedicated meditator may feel depressed and discouraged for failure in achieving mindfulness, thinking that his practice is not progressing satisfactorily. Mindfulness may not be able to pick up objects as it was in the past. At such a time it is essential for a meditator to pull out of this state and brighten the mind. He should go in search of encouragement and inspiration, perhaps to a good Dhamma book or a stimulating Dhamma discussion, which can stimulate and inspire him.

Once such a book or stimulating discussion has brought about *rapture and energy*, the meditator should use the opportunity to commence focusing the mind very clearly on the objects of observation so that the objects appear very clear to the mind's eye.

At other times, meditators may have an unusual experience, or for some other reason may find themselves flooded with exhilaration, rapture and joy. The mind may then become hyperactive and over-enthusiastic. It is then necessary to restore equilibrium by developing the three enlightenment factors of *tranquillity, concentration* and *equanimity*.

A good way to start is by realizing that one's energy is excessive and then to reflect: "There is no point in hurrying. The Dhamma will unfold by itself. I should really sit back and watch with gentle awareness". This stimulates the factor of tranquillity. Then, once the energy is cooled, one can begin to apply concentration once again. The practical method of doing this is to narrow down the meditation from attempting to focus on many objects to focus fully on a few. The mind will soon renew its normal, slower pace. If one could keep one's mind in balance, soothing excitement and lightening up depression, one can be sure that wisdom will shortly unfold on its own.

These *bojjhaṅgas* or factors of enlightenment are described in three suttas, one of which is the *Mahā Kassapathera Bojjhaṅga sutta (Samy. vol.2),* which is reproduced below:

Thus have I heard:

On one occasion the Blessed One was living near Rājagaha, in the Bamboo Grove, in the Squirrels' feeding-ground. At that time Venerable Mahā Kassapa, who was living in the Pipphali Cave, was afflicted with a disease and was suffering therefrom, and was gravely ill.

Then the Blessed One, arising from his solitude at eventide visited Venarable Maha Kassapa and sat down on a seat made ready (for him). Thus seated the Blessed One spoke to Venerable Kassapa:

'Well Kassapa, how is it with you? Are you bearing up, are you enduring (your suffering)? Do your pains decrease or increase? Are there signs of your pains decreasing or increasing?'

'No, Ven. Sir, I am not bearing up, I am not enduring: the pain is very great. There is a sign not of pains decreasing but of their increasing.'

'Kassapa, these Seven Factors of Enlightenment are well expounded by me and are cultivated and fully developed by me. They conduce to perfect understanding, to full realization and to Nibbāna. What are the seven?'

i. 'Mindfulness, the factor of enlightenment, Kassapa, is well expounded by me, and is cultivated and fully developed by me. It is conducive to perfect understanding, to full realization and to Nibbāna.
ii. 'Investigation of the Dhamma, the factor of enlightenment, Kassapa, is, ... to Nibbāna.
iii. 'Persevering effort, the factor of enlightenment, Kassapa, is ... to Nibbāna.
iv. 'Rapture, the factor of enlightenment, Kassapa, is ... Nibbāna
v. 'Calm, the factor of enlightenment, Kasspa, is ... Nibbāna
vi. 'Concentration, the factor of enlightenment, Kassapa, is ... Nibbāna
vii. 'Concentration, the factor of enlightenment, Kassapa, is ... Nibbāna
vii. 'Equanimity, the factor of enlightenment, Kassapa, is ... Nibbāna.

'These seven Factors of Enlightenment, Kassapa, are well expounded by me and are cultivated and fully developed by me. They conduce to perfect understanding, to full realization and to Nibbāna.'

'Most assuredly, O Blessed One, they are Factors of Enlightenment. Most assuredly, O Welcome Being (Sugata), they are Factors of Enlightenment.'

'Thus said the Buddha, and Venerable Mahā Kassapa glad at heart approved the utterances of the Buddha. Thereupon Venerable Kassapa recovered from that affliction, and that affliction of Venerable Kassapa was no more: it had disappeared. (fn. 1). *Samy.*vol 2.

2. Some quotations from the suttas relating to the Jhānic experience:

From the *Poṭṭhapāda sutta*. DN 9.

" . . . Having reached the first *jhāna*, he remains in it. And whatever sensations of lust that he previously had would disappear. At that time there is present a true but subtle perception of delight and happiness, born of detachment, and he becomes one who is conscious of this delight and happiness. In this way some perceptions arise through training, and some pass away through training . . .

"Again, a monk, with the subsiding of thinking and pondering, by gaining inner tranquillity and unity of mind, reaches and remains in the second *jhāna*, which is free from thinking and pondering, born of concentration, filled with delight and happiness born of detachment vanishes. At that time there arises a true but subtle perception of delight and happiness born of concentration, and he becomes one who is conscious of delight and happiness . . .

"Again, after the fading away of delight he dwells in equanimity, mindful and clearly aware, and he experiences in his body that pleasant feeling of which the Noble Ones say: "Happy dwells the man of equanimity and mindfulness", and he remains in the third *jhāna*. His former true and subtle sense of delight and happiness born of concentration vanishes, and there arises at that time a true but subtle sense of equanimity and happiness, and he becomes one who is conscious of this true but subtle sense of equanimity and happiness. In this way some perceptions arise through training, and some pass away through training.

"Again, with the abandonment of pleasure and pain, and with the disappearance of previous joy and grief, he reaches and remains in the fourth *jhāna*, a state beyond pleasure and pain, purified by equanimity and mindfulness. His former true and subtle sense of equanimity and happiness vanishes, and there arises a true but subtle sense of neither happiness nor unhappiness, and he becomes one who is conscious of this true but subtle sense of neither happiness nor unhappiness. In this way some perceptions arise through training, and some pass away through training. . . "

From the *Pāsādika sutta*, DN. 29.

" ... There are, Cunda, these four kinds of life which are entirely conducive to disenchantment, to dispassion, to cessation, to tranquillity, to realization, to enlightenment and to Nibbāna. What are they? Firstly, a monk, detached from sense-desires, detached from unwholesome mental states, enters and remains in the first *jhāna*, which is endowed with thinking and pondering, born of detachment, filled with delight and happiness. And with the subsiding of thinking and pondering, by gaining inner tranquillity and oneness of mind, he enters and remains in the second *jhāna*, which is devoid of thinking and pondering, born of concentration, filled with delight and happiness. Again, with the fading away of delight, remaining imperturbable, mindful and clearly aware, he experiences in himself that joy of which the Noble Ones say: "Happy is he who dwells with equanimity and mindfulness", and he enters and remains in the third *jhāna*. Again, having given up pleasure and pain, and with the disappearance of former gladness and sadness, he enters and remains in the fourth *jhāna*, which is beyond pleasure and pain, and purified by equanimity and mindfulness.

"These are the four kinds of life devoted to pleasure which are conducive to disenchantment, to dispassion, to cessation, to tranquillity, to realization, to enlightenment, to Nibbāna. ... "

From the Mahāsakuludāyī sutta, (MN.77).

" . . . Again, Udāyin, I have proclaimed to my disciples the way to develop the four *jhānas*. Here, quite secluded from sensual pleasures, secluded from unwholesome states, a bhikkhu enters upon and abides in the first *jhāna*, which is accompanied by applied and sustained thought, with rapture and pleasure born of seclusion. He makes the rapture and pleasure born of seclusion drench, steep, fill, and pervade his body, so that there is no part of his whole body unpervaded by the rapture and pleasure born of seclusion. ..

"Again, with the stilling of applied and sustained thought, a bhikkhu enters upon and abides in the second *jhāna*, which has self-confidence and singleness of mind without applied and sustained thought, with rapture and pleasure born of concentration. He makes the rapture and pleasure born of concentration drench, steep, fill, and pervade his body ... pleasure born of concentration. ...

"Again, with the fading away as well of rapture, a bhikkhu abides in equanimity, and mindful and fully aware, still feeling pleasure with the body, he enters upon and abides in the third *jhāna*, on account of which noble ones announce: 'He has a pleasant abiding who has equanimity and is mindful'. He makes the pleasure divested of rapture drench, steep, fill, and pervade his body, so that there is no part of his whole body unpervaded by the pleasure divested of rapture. ...

"Again, with the abandoning of pleasure and pain, and with the previous disappearance of joy and grief, a bhikkhu enters upon and abides in the fourth *jhāna*, which has neither pain-nor-displeasure and purity of mindfulness due to equanimity. He sits pervading his body with a pure bright mind, so that there is no part of his whole body not pervaded by the pure bright mind. . . . And thereby many disciples of mine abide having reached the consummation and perfection of direct knowledge. ... "

From the Laṭukikopama sutta, (DN. 66).

"Here, Udāyin, quite secluded from sensual pleasures, secluded from unwholesome states, a bhikkhu enters upon and abides in the first *jhāna* ... With the stilling of applied and sustained thought, he enters upon and abides in the second *jhāna* . . . With the fading away as well of rapture ... he enters upon and abides in the third *jhāna* ... With the abandoning of pleasure and pain ... he enters upon and abides in the fourth *jhāna*. ...

"This is called the bliss of renunciation, the bliss of seclusion, the bliss of peace, the bliss of enlightenment. I say of this kind of pleasure that it should be pursued, that it should be developed, that it should be cultivated, that it should not be feared.... "

A word of caution on the jhānas

The discerning meditator should remember that *jhānas* should always be considered only as a 'means to an end' and not as ends by themselves. For, while they are a source of 'super-blissful experiences' they do not lead to realization of the ultimate truth of the human condition.

It will be recollected that the Buddha himself, while yet an ascetic, learnt the higher *jhānas* under the tutelage of Udakka Rāmaputta and Āḷāra Kālāma, but left them because these absorptions (*jhānas*) did not lead him directly to the supreme knowledge and Nibbāna.

Letter from Māra

by

Ajahn Puṇṇadhammo

The Wheel Publication No. 461

First published 2006

Acknowledgement:

The author expresses his gratitude to the late C.S. Lewis, author of *The Screwtape Letters,* from whose work he obtained the idea for this book.

Ajahn Puṇṇadhammo

Letter from Māra

The Squadrons

Your first squadron is Sense-Desires,
Your second is called Boredom, then
Hunger and Thirst compose the third,
And Craving is the fourth in rank,
The fifth is Sloth and Accidie,
While Cowardice lines up as sixth,
Uncertainty is seventh, the eighth
Is Malice paired with Obstinacy;
Gain, Honour and Renown, besides,
And ill-won Notoriety,
Self-Praise and Denigrating Others—
These are your squadrons, Namuci;
These are the Black One's fighting squadrons;
None but the brave will conquer them
To gain bliss by the victory.

Suttanipāta III.2
Translated by Bhikkhu Ñāṇamoli
Life of the Buddha

In a faraway realm there is the most intoxicatingly beautiful pleasure park in all the vast swarm of universes. Lovely maidens and carefree youths stroll through groves of ever-flowering trees. Golden leaves swayed by gentle breezes tinkle with soft and lazy melodies. Gorgeous birds and enormous butterflies flutter through the shady groves. The ground slopes up gently and in the distance a fairy castle is visible atop a craggy peak, a marvellous structure of twisting towers and intricate parapets. Its very geometry dazzles the senses, no need to speak of the jewel-encrusted walls, the golden roofs, or the gargoyles of alabaster and jade.

In the highest tower of this dazzling construction there is a large and tastefully appointed room, an office if you will. Behind a massive desk of rarest wood and cunning joinery reclines an elegant figure in a comfortable leather chair. He is tall and handsome, impeccably dressed and groomed. His style is timeless yet fashionable, his demeanour polished and suave. A goddess of unearthly beauty sits beside him on a low stool, doing his nails. Another one sits across from him with a dictation pad on her lap.

The being behind the desk glances out the huge picture window with a smile of contentment. He watches the happy godlings at play with a paternal satisfaction. After a while he turns to the lovely goddess across from him, the heavenly secretary, and speaks: "I'll want to dictate a letter in a moment, my dear. In the meantime, would you be a sweetheart and prepare a cup of coffee while I survey the state of my empire." The manicurist gathers up her implements and exits with a smile and a wink.

As his secretary glides gracefully towards the celestial coffee-maker, the Prince of the Sense-Realms allows himself the pleasure of a lascivious glance before getting down to business. His now perfectly manicured hand rests upon a computer mouse (of unicorn ivory with a ruby button); with a few deft manoeuvres he reprograms the view in the window.

First he checks out the various heavens within his dominion, the worlds of pleasure where gods and goddesses sport in gardens and groves. Wandering about in heavenly chariots, they travel from party to party, from festival to feast. Clothed in gorgeous raiment and bedecked with garlands and jewels, they are intoxicated with their own beauty. Heavenly musicians play constantly and celestial nymphs of bewitching loveliness dance for aeons without a pause. Of course every now and again one of these beings disappears—poof!—like a Christmas tree light burning out. The others seem barely to notice; the more thoughtful may pause momentarily and blink once or twice, but they are soon diverted from any momentary melancholy.

"Ah...my children, how they do like to play! But some don't play as nicely as they might..."

Another flick of the mouse and the window displays beings in the animal realm—running and chasing, hunting and devouring, mating and giving birth. Caught in traps or dying through cold or heat, they pass briefly in and out of existence.

Again the view changes. The ghost realm appears, shadowy and dark. Beings move about moaning and wailing, misshapen beings coarse and ugly; many have bloated bellies and tiny heads, some are like living skeletons, others creep pathetically around refuse piles.

Then the hell realms come into view: realms of fire and pain; worlds of unspeakable cruelty and horror—beings impaled on red-hot iron stakes, or beings thrown into pits of fire and fished out again with hooks; beings boiled in cauldrons or skewered with knives.

The Prince's mouth curls into a faint frown of disgust. He receives his cup of steaming coffee gracefully as a swarm of writhing beings falls into a pit full of blazing coals. The secretary says with a divine pout: "That's simply awful, Māra sweetie. I don't know why you keep that place going."

A black eyebrow is raised; "My goodness! As if it were my fault! Hell isn't exactly my favourite subsidiary either. I'd much rather prefer that all these wretched beings had the good sense to live properly, but they will carry on in that evil way of theirs, so what can I do about it? Heaven or hell, it's all their own doing you know; I just, let's say, facilitate matters by helping them to see the inestimable value of a sense realm existence. Hmm, excellent coffee as usual, my dear."

"You're wicked. Do change the channel."

With a frown Māra flicks the mouse.

The goddess laughs; "Oooh...the human world! So amusing, these silly little people."

Māra frowns a little deeper and studies the flickering images: people hurrying along a subway platform; a family mindlessly watching television; a young girl selling herself in the street; soldiers burning a village.

He sips the coffee thoughtfully. "Very good. Most of this realm, too, is well and truly mine..."

On the window, now, a dusty village street, where some chickens run about and here and there a mangy dog or two. A boy walks by, leading a buffalo by a rope through its nose. Some men lounge in the shade of a mango tree, smoking.

"But there is a small annoying...leakage."

Now around a bend a line of robed figures walk silently with eyes cast down. A few old women appear and reverently place lumps of sticky rice into the monks' bowls.

"Most annoying...but fortunately the leak is a small one, and it does keep us busy trying to stop it. Can't have too many beings escaping now, can we? Where would we be if the Great Saṃsāra exhausted itself? Well, time to work. Come here and sit on my lap while I dictate a circular memo to the department heads."

Māra to his Minions

FROM:	His Supreme Excellency The Māra Namuci
TO:	All Squadron Leaders
OPERATIONS AREA:	Planet Earth, Solar System, The Human Realm
REGARDING:	Present Situation And Status Of Current Projects
DATED:	26th Century Of Current Buddha-Period

Greetings to all my hard-working minions! As you are all well aware, our overall strategy seems to be working as smoothly as usual. The vast multitude of beings who wander in our little playground, the Great Saṃsāra, are by and large oblivious of the true nature of their predicament. We must continue our unceasing efforts to maintain them in our power. It is quite true that one, shall we say, very clever fish escaped our net two and half millennia ago. I fully accept responsibility for that catastrophe. As you have all studied the history in basic training, I need not go over it in great detail; remember I tried my very best. Even my daughters dancing for him didn't move him. Even my terrible aspect, which sometimes frightens even myself, had no effect. Worse, after he had penetrated the true nature of our little game, I couldn't persuade him to keep it to himself; although I thought I almost had him convinced. Alas, what's done is done and there is a small hole in our net through which beings continue to escape. Happily, all indications are the hole grows smaller with time. It is very hard for our little fishies to imagine that their true welfare lies outside the net; all we need to do is to divert them from thoughts of the canning plant!

You, my loyal squadron leaders, are doing a fine job. Let's take this opportunity to review your departments one by one.

First Army—
The Host of Sense-Desires

You well deserve the honour of being my beloved First Host. In most cases, your work alone is enough to keep beings in line. Your Five Divisions—the Division of the Sense of Sight, the Division of the Sense of Hearing, the Division of the Sense of Smell, the Division of the Sense of Taste, and the Division of the Sense of Touch—assault our victims with all the enchantments of sensory pleasure. Beings spend their lives coming to you. Your sacrificial victims come to the altar willingly, even eagerly.

But this is no reason to slacken in your efforts. There is always the danger that they will begin to see—let us be perfectly frank amongst ourselves—the shoddy nature of the goods. We know that sense pleasures are entirely unsatisfactory and illusory. In spite of all our inventiveness, we have never come up with any pleasure that is completely satisfying, lasting or substantial. Fortunately, the vast majority of humans don't realise this. The foolish little beggars all seem to imagine that only the pleasures they've had so far are like this, and that somewhere, somehow they will eventually find the magic trinket that will let them live happily ever after.

I know this sounds preposterous, but most humans don't think these things through very carefully. They like what feels good and never mind the consequences. The only trick for us is to keep them diverted and entertained. We must keep coming up with new enticements as humans tire with the old ones. Although we have a few tried and true lures, that is, sex and food primarily—even here we need to keep coming up with new variations and twists!

So far, my dear army, you've been doing a marvellous job. Take sex for example, this has been our weapon of choice for about a billion years now. For a simple biological function, it does allow for a great deal of creative possibilities. What a wonderful swindle it all is! The weird and wonderful variations they get themselves so frenzied about—all reduce to some tricky wiring and a simple bit of friction! In one sense, it isn't sex itself that keeps us in business, but all the peripheral things that go with it: all the expectations and preliminaries, all the accessories and emotional baggage. Fortunately, there's enough of this stuff to keep most of them going for a lifetime; and one lifetime at a time is all we need to concern ourselves with. They'll keep coming back for more of the same, won't they?

Lately, I must say, we have been succeeding wonderfully in this area. Technology is such an asset. As soon as they got the daguerreotype working, they were pointing it at naked women, and of course now we have colour photography, cinema and video to boot. Tantalising images are ever more easy to come by. Recently they've been distributing all this stuff on the Internet, so they don't even have to go anywhere to find it. (Perhaps I ought to get a web page—no, it would only be redundant!)

Technology itself is largely a product of sensual desire; beings create devices to make the acquisition of sensual pleasures easier, or to avoid the occurrence of sensory discomfort. This drives their whole economy and keeps them busy all of their brief lives. They want, indeed imagine they need, a car, a stereo, a computer, and then a newer car, a newer stereo, etc. We must keep them in a state of desire for all these devices—the more they work, the less time they will have for reflection.

The teachings of our Great Adversary are the only serious obstacle to this project. He has pointed out to them again and again the dangers inherent in sensual desire. However, we have, over the centuries, succeeded so well in muddling up this truth with various bogus teachings that it is becoming harder and harder for them to find the real Dhamma. There are plenty of so-called "teachers" among them who are willing to speak our line in his name. Not merely soft-pedalling the idea of renunciation, but proudly announcing that the "passions themselves are enlightenment". Of course, there are plenty of fish that like the taste of that bait!

If they do start to reflect or, worse, to practise renunciation and meditation, then we mustn't give up. They are then getting dangerously close to finding a way out of our power. Once they discover that their true happiness is not based on things/objects (in other words, our trickery), then they may escape. We must use all the resources at our disposal to distract them. Although they may be sitting quietly, their minds are still easily distracted for a long time. Fantasy is a great thing, especially as the mind can powerfully visualise and hold an object, even an unwholesome object, with a bit of concentration. The thing we must not let them do is to contemplate the real nature of the body. You would think that any being of even moderate intelligence could see the inherently foul and unstable nature of those meat-machines they drag around. After all, they have to be constantly washing and perfuming the stinking things just to bear being in each other's company! But they don't see that or they don't want to see it. We merely have to keep them looking at their bodies in a highly selective way, emphasising those largely visual characteristics identified as "beautiful." It's an easy enough trick. And don't forget to whisper all the current buzz that keeps them from doing body-meditations. You know what I mean, meditation on the unlovely is "life-denying, uptight, repressive". It's easy enough to convince them, because it's what they want to hear. Keep them imagining they can have their cake and eat it too, then we can stop worrying. Let them meditate all they want—as long as they think they don't have to let anything go, we're still in control.

Māra folds his arms behind his head and sighs, composing the next letter in his mind. The secretary, sensing a break in the work, slides off his lap and goes over to the window, the cordless mouse in her hand.

"Gee Māra, you'd sure think that the First Army would be enough." Flicking the mouse, she spies on all the gods and goddesses. She settles for a while on a scene of beautiful beings cavorting in a lotus pool as swans drift about, little barrels of intoxicating divine nectar about their delicate necks. Sometimes, when a godling reaches for a draught, the birds dart away playfully amid general splashing and hilarity. "You sure know how to throw a party!"

Māra narrows his dark eyes. "Thank you, my sweet. But even the mighty First needs some backup." He watches with a smile as she grows weary of the heavenly skinny dippers and begins flicking through the realms, faster and faster…

"Come on, back to work…"

Second Army—Boredom

To my Second Army, the Host of Boredom, I extend greetings and congratulations. Your role is to act in accord with my First Army; you are, as it were, the artillery softening up the enemy's defences for an infantry assault by sensory desire. We must keep beings in a constant state of dissatisfaction with their present reality. To be bored is primarily a state of aversion; the current input of the senses is not providing the desired kick of pleasure so that beings are irritated with what they call the dullness of their environment. They become 'bored' and seek to remedy the situation with new and exciting stimuli, which my first host is eager to provide. They become lost in sensuality and once again we have them where we want them, thus creating the basis of fresh 'becoming'.

What a scam! We keep them always craving after something exciting, something new. As a result they keep running on in the Great Saṃsāra, like one of their wretched pet hamsters on an exercise wheel. If they ever catch on and realise how long they've been at it and how there really is nothing new or fresh to be experienced…

Of course, we cannot let that happen. The trick is to keep them from paying attention to the present moment. Once they're fully present, here-and-now, then they cannot be bored. Lately we've managed to foster a social climate that positively discourages calmness and clarity. Their whole modern culture is fast and frenzied. Fashions in everything from music to clothing change rapidly and they're all eager to keep up with it. The masses prefer excitement to subtlety. The last half century or so has seen many advances in our efforts to fracture the human attention span. Television was a great help, but I think the single greatest advance in the triumph of boredom was the invention of the remote control. There are now many millions whose attention span is so pathetic that they cannot sit through a half-hour story; they cannot even be diverted that long by a single train of enticing images, let alone sit quietly by themselves!

We've succeeded so well in this department that being bored is considered one of the great evils of life. This, of course, never arose when they required all their physical energy just to survive. But now we have a generation of enervated dilettantes who cannot bear their own company—although one can scarcely blame them for that!

People create virtual hell realms of boredom for themselves. You can see them everywhere in large modern cities—riding the subways, waiting in lines, sitting in offices. The dull lethargic look on their faces, the glassy stare in their eyes indicates a mind that would rather be somewhere—anywhere—else. What pathetic creatures! If they only realised that the only place they can ever be is here-and-now!

Boredom is based on what our Great Adversary called *vibhavataṇhā*, "the craving for non-being", in the vernacular. They find their current state of existence unbearable, chiefly because of their own mental state, and they wish to blot it out. In the purest form, this leads to suicide and a consequent lower rebirth; in a milder form, it leads to the petty self-annihilation by means of drink, drugs, sleep, or mindless entertainment.

As long as we keep them trapped into these two strategies of sensuality and lethargy, they will remain in our power. Should they stray close to the true escape, which lies in the Middle[1], then we must redouble our efforts. Then you should whisper in their ears, and don't let them be still. Tell them again and again the good old lies: "This is really boring. Get out and enjoy life!"

"I'm thirsty Māra, can we take a Soma break, now?" the secretary pouts.

" 'All Beings are sustained by nutriment…' "

She pours herself a shining cup of sublime nectar from a crystal decanter. "What did you say, honey?"

"Nothing…just something I read in a book a long time ago."

"You're so intellectual," she coos, climbing back into his lap and turning the page in her memo pad.

1. The "Middle" refers to the Middle Path that the Buddha discovered and taught. It avoids the extremes of craving for sensual pleasures, the craving for non-being, and the consequent views and practices evolving out of these. Instead, it focuses on the development of the Eightfold Path that is based on the understanding of Dependent Origination and the four Noble Truths.

THIRD ARMY—HUNGER AND THIRST

My mighty and terrible Third! Greetings! Your methods may be crude compared to the refinements of my beloved First Army, but they are nonetheless effective. The cravings you engender are even more primaeval than those of sex. Sex, after all, they only imagine they cannot live without. Food and drink they really do need to sustain the body.

I will always remember that it was you, the minions of Hunger, that lured the race now called human into my clutches in the first place. Ah! How long ago was that? Two or three billion years? I remember it as if it were yesterday! The great earth was formless and void, then, and the beings at that time were glorious—self-luminous and fed on jhānic bliss. Bah! Not much we could do with them; a tedious state of affairs. So we caused the seas to develop a nutritious foam and then some of them became just a wee bit curious. Patiently and slyly we whispered in their godlike ears for many a millennium: "Mmm…tasty." One by one they dipped a fingertip and delicately licked. One by one they began absorbing the coarse physical stuff and their own forms coarsened. Gradually, imperceptibly, they took on coarser forms, and required more and grosser food.[2] Ha ha! Now we have the fools lining up for greasy burgers!

Of course, the purely physiological response of an empty belly is not our real weapon; it's the imaginary hunger—the greed for tastes, the lust for savours. They can become quite obsessed with food and the obsession can take many amusing forms: the gourmet who spends a small fortune on exotic dishes; the health-nut who makes a fetish of diet; the glutton who overloads his system with calories; and the anorexic who starves herself with a pathological vanity—all are in a state of delusion that exaggerates the importance of what is, when all is said and

---

2. Māra's discussion here is based on the cosmological myth found in the Aggañña Sutta (Dīgha Nikāya 27). This discourse describes how human beings devolved from god-like entities. The beginning of this descent occurred when the entities tasted a primeval nutritive essence floating on the surface of the sea, causing them to develop coarse physical bodies.

done, merely fuel for the organism. Very important also is the lack of fortitude in bearing with the bodily sensations. Beings are always seeking satisfaction; never let them suspect that that is precisely the one thing that is quite beyond our power to provide.

Nevertheless, the cruder forms of hunger, the real need for food, serves our purposes as well. Driven by the need to sustain their bodies, they perform actions in the world, working on farms and factories, and action is karma and karma drives sense-sphere becoming. You know this very well.

Our Great Adversary understood the dangers of the Third Army—as always in his maddeningly direct way he taught a Middle Path through this swamp. He himself tried extreme fasting, which often serves our ends quite as well as gluttony, and rejected it as a method. His rule for the monks stipulates moderation in eating and a limited form of fasting; abstaining from food for half of each day. Nevertheless, you, the Army of Hunger, are one of my chief weapons against the monks in their efforts to escape. Often we can bedevil their minds and dreams with images of delicious food. Always remember that with celibates food is their chief outlet for sensuality. With the monks of orders outside his dispensation, who do not keep the rules of Vinaya, we have often had great success in this area, creating many a jolly Friar Tuck!

The main thing to remember is to prevent them from eating mindfully. If humans keep their wits about them, and eat with awareness, contemplating the sensations and feelings aroused, then they can learn a lot. This is very dangerous for us. Fortunately, this is a difficult exercise and we all know how little humans like difficult exercises.

In surveying the state of the world today, it seems you are succeeding splendidly. Half the world is starving and the other half is obese. In both cases they are obsessed with food. Keep them that way and they will not turn their thoughts to things beyond our realm.

Māra swivels around in his chair, musing. He looks around at his well-appointed office, his beautiful secretary, his own well-groomed fingernails. How glad he is to be Māra!

Fourth Army—Craving

To my busy legions of the Fourth Army: greetings and congratulations. This army has three divisions: the Division of Sensual Desire, the Division of Being and the Division of Non-Being. Since the Fourth Army's Division of Sensual Desire duplicates the work of my beloved First Army—the Host of Sense Desires—I'm enclosing a copy of the notes I sent to them.

The secretary asks "Shouldn't we do something about that redundancy?"

"Why? This organisation is the last one in the universe that will have to consider downsizing! Now, don't interrupt me again!"

The Second Division, which promotes the craving to be, has a vital role to play. Beings exist because of your work. The technical details of this process have been aptly explained by our Adversary in his Dependent Origination, and grudgingly we must admit the accuracy and clarity of the exposition. We needn't go into the details here; those of you who are so inclined can consult the relevant literature[3]. Let us merely consider the idea from the practical angle; the beings in our power exist because they want to.

Be clear about this. They don't as a rule begin to understand what existence means; they are mostly not even fully conscious of this craving. You have done your work well and insidiously. The craving for being is usually manifested in a cruder form, a second derivative as it were—not as the simple will-to-be but the craving to be this or that thing in particular: To be loved, to be rich, to be healthy, to be the president of the United States, and so on.

Your attack should be two-pronged: as long as it is possible to do so, keep feeding the secondary manifestation in particular, the craving to be this or that. We have been doing quite well in this regard in recent times. Our possibilities were limited when society was hierarchical and stable. For the last few centuries, however, the old certainties have become less and less effective. Society is now so open as to be almost totally chaotic. Not that this so-called 'freedom' does them any real good; most of them

3. E.g., Nidāna Saṃyutta (SN 12); Nidāna Sutta (DN 15); Mahātaṇhā-saṅkhaya Sutta (MN 38).

will never be rock stars or presidents, or any of those other ridiculous things they seem to crave so much. No matter—for our purposes, it's good enough that they want it. Keep the dream alive! If things start looking too hopeless, remind them to buy a lottery ticket.

Sometimes, though, some of them do surprise us and do become something, but usually we can just up the ante. If one of them gets to be president, make sure he or she wants to be a great president. Nevertheless, in spite of our best efforts, some of them may occasionally come close to being satisfied; even in quite humble and ordinary circumstances, and this is very dangerous. In such cases, consider Plan B and bring them closer to the root craving for sheer existence.

Our principle weapon, here, has always been the Eternity View. Tell them: "You are, or can be, immortal. Your essence will continue forever." Don't let them think about death. This is easy because most of them don't want to anyway. Any version of this view will do for our purposes. It doesn't have to make too much sense; very few of them are willing to think these things through to their logical conclusions. There are a few good religions around that will serve up this soothing broth and these should be encouraged, but some of our other projects have resulted in increasing numbers of materialists and sceptics. Many of these will be better targets for the Third Division, the Forces of Craving for Non-being, but a surprising number will still buy into a version of Eternalism.

Most of the simpler-minded persons will be happy to keep artificially prolonging youth with facelifts and hair transplants, but a few will require headier medicine. The myth of the all powerful science, although quite silly really, is very seductive to these types. Many now believe that science will eventually prolong human life indefinitely. Some even get their carcasses frozen in liquid nitrogen. Remember the ancient Egyptians? I am having the boys in Research and Development do a feasibility study on starting up that game again.

Sooner or later, however, in spite of our best efforts, many of them will begin to lose the zest for existence. Life in the human realm is very often nasty, brutish and short, and wishful thinking only goes so far. That's all right if we handle it properly; that is precisely why the Forces of Craving for Non-being are needed.

On a superficial level, this can manifest as simple aversion; the craving not-to-be in debt, or the craving not-to-be married to that person next to them in bed, or the craving not-to-be whoever they are. Even more trivial forms are still useful; the craving not-to-be in the back of a long queue or not-to-be cold, etc., ad infinitum. All these mind sets produce unsatisfactoriness and this keeps them within our power.

Remember your awful final weapon! When diversion fails to beguile, then despair can enthral them. Having invested all their hopes in some pathetic illusion, when this is at last punctured, it only takes a short push from us to move them across the dangerous middle ground into hopelessness. Remember Hamlet? "To be or not to be" sums up our programme nicely; whatever you do, don't let them even suspect a third alternative.

Obviously, it's not to our advantage to have any of our subjects actually cease to be, but we need not worry, as suicides do not escape us. We can however promote the delusion that this is possible. The ideological basis for this is the Annihilation View[4]. Historically, this has been a minority philosophical position, useful only for snaring a few intellectuals, but we've had great success in the last three or four hundred years in popularising this doctrine. Some of you were sceptical when I launched "Project Descartes", but I think the results have proven my foresight. The scientists among them who work with issues related to mind and consciousness; neurologists, cognitive psychologists, and the like are absolutely blinkered by the concept that mind is an emergent property of the brain. They have no proof at all of this—how could they?—but accept it absolutely as axiomatic, so much so that they mostly seem unaware that they are assuming anything at all. This attitude is starting to percolate down to the masses.

The Annihilation View underpins many modern trends: materialism, consumerism, secularism, science, anti-clericalism, etc. Many millions believe that their bodies and minds are

---

4. The Annihilation View is one of the two principal false views. It is the idea that the living being is merely a product of matter in motion, and that consciousness is annihilated at death. Its opposite viewpoint is the Eternalist View, which holds that the living being has a permanent self-entity ("atman"; or "soul"), which, being immortal, survives the death of the body.

nothing more than meat machines. This facilitates a breakdown in morality. Given the materialist world-view, there is nothing to stop them from engaging in abortion, euthanasia, suicide (of course), or even genocide.

If they do take the final step and 'destroy' themselves, well—it's unfortunate I suppose, but it does make work for the crew downstairs.

FIFTH ARMY—SLOTH AND ACCIDIE

The secretary consults her notes: "The next army is 'sloth and accidie.' Māra, what's 'accidie?' "

"You could look it up."

She sighs, "Why bother?"

Greetings to the dull grey, heavy hordes of sloth and accidie! (Aside: 'accidie', is an old spelling of 'acedia', a pathological mental or spiritual torpor.) I hope you don't take this the wrong way, but keep up the good work!

It may seem as if your power is slipping; people have been working longer and longer hours ever since the industrial revolution, but you and I know that spiritual laziness is more prevalent than ever before. The quick fix, or instant salvation, is all they are interested in.

Nature has made our work simple. The fundamental cosmic law of entropy is our greatest ally. In the sphere of mental life, this means that the spark of consciousness is always engaged in a struggle to keep from sinking back into the darkness of unknowing. Let them but relax the effort, a simple and inviting temptation, and the level of mind will inevitably decline.

That Teacher of theirs, the one who sadly escaped my grasp, has often praised effort and diligence. This emphasis has done much to undercut the real popularity of his teachings over the centuries. I seem to recall one of his own monks who broke with the order and declared that the teaching was no good because it only worked if you followed it. We would to well the endorse the reasonableness of this view.

Every one of us engaged in the work of this organisation is aware of the great complexity of the maze we have built for our 'clients'. Layer upon layer of delusion has carefully and methodically been constructed. It is not an easy task for the worldling to cut through this timeless tangle. Not easy by any means, but regretfully still just possible. So redouble your own efforts and take the wind out of theirs! They will not cut through with a dull blade.

Let us review the techniques that have worked well in the past. Remember, the qualities we want to foster are dullness, heaviness, lethargy, idleness and mindlessness. The oldest and still very profitable method is sleep. Lots of it; in big soft, comfy beds. It's not hard to persuade them to roll over in the morning! Let them lie in bed more than six hours and they're ours!

Another wonderful tool is the whole pharmacopoeia of dulling and befuddling agents that so may of them like to pop into their mouths, lungs and veins. You almost can't beat the old perennial standard ethyl alcohol for reducing them to a sub-human level, but these days we have a much wider range of intelligence-reducing agents readily available—both natural and synthetic. Better living through chemistry! Many of them are so eager to drown their wits that they will even inhale various toxic by-products of the industrial revolution. (Now that was a great idea with all sorts of unexpected benefits!)

Speaking of technology, I cannot praise the use of television highly enough. It requires no thought or effort of any kind and completely stultifies the brain with a panorama of sensually enticing images. Some of you were sceptical when I began Project Vidiot, even citing possible undesirable educational and cultural side-effects, but now that we have whole generations weaned on the tube, we can all see that the results have more than vindicated my enthusiasm.

"That's why you make the big bucks, Māra!"

"Don't interrupt when I'm bragging. Now where was I?"

Don't neglect the simpler dodges either. Procrastination is a wonderful vice. They can diddle away several lifetimes, if properly guided. Over-eating is an effective measure; the full belly makes for a dull mind. Bad posture, soft furniture, and the lack of exercise are all to be encouraged.

Perhaps most fundamental of all is the fostering of an attitude of hopelessness. Let them think that the spiritual life is too hard for the ordinary person, the goal too far away, the effort too daunting. A sense of dull grey ennui is a miasma that chokes the spirit of contemporary humanity and keeps them in our sway. When economic times are good, they are befuddled with empty luxuries; when times are bad, they descend into the pit of despair and turn on each other with petty nastiness. Underlying all the cycles is the spirit of hollowness and futility that is our greatest contribution to the modern age.

There is a timid knock on the polished mahogany door. Silently it swings open on the oiled hinges. With his head bowed and his hands shaking a young demon scurries into the room, clutching a sheaf of papers. He holds them out to Māra and stands quaking before the desk.

With a brusque gesture, Māra snatches the papers and ruffles through them. A glint of awful fire appears in his eyes.

"You miserable worm! You call this a status report!" He flings the papers at the junior officer who, paralysed with fear, fails to catch them, letting them scatter around the floor.

"PICK THEM UP AND GET THE HELL OUT OF HERE!!!" Māra's terrible voice booms like a thunderstorm. The demon whimpers as he frantically gathers the papers and then bolts from the room.

The secretary is shocked. "Māra, you're horrible."

He calmly sips his coffee. "When I want to be, my dear, when I want to be."

SIXTH ARMY—COWARDICE

My Sixth Army, you have a special place in the task of keeping beings in a state of bondage. You weaken the beings whom you attack and render them vulnerable to my terrible aspect. I prefer to charm and delight, but will brook no opposition, so those few who fail to be seduced must be terrorised into submission!

Physical cowardice is useful in its place, but it is the spiritual and moral types who are most suitable for our purposes. Beings must be cajoled into clutching at a sense of security. This is the trick we must play. Of course, you and I know that there is no security in my realm. All beings are subject to the awful realities of birth, sickness, old-age and death. Their goods and chattels, their relations, friends and mates are all as ephemeral as chaff in the wind. No matter. The dream of security may be a hopeless one, but it is powerful. Beings everywhere are afraid to risk what they have, and can be reduced to spiritual impotence by that fear.

Encourage them often not to take risks. If they risk, they may grow; and if they grow, they may awaken. Teach them to cling to the flimsy raft of their life until it is washed over the cataract. They may be kept in this state of fear for countless cycles of birth and death. Their folk wisdom has it that a coward dies many times, and a brave man but once. Few indeed realise the deeper truth hidden in that trite proverb.

We can use this cowardice to keep them from facing the reality of existence. Even to think about it is too scary. The idea of examining it in a methodical way, as for instance in a meditation retreat, is just too much to bear. If they do come to the point of sitting down, they will need courage to finally break through the veil, and if they manage to get past the petty anxieties of their life dramas, they will encounter the real primal fears. It takes great courage to plunge into the Void and this we can undermine.

This is, after all, the golden age of cowardice. No one wants to take a chance. This manifests in a host of symptoms. As their numbers increase and the pressure on the earth's resources mounts, those who have a generous portion grow mean and afraid of those that have nothing. Their culture is one based on delightful lies of our devising, and the ugly realities are hidden away. The sick and the old are hidden from view and the dead are never seen. Insurance companies grow fat on the people's futile attempts to prevent the unpreventable.

Keep them afraid to leave the pathetic ruts of their little lives. Keep them afraid to think, to love, to give, to dare the unknown. Should they find the courage to question, it's the beginning of the end!

We can encourage them to make a virtue of their cowardice. Call it prudence. Call it responsibility. "Be sensible. Why ask for trouble? Leave well enough alone." They will get up every morning and put on their hats and take the subway to their dull grind of a job and carefully plan for their retirement. By that time, they will be so beaten down that they will slide easily and thoughtlessly the rest of the way to the grave.

What we have to watch are the ones who have a little gumption left; they may start thinking of going on a pilgrimage or, worse, to a monastery. Whisper about the dangers. "Why throw away your job in these tough economic times? Be sensible, hang in there. There are only twenty more years to your pension!"

Māra pauses in his work and strolls thoughtfully towards the picture window, his hands clasped behind his back. He watches an image of a huge city. The walls of the buildings form gigantic twisty caverns; at street level they are covered in lurid posters and glaring neon slogans. Noise and smoky fumes fill the air. Gaunt figures scurry aimlessly hither and thither through the maze, like witless ants.

"Māra, is that on earth or in one of your dreary hells?"

"It's getting harder all the time to tell the difference."

SEVENTH ARMY—UNCERTAINTY

The role of my seventh is to paralyse with doubt. You are to work closely with my Forces of Fear; with your attacks consolidated, we can keep beings in the wretched state of a deer mesmerised by oncoming headlights.

This is a generation of doubters. Whereas at one time your resources were limited and we made more use of the opposite vice, credulity, now we have whole masses of people with no sure beliefs at all. The old certainties in religion, society, politics, and even science have all had their props kicked out from underneath them. They rejoice in what they call their freedom, but then are unable to advance in any direction. If we can maintain them in this state of confusion, they will surely never escape our grip.

Doubt has been compared to wandering in the desert without a map or guide. This comparison is apt, although I am loath to admit it, considering the source. When beings have no faith, there is no basis for morality and they will fall into all manner of delicious and loathsome vices. We can see this in the present day, which in this respect is very much like late antiquity—a period I greatly enjoyed. In the Imperial Roman period, the old religion was openly scoffed at, virtue was considered a weakness, and the only object in life was the selfish pursuit of personal gratification. Indeed, a marvellous party. True, the destruction of beings was frightful, but that was a sacrifice I was willing to make.

Once again, in modern times we have convinced them to believe that a thoughtless scepticism is clever and chic. It bears repeating that the inevitable result of this is a destruction of morality. When beings don't understand that actions have results; in other words, when they disbelieve in the Law of Karma, then they will have no restraint upon their appetites (which my other departments are so admirably stirring up!). The really useful detail—from our point of view—is that their foolish disbelief has no effect at all upon the operative effectiveness of that law. (But don't let them know that!) They will proceed happily upon their debaucheries and violence, and after death they will continue in our service, albeit in a somewhat less salutary capacity.

Another result of the widespread scepticism of the age is that, should they begin to question the facts of their existence—as regrettably many of them do—they will not be able to find an effective way out or to stick with it, should they stumble upon it. In all sceptical ages we see a proliferation of sects and cults. The poor wretches seeking to find their way out of the maze will stumble from priest to guru to psychic and back again, without ever exploring any path long enough to gain real insight into their predicament. Many will abandon the whole enterprise as a hopeless fraud and lose themselves in sense pleasures, which at least offer a momentary diversion from the grim facts.

Encourage in them this cynical and dissolute frame of mind. Teach them to scoff at ancient wisdom and to place their reliance on the new and fashionable whimsies of the day. It is especially easy to undermine any teaching that puts a restraint upon their greed or lust. The doubt that keeps them lost they call rationality, but don't make the same mistake they do. A real rationality is very dangerous for our interests. A truly critical examination of the phenomena of existence is precisely the method by which a bothersome few penetrate our web of deceit. Make sure their 'critical thought' is guided by desire; don't let them ask the real questions.

If they're managed properly, they can manifest the most amusing contradictions. They will scoff at religion, but believe implicitly in the daily horoscope; they will pretend that Karma is superstition, even as they avoid stepping on cracks in the pavement. When they wish to justify an abortion, then a human organism is simply a mass of cells and electric impulses, but when they want a lottery number, they will consult a channeler and communicate with the hungry ghosts. Although they are proud of their modern rationality, most of them are quite ridiculous in their superstitions. The scientifically trained ones are often the worst of the lot; they are dogmatically attached to the materialist delusion even in the face of evidence to the contrary. (Although, I must admit, we have been having some difficulties with the physicists lately, I am beginning to suspect a leak.)

To sum up then: keep them guessing! Confuse them with a multitude of options and let them wander about life aimlessly. Call morality regimentation and restraint repression. Praise a shallow scoffing attitude as penetrating intelligence. Belittle the timeless verities and praise only the fashionable. Let them be too clever by half. By the time they begin to clear the muddle, it will be too late and we'll have them for another ride on the carousel.

As Māra pauses to review some data on his desktop monitor, there is a soft knock on the office door and another young ravishing goddess enters with a platter full of sweetmeats.

"Snack time!"

As Māra eyes her appreciatively, the secretary's eyes narrow. She snaps her fingers as the younger goddess leaves, causing her to grow a pair of donkey ears.

Māra raises an elegant eyebrow. "My dear! I'm shocked and appalled."

"I hate the bitch," she hisses.

"Mmmm. Have one of these dainties, they're literally divine!"

Eighth Army—Malice and Obstinacy

My Eighth Army is the negative image of the First. It is your duty to see to it that beings fall into the mental habits of aversion, ill will, anger, hatred and spite.

The theory is elementary in our trade, but let us review it briefly. Whenever a being makes contact with a sense object, that is at each and every conscious moment, then an associated feeling arises. This feeling may be one of pleasure or displeasure, or so subtle as to be for all practical purposes neutral. These feelings are an extremely rudimentary level of mental life and are for the most part completely natural and automatic. The simplest beings could not maintain existence without a liking for good tasting food and a disliking for harmful conditions. These basic feelings are not of our doing; we can however use them to lure beings on to the next step.

In the case of happy feelings, the job is well left to the able ministrations of the First Army. It is your job to develop mental proliferation around the unhappy feelings. If the being in question is not mindfully aware of his own mental processes (and few of them are even marginally aware), then we can turn this simple unpleasant feeling into a whole complex of aversion and resentment. The raw feeling is a momentary thing of little significance, in and of itself, but oh—what fun we can have with it!

It is of course true that, by developing these negative proliferations, beings are adding completely unnecessary suffering to whatever unavoidable physical unpleasantness they may be enduring. This is their problem, not ours. We have a job to do.

Beings engrossed in unhappiness or anger are unable to see things clearly; they cannot see their true situation and they cannot begin to work out their escape. There are many tricks we can use to encourage them in their delusions. One of the most amusing is "righteous" anger. Feed the negative mental proliferation by justifying it: "He hurt me, he robbed me, he threw me down and beat me!" This has the added twist of building up the ego image. We have made some excellent progress in this area lately, their popular psychology now praises the 'empowering' aspect of such anger. Let it remain our little secret about just who is empowered by this method.

A related syndrome is to encourage the victimised feeling. "Poor me" is a marvellous way to entrench the concept of 'me'. All types of ill will work by causing beings to understand the universe in reference to their own arbitrary ego positions. They cannot begin to see clearly so long as they operate from such an assumption.

We have a wide spectrum of emotions to work with: there is the very mild and temporary flicker of aversion towards the driver ahead of you on the highway, who is taking too long to make a turn; there is the smouldering resentment towards the inconsiderate boss at work; and there is the bitter lifelong ethnic hatred that can enflame whole nations. All of these are grist for our mill, manifestations of the same thing.

They can even be made to feel ill will towards inanimate objects, particularly objects of their own creation. Nothing is more amusing than to see humans work themselves into a frenzy of anger directed at some malfunctioning machinery. The senselessness of it hardly deters them at all!

Obstinacy is the pig-headed refusal to change. This is a tendency many of them have. Once they've invested emotional energy in a grudge, they find it hard to let go, somewhat like admitting how foolish they've been all along, and that they would never do.

Our position in this department is quite sound. As they multiply on earth, they crowd into each other more and more and get on each others' nerves. Nevertheless, we must be vigilant against the one credible antidote to ill will: the emotion of universal loving kindness. You shudder at the name, my minions, but name it I must. In the old Pali language it's called *mettā*; to the Greeks it was called *agape*. This is the one force against which we cannot stand, so stop it before it's cultivated. Discredit it as weakness. This is becoming easier, as compassion is losing its stand amongst them. It has become quite unfashionable to pity the poor, for example. Little do they know that it requires real courage of spirit to practise universal goodwill. Luckily for us, few of them possess the requisite mettle.

Should any of them begin to practise mental development, as for example by meditating, then that's the time to redouble our efforts, because here is one that might get away. I have touched upon this issue in my notes to some of the other armies, but in your speciality you have many opportunities to attack the meditator. Attack them through the body. It is inevitable that the effort to remain motionless will cause the squirmy little beggars some discomfort. It takes only a little prodding from us to turn this into aggravation or self-pity. The nuances are endless; it can take them a very long time to realise that whereas the bodily aspect of pain is inevitable, this mental self-torment is entirely superfluous. We can also encourage resentments against the teacher, the practice, the food, the weather, and numerous other external factors. They can wallow in these petty miseries for hours and hours. Don't let any of them get away!

The secretary again fiddles with the remote control and the picture window fades into a view of a darkly handsome singer wailing into a microphone as he does a loose-hipped dance. The near-hysterical roar of the crowd is plainly audible behind the plaintive song.

"Ooooh! I just love Elvis!"

Māra gets the mouse and gives it the merest flick. The famous performer is seen some years later, bloated and pasty faced he fumbles shakily in a bed-side drawer, searching amongst the unsorted rubbish for his barbiturates.

Ninth Army—Honour, Renown, and Notoriety

It is hard to understand, from a rational point of view, why humans crave fame. It seems to destroy so many of the most gifted amongst them. The pathological inflation of the ego-illusion becomes too much for the merely mortal shell, and yet crave it they do. The prudent may say that "the wise man seeks no notoriety", but their counsel is drowned by the crowd singing, "there's no thrill that'll getcha…", et cetera.

We should be clear as to the psychological basis of this syndrome. The ego-illusion is very dear to them. Nevertheless, since it is in reality a mere phantasm, it is in fact quite hard to maintain and generally requires a tremendous investment of energy. Energy that, needless to say, is not available for anything useful. If this insubstantial ego can be pumped up with external sources of energy, as the adulation of the crowd, then it can be experienced as a net-gain. Of course, it is all still illusory and very dangerous to the individual, but it is very intoxicating.

Our resources in this department have been quite limited until recently. In antiquity, fame generally meant being well known amongst the inhabitants of one's own city-state, although we could do a bit better with the occasional emperor or what-not. Now, however, the stakes are much higher. With the invention of technology to transmit images from place to place it has become possible for one individual's features to be globally recognisable.

Together with the technological possibility, there has arisen a powerful cult of celebrity. The masses seek to improve their dreary existence by living vicariously through their idols. This is a marvellous system of mutual self-destruction. The common TV addicts are able to escape having a real life of their own, instead remaining trapped in an ersatz astral plane existence.

Futile and pathetic, but well suited to our purposes. And in the not so long term they end by turning on and devouring the former objects of their worship. We win both ways.

Of course, this level of fame is necessarily restricted to the few. But we still have the older antique type of fame that can ensnare many more. This is the desire, which can be inflated to a positive obsession, to be well known and well regarded in one's own petty sphere. This is a simple way of stoking the fires of ego. As long as they are concerned about their reputations at work, amongst their friends and associates, then they are still trapped in the idea of themselves as real entities. When Joe hears that everyone saying: "Joe is the best diesel mechanic in the plant", then Joe is reassured of the reality of the concept 'Joe, the diesel mechanic'. It works just as well if everyone says, "Joe is the sloppiest excuse for a mechanic we've ever seen."

Generally, people define themselves according to the way in which others see them. This is the 'persona', the public mask. Becoming obsessed with putting on a good front they can eventually fool themselves and lose track of who they really are. As long as they are looking outward, they are not looking within, and the outward direction is our territory.

Further, Praise and Blame are yet another potent source of pleasure and pain. Let me reiterate that these are the carrot and stick by which we drive the donkeys down the garden path. It hardly seems to matter that the objects here are such ephemeral ones. The drive for recognition is a powerful source of craving and it stimulates the process of becoming quite as well as more 'substantial' rewards.

Praise and Blame are called the worldly winds. They are among our most useful tricks. The fact that they are utterly void of substance is amusing to us, but unapparent to them. Keep these winds gusting, they can blow beings round and round saṃsāra for a long, long time!

Tenth Army—Self-Praise and Denigration of Others

Māra leans back in his chair with his hands behind his head. "Sometimes I amaze myself. I mean, where would this organisation be without me? If I wasn't so modest, I'd be damned near perfect!"

"I've always thought so, Māra, and those armies of yours sure are deadly!"

"What!? Those incompetent bums! If I didn't play the nursemaid over them constantly, they'd be fouling things up all over the universe! It's so hard to get decent help these days! But never mind."

To my bold and powerful Tenth, greetings! Your task is crucial, but, fortunately for us, it is also easy. Generally, humans have a most unreasonable attitude of taking themselves so seriously. They seem unable to mentally disengage from the ego perspective. One way to reinforce this primary cognitive illusion is to foster an attitude of self-praise. Let them think of themselves as truly wonderful and righteous; fill them up with pride. This is the task of the First Division of the Tenth Army.

Self-praise fuels all the defilements. It's a masterwork of delusion; they look into the mirror with rose-coloured glasses. They become unable to see their own faults, and bristle with indignation whenever these are pointed out to them. Self-praise, of course, also fuels attachment and sensuality; after all, doesn't someone as wonderful as Me deserve a little fun? It also fires up anger, the fierce anger of the self-righteous who knows their views and opinions are correct and everyone else is an idiot. It is so amusing to watch two human egos clash.

The forces of the Tenth Army have a special role to play in those difficult cases where individuals shows signs of spiritual progress: If they begin to free themselves from the coarser snares of my other armies, we can often use their own victories against them by encouraging a spiritual pride and arrogance. Whisper in their ear about what wonderful spiritual beings they are; "Look at me, the great holy man!" This is a trap that has caught many a fish.

Don't be overly concerned about the accuracy of their grandiose opinions; they are capable of the most ludicrous self-delusion concerning their own merits. Very few of them, after all, ever develop a knack for introspection, and even fewer are truly capable of self-criticism.

However, you should be aware that there will also be a large number of them that have a very negative self-image. If handled properly, this should cause no concern. Negative or positive, a self-image is a self-image and it is the fundamental perceptual hallucination of a self-perspective that keeps them in bondage. Both the positive and the negative versions suit our purposes well. If you cannot convince them that they are wonderful, then encourage them to kick themselves for being such losers. Remember, there are three kinds of conceit: "I am better than you; I am worse than you; and I am equal to you." Any one of these is still a conceit and still reinforces duality.

In fact, there are signs that in the these times, negativity has become a common attitude. A great many humans don't like themselves very much. (Not that I can really blame them.) This is a complicated phenomenon, but it is ultimately rooted in the rise of materialism. When a human being denies the fundamental spiritual level of being, then life becomes quite hollow. Don't let them guess that this is the problem; instead, encourage them to believe that they are, as individuals, inadequate. The post-modern environment encourages this sense of self. Since the industrial revolution, humans have been seeking to create a materialist paradise with their machines, and now their own inventions are rendering them redundant by the million.

The Second Division of the Tenth Army has the job of promoting the denigration of others; this is the complement of self-praise. Many beings seek to inflate themselves by pulling others down. They don't care that this is an illogical practice; never mind that it always makes matters worse—they still do it. It is far easier to criticise someone else's defilements than to work on your own. You have many weapons and tactics: scolding, gossip, judgement, and so forth. You are a primary vehicle for the stirring up of ill will and conflict!

It has often been noted that the defects people are most ready to criticise are precisely the ones they themselves are suffer from. It is really amusing to watch, but they almost never see it for themselves when they're caught up in it. All forms of denigration of others are based on a delusion of self-righteousness.

Gossip is a popular form of this vice. Everyone loves a scandal and never mind whether it's really true or not, so long as its juicy! How righteous they feel as they cluck over someone else's peccadilloes! This is a petty vice that you can stir up wherever humans gather—at school, work, clubs, in families, etc. We have found from experience that this is a great corrupter of monasteries and other spiritual communities.

Moreover, don't forget the nastier forms of criticism. Vicious personal attacks can ruin a person's life, and even more destructive is prejudice where the hostility is based on non-personal criteria like language or skin colour. As absurd as it may sound to a rational being, humans can get so worked up over these stupidities that whole nations can be plunged into the chaos of war. War, of course, is an activity to be encouraged as it is a great devourer of all spiritual values.

Even more subtle, profound and significant than all this though, is the fundamental fact that so long as one is looking for faults outside, then one is not looking within, and that is the one thing we must never, ever let them do.

"Sign it: Māra, the Lord of Birth and Death, the Devourer of Beings, and the Spinner of the Wheel, etc. Send one copy to each of my Army Chiefs and one to my attorney."

The secretary leaves now with a giggle and a wink. Māra closes the day's business by quickly surveying his far-flung empire. He watches the screen and scans the cosmos, observing beings as they pass in and out of existence. The moral ones he watches die and reappear in heaven; the immoral drop to hell. From hell and heaven beings finish their time and reappear on earth…round and round in fruitless circles they go blasted by the winds of desire; winds fanned by Māra's efforts through the ages.

But there, on the screen—in a small bamboo hut, an old woman lies down to die. She is wearing robes and her head is shaved. With quiet dignity she stretches her frail body out on the thin woven mat, lying on her right side. Māra watches with distaste—he knows and fears what is coming but cannot look away; it is as painful and as compulsive as probing a rotten tooth with your tongue. The nun quietly and peacefully expires and the screen flickers; the automatic software searches quickly through all the realms of existence and comes back with the dreaded error message: "Being not found".

"Bah! Fortunately we don't lose many that way." Māra doesn't allow himself to speculate too long on the whereabouts of the old nun—the idea is vaguely disturbing. He continues to review the many, many more manageable cases that remain within his jurisdiction. Round and round they go; up and down the big Ferris wheel.

So Māra has been busily at work for millennia—but Māra, too, is caught in his own web. As he relaxes now with the day's tasks done, he pulls a comb from his vest pocket. The elegant demon-god combs his shiny black hair reflectively, vanity of course being one of his vices. After a few minutes, Māra casually glances at the platinum and tiger-bone comb; suddenly his eyes narrow, his breath stops, and he gets a sick feeling in the pit of his stomach—among the black hairs is a grey one...

The Four Planes of Existence in Theravada Buddhism

by

Dr. Sunthorn Na-Rangsi

The Wheel Publication No. 462

Preface

The following essay on the four planes of existence is a general introduction to Buddhist cosmology, in specific to the different realms of rebirth. Buddhist cosmology has played an important role in traditional Asian Buddhist practice and thought right since the Buddha started teaching. For example, one of the subjects of meditation the Buddha taught is the recollection of the qualities of the gods (*devatānussati*).[1] Nevertheless, Buddhist cosmology has generally been unpopular with Western Buddhists who often find it difficult to come to terms with rebirth because of their materialistic background. Since the final goal of the Buddha's teaching is the cessation of rebirth, by putting an end to the kamma that leads to it, a basic knowledge about the different planes of rebirth and the types of kamma that lead to them is important. For example, contemplating the impermanence and the suffering of the realms of rebirth makes one realise how fortunate one is to have been reborn in the human world, to have encountered the Buddhist teachings, and to be able to practise them. The practice of the Dhamma is impossible or more difficult in other realms of existence unless one is a stream-winner. It will therefore lead to more urgency in one's practise and a quicker realisation of the ultimate goal.

Dr. Sunthorn Na-Rangsi elucidates this complicated subject in a clear and accessible way and this essay is useful for both average readers and scholars alike.

In the original edition of this essay the references to Pali texts are to the Thai editions, but these are of no use to most non-Thais and therefore have been changed the refer to the Roman script editions of the Pali Text Society and their translations. While searching for the corresponding references, sometimes related references information were found and these, sometimes together with some supplementary information, have been added in the footnotes, which are now entirely the work of the editor as there were only references in the footnotes of the original text.

1. AN 6:10. Cf. Vism 7.115-128.

Dr. Sunthorn Na-Rangsi regularly refers to a work that is popular in Thailand but virtually unknown and unavailable outside of it—the *Paramatthajotikā*, a modern commentary on the Abhidhammatthasaṅgaha composed by Phra Saddhammajotika, a Burmese Abhidhamma teacher in Bangkok. The editor traced the quotations of this work in other Pali texts and put the references to these in the footnotes.

Tables describing the thirty-one different realms of existence have been included as an Appendix.

This essay was earlier published as Chapter IV (called "Rebirth and Planes of Existence") of Dr. Sunthorn Na-Rangsi's *Karma and Rebirth* (Bangkok, 1976) and has been republished by the BPS with the kind permission of the author.

Editor
Buddhist Publication Society

INTRODUCTION

Buddhists believe that the human world is not the only world where living beings exist, but that there are many other planes of existence where some forms of life flourish. These planes of existence, despite the fact that some of them are invisible to human eyes, are closely related to our world. They are places where rebirth takes place. According to Buddhism, the nature of one's future birth is conditioned by kamma performed in the present life. From here one may, after death, go "upwards" to the plane of happiness or "downwards" to the realm of misery. So far as kamma is concerned, our present world seems to be the centre of all other worlds and this present life is the determining factor of future lives. Viewed from the point of view of rebirth, the human world and other worlds or planes of existence are reciprocally related. Not only do the beings of this world pass away to take rebirth in other planes, but the beings of those planes also come to take rebirth in the human world.

The Pali Canon speaks of three planes of existence called *bhava*. The Pali term *bhava* literally means "becoming", "state of existence" or "plane of existence". The three planes of existence are: (1) *kāmabhava*, the plane of desires, (2) *rūpabhava*, the plane of form, and

(3) *arūpabhava*, the plane of the formless or incorporeal beings.[2]

In the Sammādiṭṭhi Sutta the Venerable Sāriputta speaks of the cause, the cessation and the path leading to the cessation of *bhava* for each and every individual. Attachment (*upādāna*) is described as the cause of *bhava*. Because of attachment one is to be reborn again after death, and because one is to be reborn, there is *bhava*. The cessation of *bhava* is nothing but the cessation of attachment, which is its cause. The Noble Eightfold Path is said to be the way leading to the cessation of *bhava*.[3]

In the Abhidhammatthasaṅgaha the classification of the planes of existence is slightly different from that of the Pali

2. E.g., MN 9.30; SN 12.2.
3. MN 9.30.

Canon. Here the planes of existence are called *bhūmi*.[4] The Pali term "*bhūmi*" literally means "ground, soil, plane, or stage". The Abhidhammatthasaṅgaha classifies planes of existence into four sub-divisions: (1) *apāya-bhūmi*, the plane of misery, (2) *kāma-sugati-bhūmi*, the sensual happy plane, (3) *rūpāvacara-bhūmi*, the plane of form, and (4) *arūpāvacara-bhūmi*, the plane of the formless.[5] The *apāya-bhūmi* and *kāmasugati-bhūmi* are included in the sensual-plane (*kāmāvacara-bhūmi*), the plane of the beings whose consciousness is restless under the influence of diverse worldly desires. Classification is made here merely to distinguish the plane of misery (*duggati*) from the plane of happiness (*sugati*). Our consideration of the planes of existence will follow the classification as given in the Abhidhammatthasaṅgaha.

The Pali Canon speaks of four types of birth in different planes of existence.[6] The first type is that of a being born from an egg (*aṇḍaja*). Whatever being comes into life by breaking through an eggshell is called a "being born from an egg". The second type is that of a being born from a womb (*jalābuja*). The being born by breaking through a membranous sheath, like human beings, or some kinds of animals like cows, etc., belongs to this type of birth. The third type is that of the being born of moisture (*saṃsedaja*). Whatever being is produced out of rotting fish or rotting corpses or in a dirty pool, is called a "being born of moisture". The fourth type is that of spontaneous uprising (*opapātika*). The devas or gods in heaven, and those who are born in hell belong to this type of birth.

We may roughly say that human beings belong to the second type of birth (*jalābuja*); some of the beings in the animal kingdom belong to the first type of birth (*aṇḍaja*), some belong to the second type or *jalābuja*, and some belong to the third type (*saṃsedaja*); the beings in heaven and in hell belong to the fourth type (*opapātika*).

---

4. This usage of *bhūmi* already found in the Canon; i.e., *apāyabhūmi* in DN 20.3.
5. Abhidh-s 5.3. (CMA p. 189ff.)
6. MN 12.32.

CHAPTER I.
PLANE OF MISERY

The first plane of existence is the plane of misery or *apāya-bhūmi*. It is where the doer of evil deeds is born after death to suffer the consequences of his wicked actions. This plane is further divided into four sub-divisions according to different types of beings. The four sub-divisions are: (1) hell or *niraya*, (2) the realm of animals or *tiracchānayoni*, (3) the realm of the hungry ghosts or *petayoni* and (4) the realm of the Titans or *asurayoni*.[7] These four realms of *apāya-bhūmi* will be discussed separately.

1. Hell

The Pali term *niraya* is defined in the *Paramatthajotikā*[8] as a place completely devoid of happiness.[9] It is one of the four realms of misery where evildoers are reborn after death according to their evil kamma. It is explained that the beings in niraya will never have even a single moment of happy feeling; they have to suffer the painful results of their evil kamma from the beginning to the end of their lives in that realm. There is no time limit for one who is born in hell. Some may have to suffer there for a short period of time and some for numberless years. This depends on the power and efficacy of evil kamma done by each individual.[10] But however long one may suffer in hell, life there is still temporary; one day, upon the exhaustion of the power of one's evil kamma, one will be freed from the hellish suffering. Bhikkhu Devadatta is an example in this connection. Because of his ill will and misdeeds directed towards the Buddha and the Sangha, he is said to have been born, after death, in the lowest hell called Avīci. It was prophesied by the Buddha that Devadatta, upon the

7. Abhidh-s 5.4. (CMA p. 189.) In the sequence in MN 97.30 the *asurayoni* is not given.

8. *Paramatthajotikā*, a modern Thai commentary on the *Abhidhammatthasaṅgaha*, composed by Phra Saddhammajotika, Bangkok, 1963.

9. Pmd § 143. Cf. MN 129.7; Sp-ṭ II § 38 (Be p. 19).

10. Dhp-a III 121; Vibh-a 521.

exhaustion of his evil kamma after the lapse of a long period of time, would, as a result of his previous meritorious actions, become in the future a Pacceka-Buddha named Aṭṭhissara.[11]

In the *Paramatthajotikā*, eight great hells (*mahāniraya*) are mentioned.[12] They are said to be located under the realm of human beings. The eight great hells are as follows:[13]

12. Sañjīva: It is explained that in this hell, the guardians of the hell (*niraya-pāla*) chop and cut the hell-beings with glowing weapons. But as long as their evil deeds remain unexhausted, they regain their lives after the punishment is over. Hence this hell is called Sañjīva—'the reviver".

13. Kālasutta: It is explained that the beings born in this hell are placed on a floor of heated iron, marked with a black thread, and made red hot. The guardians of hell then plane them with adzes along the markings and hence the name Kālasutta—"the black thread."

14. Saṅghāta: This hell is so called because the beings born here are crushed into dust by glowing mountains.

15. 4. Roruva or Dhūmaroruva: This hell is so called because the beings born here are all the time crying with a loud noise, or because they have noxious gases blown into their bodies and painfully cry with a loud noise and hence the name Dhūmaroruva.

16. Mahāroruva or Jālaroruva: This hell is called Mahāroruva because the beings born here are crying louder than the beings born in the Roruva hell, or it is called Jālaroruva because the beings born here have hellish flames blown into their bodies and they cry loudly.

17. Tāpana or Cullatāpana: It is said that the beings born in this hell are pierced by red-hot stakes and they remain transfixed, motionless as long as the results of their evil deeds last and hence the name.

18. Mahātāpana: It is explained that the hell in which the beings are heated with more suffering than in the Cullatāpana is called

---

11. Mil 111; Dhp-a I 147.
12. Pmd § 143. Cf. Kv p. 622; Ja 530 v. 83.
13. The descriptions are also found in the commentary to the Saṃkicca Jātaka, J 530.

Mahātāpana. The *niraya-pāla* (hell-guardians) of this purgatory force the hell-beings to climb up a burning iron mountain and then they are slipped down by strong winds, falling to the red-hot stakes below. There they experience feelings that are painful, sharp, severe, as long as the power of their evil kamma lasts.

19. Avīci: This great hell is the lowest and the most terrible of all. The chief suffering endured in this hell is that of heat. It is explained that there is no space between the beings and the flames and there is no gap of suffering experienced in this hell and hence it is called Avīci—"gapless." It seems to have been specially designed for those who had committed very grievous crimes, such as the five great sins, etc. In the Pali scriptures many names are mentioned as to those who had to suffer the fruition of their evil deeds done in their human life. Among them are, for instance, Nanda, who raped his cousin, the Therī Uppalavaṇṇā; Devadatta, who tried to assassinate the Buddha and caused a schism in the Order; Cunda, the pork butcher; Suppabuddha who insulted the Buddha; etc. It is said that when Devadatta entered the great hell Avīci, his body became one hundred leagues (*yojana*) in height; his head, as far as the outer ear, entered into the glowing iron ceiling and his feet entered into a glowing iron floor up to the ankles; and an iron stake as big as the trunk of a palmyra tree coming from the west wall pierced him from the back through his breast entering the east wall. Other similar stakes coming from the right wall pierced through his body entering the left wall and from the ceiling pierced his head penetrating through the whole body and entering the red-hot iron ground below. Both of his hands were fixed with red-hot iron stakes. He is thus standing motionless amidst the hellish flames until his evil kamma is exhausted in the future.[14]

The above mentioned great hells are said to be located farther downwards respectively from the human world, the Sañjīva being the nearest and the Avīci is the farthest or the lowest. The hell-beings may undergo the severest punishments, but they will retain their lives as long as the power of their evil kamma lasts.

---

14. Dhp-a I 148.

Apart from the eight great hells, the *Paramatthajotikā* mentions also five small hells called *ussada-niraya*. The Pali term *ussada* literally means "plenty" or "abundance". It is explained that suffering is abundant in these small hells. They are therefore called *ussada*. The *ussada-niraya* surround each great hell in four directions.

The Devadūta Sutta[15] describes the great hell as being square in shape encircled by an iron wall and covered by an iron roof; the floor is made of glowing iron of a hundred leagues square; there are four big gates in four directions. Next to each gate in each direction are situated in respective order the five small hells or *ussada-niraya*. The five small purgatories are: (1) Gūtha-niraya or the Filth Hell, (2) Kukkuḷa-niraya or the Ember Hell, (3) Simpalīvana-niraya or the Silk-cotton-tree Hell, (4) Asipattavana-niraya or the Sword-leafed-forest Hell; and (5) Vettaranī-niraya or the Caustic River Hell. Thus one great hell is surrounded in four directions by twenty small hells. Counted together the total number of hells becomes 168, i.e., eight great hells and 160 small hells. But since each great hell is surrounded by five varieties of small hells, the same kinds of hells in the four directions may be counted as one and thus one great hell has only five surrounding small hells. In this way the total number is 48—eight great hells and 40 small hells.

The ruler of the great hell is called *yama* (determiner) or *yamarāja* (determiner-king).[16]But there is not only one yamarāja for one great hell; there are actually four yamarājas who are in charge of the four gates. Thus for eight great hells there are altogether thirty-two yamarājas. Apart from these yamarājas, there are a number of hell-guardians called *niraya-pāla*. The duty of the *yamarāja* is to consider the case of each hell-being and give orders for punishment; the hell-guardian's duty is to inflict the penalties typical of each hell on the hell-beings. Yamarāja and niraya-pāla are actually not hell-beings, but belong to the heaven of the Four Great Kings or Cātumahārājika. They are described as *vemānikapeta*, the beings that sometimes enjoy the fruitions of their meritorious kamma in heaven and sometimes suffer the results of their evil deeds in hell. Because of particular

15. MN 130.

16. A-ṭ II 114 (Be): *Devadūtasarāpanavasena satte yathūpacite puññakamme yameti niyametīti yamo.*

kinds of kamma they are sent to perform their duties in this realm of misery by inflicting penalties on the hell-beings.[17]

It is said in the Devadūta Sutta that the hell-guardians seize the person who has just passed away from the human world and present him to the yamarāja, saying:

> "This man, sire, has no respect for his mother, no respect for his father; he does not honour recluses; he does not honour Brahmins; he does not pay due respect to the elders of the family. Let your majesty decree a punishment for him."

Then the yamarāja cross-questions him, asking about the five divine messengers (*devadūtā*). The five divine messengers are: (1) a newly born baby, (2) an aged man or woman, (3) a sick person, (4) a person subjected to various punishments, and (5) a dead man or woman. The yamarāja questions him about these five divine messengers one by one respectively. In asking about the fifth messenger, for instance, he says:

> "My good man, did you see the fifth divine messenger who appeared among men."
>
> He replies: "I did not see him revered sir."
>
> The yamarāja speaks to him thus: "My good man, did you not see among men a woman or a man dead for one, two or three days, swollen, discoloured, decomposing?"
>
> He replies: "I saw this, revered sir." Then yamarāja says: "My good man, although you are sensible and grown up, did it not occur to you that you too were liable to death, that you had not outstripped death and that you should do what is lovely in body, speech and thought?"
>
> He speaks thus: "I was not able, revered sir. I was indolent, revered sir."
>
> Yamarāja then speaks to him: "If it was because of indolence, my good man, that you did not do what is lovely in body, speech and thought, they will undoubtedly deal with you, my good man, in accordance with that indolence. For this evil deed is yours; it was neither done by your mother, nor by your father, nor by your brother, nor by your sister, nor by your friends and acquaintances, nor by kith and kin, nor by recluses and brahmins, nor by

17. MN-a IV 230; AN-ṭ II 114 (Be).

> gods. This evil deed was done by you; it is you yourself that will experience its ripening."
>
> Yamarāja, having thus spoken, remains silent. The guardians of the hell then subject him to what is called the fivefold pinion. They drive a red-hot iron stake through each hand and each foot and a red-hot iron stake through the middle of his breast. There he experiences feelings that are painful, sharp and severe. But his term does not expire until an end is made of his evil kamma.
>
> Then the guardians of the hell lay him down and plane him with adzes. There…
>
> Then the guardians of the hell place him feet up and head down and plane him with razors. There...
>
> Then the guardians of the hell bind him to a chariot and drive him up and down over ground that is burning, aflame, ablaze. There....
>
> Then the guardians of the hell push him up and down a great mountain slope of glowing cinders, burning, aflame, ablaze. There....

Then the guardians of the hell take him feet up and head down, and plunge him into a glowing brazen cauldron, burning, aflame, ablaze. There he is boiled and rises to the surface with the scum. Boiling there and rising to the surface with the scum, he once comes up and once goes down and once he goes across. There he experiences feelings that are painful, sharp and severe. But his term does not expire until an end is made of his evil kamma. Then the guardians of the hell toss him into the great hell."

The Devadūta Sutta describes the penalties inflicted on the hell-beings in the great hell (*mahāniraya*) as follows:

> "The flames that leap up by the eastern wall of this great hell are hurled against the western wall; the flames that leap up by the western wall are hurled against the eastern wall; the flames that leap up by the northern wall are hurled against the southern wall; the flames that leap up by the southern wall are hurled against the northern wall; the flames that leap up from below are hurled above, the flames that leap up from above are hurled below. There he experiences feelings that are painful, sharp, severe. But he does not expire his term until his evil kamma has become exhausted.

There comes a time after the lapse of a very long period when the eastern gateway of this great hell is opened. That being rushes there swiftly and speedily; while he is rushing swiftly and speedily his skin burns and his hide burns and his flesh burns and his tendons burn and his eyes are filled with smoke—such is his plight.

When at long last he reaches the gateway, then it is nevertheless closed against him. There he experiences feelings that are painful, sharp, severe. But he does not expire his term until he makes an end of his evil kamma.

There comes a time after the lapse of a very long period when the western gateway... the northern gateway... the southern gateway of this great hell is opened. He rushes there swiftly and speedily; while he is rushing swiftly and speedily his skin burns... the gateway is nevertheless closed against him. There he experiences feelings that are painful, sharp, severe. But he does not expire his term until his evil kamma has become exhausted.

There comes a time after the lapse of a very long period when the eastern gateway of this great hell is opened. He rushes there swiftly and speedily... such is his plight. He issues forth by this gateway.

However, surrounding this great hell is the Filth Hell (*gūtha-niraya*). He falls into it. And in the Filth Hell needle-mouthed creatures cut away his skin; having cut away his skin they cut away his hide...his flesh... his tendons... his bones; having cut away his bones, they devour the marrow of the bones. There he experiences feelings that are painful, sharp, severe. But he does not expire his term until his evil kamma has become exhausted. And surrounding this Filth Hell is the Ember Hell (*kukkuḷa-niraya*). He falls into it. There he experiences feelings that are painful, sharp, severe. But he does not expire his term until his evil kamma has become exhausted.

And surrounding this Ember Hell is the Silk-Cotton Trees Forest (*simpalīvana*) towering a league (*yojana*) high with prickles of sixteen finger-breadths long, burning, aflame, ablaze. The hell guardians make him climb up and down. There he experiences feelings that are painful, sharp, severe. But he does not expire his term until his evil kamma has become exhausted.

And adjacent to that Silk-Cotton Trees Forest is the great Sword-Leafed Forest (*asipattanavana*). He enters it. Its leaves, stirred by the wind, cut off his hands and cut off his feet and cut off his hands and feet... ears... nose, and cut off his ears and nose. There he experiences feelings that are painful, sharp, severe. But he does not expire his term until his evil kamma has become exhausted.

And adjacent to that Sword-Leafed Forest is the great River of Caustic Water (*khārodaka-nādi*). He falls into it. There he is carried with the stream, against the stream and with and against the stream. There he experiences feelings that are painful, sharp, severe. But he does not expire his term until his evil kamma has become exhausted.

The guardians of the hell haul him out with a fish-hook, set him on dry ground and speak thus to him: "My good man, what do you want?"

He replies: "I am hungry, revered sirs."

The guardians of the hell, opening his mouth with a glowing iron spike, burning, aflame, ablaze, then push into his mouth a glowing copper pellet, burning, aflame, ablaze. It burns his lips, his mouth, his throat, his chest and it passes out below taking with it his bowels and intestines. There he experiences feelings... But he does not expire his term until his evil kamma has become exhausted.

Then, the guardians of the hell ask him: "My good man, what do you want?"

He speaks thus: "I am thirsty, revered sirs."

The guardians of the hell, opening his mouth... pour glowing copper liquid into his mouth...

There he experiences feeling .... But he does not expire his term until his evil kamma has become exhausted. Then, the guardians of the hell toss him back again into the great hell."

The Great Hell as described in the Devadūta Sutta is probably the Avīci-mahāniraya since the chief suffering endured in this hell is that of heat. But the Avīci-mahāniraya seems to consist of more than one great hell and five small hells as appears in the Devadūta Sutta.

The Venerable Saddhammajotika in his *Paramatthajotikā*, quoting the commentary on the Saṃyutta Nikāya and Aṅguttara Nikāya[18], says that there are twelve different hells under the common name *avīci*: (1) Pahāsa, (2) Aparājita, (3) Ambuda, (4) Nirabbuda, (5) Ababa, (6) Ahaha, (7) Aṭaṭa, ((8) Kumuda, (9) Sogandhika, (10) Uppala, (11) Puṇḍarīka, (12) Mahāpaduma or Paduma. The last one or Paduma-niraya is known as where Bhikkhu Kokālika—a close friend of Devadatta, who falsely accused the Venerable Sāriputta and Moggallāna of having a wicked thought—was born after his human life.[19]

In the small hells (*ussada-niraya*), apart from suffering caused by the nature of punishment particular to each hell, the hell-beings are said to suffer also from the attack of four kinds of hell beasts: giant vultures, giant crows, giant hawks and giant dogs. These animals are said to be very fierce and will furiously attack the hell-beings at first sight.[20]

Among the four realms of the plane of misery (*apāya-bhūmi*), niraya appears, as we have seen, to be the most horrible of all. The birth of the being in hell is spontaneous (*opapātika*) and is purely brought about by evil kamma. The body of the hell-being may be completely destroyed by hellish punishment, but as long as his evil deeds have not been recompensed it will always be created anew.[21] It is said that when the power of evil kamma becomes weaker he will be free from the great hell, but he still continues to suffer in the small hell (*ussada-niraya*).

During this period, if his meritorious kamma performed in the past is very powerful, he may immediately move from hell and assume rebirth in heaven or in the realm of human beings. If, on the other hand, his evil kamma still remains, but not strong enough for his suffering in hell, he may move from there and take rebirth in the realm of the hungry ghost (*peta*) or as an animal, whatever will suit the case.

2. Animal Realm

Buddhism regards animal existence as a state of life belonging to the plane of misery or *apāya-bhūmi*. It maintains that there is no certainty in the state of being, a man may be reborn as an animal, and vice versa or an animal may attain the state of

18. SN-a I 167f, AN-a II 850.
19. SN 6:10.
20. J 541.
21. Mil 67; MN 130.

divine being in heaven and the divine being may be degraded and be reborn as an animal. This depends on the kamma performed by each individual in his previous and present life. Whatever action has been done by him, he himself is to receive its consequences. As the Buddha said:

> "Owners of their kamma are living beings, heirs to their kamma, have kamma as the wombs from which they spring, have kamma as their kinsmen, have kamma as their refuges. Whatsoever kamma they will do, be it wholesome or unwholesome, of that they will be the heirs."[22]

Now, what type of person will attain, after death, animal birth? To this question we find the answer in the Aṅguttara Nikāya[23] where the Buddha is reported to have said:

> "Some person in this world, bhikkhus, takes life, he is a hunter, bloody-handed, given over to killing and slaying, void of compassion for all living creatures... takes what is not given... commits adultery... is a liar, a slanderer, of harsh speech, of idle babble... covetous... of harmful thoughts... of wrong view.... He goes crookedly in body, crookedly in speech, crookedly in mind. His physical action is crooked, verbal action is crooked and mental action is crooked; crooked in his bourn and crooked in his rebirth. I declare, bhikkhus, any one of the two bourns, viz., a woeful state of hell or birth as an animal that creeps crookedly along, for him whose bourn is crooked and whose rebirth is crooked.
>
> Of what sort, bhikkhus, is that animal birth, one that creeps crookedly along. It is of a snake, a scorpion, a centipede, a mongoose, a cat, a mouse, an owl or whatsoever other animal, one that goes stealthily on seeing human beings."

In the Jātaka we are told that the Buddha himself had been born as an animal in many of his previous births. Thus, for ordinary men like us it is no doubt that in the course of our wandering in saṃsāra we might have been born as an animal, since no one who is still in bondage has never performed evil deeds in the past.

---

22. AN 10:205.
23. Ibid. Cf. MN 129.19-26.

Some modern Buddhists, however, are of the opinion that it is not possible for a well-developed being like man to be reborn as a low creature like an animal. This view is definitely not in accordance with the Buddha's teachings and it will never be accepted by a serious Buddhist.

From the Buddhist point of view, the interchange of beings between the plane of misery and the plane of happiness is a common phenomenon in the world of saṃsāra. Buddhism maintains that only one who has attained the holy stages ranging from the Stream-Enterer (*sotāpanna*) to the Non-Returner (*anāgāmi*) will be no more reborn as an animal.[24]

There is nothing to be said about one who has attained the stage of Arahat-ship, as the root-cause of his rebirth has been totally uprooted. However, for the worldly man (*puthujjana*) like us, rebirth in the plane of misery, e.g., as an animal, as a hell-being, etc., is as possible as rebirth in the plane of happiness.

The animal kingdom, unlike other realms, is in the same world as human beings. It is not difficult to see the reason why Buddhism regards animal birth as a state of life included in the plane of misery. First of all, there is no morality in the animal kingdom; animals live according to the wild law of nature. Among animals, the strongest is the survivor; the bigger eats the smaller. Danger to life is the crucial problem for them; it may come at any moment from animals themselves as well as from human beings. They have to struggle hard for their survival, especially for food which is not always certain. Sometimes they have enough to eat, but sometimes they have to starve for many days. Moreover, they have to bear nakedly the hot and cold, the wet and dry seasons of the year without proper protection. With all these difficulties, animal life, although it is not as much suffering as that of the beings in hell, is rationally included as one of the miserable existences.[25]

Another reason why Buddhism includes animal birth in the *apāya-bhūmi* is that whosoever, because of his evil kamma; attains the birth of animal is naturally obstructed from realising the ultimate truth, from following the path of virtue which leads to emancipation. This is because animal existence is the negation of such realisation and practice. Lacking the capacity for

---

24. DN 16.8; SN 12:41.
25. Cf. MN 129.18-26.

realising the ultimate truth is considered critical since such realisation is the prime aim of life that we struggle for.

3. Realm of Unhappy Ghosts

Pettivisaya literally means "the realm of the unhappy ghosts (*peta*)." It is a realm included in the plane of misery according to Buddhism. It is said that there is no particular place for the *petas* to live; they live in the same world as human beings, such as in forests, on mountains, on islands, in cemeteries, etc. However, since they belong to a different realm of existence they are, therefore, invisible to human eyes. They may be seen only when they want themselves to be seen by human beings. Another means of seeing the petas is by clairvoyance (*dibbacakkhu*) developed by meditation.

The *Paramatthajotikā* quotes the commentary on Petavatthu[26] and mentions four kinds of peta, namely, (1) *paradattūpajīvika-peta* (peta who lives on the gifts of others), (2) *khuppipāsika-peta* (hungry and thirsty peta), (3) *nijjhāmataṇhika-peta* (peta consumed by craving), and (4) *kāḷakañcika-peta*[27] (black-eared peta).The *paradattūpajīvika-peta* (peta who lives on the gifts of others) is an unhappy ghost who lives on the *dakkhiṇa* or sacrificial offerings of others. It is because of this type of peta that Buddhism encourages its followers to perform a merit-making by offering food, clothing, shelter, etc., to virtuous persons, such as a bhikkhu or a group of bhikkhus, and then to dedicate the merit acquired there from to deceased relatives. This is done on the basis of the belief that if the deceased relatives have attained the life of the paradattūpajīvika-peta, their suffering, on the appreciation of the sacrifice done and dedicated to them, will be abolished and they will thereby attain to the plane of happiness. This belief is affirmed by many stories of the petas, which appear in the Petavatthu of the Pali Canon.

In one story, for instance, it is said that the Venerable Sāriputta came across a female peta appearing as an ugly, bony-thin and naked woman. The Elder questioned her and she replied that she was a peta born in the miserable peta-world. She reported that when she was a human being neither her father,

---

26. Untraced, but see Ud-a 140.
27. Also called *kāḷakaṇṇika-peta*.

mother nor relatives persuaded her to perform any good kamma like giving alms, observing precepts, etc. Because of lacking such meritorious deeds she was, after her human existence, consequently born as an unhappy peta tortured by hunger and thirst for five hundred years. At last, she begged for help from the Venerable Sāriputta. The Elder accepted her request and later offered a certain amount of food, a small piece of cloth, and water to one bhikkhu. He particularly dedicated that offering (*dakkhiṇa*) to that peta. On appreciating the offering specially consecrated to her, she immediately acquired food, clothes and other properties and became released from suffering. Having attained the state of a celestial being, she came and appeared before the Venerable Sāriputta. Being unable to recognise her, the Elder asked her who she was. The *devadhītā* (goddess) informed him and said that she had come to pay her homage to him.[28]

The peta in the above story was obviously a *paradattūpajīvika-peta*. It should be noted here that according to Buddhism only the peta of this sort are able to enjoy the outcome of an offering dedicated by their relatives. The peta of other sorts are not affected by such a dedication.[29] The offering (*dakkhiṇa*) will become fruitful to the peta, however, only when three conditions are met. The three conditions are: (1) the offering is given to a virtuous person; (2) the performer of the offering dedicates it particularly to his deceased relative; and (3) his deceased relative has been born as a *paradattūpajīvika-peta* and that peta knows and appreciates that offering particularly consecrated to him.[30] If any of these three conditions is lacking, the deceased relative will not be able to enjoy the outcome of the offering. But whatever the case may be, the performer of the offering will never be without the result of his meritorious action.

The second kind of peta is the *khuppipāsika-peta* (hungry and thirsty peta). This sort of peta suffers from hunger and thirst. The offering dedicated by relatives in the human world cannot bear fruit to one born as this kind of peta. He will suffer in the peta-realm as long as his evil kamma lasts.

The third kind of peta is the *nijjhāmataṇhika-peta* (peta consumed by craving). The suffering of this sort of peta is

28. Petavatthu II.1: Saṃsāramocakapetivatthu.
29. AN-a V 74 to AN 10: 177.
30. Cf. Pv-a on the Tirokuḍḍasutta.

caused by his own craving or taṇhā. It is said that fire burns in his mouth all the time and this results in his burning desire which can never be fulfilled. He will continue to suffer in the peta-world unless and until his evil kamma performed in the past becomes exhausted.

The fourth kind of peta is the *kāḷakañcika-peta* (black-eared peta). It is explained that this sort of peta has a body three leagues (*yojana*) tall. However, his body appears to be like a dry leaf with only skin covering the skeleton; his eyes protrude like those of the crab and his mouth is extremely small. He suffers from hunger and thirst like the other types of peta.

The *Paramatthajotikā* also mentions many other types of peta, but after careful consideration we may conclude that the differences between the beings in the peta-world are characteristically dependent on the particular nature of the evil kamma formerly performed by each peta. One peta is always different from the others in the way and manner of suffering and this different is solely determined by the peta's particular evil kamma. Another type of peta which should also be mentioned here is the *vemānika-peta* (a peta who has a celestial palace).[31] According to the Buddhist texts,[32] this peta appears at night as a god of the lower grade, enjoying the fruition of his previous good kamma in a celestial palace called *vimāna*. However, during the day his previous evil kamma forces him to leave his happy *vimāna* and suffer its unhealthy result at a certain place until the end of the day when he then returns to his celestial residence. His cycle of life will continue in this way unless and until his previous evil kamma has been recompensed. Since one half of his life is spent in happiness in the *vimāna* and the other half in the painful experience of the peta, hence he is called *vemānika-peta*.

We are further told that there is no certain limit or duration to existence in the realm of the peta.[33] One may suffer in this miserable world for a very long period of time and another may exist there only for a number of days. This is because existence in the peta-world is solely determined by evil kamma previously performed by each individual. In the human world

31. E.g., Pv-a 204.
32. Ibid.
33. Abhidh-s 5.12.

one may pass away due to the expiration of life, but in the peta-world the end of life occurs only with the exhaustion of evil kamma.[34] This realm is included in the plane of suffering (*duggati*) because life there is dominated entirely by the suffering of pain and torture.

4. Realm of the Titans

The last type of birth included in the plane of misery is birth as a Titan or *asura*. The being called *asura* here is to be distinguished from the *devāsura* (*deva-asura*) who does not exist in the plane of misery. The *devāsura* (god-titan) is a class of god belonging to the same realm of Tāvatiṃsa heaven. Vepacitti is said to be the king of this sort of *asura*.[35] The *devāsura* is definitely not included in the type of being in the plane of misery. Only the *peta-asura* and *niraya-asura* are accounted as beings of the *apāya-bhūmi*.

The Paramatthajotikā[36] says that the being which is called *asura* or *asurakāya* of the *apāya-bhūmi* is but the *kāḷakañcika-peta* (black-eared peta), one of the four sorts of peta we have already considered.[37] These *kāḷakañcika-peta* have, like other sorts of peta, no particular place of their own; they live in the human world, i.e., in forests, in the sea, on islands, in valleys, etc.

The niraya-asura (hell-titan) is described as a type of hell-being. They have a particular realm of their own called Lokantarika-niraya (World-interspace Hell). This type of niraya is said to be situated between each three world-spheres (cakkavāḷa).[38] In between these three worlds there is a dark sea of acid water surrounded by rocky mountains. This sea is covered with eternal darkness; no ray of light can reach this place. The creatures of the World-interspace Hell hang themselves on cliffs like bats. They are tortured by hunger and

---

34. Vibh-a § 1028/p. 521.
35. SN 11:4; 35:207; M I 251.
36. Cf. DN 20.12; 24.1.7; Kvu p. 360 § 503; Pv-a 272; J-a V 455. In DN 24.1.7 it is said that they are the lowest class of asuras.
37. In *apāya* sequence in MN 97.30 the *asurakāya* is not mentioned and seems to be included in the *pettivisaya*.
38. E.g., MN-a IV 176: *tiṇṇaṃ tiṇṇaṃ cakkavāḷānaṃ antarā ekeko lokantarikā hoti.* J-a I 76; Vbh-a p. 4/§ 2; Vism 7.44, Bv-a p. 30; MN-a IV 176. For a description of *cakkavāḷa*, see PP pp.218-19 n. 14.

thirst as there is no food for them. While moving along the cliff they sometimes come across each other. Thinking that they have come across food, they jump upon each other and start fighting. As soon as they start fighting, they let loose their grip on the cliff and as a result they fall into the sea below and their bodies melt away just like salt melting away in water.[39]

It is explained that the creatures of the Lokantarika-niraya are called "asura" because their lives are contrary to the gods in the Tāvatiṃsa heaven who are called "sura", i.e., life in Lokantarika-niraya is entirely unpleasant while that of the Tāvatiṃsa gods is entirely pleasant. The reason why the asura or asurakāya is spoken of separately as another sort of being in the plane of misery is probably because this type of creature possesses special characteristics unlike other beings of the peta world.

Now, we have seen that in the plane of misery (*apāya-bhūmi*) there are four principal births: birth as a hell-being, as an animal, as a peta or hungry ghost, and as an asura. Among these four sorts of beings, the three principal births, namely, the birth of the hell-being, the peta and the asura, belong to what is called spontaneous uprising (*opapātika*). The birth of animals varies from one type to another according to its kind, i.e., some kinds belong to the *aṇḍaja* (born from eggs) some belong to the *jalābuja* (born from a womb) and some belong to *saṃsedaja* (born from moisture). All these four principal births are brought about entirely by evil kamma and hence they are regarded as miserable existences.

---

39. AN-a II 532.

CHAPTER II. SENSUAL HAPPY PLANE

The second plane of existence to be considered here is the sensual happy plane or *kāmasugati-bhūmi*. The Pali term *kāmasugati-bhūmi* can be translated as "the plane of happiness connected with desires." This implies that the life of the being born in this plane is mainly dominated by the influence of diverse worldly desires. The happiness of the beings of this plane arises from the six sense-object contacts generally termed as sensual pleasures. The desire to acquire this type of pleasure is the common characteristic of all beings of the sensual happy plane.

According to Buddhism, there are actually twenty realms of happy existence. These twenty realms are distinguished into three groups in accordance with their common characteristics: (1) the sensual happy plane (*kāmasugati-bhūmi*), (2) the plane of form (*rūpāvacara-bhūmi*); and (3) the plane of the formless (*arūpāvacara-bhūmi*). The plane of form and the plane of the formless will be discussed later.

The *kāmasugati-bhūmi*, the sensual happy plane, is classified into seven realms: (1) the realm of human beings and the other six being the six realms of the sensual-plane (*kāmāvacara*) heavens, viz., (2) Cātumahārājika, (3) Tāvatiṃsa, (4) Yāmā, (5) Tusita,

(6) Nimmānaratī and (7) Paranimmitavasavattī. This classification is hierarchically arranged from the lowest to the highest realm respectively.[40] Birth or rebirth in these seven realms is conditioned by meritorious kamma.

1. The Realm of Human Beings

Buddhism regards human existence as one of the twenty happy existences. In human beings the degree of happiness varies from one individual to another. This depends on one's kamma, which affects one's life. One is born rich and another is born poor; one is born blind or deaf and dumb and another is born normal.

40. SN 56:12; Abhidh-s 5.12.

Although the abnormal seems to be less happy than the normal, no one can deny that the abnormal individual has a chance to be happy. As long as his body is capable of sense-object contacts, even though not through all of his senses, he is still capable of enjoying sensual pleasures. The beggar appears to experience more suffering than happiness, but he still has a chance for worldly pleasures in his life. In the human world, however lofty or humble one's life is, happiness is always possible and this is one reason why it is regarded as one of the twenty realms of happy existence.

The main reason the realm of human beings is regarded as one of the sensual happy plane (*kāmasugati-bhūmi*) is that human birth is the result of meritorious kamma. And everyone born as man, however high or humble his birth may be, has an equal chance of realising the ultimate truth and attaining emancipation. Moreover, although the human world is the lowest of all the happy realms of existence, it possesses many significant characteristics that many other realms do not have. Firstly, it is the realm situated between the plane of misery (*apāya-bhūmi*) and the higher realms of happiness, the worlds of the gods (*devaloka*). In this sense it may be said to be the centre of all realms from which man may go "upwards" or "downwards" after death according to the nature of his kamma. Secondly, it is the only realm where the life of a recluse, an ethical life that leads directly to the realisation of the ultimate truth, is made possible. Thirdly, it is where the fulfilment of the ten perfections (*dasa-pāramī*) of the Buddha-to-be or Bodhisatta is made possible. Fourthly, it is the only realm where the Bodhisatta attains to Buddhahood and preaches the ultimate truth to the world. With all these significant characteristics, the human world may be regarded as the most important realm of happy existence although happiness here is mixed with suffering.

As regards the kinds of kamma which cause rebirth in the realm of human beings, an explanation can be found in the Aṅguttara Nikāya where the Buddha is reported to have said to his disciples:

> "There is, O bhikkhus, someone in this world who only on a small scale performs meritorious action founded on charity (*dāna*), only on a small scale performs meritorious action founded on virtue (*sīla*) and does not perform

meritorious action founded on mind-development (*bhāvanā*). He, on the dissolution of the body after death, is reborn among men of ill luck.

There is, O bhikkhus, someone in this world who performs meritorious action founded on charity to a medium degree, performs meritorious action founded on virtue to a medium degree and does not perform meritorious action founded on mind-development. He, on the dissolution of the body after death, is reborn among men of good luck." [41]

The above passages clearly show that charity (*dāna*) and virtue (*sīla*) are the determining factors in bringing about rebirth in the realm of human beings. These two kinds of wholesome action still have their roles to play in conditioning more or less happiness and prosperity in a man's life after birth according to the degree of their power and efficacy. But, since circumstances in human life are more complicated, other kinds of wholesome and unwholesome actions performed in his previous birth also fruit for him who has been born as a human being.[42]

2. Heaven of the Four Great Kings

Cātumahārājika is the name of the lowest realm of the twenty-six heavens. It is so called because this heaven is ruled by the Four Great Kings in four different directions, i.e., in the East, in the South, in the West and in the North. The problem arises about the centre of this realm, which divides the regions of the Four Great Kings. The *Paramatthajotikā* mentions a mountain called Sineru as the centre of this heaven.[43] However, at present we cannot locate any mountain by this name anywhere in the world. It is said that Sineru is the highest mountain in the world and it may therefore be the highest peak of the Himalaya range called Everest at present.

In the Āṭānāṭiya Sutta[44] we are informed that a Devarāja called Dhataraṭṭha rules over the eastern region of Cātumahārājika heaven. He is the king of the *gandhabbas*. A

41. AN 8:36. Cf. MN 135.
42. Cf. MN 136.8.
43. Cf. Vism 7.42.
44. DN 32.4.

Devarāja named Virūḷhaka rules over the southern region; he is the king of the *kumbhaṇḍas.* In the western region a Devarāja named Virūpakkha is the ruler and he is the king of the *nāgas.* In the northern region a Devarāja named Kuvera or Vessavaṇa is the ruler; he is the king of the *yakkhas.* These Four Great Kings are also said to be the protectors of the human world and thus they are sometimes called *lokapālā*—the protectors of the world.[45]

It should be noted that each of the Four Great Kings rules over one type of god of the Cātumahārājika heaven.[46] The *gandhabbas,* the attendants of King Dhataraṭṭha, are described as the god-musicians. They are said to be well-versed in music. Pañcasikha, whose name is often mentioned in the Pali scriptures, belongs to the Gandhabba community. He always goes with his yellow lute (*vīṇā*) in his hand. The *kumbhaṇḍa* is described as a type of being with a big belly and big red eyes.[47] As the retinue of King Virūḷhaka, their duty is to take care of forests, mountains, underground riches, hidden treasures, etc. The *nāgas,* the inhabitants under King Virūpakkha's administration, are another type of celestial being in the Cātumahārājika heaven. *Nāga* literally means "snake", but as the inhabitants of this heaven, they are demigods endowed with divine power. The *yakkhas* are the retinue of King Vessavaṇa. They are also a type of god inhabiting this heaven. In the Janavasabha Sutta[48] it is said that King Bimbisāra of Magadha was born after his human existence as a high ranking yakkha of this realm. In the *Paramatthajotikā,* distinctions are made among the three types of gods of the Cātumahārājika heaven according to the nature of their residences (*vimāna*). The three types are: (1) *bhummaṭṭha-devatā* or gods living on the ground, (2) *rukkhaṭṭha-devatā* or gods living in trees and (3) *ākāsaṭṭha-devatā* or gods living in the sky.[49]

The ground-gods or *bhummaṭṭha-devatā* are said to reside on mountains, in pagodas, in public houses like temples, etc. They do not have palaces (*vimāna*) of their own. The tree-gods or

---

45. J 442; Ap v. 262. Cf. AN 3:36.

46. DN 32.

47. DN-a 964, J-a to J 347. Their name literally means "pot-testicles", because their testicles are as big as pots.

48. DN 18.

49. Pmd § 143. Cf. DN 16.5.6

rukkhaṭṭha-devatā are distinguished into two types, one being those who have palaces of their own on the tops of trees and the other being those who have no palaces (*vimāna*) but reside in trees. Since their residences are in connection with trees, when those trees are chopped down they have to shift to other unoccupied ones. The *ākāsaṭṭha-devatā* or the gods living in the sky are said to have vimānas of their own. The magnificence of their palaces varies from one to another, depending on the karmic results of the owners.[50]

It should be noted that the Cātumahārājika heaven is actually on the same level as the human world. It may be regarded as a sub-world which is invisible to human eyes. The reason for its invisibility is that it belongs to a different realm of existence. The birth of a being in this realm is, as is birth in all the other realms of happiness, conditioned by meritorious kamma.

In the Aṅguttara Nikāya[51] we are told that the age of the beings in the Cātumahārājika heaven is about five hundred divine years. Fifty years in the realm of human beings is equal to a single day and night of that realm; thirty such days and nights make one month; twelve such months make a year. Five hundred years of that realm are, therefore, equal to nine million years in the human world. However, it should not be understood that all beings of this heaven always live long, up to the expiration of their span of life. The life of the beings in every realm of existence is actually the same as that of human beings, i.e., some may die at a young age, some may live up to middle age and then die, and some may pass away at the expiration of their span of life. This depends on the power and efficacy of the kamma done by each individual which governs and determines the nature and duration of his life in the plane where he is born.[52]

3. Heaven of the Thirty-three

The second realm of the sensual-plane (*kāmāvacarabhūmi*) heaven and the third realm of the plane of happiness is the

---

50. Cf. Vv-a on v. 3 and 318.
51. AN 3:70.18. Cf. Abhidh-s 5.12.
52. DN 1.2.4; DN-a I 110; Vibh-a 521 (§ 1028). Dhp-a I 173: *devalokato hi devaputtā āyukkhayena puññakkhayena āhārakkhayena kopenāti catūhi kāraṇehi cavanti.*

Tāvatiṃsa heaven. The term "*tāvatiṃsa*' means "thirty-three". This heaven is named after the number of a group of people who collectively performed meritorious kamma and who were born after death in this realm of happiness.

According to the legend,[53] it is said that once in the far past there was a group of thirty-three men in a village called Macalagāma. The leader of the group was a young man named Magha. These thirty-three men collectively dedicated their efforts to the happiness and well-being of other people. They built and repaired roads, dug wells and ponds at road-sides for travellers who needed water, built rest houses at cross-roads, etc. They passed their whole life with such wholesome actions and on the dissolution of their bodies, after death, they attained to this third realm of happiness. The leader of the group became the ruler of this heaven and acquired the name Sakka or Indra. His thirty-two friends were reborn as high ranking gods. Since the thirty-three friends were born in this realm, it is, therefore, called Tāvatiṃsa or the heaven of the Thirty-Three Gods. In fact, there are many other gods who attained to this realm before and after the thirty-three friends, but when Magha was born here, because of his excellent virtues and marvellous meritorious kamma, he acquired supreme power and became the ruler of the realm.

The Tāvatiṃsa heaven is said to be situated on the top of Sineru mountain.[54] It is just above the Cātumahārājika or the heaven of the Four Great Kings. At the middle of this realm there is a city called Sudassana. The palace or vimāna of Sakka the Devarāja, called Vejayanta,[55] is in the eastern part of the city. In the city there are many parks, lotus ponds and flower gardens which serve as the places of enjoyment and recreation of the gods in Tāvatiṃsa heaven. There is also a Pārijāta (or Pārichattaka) tree, which is the landmark of this realm, and an assembly hall called Sudhammā serving as the meeting place of the Tāvatiṃsa gods.

It is explained that all gods and goddesses in this heaven are always in their youthful stage of life. No old age, sickness and disfigured parts of the body appear among them. Their foods are so subtle that no excretions are produced from their

53. Dhp-a I 263. Cf. J 31.
54. Sn-a II 485.
55. MN 37.10.

bodies. Their birth in heaven is one of spontaneous uprising (*opapātika*), i.e., the being born in heaven spontaneously appears as a young man or woman. When the god's death occurs, because of the exhaustion of the kamma that leads him to take rebirth in heaven, he just disappears from the celestial world leaving no trace of his corporeal body.

In the Itivuttaka[56] it is said that when the end of his term of life in heaven is drawing near, the five signs appears to the god who is to pass away to take rebirth in another realm of existence. The five signs are: (1) his decorating flowers wither away, (2) his clothes become faded, (3) sweat comes out of his armpits, (4) his complexion becomes ugly, and (5) he becomes displeased with his heavenly seat. When these five signs appear to any god, he himself, as well as others, realises that the end of his life in that realm is close at hand and he is consequently overcome with grief. Having seen the five signs his friends try to console him with their wishes: they wish him attainment to the realm of happiness, attainment to that which is beneficial for him and to be well-established in what has been attained. To attain to the realm of happiness for a god in heaven is explained as obtaining rebirth as a human being; to attain to what is beneficial for him is to have faith in the teachings of the Buddha who preaches his doctrine in accordance with the natural law of cause and effect or the law of kamma; and to be well-established in what has been attained is to have an unshakable faith therein.

It is also said that the gods of the higher heavens are invisible to the gods of the lower ones but not vice versa.[57] This is because the bodies of the gods of the higher realms are more subtle than those of the beings in the lower realms. The celestial beings of the higher heavens are visible to the beings of the lower realms only when they want themselves to be seen by transforming their subtle bodies into grosser bodies. Moreover, although all gods are endowed with divine power, the beings of the lower realms cannot travel to realms higher than their own. This is because of the limitation of their power. However, in travelling to the lower realms there is no such obstruction; they can go any time they wish. These two general characteristics, i.e., the invisibility of the higher gods to the lower gods and the

---

56. It 83.
57. Cf. MN 49.9-10.

incapability of the lower gods to travel to the higher realms, are common to all the heavens excepting the Cātumahārājika and the Tāvatiṃsa heaven which appear to be closely related. The Buddhist scriptures reveal to us that gods of the Cātumahārājika heaven can go to Tāvatiṃsa heaven, although in the hierarchy of gradation Tāvatiṃsa is a higher realm of existence. The evidence for this appears in the Janavasabha Sutta and Mahāgovinda Sutta[58] of the Dīgha Nikāya.

In the Mahāgovinda Sutta we are told that a gandhabba named Pañcasikha came to visit the Buddha one night while the latter was staying at Gijjhakūṭa hill near the city of Rājagaha. He told the Buddha of the event experienced by him in the heaven of Tāvatiṃsa. He said that on a certain occasion on a full moon day, all the gods of Tāvatiṃsa assembled in Sudhammā assembly-hall. The Four Great Kings of Cātumahārājika heaven were also present in the assembly.

In the East King Dhataraṭṭha, the king of the Gandhabbas, sat facing the western direction; in the South King Virūḷhaka, the king of the Kumbhaṇḍas, sat facing the northern direction; in the West King Virūpakkha; the king of the Nāgas, sat facing the eastern direction; and in the North King Vessavaṇa, the king of the Yakkhas, sat facing the southern direction. Pañcasikha said that just behind the seats of the Four Great Kings was his own seat. Sakka the Devarāja, the lord of Tāvatiṃsa heaven, presided over the meeting.

Pañcasikha continued his narration, saying that all the gods in the assembly were delighted with the increasing number of new gods in the realm. There were some gods who had observed the practice of the Buddha's teachings in their human lives. When they attained to this realm of existence, they surpassed the other gods with their splendour and glory. King Sakka, realising the delighted minds of his fellow gods, addressed them and narrated to them the eight wonderful qualities of the Buddha. At the end of his narration, a splendid ray of light appeared in the northern direction with its great brightness beyond the power of all the gods in that assembly. He told the god assembly that such a splendour of light was the antecedent of the appearance of a Brahmā.

---

58. DN 18 & 19.

At that moment a Brahmā named Sanaṅkumāra from the Brahmā world appeared before the gods of Tāvatiṃsa heaven. He surpassed all the assembled gods with his ordinary splendour and glory. Realising the delightful minds of the other gods with his mind, Sanaṅkumāra the Brahmā addressed them and requested King Sakka to repeat to him the eight wonderful qualities of the Buddha. Sakka the Devarāja yielded to his request and when he finished his narration Sanaṅkumāra the Brahmā related to the assembly the story of Mahāgovinda, which is said to be one of the Buddha's previous births.

The story of Pañcasikha the gandhabba given above adds some facts to our knowledge of the heaven world: that the Four Great Kings and Pañcasikha himself belong to the lowest heaven or Cātumahārājika; that their appearance in Tāvatiṃsa on some occasions shows the close relations between these two grades of heaven. The Four Great Kings, although they rule over other different heavens, seem to be among the god-retinue of Sakka the Devarāja.

According to the Sakkapañha Sutta,[59] Pañcasikha the gandhabba appears to be King Sakka's favourite attendant; he was made a guide and messenger when King Sakka went to visit the Buddha at Indasāla cave of Vediyaka mountain near the city of Rājagaha. The Sakkapañha Sutta also reveals that the goddesses (*devadhītā*) of Cātumahārājika went occasionally to entertain the Tāvatiṃsa gods with dancing and singing. This indicates the accessibility of Tāvatiṃsa heaven to the gods of Cātumahārājika.

In the heavenly hierarchy beginning from the lowest to the highest realm, Tāvatiṃsa ranks second of the six sensual-plane (*kāmāvacara*) heavens and the third of seven realms of the sensual happy plane (*kāmasugati-bhūmi*). Life in this realm is described as predominantly consisting of enjoyment. The span of life in this heaven is very long. It is said in the Aṅguttara Nikāya[60] that one hundred years in the world of human beings is equal to a single day and night of that realm; thirty such days and nights make one month; twelve such months one year; and one thousand such years is the approximate age of the gods in Tāvatiṃsa heaven.

59. DN 21.
60. AN III 70.19. Cf. Vibh? 1023.

It should be mentioned here that not every god of this heaven has a palace or vimāna of his own. Many gods were born here as personal attendants of other gods. It is said in the *Paramatthajotikā* that if a new god or goddess is born on the lap of the owner of a palace, he or she will be regarded as the son or daughter of that god; if a goddess is born in his bed, she will be his wife; if a new god or goddess is born in the precinct of his palace, he or she will become his personal attendant.[61] In some cases, if a new god or goddess is born in between the boundaries of two palaces, the owners of those palaces will try to possess that newcomer. If they cannot settle the dispute among themselves, they will approach King Sakka for necessary judgment. King Sakka will give his judgment according to the rules of heaven. According to the rules, if, at the beginning, a new god or goddess casts his or her eyes on any palace, he or she will be given to the owner of that palace, or otherwise he or she will be given to the owner of the palace which his or her birthplace is near. In some cases, the distance from the birthplace of the newcomer to both the palaces is equal and he or she does not particularly look at any palace. In a case such as this, King Sakka, in order to prevent a dispute among his citizens, will take for himself possession of the newcomer. His judgment is always deemed final in all cases.[62] Here there is nothing to be said about the god who is born with his own *vimāna*, as he acquires an independent status from the beginning of his existence in the realm.

This explanation is applied to the status of the gods in all realms of the sensual-plane heavens. Life in heaven seems to be very desirable since it is free from all the hardships and pains of human life. However, it should be mentioned here that individual differences exist even among gods of the same realm. The quality and quantity of happiness and glory vary from one individual to another. This depends on the nature of the meritorious kamma performed by each god in his previous human life.[63]

---

61. Cf. DN-a III 705.
62. DN-a III 705.
63. See, for example, Vv-a I.1 & 6, and II.5.

4. Heaven of the Easeful

The third realm of sensual-plane heavens and also the fourth of the sensual happy plane (*kāmasugati-bhūmi*) is called Yāmā. It is explained that this realm is the abode of the gods whose lives are without hardship, and thus it is called Yāmā; or it is called Yāmā because it is the abode of a Devarāja named Yāmā.[64]

In the Buddhist Pali scriptures we find very little description of this realm of happiness. It is said to be the next higher heaven from Tāvatiṃsa. If Tāvatiṃsa heaven is on the top of the Sineru mountain, which is the highest point of the human world, this heaven must, therefore, be in the sky. This is looked at, however, from the human point of view. But it is said that a garden or park called Nandavana exists in every heaven. This garden or park is so called because it gives enjoyment to those who come to it. If there is a park, there must, therefore, be a ground, for it is not possible for the trees in the park to grow up from the empty space. But what is seen as air or empty space by human beings may be seen otherwise by other beings whose bodies are not visible to human eyes. This point of view is affirmed by the statement which appears in the Mahāparinibbāna Sutta.[65] It is said in that Sutta that many of the gods from the ten thousand worlds came to pay their last visit to the Buddha before he passed away into Nibbāna in the Sāla park near the city of Kusināra. Among the gods assembled in the park, some of them took the air for the ground and some took the ground as ground.[66] This apparently indicates not only the differences between human beings and gods but also the differences among the celestial beings themselves.

However, the Yāmā heaven is a realm of happiness better and higher than Tāvatiṃsa. The ruler of this realm is a *devarāja* named Yāmā or Suyāmā. We are told in the Aṅguttara Nikāya[67]

64. Vibh-a 519.

65. DN 16.5.5-6.

66. The proper translation of the Pali is "devatās in the sky who perceive earth … devatās in the earth who perceive earth …" and it might rather refer to devas different in body and different in perception (DN 15.33) or to devas with a meditative attainment (DN 16.3.14; MN 1; 121).

67. AN 3:70.

that two hundred years in the world of human beings is equal to a single day and night in the heaven Yāmā; thirty such days and nights make one month; twelve such months make one year, and two thousand such heavenly years is the approximate age of the Yāmā gods. Thus the span of life in this realm of existence is much longer than that of the gods in Tāvatiṃsa heaven.

5. Heaven of the Contented

Tusita is the fourth realm of sensual-plane heavens, just higher than the Yāmā-bhūmi. Like other happy realms of existence, it is a place where virtuous persons are born after their human lives. It is explained that this heaven is called "Tusita" because it enables those who are born there to always enjoy the pleasures of life.[68]

The significance of this realm seems to lie in the fact that every Bodhisatta is said to be born here in his existence before the last one in which he attains to Buddhahood. From here he will be born as a human being, become the Buddha through enlightenment, preach and establish his doctrine in the human world and then pass away into Nibbāna.[69]

The Buddha's mother, who died on the seventh day after he was born, is said to have been reborn in this Tusita heaven.[70] The Abhidhamma, a portion of the Buddha's teachings contained in the Tipiṭaka, is generally believed to have been first preached to her by the Buddha in Tāvatiṃsa.[71] Why did the Buddha not go to Tusita heaven directly but instead chose Tāvatiṃsa as the place for preaching the Abhidhamma to his mother? The answer to this is that the Tāvatiṃsa is accessible to the gods of all realms, lower as well as higher heavens. The Buddha wanted his sermon to benefit not only his mother, but also gods of other realms who were interested in his teachings. If he chose to preach to his mother in Tusita, only the gods of the same realm and of the higher heavens could attend his sermon, but not the gods of lower realms since Tusita is inaccessible to them.

---

68. Nidd II 447; DN-a 1001; Vibh-a 519.
69. AN 4:127; AN 8:70.
70. Th 533f.; Th-a II 225. Cf. DN 1417.
71. J 483/J-a IV 265; Dhs introduction.

The ruler of this heaven is said to be a Devarāja named Santusita.[72] According to the Aṅguttara Nikāya[73] the span of life in this realm is much longer than that of the Yāmā gods. Four hundred human years are equal to a single day and night of the Tusita gods; thirty such days and nights make one month; twelve such months make one year; and four thousand such years make up the life period of the Tusita gods. This shows that the whole of one life of a human being is less than a quarter of one day in this realm.

6. Heaven of Those who Delight in Creation

The next realm higher than Tusita is a heaven called Nimmānaratī. It is explained that the gods of this realm enjoy the objects of the senses created by them and thus it is called Nimmānaratī.[74] One common characteristic of all the realms in the world of sensual desires (*kāmāvacara*) is that happiness is enjoyed in the form of sensual pleasures. However, in this connection there is a distinction between the gods of Nimmānaratī heaven and the gods of the other lower realms. In the lower heavens the objects of sensuous enjoyment exist by their own nature, but in Nimmānaratī heaven the beings of the realm create for themselves the objects of sense and enjoy them as they like. In this way we may say that the Nimmānaratī gods can enjoy the pleasures of life at will.[75]

In the Aṅguttara Nikāya and the Abhidhamma[76] we are told that the span of life in Nimmānaratī heaven is still much longer than that of the Tusita gods. Eight hundred human years is said to be a single day and night of Nimmānaratī; thirty such days and nights make one month; twelve such months make one year and eight thousand such heavenly years make the life period of the gods of Nimmānaratī heaven. This realm of happiness has a Devarāja named Sunimmita or Nimmita as ruler.[77]

---

72. DN 11.73; Bv-a 45.
73. AN 3:70.
74. DN-a 1001. Cf. DN 33.1.10.40.
75. It-a II 122; Vibh-a 519.
76. AN 3:70; Vibh. § 1023.
77. DN 11.73; Bv-a 45.

7. Heaven of Those who Wield Power over the Creations of Others

The sixth and the last realm of the sensual-plane heavens is Paranimmitavasavattī. This is the highest of all the realms characterised as the sensual happy plane. It is explained that this heaven is so called because it is the abode of the beings who enjoy the objects of sensual pleasures created by others.[78] Unlike the gods of Nimmānaratī heaven, the Paranimmitavasavattī gods themselves have nothing to do with the creation of the objects for sensuous enjoyment. Their duty is only to enjoy such ready-made objects of others' creations. It is said that their god-attendants who realise their desires do such services for them.[79]

The *Paramatthajotikā* mentions a Devarāja named Paranimmita as the ruler of this realm.[80] A heretic god named Vasavattī who is a Māra (demon) is also said to live in this heaven.[81] He has no faith in the Buddha and Buddhism. He tried many times to create obstacles for the Buddha, but he always met with failure. His power, however, surpasses that of the gods in the six sensual-plane heavens.[82]

According to the Aṅguttara Nikāya and the Abhidhamma[83] the span of life in Paranimmitavasavattī heaven is very long. One thousand and six hundred human years are but a single day and night of this realm thirty such days and nights make one month; twelve such months make one year; and sixteen thousand such

78. DN-a 1001. Cf. DN 33.1.10.40.

79. It-a II 122; DN-a III 1001; Vibh-a 519.

80. No god with this name has been traced and there seems to be a confusion. In AN 8:36, DN 11.79, and MN-a I 34 Vasavattī is said to be the chief of this realm. SN-a I 158 states that Vasavattī is a name for Māra.

81. According to MN-a I 34 (RE 52) Vasavattī is king here and Māra lives in one district wielding power over his own retinue like a rebel prince in a border area. MN-a also mentions that Māra and his retinue are not devas of the sensual-plane heavens. Other commentaries (e.g., Sn-a I 44) state that Māra is a "son of a god" (*devaputta*). A devaputta according to other commentaries can be a demon (*yakkha*) (e.g., J-a VI 118). In DN 20.13 Namucī, another name of Māra, is placed among the asuras. Cf. DN-a 689.

82. AN 4:15. For more on Māra, see DPPN.

83. AN 3:70; Vibh. § 1023.

heavenly years make a life-period of the gods in Paranimmitavasavattī heaven.

Now, we have seen that the sensual happy plane (*kāmasugati-bhūmi*) consists of seven realms, i.e., the realms of human beings and the six realms of sensual-plane heavens. According to Buddhism, birth or rebirth in any of these realms is caused by meritorious actions that one has performed in one's previous births. The type of good kamma that will bring one to rebirth in a certain one of these realms of happiness, is found explained in the Aṅguttara Nikāya.[84] According to this source, the Buddha gave his explanation as follows:

> "There is, O bhikkhus, someone in this world who performs meritorious action founded on charity (*dāna*) to a high degree, performs meritorious action founded on virtue (*sīla*) to a high degree and does not perform meritorious action founded on mind-development (*bhāvanā*). He, on the dissolution of the body after death, is reborn among the company of gods in the realm of the Four Great Kings (Cātumahārājika)....
>
> There is, O bhikkhus, someone in this world who performs meritorious action founded on charity to a high degree, performs meritorious action founded on virtue to a high degree and does not perform meritorious action founded on mind-development. He, on the dissolution of the body after death, is reborn among the company of gods in the realm of Tāvatiṃsa...."

In the above passages it is noteworthy that there is no difference in regard to the kinds of kamma that cause rebirth in Cātumahārājika and Tāvatiṃsa heavens. The same explanation is used for rebirth in the higher realms of Yāmā, Tusita, Nimmānaratī and Paranimmitavasavattī.

It is rather difficult to see the reason as to why the Buddha used the same explanation for rebirth in all the sensual realms (*kāmāvacara*) of heavens. Viewed from the hierarchical point of view of those realms, Tāvatiṃsa is hierarchically higher and superior in happiness than Cātumahārājika. To be reborn in Tāvatiṃsa requires a higher degree of meritorious actions than

84. AN 8:36.

those which bring about rebirth in Cātumahārājika heaven. Rebirth in the higher realms such as Yāmā, Tusita, etc., certainly requires even higher and higher degrees of wholesome kamma. If such is the case, the conditions for rebirth should vary in degree according to the hierarchical variation of the realms.

However, although we cannot find a satisfactory explanation about this anywhere, there is one reason that should not be overlooked. The degree of meritorious actions is not like the distance from one place to another place, which can be easily measured and divided. What we can say about the degree of good kamma is just to describe it by employing the adjective terms of distinction such as "low", "medium", "high", etc. Although the adjective "high" can be distinguished as "high", "higher" and "highest", it is still impossible to give a definite determination as to what is exactly high, higher and highest good kamma.

It might be due to this reason that when the Buddha explained the conditions of rebirth in the six sensual-plane realms, he merely said, "... meritorious action founded on charity and virtue to a high degree..." This may not be clear to common people, but for those who have real insight in the law of kamma with proper knowledge of rebirth and planes of existence, it is as clear as seeing different objects appearing just before their eyes.

This interpretation and argument may, however, still not be satisfactory. The writer wishes to leave this problem to the discretion of Buddhist scholars for further investigation. It should be noted also that the span of life in these happy realms of existence is much longer than that of human beings. The higher the realm the longer is the life-period and the better or superior is life and happiness. The higher heavens are generally inaccessible to the gods of the lower ones and the beings living there are invisible to the beings of the lower realms. These are the general characteristics of all heavens except the Cātumahārājika and Tāvatiṃsa which are closely connected.

Apart from the six sensual-plane heavens, Buddhism speaks of some higher and better realms of happy existence under the categories of plane of form (*rūpāvacara-bhūmi*) and the plane of the formless (*arūpāvacara-bhūmi*), respectively.

Chapter III.
The Plane of Form

The third plane of existence as classified in the Abhidhammatthasaṅgaha is the plane of form or *rūpāvacara-bhūmi*. This plane is distinguished in contrast to the plane of the formless (*arūpāvacara-bhūmi*). The distinction of the divisions of this plane of existence is made in connection with the four jhānic stages of meditation.[85] The plane of form consists of sixteen categories or sorts of celestial beings beginning from the lowest to the highest in hierarchical order. This hierarchical distinction cannot be fully comprehended without an understanding of the four stages of jhāna or absorption.

Buddhism regards meditation as an indispensable practice for the realisation of the ultimate truth. It is the second practice of the three-fold course of practice, viz., (1) *sīla,* moral practice or code of morality, (2) *samādhi,* meditation and (3) *paññā,* knowledge. *Jhāna* is the state of mind absorbed in meditation through concentration. Jhāna in this regard is technically called *rūpa-jhāna* (material-jhāna) the jhāna that the meditator attains by concentrating his mind upon material objects such as earth, water, fire, etc. On attaining jhāna the five hindrances (*nivaraṇa*), which are incompatible with the one-pointedness of mind, are completely suppressed.

Rūpa-jhāna, as described in the Abhidhamma Piṭaka,[86] consists of four stages as follows:

(1) The first stage, called first jhāna (*paṭhama-jhāna*), consists of five jhānic factors, viz., *vitakka* (applying the mind to the object of meditation), *vicāra* (sustaining the mind in the object), *pīti* (the joy of pleasant sensation), *sukha* (ease), and *ekaggatā* (one-pointedness of mind).

(2) The second stage, called second jhāna (*dutiya-jhāna*), consists of three factor, viz., *pīti, sukha and ekaggatā* (*vitakka and vicāra* have faded away).

---

85. Abhidh-s 5.31.
86. Vibh § 623. Cf. DN 2.75ff; 33.1.11.4; SN 45:8; MN 43.20.

(3) The third stage, called third jhāna (*tatiya-jhāna*), consists of two factors, viz., *sukha* and *ekaggatā* (*pīti* has faded away).
(4) The fourth stage called fourth jhāna (*catuttha-jhāna*), consists of two factors, viz., *upekkhā* (equanimity of the mind) and *ekaggatā* (*sukha* has faded away).

Rūpa-jhāna is sometimes divided into five stages and called *pañcama-jhāna*.[87] The difference between the *catuttha-jhāna* and the *pañcama-jhāna* is that in the latter each of the four jhānic factors, viz., *vitakka, vicāra, pīti* and *sukha,* disappear in the second, third, fourth and fifth stages respectively. The fifth stage of the *pañcama-jhāna* is identical with the fourth stage of the *catuttha-jhāna.*

1. Rebirth in the First Jhāna Plane

Unlike rebirth in the lower planes of existence, birth or rebirth in the plane of form is caused by kamma that is definitely known. The first realm of this plane is where those who attain the first stage of rūpa-jhāna in their previous lives are born.[88] Hence this realm is called the first jhāna plane (*paṭhama-jhāna-bhūmi*). In this realm there are three sorts of beings, namely; (1) members of Brahma's assembly (*brahmapārisajja*), (2) Brahma's ministers (*brahmapurohita*) and (3) Great Brahmā's (*mahābrahmā*).[89] It is explained in the Vibhaṅga of the Abhidhamma Piṭaka that one who attains the first jhāna with the inferior strength of meditation will be reborn, after death, among the Brahmapārisajja gods; the one who attains this jhāna with the medium strength of meditation will be reborn among the Brahmapurohita gods; and one who attains this jhāna with the superior strength of meditation will be reborn among the Mahābrahmā gods.[90] The span of life of the Brahmapārisajja is

87. This five stage jhāna sequence is already given in the Canon; i.e., MN 128.31; AN 8:63. Cf. SN 43:3; DN 33.10.50. The normal first jhāna is divided into two jhānas in this sequence.
88. Cf. AN 4:123.
89. In the Canon these three types of devas are classified as *brahmakāyikā devā*, e.g., DN 15.33; AN 4:123. The first two types are only mentioned in a few places in the Canon; e.g., SN 6:2.4; MN 49; DN 21.12; Th 1187. MN 49 also mentions *brahmaparisā* (Brahma's Assembly).

one-third of an aeon (*kappa*), that of the Brahmapurohita is one half of an aeon, and that of the Mahābrahmā is one aeon.[91]

According to the *Paramatthajotikā* these three sorts of celestial beings live on the same plane of the first jhāna plane. It further explains that Mahābrahmā is the ruler of this realm and that there is one Mahābrahmā. This seems, however, to contradict the explanation of the Vibhaṅga, which says that one who attains the first jhāna with the highest or superior strength of meditation will be reborn among the Mahābrahmās. It is true that there is one Mahābrahmā who is the ruler of the realm and this is, according to the Brahmajāla Sutta,[92] the Mahābrahmā who was born in the realm before all others. Since the first jhāna with the superior strength of meditation can be attained by anyone who follows the course of mind-development (*bhāvanā*), there must be, therefore, many other gods of the same class with Mahābrahmā.[93] The distinction in this regard is only that those who are born in the realm after the first Mahābrahmā regard and respect him as the superior and the ruler of the realm.[94]

2. Rebirth in the Second Jhāna Plane

The higher, the subtler and the better sort of life and happiness than that of the being of the first jhāna plane is that of the beings in the second jhāna plane (*dutiya-jhāna-bhūmi*). As in the first realm of the plane of form, the celestial beings of this second realm are of three different sorts, viz., (1) gods of limited radiance (*parittābhā devā*), (2) gods of unlimited radiance (*appamāṇābhā devā*) and (3) gods of brilliant radiance (*ābhassarā devā*).[95]

With regard to kamma that brings a person to rebirth in this realm, the Vibhaṅga gives a similar explanation as in the case of one who is born in the first realm. It is said that one who attains the second stage of *rūpa-jhāna* with the inferior strength

90. Vibh § 1024; Abhidh-s 5.31.
91. Ibid. Cf. AN 4:123.
92. DN 1.2.5; cf. DN 15.33.
93. Cf. MN 120.
94. Cf. MN 49.
95. MN 111; 41.18-42 & 120.19-32 add another type, the Gods of Radiance (*ābhā devā*), but MN-a I 32 states that this a collective name for the 3 other classes.

of meditation will be reborn, after death, as a God of Limited Radiance, with the medium strength of meditation as a God of Unlimited Radiance, and with the highest strength of meditation as a God of Brilliant Radiance.[96]

The period of life of the Parittābha god is two aeons (*kappa*), of the Appamāṇābha god is four aeons and of Ābhassara god is eight aeons.[97] These three types of celestial beings are said to live in the same plane of the realm.[98]

3. Rebirth in the Third Jhāna Plane

The third realm of the plane of form is the third jhāna plane (*tatiya-jhāna-bhūmi*). This is the realm where one who attains the third stage of rūpa-jhāna will be born after death. As in the two lower realms, beings in this realm there are also three sorts, namely; (1) gods of limited beautiful splendour (*parittasubhā devā*), (2) gods of unlimited beautiful splendour (*appamāṇasubhā devā*) and (3) gods of refulgent splendour (*subhakiṇha* or *subhakiṇṇā devā*).[99]

The differences between these three types of divine beings depend on the differences of the strength of meditation, as in the cases of the beings of the first and second realms discussed above.[100]

The Vibhaṅga says that the life-period of the Parittasubha god is sixteen kappas, of the Appamāṇasubha god thirty-two kappas, and of the Subhakiṇha god sixty-four kappas.[101]

4. Rebirth in the Fourth Jhāna Plane

The fourth and the last of all the realms in the plane of form is the fourth jhāna plane (*catuttha-jhāna-bhūmi*). It is the realm where those who attain the fourth stage of rūpa-jhāna are born.

---

96. Vibh. § 1025.
97. Ibid. Cf. AN 4:123.
98. Vibh-a 520.
99. MN 41.18-42; 120.19-32 add another type, the Gods of Splendour (*subhā devā*), but MN-a states that this a collective name for the three other classes.
100. Vibh § 1026.
101. Ibid. Cf. AN 4:123. They share the same plane like the beings in the preceding jhāna planes.

In this bhūmi there are seven sorts or groups of beings, viz., (1) gods of great reward (*vehapphalā devā*), (2) non percipient gods (*asaññasattā devā*), (3) durable gods (*avihā devā*), (4) serene gods (*ātappā devā*) (5) beautiful gods (*sudassā devā*), (6) clear sighted gods (*sudassī*) and (7) supreme gods (*Akaniṭṭhā*). In each of the former three realms, although the beings are classified into three groups, they are said to live on the same plane of the realm. However, in the fourth jhāna plane, different groups of beings live in different realms. Thus the fourth jhāna plane is subdivided into six different realms as the abodes of seven different sorts of beings.

It is to be noted that the particular names like Parittābha, Subhakiṇha, Vehapphala, Avihā, Atappā, etc., are the collective names of the beings born in the same realm, just as the term "Indian" stands for the people of Indian stock born in India. Such a name as Vehapphala is also used as the designation of the realm.

The Vehapphala and the Asaññasatta devas, although they are different sorts of beings, are said to live on the same plane.[102] An ordinary man who practises meditation and attains the fourth stage of rūpa-jhāna, and who can maintain it up to the last moment of his life, will be reborn in this realm.[103] The Asaññasatta (non-percipient being) is the particular type of rebirth for one who develops meditation with the feeling of dispassion (*virāga*) towards perception (*saññā*). As a result of this, if he dies when his mind is absorbed in the fourth stage of jhāna, he is born as a unconscious or non-percipient being in the world of form.[104] This being is said to be actually a one-aggregate being, i.e., a being who possesses only the *rūpakkhandha*, with the absence of all the other four aggregates, namely, feeling (*vedanā*), perception (*saññā*), disposition (*saṅkhāra*) and consciousness (*viññāṇa*). The non-percipient being (*asaññasatta*) is, therefore, a being without all mental activities.[105] The being remains like a motionless stone in the realm from the beginning up to the end of his life. It is said that at the end of its life the being will regain consciousness, but as

102. MN-a I 35.
103. AN 4:123.
104. Abhidh-s 5.31; DN-a to DN 1.31/DN-a I 118; AN 9:24.
105. Vibh § 1017.

soon as consciousness arises, it moves from that realm and takes rebirth in another realm suitable to his previous kamma.[106]

The five other realms of the fourth jhāna plane—Avihā, Atappā, Sudassā, Sudassī and Akaniṭṭhā—are collectively called the Suddhāvāsa or the Abode of the Pure.[107] According to Buddhism, only one who attains the third holy stage of Buddhism—the non-returner (*anāgāmi*)—is rèborn, after death, in these realms. One who is born in any of the other heaven worlds may be reborn again in the human world or even in the plane of misery (*duggati*),[108] but one who is born in the Suddhāvāsa will never return to rebirth in any lower realms.[109]He will attain final release in and enter into Nibbāna from this Abode of the Pure.[110]

Now, the question arises as to why different individuals who attain the same fourth stage of jhāna are born, after death, in different realms of existence. In this connection we find the answer in the Vibhaṅga, which says:

> "Among those who develop and sustain the fourth stage of jhāna some are born among the Asaññasattā, some are born among the Vehapphala gods... among the Avihā gods... among Atappā gods... among the Sudassā gods... among the Sudassī gods... among the Akaniṭṭhā gods. This is so because of the individual differences as regards the objects of concentration, the manners of concentration, as regards impulse (*chanda*), resolve (*paṇidhi*), determination (*adhimokkha*), way of endeavour (*abhinīhāra*), and knowledge (*paññā*)."[111]

The *Paramatthajotikā*[112] explains that one who is destined to be born in the Suddhāvāsa must attain the fifth stage of jhāna and

---

106. DN 1.31 & DN-a I 118.
107. DN 33.2.17; Abhidh-s 5.6. AN-a IV 190: "The Suddhāvāsā are like a campsite (*khandhāvāraṭṭhāna*) of Buddhas. When no Buddhas arise in an immeasurable aeon, this place remains empty."
108. AN 3:114; 4:123. These suttas state that the worldling, although he has been reborn in a *rūpa-loka*, can fall back into a bad bourn, but the *ariyapuggala* (noble person) attains full Nibbāna there.
109. MN 12.56/M I 82; AN 4:172; 7:15; 7:52.
110. Ibid.
111. Vibh § 1027.

must be an *non-returner (anāgāmi)*. The controlling principle or the directive force (*indriya*), which is the predominant character of each individual, will determine the realm where he is to be reborn. One whose directive force is faith (*saddhā*) will be reborn in the realm of Avihā; one whose directive force is energy (*viriya*) will be reborn is the realm of Atappā; one whose directive force is mindfulness (*sati*) will be reborn in the realm of Sudassī; one whose directive force is concentration (*samādhi*) will be reborn in the realm of Sudassī; and one whose directive force is wisdom or reason (*paññā*) will be reborn in the realm of Akaniṭṭhā.[113]

The following are the approximate life-periods of the beings born in the fourth jhāna plane given in the Vibhaṅga: the life-period of the Vehapphala gods and the Asaññasattā (non-percipient beings) is five hundred kappas, of the Avihā gods one thousand kappas, of the Atappā gods two thousand kappas, of the Sudassī gods four thousand kappas, of the Sudassī gods eight thousand kappas, and of the Akaniṭṭhā gods sixteen thousand kappas.[114]

It is said in the Mahāpadāna Sutta of the Dīgha Nikāya[115] that the Suddhāvāsa is the only plane of existence where the Buddha, in his long wandering in saṃsāra before attaining Buddhahood, had never been born.[116] According to the sutta, one day when he was in seclusion under the Sāla tree in Subhāvanā forest near the city of Ukkaṭṭhā, the Buddha thought of this and wanted to visit this Abode of the Pure. He then disappeared from under the tree and reappeared among the gods of the Suddhāvāsa in a single moment. Many gods of the realm came to him and told him of the important events which

---

112. Pmd § 154, Abhidh-s 5.31. Cf. AN 4:136; 9:35: *samādhismiṃ paripūrakārī hoti*. AN 4:124 states that one who practices insight (supposedly an *anāgāmin*) and who has attained any of the four jhānas can be reborn in the *suddhāvāsā*. An *anāgāmin* is not necessarily reborn in the *suddhāvāsā*, but can be reborn in any *rūpa-* or *arūpa-loka*. See AN 4:172 and CMA 5.31/p.218-19.

113. The suttas (MN 41; 120; AN 4:123; 4:172; 8:35; etc.) indicate that the resolve (*adhiṭṭhāna*) of one endowed with virtue, generosity, wisdom, etc, is a determining factor for being reborn in a particular realm.

114. Vibh § 1027. Cf. AN 4:123.

115. DN 19.29.

116. Cf. MN 12.56/M I 82; Bv-a 224.

had occurred in the periods of many previous Buddhas, beginning from the time of the Buddha named Vipassī who enlightened the world with his teachings ninety-one aeons before the present one.

Now, we have seen that in the plane of form there are sixteen sorts or categories of beings living in different realms according to the nature of their previous kamma. Life in this plane of existence is subtler and happier than that of the sensual-plane heavens where sensual pleasures dominate.

The differences between the beings in the sensual-plane and those in the plane of form are that the beings in the sensual-plane consist of two different sexes—male and female—while no differences in sex appear among the beings in the plane of form.

Happiness in the plane of form is without, and superior to, sexual delight. The reason for this is that the rūpāvacara beings' feeling of sensual pleasures in which sexual enjoyment plays the dominant role has been absolutely eliminated when they were human beings. This eventually leads to the disappearance of the sex organs since they haven't any function for the beings in this plane. It is said, however, that although the beings of the rūpāvaçara heaven possess no sex, their physical appearance is of human male predominance.[117]

---

117. Vibh-a 437.

Chapter IV. The Plane of the Formless

The last plane of existence where living beings are born according to the result of their kamma is the plane of the formless or *arūpāvacara-bhūmi*. Similar to the plane of form, the plane of the formless is closely connected with the *arūpa-jhāna* (the non-material jhāna). This jhāna can be developed only when a person has experienced all the four stages of rūpa-jhāna. The practitioner of meditation intending to rise higher in the levels of jhāna, gives up the form-meditation-subject (*rūpa-kammaṭṭhāna*) and practises the formless-meditation-subject (*arūpa-kammaṭṭhāna*) that will lead him to the attainment of arūpa-jhāna.[118]

There are four stages of arūpa-jhāna which the meditator will attain one by one, as follows:

1. *Ākāsānañcāyatana* (the base of infinite space): The meditator, having obtained and then abandoned the fourth stage of rūpa-jhāna, applies his mind to the infinity of space (*ananta-ākāsa*). He thereby attains the first stage of arūpa-jhāna called *ākāsānañcāyatana*.
2. *Viññāṇañcāyatana* (the base of infinite consciousness): He, having obtained the first stage, gives up concentrating on the infinity of space and switches his mind over to concentration on the infinity of consciousness (*ananta-viññāṇa*). He thereby attains the second stage of arūpa-jhāna called *viññāṇañcāyatana*.
3. *Ākiñcaññāyatana* (the base of nothingness): The meditator, having attained and dwelled in the second stage, gives up concentrating on the infinity of consciousness and switches his mind over to the concentration on nothingness of consciousness (*ākiñcañña*). He thereby attains the third stage of arūpa-jhāna called *ākiñcaññāyatana*.

---

118. E.g., AN 9:33. The term *arūpa-jhāna*, such as *rūpa-jhāna*, is a commentarial term that is not used in the suttas, where only the term *āyatana* (base) is used to denote these states.

4. *Nevasaññānāsaññāyatana* (the base of neither-perception-nor-non-perception): He, having attained and dwelled in the third stage, gives up concentrating on the nothingness of consciousness. His mind then enters a state in which cognition is so extremely subtle that it cannot be said whether it is or not. At this point he is, regarded as having attained the fourth stage of arūpa-jhāna called *nevasaññānāsaññāyatana*.

A person who has developed any of these four stages of arūpa-jhāna and sustained it up to the last moment of life will, at the breaking up of his body, after death, be reborn in the world of the formless (*arūpaloka*).[119] The plane of the formless is classified into four realms in accordance with the four stages of the arūpa-jhāna. One who attains the first stage will be reborn, after death, in the first realm; one who attains the second stage will be reborn in the second realm; one who attains the third stage will be reborn in the third realm and one who attains the fourth stage will be reborn in the fourth realm.[120] The four realms of the plane of the formless bear the same names as the four stages of the arūpa-jhāna, i.e., (1) Ākāsānañcāyatana, (2) Viññāṇañcāyatana, (3) Ākiñcaññāyatana and (4) Nevasaññānāsaññāyatana.

The Vibhaṅga gives the following approximate life-periods of the formless gods in the plane of the formless: The life-period of the Ākāsānañcāyatana gods is twenty thousand kappas; of the Viññāṇañcāyatana gods forty thousand kappas; of the Ākiñcaññāyatana gods sixty thousand kappas; and of the Nevasaññānāsaññāyatana gods eighty-four thousand kappas.[121]

The problem now arises as to how long one aeon or kappa is. To this question we find a parable explaining the duration of an aeon in the Pali Piṭaka itself. According to the Saṃyutta Nikāya[122] it is said that a bhikkhu put to the Buddha a question about the duration of an aeon. The Buddha replied that an aeon is exceedingly long. It is not easy to reckon how long by saying so many years, so many thousand years, so many hundred thousand years.

---

119. AN 3:114.
120. Ibid.
121. Vibh § 1028. Cf. AN 3:114.
122. SN 15:5.

> "Suppose there were a mountain of solid mass one *yojana* (league) wide, one yojana across and one yojana high, and at the end of every hundred years a man were to stroke it once each time with a kasi cloth. That mountain in this way would be sooner done away with and ended than would an aeon (*kappa*)."

This simile indicates that the duration of an aeon or kappa is immeasurable.[123] The *Paramatthajotikā* explains that an aeon is the span of time counted from the beginning of the world's evolution up to its destruction. At the end of its cosmic life the world will be destroyed by fire, water or wind. After its destruction it starts forming again by gradual evolution and it will be again destroyed at the end. The span of time from the beginning to the end of the world is regarded as one kappa.[124] In eight kappas the world will be destroyed seven times by fire and one time by water. The cycle of destruction will repeat itself in this way up to the sixty-fourth kappas and then the world is destroyed by wind.[125] One round of sixty-four kappas is called an incalculable aeon (*asaṅkheyya-kappa*).

It is said that when the world is destroyed by fire the heavens are destroyed up to the first jhāna plane; when it is destroyed by water the second jhāna plane is also destroyed; and when it is destroyed by wind the heavens are destroyed up to the third jhāna plane. Only the fourth jhāna plane and the four realms of the plane of the formless remain undisturbed by the destructions of the world.[126]

The life-period of the beings in the plane of the formless appears to be exceedingly long. It is very difficult even to imagine how long it is. Even one kappa is still immeasurable. There is, therefore, nothing to say about the eighty-four thousand kappas that are said to be the span of life in the Nevasaññānāsaññāyatana realm. But although the life-period in the plane of the formless is so long, the beings born there still have to be reborn in other planes of existence when their span of life in that particular realm expires. They may obtain rebirth in

---

123. Cf. AN 4:156.
124. Vism 13.55-63.
125. Vism 13.65.
126. DN 1.2; 27.10; AN 7:42; Vism 13.20-65. Cf. CMA ch. 5 § 14.

other planes of happiness or in the plane of misery, depending on the nature of their previous kamma.

The plane of form and the plane of the formless are collectively called Brahmaloka or the world of Brahmā.[127] It should be noted that the formless beings of the plane of the formless are just opposite to the non-percipient beings (*asaññasattā*) of the plane of form: the formless being is born without form or corporeal body (*rūpa*) while the non-percipient being is born without mental faculties (*nāma*). In the case of the non-percipient being we can imagine a being subsisting in an unconscious state from the beginning up to the end of his life in this realm. However, in the case of the formless beings in the plane of the formless, it is very difficult to see how life subsists without a material body. Nevertheless, the cases of the non-percipient beings and the formless beings in the plane of the formless demonstrate the two extreme types of kamma that yield results just opposite to each other.

Conclusion

We may conclude that rebirth and the planes of existence are closely connected, since to be reborn means to exist somewhere. Buddhism speaks of rebirth and the planes of existence in three different ways. (1) Viewed in terms of happiness and suffering, which are the results of good and evil kamma, there are only two planes of existence, viz., the plane of happiness (*sugati*) and the plane of suffering (*duggati*). (2) Viewed in terms of kamma which brings about rebirth in different planes of existence suitable to its nature, there are three planes, namely, the plane of sensual existence (*kāmabhava*), the plane of form existence (*rūpabhava*) and the plane of formless existence (*arūpabhava*).[128] (3) Viewed from the same ground, the Venerable Anuruddhācariya in his *Abhidhammatthasaṅgaha*[129] classifies the planes of existence into four groups, namely, the plane of misery (*apāya-bhūmi*), sensual happy plane (*kāmasugati-bhūmi*), the plane

127. E.g., MN 97.31; Vibh-a 521 (§ 1028).
128. MN 9.30.
129. Abhidh-s ch. 5 § 9.

of form (*rūpāvacara-bhūmi*) or, and the plane of the formless (*arūpāvacara-bhūmi*).

All these are the planes of existence where an unemancipated individual is to be reborn again and again in the course of his wanderings in saṃsāra. To be born here and die here and be born elsewhere, to be born there and die there, to die there and be born elsewhere, is what Buddhists call the Wheel of Becoming (*bhavacakka*).

Appendix

The Four Planes of Existence and Thirty-one Realms of Rebirth

For the durations of existences and causes for rebirth, see AN 4:123; Vibh § 1022-28; Abhidh-s ch. V.

The realms are given according to the sequence given the Pali Canon (e.g., DN 33.3.4). [130*]

Tables

1. The Woeful Plane *(apāyabhūmi)*
2. The Sensual Happy Plane *(kāmasugatibhūmi)*
3. The Plane of Form *(rūpa-bhūmi)*
   a. The Plane of the First Jhāna *(paṭhama-jhānabhūmi)*
   b. The Plane of the Second Jhāna*(dutiyajhānabhūmi)*
   c. The Plane of the Third Jhāna *(tatiyajhānabhūmi)*
   d. The Plane of the Fourth Jhāna *(catutthajhānabhūmi)*
   e. Plane of Pure Abodes *(suddhāvāsabhūmi)*
4. The Plane of the Formless *(arūpabhūmi)*

130. The sequence (*niraya, pettivisaya, asurakāya,* and *tiracchānayoni*) that is given in the introduction (pp. 39) of *Long Discourses of the Buddha* by Maurice Walshe is incorrect.

I. THE WOEFUL PLANE (*APĀYABHUMI*)

Duration of existence is indefinite. Only when their evil kamma is exhausted, can beings leave these realms.

Realm of Rebirth	Inhabitants	Cause of rebirth here
(1) Hell (*niraya*) **Great Hells** (*mahāniraya*): Gapless One (*Avīci*) Great Tormenter (*Mahātapana*) Tormenter (*Tāpana*) or Small Tormenter (*Cullatāpana*) Great Roarer (*Mahāroruva*) or Flamy Roarer (*Jālaroruva*) Roarer (*Roruva*) or Smoky Roarer (*Dhūmaroruva*) Crusher (*Sanghāta*) Black-thread (*Kāḷasutta*) Reviver (*Sañjīva*) **Subsidiary hells** (*ussada-niraya*) are surrounding each of the Great Hells on each of its four sides: Caustic River Subsidiary (*Vettaranī-ussada*) Sword-leafed-forest Subsidiary (*Asipattavana-ussada*) Silk-cotton-tree Subsidiary (*Simpalīvana-ussada*) Ember Subsidiary (*Kukkuḷa-ussada*) Filth Subsidiary (*Gūtha-ussada*)	Hell beings (*nirayasatta*), hell-guardians (*nirayapāla*), determiner kings (*yamarāja*).	• Unwholesome actions (MN 41; 129) • Lack of virtue, holding to wrong views (AN 10:177) • Telling lies, not keeping word deceit, abuse of ascetic state, adultery, wrong views • (Dhp chapter 22) • Murdering parents or an arahant; injuring the Buddha; creating a schism in the Sangha (AN 5:129)

(2) Animal Birth (*Tiracchānayoni*)	Animals (*tiracchāna*)	Animals (*tiracchāna*) • Lack of virtue, holding to wrong views. If one is generous to monks and nuns, however, one may be reborn as an "ornamented" animal (i.e., a bird with bright plumage; a horse with attractive markings, etc.). (AN 10:177) • Behaving like an animal (MN 57)
(3) Region of Ghosts (*Pettivisaya*)	Ghosts (*peta*) – 4 types: a. petas who live on the gifts of others (*paradattūpajīvīka-peta*), b. hungry and thirsty petas (*khuppipāsika-peta*), c. petas consumed by craving (*nijjhāmataṇhika-peta*), d. black-eared peta (*kāḷakañcika-peta*).	• Unwholesome actions (MN 41; 129) • Lack of virtue, holding to wrong views (AN 10:177)
(4) Titan Group/Titan Birth (*Asurakāya/Asurayoni*)	Titans (*asura*)	• Unwholesome actions (MN 41; 129)

II. THE SENSUAL HAPPY PLANE (*KĀMASUGATIBH√MI*)

Realm of Rebirth	Inhabitants	Duration	Cause of rebirth here
(5) World of humans (*manussaloka*)	Human beings (*manussa*)	About 100 years.	• Wholesome actions (MN 41; 129) • Virtue and wisdom (AN 10:177)
(6) The Heaven of the Four Great Kings (*Cātummahārājika-devaloka*)	Four Great King Gods (*cātummahārājikā devā; gandhabbas, yakkhas, nāgas, kumbhaṇḍas, garulas/supaṇṇas, devāsuras, accharās.*)	500 divine years 9 million human years.	
(7) The Heaven of the Thirty-t hree (*Tāvatiṃsa*)	The Thirty-three Gods (*tāvatiṃsa-devā*)	1,000 divine years 36 million human years.	
(8) Heaven of the Easeful (*Yāmā-devaloka*)	Devas Wielding Power over the Creations of Others (*paranimmita-vasavatti-devā*)	16,000 divine years 9,216 million human years	

III. The Plane of Form (*R∨PA-BH∨MI*)

Strictly speaking, the realms in the four jhānic subdivisions of this plane are not separate because the beings share the same jhāna or anāgāmin attainment realms, e.g., the *Brahma-purohita devā* and *Brahmapārisajja devā* are Mahābrahmā's ministers and retinue. See MN 49 and Vibh-a 520. All beings in this plane are Brahmā gods (*brahmakāyika-devā*).

a. The Plane of the First Jhāna (*paṭhamajhānabhūmi*)			
Realm of Rebirth	**Inhabitants**	**Duration**	**Cause of rebirth here**
(12) World of the Retinue of Brahma (*Brahmapārisajja-devaloka*)	Gods who are members of the Retinue of Brahma (*brahmapārisajja devā*)	1/3 aeon	Attainment & maintenance of 1st jhāna (AN 4:123) in minor degree (Vibh. § 1024)
(13) World of Devas who are ministers of Brahma (*Brahmapurohita-devaloka*)	Gods who are ministers of Brahma (*brahma-purohita devā*)	1/2 aeon	Ditto, medium degree. (Vibh. § 1024)
(14) World of Great Brahmā (*Mahābrahmā-devaloka*)	Great Brahmās (*Mahābrahmā*)	1 aeon	Ditto, highest degree. (Vibh. § 1024)
b. The Plane of the Second Jhāna (*dutiyajhānabhūmi*)			
Realm of Rebirth	**Inhabitants**	**Duration**	**Cause of rebirth here**
(15) Limited Radiance Heaven (*Parittābha-devaloka*)	Devas of Limited Radiance (*parittābha devā*)	2 aeons	Attainment & maintenance of 2nd jhāna (AN 4:123) in minor degree. (Vibh. § 1025)
(16) Unlimited Radiance Heaven (*Appamāṇābha-devaloka*)	Devas of Unlimited Radiance (*appamāṇābha devā*)	4 aeons	Ditto, medium degree. (Vibh. § 1025)

(17) Brilliant Radiance Heaven (*Ābhassara-devaloka*)	Devas of Brilliant Radiance (*ābhassara devā*)	8 aeons	Ditto, highest degree. (Vibh. § 1025)
c. The Plane of the Third Jhāna (*tatiyajhānabhūmi*)			
Realm of Rebirth	**Inhabitants**	**Duration**	**Cause of rebirth here**
(18) Limited Glory Heaven (*Parittasubha-devaloka*)	Devas of Limited Glory (*Parittasubha devā*)	16 aeons	Attainment & maintenance of 3rd jhāna (AN 4:123) in minor degree (Vibh. § 1026)
(19) Unbounded Glory Heaven (*Appamāṇasubha-devaloka*)	Devas of Unlimited Glory (*Appamāṇasubha devā*)	32 aeons	Ditto, medium degree. (Vibh. § 1026)
(20) Refulgent Glory Heaven (*Subhakiṇṇa-* or *Subhakiṇha-devaloka*)	Devas of Refulgent Glory (*Subhakiṇhā devā*)	64 aeons	Ditto, highest degree. (Vibh. § 1026)
d. The Plane of the Fourth Jhāna (*catutthajhānabhūmi*)			
Realm of Rebirth	**Inhabitants**	**Duration**	**Cause of rebirth here**
(21) Abode of Great Reward (*Vehapphala-āvāsa*)	Devas of Great Reward (*Vehapphalā devā*)	500 aeons	Attainment & maintenance of 4th Jhāna (AN 4:123; Vibh. § 1027)
22) Base of non-percipient beings (*Asaññasattāyatana*) or Abode of the non-percipient beings (*Asaññasattāvāsa*)	Non-percipient-being Devas (*Asaññasattā devā*)	500 aeons	Attainment & maintenance of 4th Jhāna (Vibh. §1027 & D-a to DN 1.31.); DN 15.33 calls it an *āyatana*.

e. Plane of Pure Abodes (*suddhāvāsabhūmi*)

Only those who have attained to the stage of non-return (*anāgāmi*) are reborn in these abodes, where they eventually attain arahatship. This plane is only accessible for anāgāmis and arahats. In the Abhidhamma classification this plane is a subdivision of the Plane of the Fourth Jhāna.

Realm of Rebirth	Inhabitants	Duration	Cause of rebirth here
(23) The Durable Abode (*Avihā-bhavana*)	Durable Devas (*Avihā devā*)	1,000 aeons	Attainment & maintenance of 4th jhāna and attainment of non-return (Vibh § 1027; Abhidh-s 5.31. Cf. AN 4:124; 4:136; 9:35)
(24) The Serene Abode (*Atappā-bhavana*)	Serene Devas (*Atappā devā*)	2,000 aeons	
(25) The Beautiful Abode (*Sudassā-bhavana*)	Beautiful Devas (*Sudassā devā*)	4,000 aeons	
(26) The Clear-sighted Abode (*Sudassī-bhavana*)	Clear-sighted Devas (*Sudassī devā*)	8,000 aeons	
(27) The Supreme Abode (*Akaniṭṭhā-bhavana*)	Supreme Devas (*Akaniṭṭhā devā*)	16,000 aeons	

IV. THE PLANE OF THE FORMLESS (*AR√PABH√MI*)

Realm of Rebirth	Inhabitants	Duration	Cause of rebirth here
(28) The Base of Infinite Space (*Ākāsānañcāyatana*)	Gods attained to the Base of Infinite Space (*ākāsānañcāyatanūpagā devā*)	20,000 aeons	Attainment & maintenance of the Base of Infinite Space
(29) The Base of Infinite Consciousness (*Viññāṇañcāyatana*)	Gods attained to the Base of Infinite Consciousness (*viññāṇañcāyatanūpagā devā*)	40,000 aeons	Attainment & maintenance of the Base of Infinite Consciousness
(30) The Base of Nothingness (*Ākiñcaññāyatana*)	Gods attained to the Base of Nothingness (*Ākiñcaññāyatanūpagā devā*)	60,000 aeons	Attainment & maintenance of Base of Nothingness
(31) The Base of Neither-perception-nor-non-perception (*Nevasaññānāsaññāyatana*)	Gods attained to the Base of Neither-perception-nor-non-perception (*nevasaññānāsaññā-yatanūpagā devā*)	84,000 aeons	Attainment & maintenance of the Base of Neither-perception-nor-non-perception

Wise Reflection

The Importance of
Wise Reflection in Meditation

by

Steve Weissman

THE WHEEL PUBLICATION NO. 463

First published 2006

INTRODUCTION

The purpose of this essay is to explain the value of wise reflection, *yoniso manasikāra*, and to encourage readers to use their own thought processes for the growth of wisdom in their formal meditation practice. The majority of experienced Buddhist meditators whom I have met during thirty years of meditation and eighteen years of teaching were unfamiliar with formal reflective meditation. By way of this essay I hope to correct this lack of understanding.

The Buddha himself greatly stressed the importance of wise reflection. In an important discourse on the topic of wise reflection, the Sabbāsava Sutta (MN 2), the Buddha says:

> "I say that the getting rid of anxieties and troubles[1] is possible for one who knows and sees, not for one who does not know and see. What must one know and see in order to get rid of anxieties and troubles? Wise reflection and unwise reflection.
>
> For one who reflects unwisely, there arise anxieties and troubles that have not yet arisen, and those that have already arisen increase. But for one who reflects wisely, anxieties and troubles that have not yet arisen do not arise, and those already arisen disappear."

What is *yoniso manasikāra*? Yoniso manasikāra is a Pali term that can be translated as wise reflection. This includes systematic attention, careful attention, reasoned attention, having thorough method in one's thought, proper consideration, wise consideration, critical reflection, analytical reflection, or thinking in terms of causal relations or by way of problem

---

1. I have adapted this translation of the word *āsava* from the one by Venerable Dr. W. Rāhula in his book *What the Buddha Taught*. Regarding my general agreement his translation, I add his footnote: "The term *āsava* in this Sutta has wider senses than its usual psychological and ethical meanings such as 'influx,' 'outflow,' 'defilement,' 'impurity.' It is here used figuratively and embraces both psychological cares and physical troubles and difficulties as can be seen in the sequel."

solving. Yoniso manasikāra is a significant factor leading to the arising of insight or wisdom.

What causes our mental suffering? Simply stated, it is wrong thinking that produces our mental *dukkha* (suffering).[2] Right thinking will end our mental dukkha. Thus, it is important to use formal reflective meditation in order to develop right thinking.

In helping the reader to understand the importance of reflective meditation, much of this booklet is devoted to trying to correct meditation "myths." By "myths" I mean certain misunderstandings that many Buddhists have acquired. These misunderstandings are widespread, and as a result, many meditators do not realise the importance of reflective meditation and may even doubt some of the things written here. To support my understanding, I have included several relevant teachings from the scriptures that emphasise the importance of wise reflection.

For any of you who may experience doubts concerning what is written here, I ask you to follow the Buddha's advice to all of us, to seek the truth in order to dispel ignorance. If you are going to follow the Buddha in this way, then it is important that you stay open to what is presented. If you stay open, yet after reading find that you still have remaining doubts, feel free to contact me at the address at the end of this booklet. I welcome any wise discussion on anything presented here. I do believe, though, that if you are seriously interested in ending your mental dukkha, then what is written here will help you greatly.

---

2. It is assumed that the reader is already practising Buddhist meditation and is familiar with basic Buddhist Pali terms.

PART 1

Meditation and Concentration

Over thirty years ago I read my first meditation book—a yoga book. It was mainly about the physical exercises, but in the back was a small section on meditation.

At first I was not at all interested in the meditation part. As a typical young Western man, religion was not my interest and anything related to religion was a very low priority in my life. Yet as a professional swimming coach, I quickly saw the benefits of yoga exercises. I incorporated these into my own training sessions and also used many of them with my swimmers. They produced clear benefits. Having seen those physical benefits, my interest in the meditation section was stimulated. I tried it and it felt good. In fact, the very first time I did it, it felt more than good. Indeed, there was a very familiar feeling to it, as if I had done it before.

Thus my meditation practice began, but now I would like to discuss the word "meditation." In some dictionaries, the definition of the word "meditation" is similar to this: "The emptying of the mind of thoughts, or concentration of the mind on just one thing."

To me, at that time, meditation meant concentration. So for my meditation sessions, I practised how to concentrate. It seemed useful. After all, every great swimmer needs to be able to concentrate. Every great athlete needs to be able to concentrate. Every great musician and many other "greats" need to be able to concentrate. And so do "great" thieves and murderers.

This is a clear reason why the Buddha said, "right view comes first" in the Mahācattārīsaka Sutta (MN 117). In fact, in that sutta, he said those words fourteen times! It takes about fifteen minutes to recite the sutta, yet the Buddha said, "right view comes first" fourteen times. Obviously, this statement is of great importance. I have often told meditators in retreats that if there is a thief who has been robbing homes, banks, etc. for fifteen years and has never been caught, then that person would probably have better concentration than all of the retreatants. The thief would have better concentration, which is sharper, stronger, super-focused and fully present; however the thief would not have right concentration. Why? Because *right* view is not present.

Right view includes the understandings of the Four Noble Truths and the Law of Kamma, that there are results of wholesome and unwholesome actions. These understandings are essential to our practice. To be a good meditator, to have right concentration, right view needs to come first, and is the most important condition for wisdom development. Unfortunately, many meditators don't understand this. A huge percentage of meditators believe that if they can concentrate very well, empty the mind of thoughts, or concentrate on just one thing, then wisdom will automatically come later. I believed the same thing thirty years ago. This is a major wrong view that stands in the way of right view.

Does concentration automatically lead to wisdom?

We only have to look at the account of the Buddha's life to see how wrong this belief is. One of the main reasons many Buddhists believe this myth is that they have not carefully read a good biography of the Buddha. Nearly every biography, large or small, relates how the Buddha practised prior to enlightenment.[3]

When Siddhattha Gotama stayed with his first teacher he was taught how to concentrate to a very high level, called the base of nothingness—almost the highest possible. However, Siddhattha came to realise that this was not the way to enlightenment because sufficient wisdom had not developed from this high level of concentration. He had not yet fully let go of greed, hatred and ignorance. He then went to a second teacher who taught him the highest possible level of concentration. If very deep concentration produces wisdom, then Siddhattha would have become enlightened at that time. Yet again, Siddhattha saw that this was not enough to give him the wisdom needed for enlightenment.

---

3. See, for example, chapter 2 of *The Life of the Buddha* by Ñāṇamoli Thera, published by the BPS.

The Buddha's own account, in the suttas, of his struggle for enlightenment clearly demonstrates the fallacy of this myth, yet even many Buddhists who have read biographies of the Buddha still believe it. Why? The answer may lie with another even more important reason, that is the difficulty with correctly translating the Pali word *samādhi*. Most of the time it is translated simply as concentration. However, in certain contexts, *samādhi* has a much broader meaning.

An important example occurs in the Mahāparinibbāna Sutta (DN 16), which relates the Buddha's last three months, and how he went from village to village teaching a gradual training of *sīla* (morality) as being the basis for the development of *samādhi*, and *samādhi* being a basis for the development of *paññā* (wisdom). In this sutta, the phrase *"sīla, samādhi, paññā"* is used over twenty times. In two noted translations of the sutta, the word *samādhi* is translated as concentration, making the translation of *"sīla, samādhi, paññā"* to mean morality, concentration, wisdom.

The translation of *samādhi* as "concentration," both here and in other suttas such as the Samādhi Sutta (SN 22:5), has contributed greatly to the misunderstanding about how wisdom arises. In fact, *samādhi*, in Pali, is used in two ways, and I do not believe the phrase *"sīla, samādhi, paññā"* should be translated as "morality, concentration, wisdom." When the phrase *"sīla, samādhi, paññā"* is used, it indicates the Noble Eightfold Path divided into three sections. *Sīla* indicates right speech, right action and right livelihood. *Samādhi* indicates right effort, right mindfulness and right concentration. *Paññā* indicates right view and right intention. Taken as a whole, these eight factors constitute the Noble Eightfold Path—the path for training the mind to develop the wisdom necessary for the ending of dukkha.

As "right concentration" is the widely accepted translation of *sammā samādhi*, the eighth factor in the Noble Eightfold Path, this demonstrates that the word *samādhi* is being used in two contexts; one to indicate the eighth factor of the Noble Eightfold Path and the other to indicate right effort, right mindfulness and right concentration working together as a group. Yet, often *samādhi* is simply translated as "concentration" in both contexts. This use of the word "concentration," to indicate these two different meanings, has occurred in many other translations as well.

So here is a question for every Buddhist meditator to contemplate: should the word *"concentration"* be used to describe the grouping of effort, mindfulness and concentration when it has already been used as one of three parts of the group? Some people will say, "Yes, why not? *Samādhi* is being used that way in Pali so we can do the same in English." But no, this is not actually the case and this is why when we translate *samādhi,* it is extremely important not to always use the one word "concentration."

"Sīla, samādhi, paññā" is a grouping together of three subgroups. When used together, it always means this grouping of, first, right speech, right action and right livelihood; second, right effort, right mindfulness and right concentration; and third, right view and right intention. Therefore the term *samādhi* here is understood in the context of these three subgroups of *"sīla, samādhi, paññā."*

However, the use of the word "concentration" for the translation of the second of these three subgroups has led to the myth that if a person develops strong concentration, then wisdom will automatically follow. This myth is very important, because it often stops meditators from using wise reflection in even the most basic way.

The leading Thai scholar monk Phra Prayut Payutto has translated *"sīla, samādhi, paññā"* in a different way.[4] He uses "morality, *mental discipline,* wisdom."

Thus mental discipline covers right effort, right mindfulness and right concentration as a group. This brings more clarity to understanding *"sīla, samādhi, paññā." Sīla* (morality) is a basis for the development of *samādhi* (mental discipline); *samādhi* is a basis for the development of *paññā* (wisdom). So if we use the words "mental discipline" as a translation of *samādhi* when it is used in the context of *"sīla, samādhi, paññā,"* this will help correct the wrong view that concentration automatically leads to wisdom.

No less than ten prominent Western scholars and translators have used "concentration" in this sense.[5] This has contributed to countless teachers doing so too. I hope teach-

4. *Dictionary of Buddhism,* Phra Prayut Payutto, Bangkok 1985

5. See, however, the entry *samādhi* in the *Pali–English Dictionary,* T.W. Rhys Davids and W. Stede, Pali Text Society, London.

and scholars will now think deeply about this and stop using the word "concentration" when translating *"sīla, samādhi, paññā."* If this booklet helps in only this small but important way to stop or prevent myths and misunderstandings, then much will be gained for many meditators.

As mentioned above, some people interpret *"sīla, samādhi, paññā"* to mean that wisdom is something that only comes after samādhi practice. However, wisdom is cumulative and begins with an intellectual understanding of cause and effect, and the Four Noble Truths. Also, without some degree of right understanding or wisdom, we will not know what is right speech compared to wrong speech, what is right action compared to wrong action, what is the right and wrong of anything. In this way, the initial right view will not be the deepest wisdom, yet it is a form of wisdom that is appropriate and necessary at that time in the practice.

Thus the eight factors of the Noble Eightfold Path are not a simple linear process of "do A, then B, then C." Instead, they are most effective when working together as a team, in more of a cyclic process where the factors are intertwined. This teamwork effort is clearly pointed out in the Mahācattārīsaka Sutta (MN 117). In order to have correct sīla, we need right view, and in order to have correct samādhi, we need right view. It is still possible to say, "morality is a basis for mental discipline, and mental discipline is a basis for wisdom;" while at the same time implying that all of the factors need to work together integrally.

Is wise reflection a requisite for enlightenment?

Let's look at another myth that tends to make many meditators believe that concentration produces wisdom. This is the belief that the Buddha's enlightenment came from a concentration practice, such as mindfulness of breathing, *ānāpānasati.*

This myth is also false. Although the Buddha began his meditation with concentration practice on the evening of his enlightenment, this was not the actual technique he was using at the moment of enlightenment. Rather, he was contemplating dependent origination using wise reflection in order to develop the wisdom necessary for Buddhahood. He was reflecting on a very profound level.

So is wisely reflecting, using yoniso manasikāra, *the* prerequisite for enlightenment? Will enlightenment automatically follow the use of wise reflection? This is an interesting question that I cannot answer. However, there's another important question that I think I can answer. Is wise reflection *a* prerequisite for enlightenment? According to the teachings, the answer is yes.

This is what the Buddha said:

> "This is the forerunner and precursor of the rising of the sun, that is, the dawn. So too this is the forerunner and precursor of the arising of the seven factors of enlightenment, that is, wise reflection. When one is accomplished in wise reflection, it is to be expected that one will develop and cultivate the seven factors of enlightenment." (SN 46:13)

And this is what Phra Prayut Payutto writes:

> "Yoniso manasikāra is a mental factor that assists in the birth of wisdom and is consequently of great importance in *vipassanā*. In *vipassanā*, yoniso manasikāra is a singularly important step on the path to wisdom, and is thus an essential principle of Dhamma. Yoniso manasikāra directly precedes wisdom. It is that which paves the way for wisdom, or opens up a space in which wisdom can mature...
>
> Yoniso manasikāra acts as a link between *sati*, mindfulness, and *paññā*, wisdom. It is that which guides the stream of thought in such a way that wisdom is able to get down to work and achieve results. It is that which provides wisdom with its method. It is the skilful means employed in the efficacious use of wisdom. As the term is commonly used, it implies both reflection and wisdom. In other words 'wise reflection.'"[6]

So when we consider the practice, with concentration as one aspect and wise reflection as another, which is more important? This is another question I will sidestep. Let's consider the matter in a different way.

If meditators spend their time practising only concentration, without the assistance of the other seven factors of the path, will this guarantee any development of the understanding of right speech and wrong speech, right action and wrong action, right livelihood and wrong livelihood? No, it

---

6. *"Right Mindfulness,"* Phra Prayut Payutto, Bangkok 1988.

does not. But if meditators spend their time practising only wise reflection, will this guarantee any development of the understanding of right speech and wrong speech, right action and wrong action, right livelihood and wrong livelihood? The answer is yes, definitely, but if you have never practised wise reflection meditation you may not believe me.

At this point, I'd like to divert a little to discuss the Kālāma Sutta (AN 3:65), as this sutta, in my opinion, is a very important sutta in relation to our topic of wise reflection, and also in relation to the entire practice. If the Kālāma Sutta is ever lost, the decline of Theravada Buddhism will certainly be hastened. If you do not know what the Kālāma Sutta is, I wholeheartedly encourage you to find out as soon as possible.

For it is only those meditators, who adopt the approach outlined in the Kālāma Sutta, who will be open enough to investigate and understand the importance of wise reflection. Why do I make such a strong statement? Because every meditator I have met who believed that the development of concentration will automatically bring wisdom, did so as a result of hearing it from another teacher, or reading it in a book. This is not what the Kālāma Sutta teaches us.

To these meditators I have always mentioned the example above of the thief who has never been caught. Despite having strong concentration, the thief is involved in wrong action and wrong livelihood. This example has helped most of these meditators to quickly understand the falsity of this myth.

So, for those of you who may not yet believe me when I say practising wise reflection will guarantee developing the understanding of right and wrong speech, right and wrong action, right and wrong livelihood, I encourage you to try it, test it out and see for yourself—as the Kālāma Sutta teaches us. Then, when you know for yourself through experiential understanding, you will see the importance of wise reflection, wise thinking.

The word *vipassanā* was mentioned above. It is helpful to remove another wrong view that surrounds this word. As Theravada Buddhism is relatively new in the West, the word *vipassanā* is not always being used i[illegible]e proper way. Some meditators wrongly believe that *vipas*[illegible] meditation means a specific technique, such as sweeping the body, mental noting, etc., but this is not true. Rather, it means the resulting wisdom or insight that comes from using skilful techniques.

There are many different techniques taught which support the development of wisdom. Wise reflection is one of these. And if you look deeper, you may see that wise reflection is the basis of all skilful techniques.

Thinking can be meditating

If you practise wise reflections, you will dispel another big myth, which many meditators believe: "thinking is not meditating." This wrong view often stands in the way of understanding clearly that "right view comes first" and that wise reflection is a crucial tool that we all need.

Let's look again at the word "meditation." What exactly is meditating? Why would someone claim, "thinking is not meditating"? After all, the Buddha was contemplating dependent origination when he got enlightened. Again, part of the reason people believe this is because they are not aware of how the Buddha became enlightened. Another reason is that they believe they have to blank the mind of all thoughts, or get concentrated on a single object, keeping all thoughts suppressed.

Let's look more closely at the belief that one has to "blank the mind of all thoughts." One reason for this myth is the way in which translators use the word "mindfulness." This issue is similar to the one discussed earlier, that is, why samādhi should not always be translated as "concentration."

There are two main types of mindfulness and it is very important to know the difference: one is a "small/narrow" mindfulness and the other is a "big/broad" mindfulness.

In the Pali language there is the word *sati*, which is used both as a single word and in the compound *sati-sampajañña*, and although both are often translated as "mindfulness," this is not totally accurate as they have different meanings. In my understanding, "mindfulness," as *sati*, is just basic moment-to-moment awareness, knowing what you are doing in the moment. Yet, *sati-sampajañña* is broader than *sati* and better translated as "clear comprehension" or "wisdom in action."

Here is an example of the difference between *sati* and *sati-sampajañña*: Suppose I want to practise *sati* and I am sitting and moving my arm up and around, just feeling my muscles. I mindfully move my arm up and mindfully move my arm over to the right, all the way over, just feeling the muscles in the whole arm, just practising *sati* in the moment. Now, if somebody is sitting next to me on the right and I hit him or her in the face, then this is a "small/narrow mindfulness," not *sati-sampajañña*.

So, if I am sitting next to someone and wish to practise *sati* in a wise way, *sati-sampajañña* has to be there also. Thus I recognise, "Oh, someone is sitting next to me on my right, so okay, I am going to practise *sati* by moving my arm to the left." This is an example where our mindfulness is broader, understanding cause and effect. This is what I mean by "big/ broad" mindfulness.

Another example of using narrow mindfulness is doing walking meditation in a retreat as compared to broad mindfulness walking along a busy roadside. In a retreat we can narrow down our mindfulness to only being aware of our footsteps, disregarding or simply noting distractions of sights, sounds, etc., and returning to just the footsteps. We need not even care what a particular sound actually is. But while walking along a roadside, we certainly do need to know the sounds of barking dogs, roaring motorbikes, or car horns blaring! So mindfulness can be narrow or broad.

It is also important to understand that narrow mindfulness does not guarantee wisdom. This is similar to what was said earlier about concentration. Many meditators who are very good at narrow mindfulness are also very good at suppressing thoughts. Even the technique of mental noting that can help us greatly to understand or let go of thoughts is often used to "shoot down thoughts" or simply "keep them at bay."

Unfortunately, many of the meditators who practise in this way, just suppressing thoughts, believe they are doing mindfulness meditation and think they are following the Satipaṭṭhāna Sutta's teaching.

Wise reflection in the Satipaṭṭhāna Sutta

Let's now examine the Satipaṭṭhāna Sutta (MN 10) and see how, in this very important sutta, the Buddha teaches us to think wisely and use both narrow and broad mindfulness.

First, it is clear that the Buddha is teaching narrow mindfulness and this is certainly what most, if not all, mindfulness meditators incorporate into their practice. But why isn't every one of these meditators also practising broad mindfulness by using wise reflections both formally and informally, as also taught in the Satipaṭṭhāna Sutta? Consider this reflection from the sutta, which the Buddha wants us to use whenever we see a dead body:

> "This body, too, is of the same nature, it will be like that, it is not exempt from that fate."

This sentence is repeated not just once, but nine times in the Satipaṭṭhāna Sutta. Nine times the Buddha describes dead bodies and nine times he teaches us to reflect—to think wisely—when seeing a dead body. This brings more to our awareness than simply seeing a sight with colour and form, but actually deepens our understanding of the significance of the sight and how it connects to us. This reflection helps us to gain deeper insight into the three characteristics of life; *anicca, dukkha* and *anattā*, and helps us to let go of our attachment to our body.

The Buddha also teaches us to reflect about the four elements:

> "And further, one reflects on this very body, however it be placed or disposed, by way of the material elements..."

About the thirty-two parts of the body, he says:

> "And further, one reflects on this very body ... from the soles up, and from the top of the head-hair down, thinking thus, "There are in this body, hair of the head, hair of the body, nails, teeth, skin..."

With reference to the hindrances mentioned in the fourth foundation of mindfulness he says:

> "One knows how the arising of the non-arisen sense-desire comes to be; one knows how the abandoning of the arisen sense-desire comes to be; and one knows how the non-arising in the future of the abandoned sense-desire comes to be."

He speaks similarly regarding the other hindrances, as well as with the fetters, which arise dependent on the sense doors.

We are also taught, in reference to the seven factors of enlightenment:

> "One knows how the arising of the non-arisen enlightenment-factor of mindfulness comes to be, and how perfection in the development of the arisen enlightenment-factor of mindfulness comes to be."

The Buddha speaks similarly regarding the other factors of enlightenment.

How are we to follow these instructions unless we know how to think wisely, and deliberately bring up these discursive reflections in our minds? And why shouldn't we train how to think wisely in meditation? Let's do broad mindfulness training as taught in the Satipaṭṭhāna Sutta as well as narrow mindfulness. Let's use our moment-to-moment awareness as a springboard for developing wisdom about ourselves and the world, using the objects that our senses focus on for learning about cause and effect, and the nature of the world.

We don't just want to use mindfulness to feel relaxed, "be in the moment," etc. We want to be mindful of life in order to understand life. In this way, it's always helpful to remember our practice is to centre on the Four Noble Truths.

How can we end dukkha?

Some meditators are very good at narrow mindfulness and watching things come and go, but fail to see the dukkha involved, and never let go of the causes of the dukkha.

So they may watch anger come and go, come and go. They know it is impermanent and again it comes and goes. And the anger continues to come and go, and often creates problems as well. They know it will pass but they fail to understand that the teachings, especially the Satipaṭṭhāna Sutta, teach us that we are to understand how anger will not come again in the future, not just watch it come and go. For this, *we need to know how to reflect wisely.*

There are many instructions throughout the suttas teaching us to reflect wisely: to reflect on our past generosity, to reflect on our past morality, to reflect on the Buddha, the Dhamma and the Sangha. These five are taught within the ten *anussati*, often referred to as the "recommended daily recollections" subgroup of the forty subjects of meditation (*kammaṭṭhāna*). Notice the translation used for the Pali: "recommended daily recollections." How many meditators use these as reflections every day?

And what about the very important threesome of *anicca*, *dukkha* and *anattā*? How many meditators sit in meditation and reflect for an entire meditation period about the constant changing nature of existence, impermanence, etc.? How many sit in meditation and reflect for an entire period about the unsatisfactory nature of life, suffering, pain, etc.? How many meditators sit in meditation and reflect for an entire period about the impersonal nature of the body and thoughts, non-ownership, non-self, etc.? Can you see the benefit of reflecting in this manner? What would be the result of deepening our understanding of ourselves and the world?

Maybe you are one of the many meditators who has never tried these reflections for a whole meditation session because you didn't know that it is all right to think during meditation. It is not only all right to use thought during meditation, but over and over in the suttas the Buddha encourages us to do so. The point that has to be understood is that the thoughts are to be directed towards a Dhamma theme or the Truth. Then the contemplation becomes the investigation into Truth, which is one of the seven factors of enlightenment (*bojjhaṅga*).

It is all right to think in meditation

Why aren't more teachers teaching these meditation subjects? Why aren't more meditators using them regularly? Because many of them don't yet understand or appreciate the broadness of the wonderful Dhamma. They may not have been taught enough about wise reflection and its benefits. Yet the Buddha teaches us to reflect wisely, not only in the Satipaṭṭhāna Sutta, but also in many other suttas.

Wise reflection helps us integrate the concentration and mindfulness developed during formal meditation into everyday life, and develop right view and right intention. This is especially so of right intention, which is described by the Buddha as thoughts directed towards renunciation, free from ill will and cruelty. This is the basis for developing right speech, right action and right livelihood.

Many meditators are very good at developing mindfulness and concentration while in retreat conditions, yet when they return to their normal life, they have difficulty applying the Dhamma to how they speak, act and work. On many occasions meditators have come to me who have practised ten, fifteen or more years, and have done many, many retreats, but have not found deeper happiness in their life through their meditation practice.

Here is one very sad example. A man, about fifty-five years old, came to our centre, staying about one week in between retreats. He was very experienced, having done six three-month retreats and many shorter ones, practising over ten years. In an interview, I asked him how his mindfulness and concentration was. He replied that in retreat he could get very strong mindfulness and concentration, and he could see the arising and passing away, the impermanence of phenomena very clearly. I asked him how well he could see dukkha. *He did not know what the word meant.*

I was quite surprised, he had done all this practice and yet he did not know what dukkha meant. After all, this is the first of the Four Noble Truths, which all meditators need to know in order to practise correctly, and develop right view about cause and effect on the most basic levels. I then taught him what it meant and how it is important to see not just impermanence, as he claimed he could do, but also to see dukkha. I also explained that it was even more important to be able to understand dukkha, as this is the core understanding of the Four Noble Truths.

Each day he would go for a walk after lunch down the hill, returning before the afternoon meditation period. After one week he said that he had to go for his visa trip and would return for a retreat with us. He asked if he could leave a small bag so he did not have to carry everything on the trip. We allowed it. Six months later, he had not returned, so we decided to open the bag and dispense with whatever was inside. We found illegal drugs. This man, who had done so much meditation, had stashed drugs at a monastery so that he would not be caught with them.

Although this meditator was experienced in doing retreats, he was not experienced in wisdom; he was not experienced in understanding dukkha, the cause of dukkha, the ending of dukkha and the way out of dukkha. *He did not know how to think wisely.* In retreat he could get very strong mindfulness and concentration, but he had not grown in wisdom or compassion, either for himself or others, in the way the Buddha wished us to.

On the other hand, there have been other people, addicted to drugs, who came to our centre and learned the meditation techniques taught here, including wise reflection. They made a commitment not to take drugs during the retreat. Many of them made the resolution after the retreat never to take drugs again and kept to that resolution. This resolution did not come from the mindfulness practice, but from wise reflection on the suffering, dukkha, of using drugs, not only for themselves, but also for others. They gave it up through compassion to themselves and others. They may not have had strong concentration, but more importantly, they used their practice to develop their wisdom and compassion, changing their lives in a positive way.

Yet, many meditators are not using wise reflection in their formal meditation training because there are many teachers who are actually telling their students not to do it. Some are even proclaiming the myth "thinking is not meditating." Why? Why are many teachers teaching something which is not true? Because they just don't understand the broadness of the wonderful Dhamma. They have a limited view of what meditation is within Theravada Buddhism and they have not yet been taught enough about wise reflection.

The Buddha teaches wise reflection throughout the suttas, and, most important—it works. It works to help us end dukkha. And if it is a wonderful tool to help us end dukkha, shouldn't we use it? Yes, of course we should.

Does experience automatically lead to wisdom?

The above example clearly demonstrates the futility of another common myth that if you "experience life," using concentration and mindfulness in the present moment, then wisdom will automatically arise. This wrong view is yet another misunderstanding which encourages many meditators not to use reflective meditation.

Regarding this myth, I'd like to quote the late United States Supreme Court Justice, Earl Warren, "The only thing we learn from history, is that we don't learn." Do you understand what he was saying? Here was a man hugely experienced in the difficulties people have in dealing with each other, who was also required to have an intimate knowledge of political, social and legal history, making a considered statement about the problem of learning from experience. Simply put, *humans have an extremely hard time learning from experience.*

Yet, can we increase our ability to learn from experience? Yes, but to do so we have to reflect about our experience. We have to think about it; as to whether it was beneficial or not, examine it, investigate it, understand what actually happened, and then consider whether we would like it to happen again in the future or not. Regarding this the Ambalaṭṭhikā Rāhulovāda Sutta (MN 61) is important. In this sutta the Buddha teaches his own son, Rāhula, at the age of seven. He encourages Rāhula to think wisely about what he had done, what he is doing, and what he will do. As well, he encourages Rāhula to do this not only for every physical activity, but also for every verbal and mental activity.

Regarding any activity, one should reflect:

> "Is it leading to self-affliction, to the affliction of others, or to both? Is it an unskilful activity, with painful consequences, painful results? If, on reflection, you know that it is leading to self-affliction, to the affliction of others, or to both, it is an unskilful activity with painful consequences, painful results, then any activity of that sort is absolutely inappropriate for you to do. But if, on reflection, you know that it is not leading to self-affliction, to the affliction of others, or to both; it is a skilful activity with happy consequences, happy results, then any activity of that sort is appropriate for you to do."

The Buddha taught his own son to *think wisely* about all of his activities, whether already done, in the process of being done, or yet to be done.

Another example of how experience by itself does not produce wisdom, but reflecting about experience can, is the following: Friends invite a man to drink with them one Friday night. He gets drunk, goes home and hits his wife. The next day he finds out what he did and regrets the action. He apologises to his wife, but he does not think about it any further. The next Friday night he gets drunk again and hits his wife again. The same cycle repeats itself.

A second man is invited by friends to drink with them one Friday night. He gets drunk, goes home and hits his wife. The next day he finds out what he did and regrets the action. He apologises to his wife. He feels absolutely ashamed of what he did. He thinks about it continuously and wishes he had never done it. It is in his thoughts regularly. His friends ask him to drink with them again. Now, however, not wishing to confuse his mind with intoxicants so that the same suffering arises for himself and his wife again, he refuses.

Experience itself does not guarantee wisdom. We have to reflect about experience. These two men had the same experience, one reflected wisely and one did not. Experience by itself doesn't guarantee wisdom, but reflecting about it can.

Remember the quote at the beginning of this booklet? Getting rid of our anxieties and troubles is possible, but a person must know how to reflect wisely in order to do it.

Also, and very importantly, we don't even have to have the experience in order to develop wisdom. That is, if we can reflect wisely beforehand, as the Buddha taught his own son. We don't have to experience the same dukkha as everybody else, just to know the pain of that dukkha. That's where wise reflection helps, so we can avoid having the same dukkha. If we hear a story about someone getting drunk, coming home and hitting his wife, we can say, "Oh my gosh! Getting drunk? Forget it!" Because we understand the dukkha that happened to somebody else, we don't even want to risk clouding our awareness so that we can't make wise choices.

Four types of thoroughbred horses

The Buddha once likened human beings to four types of thoroughbred horses, in relation to how quickly they can "wake up" to the reality of dukkha and start to purify their minds and hearts (AN 4:113). He said that for the first type of horse, you wave the stick, it only sees the shadow of the stick and it's ready to go. For the second type, you wave the stick, it does nothing, then you touch it lightly with the stick and it's ready to go. For the third type, you wave the stick, it does nothing, you touch it lightly with the stick, it does nothing, then you poke it sharply with the stick and it's ready to go. For the fourth type, you wave the stick, it does nothing, you touch it lightly with the stick, it does nothing, you poke it sharply with the stick, it still does nothing, then you pierce the horse with the stick right through to the bone and only then is it ready to go.

In the same way the Buddha likened humans who have woken up to dukkha. They can be viewed like this: some hear about dukkha in the world and consider, "Oh, it may happen to me!" and they wake up quickly. Others see someone in the world who has some dukkha, "Oh, there it is for real, it could be me!" and they wake up quickly. Still others have a relative or friend with dukkha and they think, "Oh, it is even closer to me!" and they wake up. While the fourth type experiences dukkha themselves, "Oh, here it is!" and they wake up.

Unfortunately though, most human beings are even worse off than the fourth type of horse. You only have to look at the world. So many people have so much dukkha, yet they won't wake up. You want to help them, but generally you can't, and sure enough they have more dukkha tomorrow, and more dukkha next week. They get hit by dukkha again and again and again, yet still never wake up.

I would rather be one of the thoroughbred horses. Wouldn't you also?

Wise reflection can help us to avoid dukkha in the future. Why do so many suttas, including the Mahācattārīsaka Sutta and Sabbāsava Sutta, have a statement by the Buddha or an enlightened disciple prior to beginning the teaching similar to this, "Listen and heed well to what I shall say?"

What does "heed well" mean? Reflect and follow this advice. In other words, they could have easily said, "If you wish to avoid dukkha, you must listen carefully to what I say, you must reflect wisely on it and you must follow it accordingly."

Moral shame and moral dread

When we train our minds to think wisely, it is very helpful to be aware of the "two virtues which protect the world," the *lokapāla dhamma* (It 42). These two virtues are moral shame and moral dread. In order to use these two virtues to protect "our world," we must know how to think wisely. And in order to know how to think wisely, we must train our minds to think wisely.

I believe that if a person could perfect moral shame and moral dread, then enlightenment would soon follow. This is quite a claim, especially coming from someone who is not yet enlightened. Why do I believe this so strongly that I would state it? I will leave the answer for now, as I will first explain these two wonderful virtues and how they work.

Moral shame and moral dread are a pair. A wonderful and very important pair. They each have a different job and are responsible for two different things. Yet they work together protecting the world—our world.

Moral shame's job is to look into our past. It just looks at everything and is objective about it. Looking into the past, it thinks, "Okay, what did I do that wasn't so wise? What was not skilful? What was basically wrong?" It does this objectively, like a scientist, not in order to come back later and beat us over the head with guilt, fear and all of that, but simply to look objectively into our past and consider, "What did I do wrong?"

Moral shame is like a computer database. It looks back and says, "When I was twelve I did this, when I was fourteen I did that," and so on. It records everything that we did that was not wise.

Now, if that's all we use moral shame for, we've got a nice file tucked away in a folder and that's it. Yet, moral shame has more to do; it turns to moral dread and says, "Here, moral dread, here's your stuff. Study it. Learn from it and don't let it happen again." Moral dread is a type of wise fear, linked with compassion for ourselves and others, that ignites *right effort*, in this case the effort to prevent, the first of the "four great efforts," to prevent the same dukkha from arising for ourselves and others again. Through compassion for the person we will become, we make a determination to be more aware of our actions, speech and thoughts to avoid similar dukkha. This is moral dread's job, to bring up the wise fear that says, "I don't want to cause dukkha again."

However, moral dread can't stop us from doing anything again in the future unless it knows what was done in the past, that's why moral shame hands over the file to moral dread. Moral dread has to study it. It's got to really study it; it's got to learn, "What did I do which led to problems? What did I do which was unskilful?" Moral dread must think about, reflect about all that moral shame has recorded. It has to understand everything it can about moral shame's database.

Then moral dread starts watching out, because we have compassion for ourselves and for others. We don't want to create the same dukkha again. That's moral dread's job: "Don't do it again." This is how the two work together. Do you see what these two virtues can do for each one of us? They can help us understand how not to do a similar unbeneficial action in the future. Do you see how this would certainly take a person toward enlightenment, the ending of all dukkha? This is not hard to understand because every defilement would be uprooted. This is why I believe, "If a person could perfect moral shame and moral dread, then enlightenment would soon follow."

So what do the "two virtues which protect the world" have to do with wise reflection? We must be able to think wisely in order for moral shame and moral dread to do their work efficiently. We must train our minds to focus directly on our dukkha: "Does dukkha exist or not? Where does the dukkha come from? How can the dukkha go away?" And most important, "How does similar dukkha not come again in the future?" In order to apply the Four Noble Truths to our practice and our life, we must know how to think wisely.

Along with the "two virtues which protect the world," I would like to mention a few more groupings in which the Buddha emphasised wise reflection, yoniso manasikāra. One is the "two causes for the arising of wisdom," the *sammādiṭṭhi-paccaya* (MN 43). The first of these is wise reflection and the second is hearing teachings or advice from a wise spiritual friend, *kalyāṇamitta*.

Wise reflection is also listed among the four "virtues conducive to growth," the *vuḍḍhi dhamma* (AN 4:246). These four are 1) association with a wise friend (*kalyāṇamitta*); 2) listening to good teaching; 3) wise reflection; and 4) practise in accordance with good teaching. These appear to be exactly the same as another grouping, the "factors for attaining stream-entry," *sotāpattiyaṅga* (SN 55:5).

A cause for the arising of wisdom, a virtue conducive to growth, a factor for attaining stream-entry, these are just three of the groupings in which the Buddha included wise reflection. Is it worth practising? Is it worth developing? Is it worth perfecting?

My answer to all of these three questions is "yes." But let's now consider the way in which many other meditators would answer, and I'll do this in reverse: Is it worth perfecting? Many would answer, "Yes." Is it worth developing? Many would answer, "Yes." Is it worth practising? Many would answer, "But thinking is not really meditating..."

It's time for all those meditators to take the "but" out of their practice; it's time to blow away those incorrect myths; and it's time to practise more fully as the Buddha is recorded to have taught us.

Yoniso manasikāra—wise reflection

Now, let's return to the dictionary definition of meditation as given at the beginning of this essay: "The emptying of the mind of thoughts, or concentration of the mind on just one thing."

It is clear from everything written here that our meditation training to develop wisdom and to end dukkha includes much more than this. It is also clear that concentration, by itself, does not guarantee the development of wisdom.

So let us now consider two other dictionary definitions of meditation:

5. The act of thinking about something deeply and carefully
6. An extended and serious study of a particular topic

Can you see how these two definitions appear very similar to the one of wise reflection, yoniso manasikāra?

In the suttas the Buddha teaches *citta-bhāvanā*. *Citta* generally means "mind-heart" and *bhāvanā* means "development." So *citta-bhāvanā* is normally translated as "mental development." In our retreats my wife, Rosemary, and I emphasise mental development, trying to develop beneficial mental qualities and to lessen unbeneficial mental qualities. All of the meditation methods taught in our retreats are concerned with mental development. And as we use the words, "meditation" and "mental development," they mean basically the same thing.

For many years we have been trying to help our students see the broad, practical nature of Theravada Buddhism, to see that it is a training for every moment of the day; and to understand that a significant part of these wonderful teachings include formally training our minds to think wisely in order to end our mental dukkha and find deeper peace within.

In the balanced practice that we teach, concentration and mindfulness are important tools to develop and use. The point is, though, that we must know how to use them wisely and this is where wise reflection helps greatly. With wise reflection we can develop a balanced practice with right view, which will guide the other factors of the noble eightfold path, and bring us to deeper wisdom and peace. "Right view comes first."

As the Buddha has taught:

> "With regard to internal factors, I do not perceive any other single factor as helpful as wise reflection in doing so

> much benefit for one in training, who has not attained the heart's goal but remains intent on the unsurpassed safety from bondage. One who reflects wisely abandons what is unskilful and develops what is skilful." (It 16)

I sincerely hope that this essay has helped you to understand more fully how important it is to train your mind to think wisely, with wise reflection, yoniso manasikāra.

PART 2

Wise Reflection Meditations

For those who wish to put some of these ideas into practice, the following list includes many of the wise reflection meditations we teach, along with brief notes about them. When practising wise reflection meditation, we use our thoughts to develop our understanding of the nature of the world and ourselves, and to cultivate beneficial states of mind. We try to keep our minds centred on the topic being examined and not wander to new subjects, getting lost in other thoughts. It's very normal for the mind to wander off, here and there, so we must make a concerted effort to stay on the topic.

For some, using visualisation of situations and people can be very helpful. For others, using reflection and analytical thinking helps them develop the appropriate states of mind and understanding. Nearly all of the systematic methods we teach have been designed for the purpose of developing wisdom. This is not a complete listing, but it will certainly give you plenty to work with:

Eating and our relationship to food

This is based on traditional advice from the Buddha. To reflect wisely in the following ways prior to eating our food helps greatly to avoid the excessive reactions to pleasant and unpleasant tastes:

- Why do we eat?
- How fortunate we are to have sufficient food.
- The dukkha involved in producing the food and how it came to us.

By reflecting in these ways, we come to deeper understandings that include:

- The basic reason why we eat is to keep our body alive and healthy, to alleviate discomfort and to enable us to continue on with our inner development.

- The appreciation that we have so much food at a time when many people around the world are starving. We can use this reflection to help us to be more content with whatever food we have, whether pleasant or unpleasant, knowing how very fortunate we are.
- That many beings suffer just for us to have our food. Even whether or not we are a vegetarian, numerous beings die so we may eat. When the fields are ploughed for planting rice or vegetables, many, many animals and insects are killed. The growing and producing of nearly all foods causes the deaths of other beings.
- As well, to reflect upon the hardships of the farmers, transport people, store owners and all of the people who have helped get our food to us, all the way to the people who are cooking and preparing the food for us. In this way we can see how interrelated we are with the rest of the world.

Compassion and loving kindness

This approach to compassion and loving kindness differs from the more usual *metta-bhāvanā* meditation in that it is intended to develop wisdom. These meditations are therefore closer to vipassanā type practices rather than *samatha* or concentration. With these meditations, we start by focusing our attention on a particular subject, whether ourselves, another person, an animal or any other living being, and reflect on the difficulties that the subject is, or might be, experiencing, allowing our compassion to arise for them. We then wish them compassion and loving kindness, a combined expression of a sincere hope that the person, persons, or beings will be free from their difficulties and find inner peace and happiness.

There are several different systems that can be used to guide this reflection, for example:

- Start with yourself, then reflect about someone you like, someone who is neutral to you and someone you don't like.
- Start with yourself, then with your closest family and relatives: husband, wife, children, parents, brothers, sisters, expanding to the rest of your relatives, friends, teachers and, depending on how much time you have,

you could continue expanding to other people and creatures. Upon finishing, it can be helpful to come back to yourself.

- Start with yourself, then the person who is spatially closest to you (next to you or in the next room), then expand to all the people in your building or on your street. Expanding again to all in your town, all in your country and so on. Again, when finishing, it can be helpful to come back to yourself.
- Use grouping systems such as ages (one year at a time 0–100), people with different occupations (the alphabet helps; airplane pilots, barbers, cooks, etc.), mental problems (anger, boredom, etc.), countries, or any other way of grouping people. This gives the mind a "map" to follow for what subjects to think of, making it less likely that the mind wanders off, thinking, "Oh, whom should I do next?"

There are also some special systems for doing compassion and loving kindness meditation, designed to help with particular situations.

D/D (defusing and diffusing)

D/D is a play on two English words, defusing and diffusing. With this technique we are going to defuse the "bomb" we create within ourselves by negatively attaching to experience and diffuse or universalize our compassion and loving kindness. This technique is extremely useful for letting go of self-pity and other unbeneficial mental states when experiencing any type of dukkha, whether physical or mental. This method has its roots in the story of Kisā Gotamī and the mustard seed.

This is a a systematic way of doing the defusing and diffusing reflection:

- In the first part of the meditation start with yourself; reflect on the dukkha you're experiencing and wish yourself compassion and loving kindness. Then reflect on someone else, same age and sex with similar dukkha, giving them the compassion and loving kindness wish. Then the same age but opposite sex, then add 10 years and include both sexes, then go down 10 years for both sexes, then up 20, down 20 and

continue until you have gone down to little children and up to 100 year olds.
- In the second part of the meditation, use your own age and sex only. Consider many people similar to you, but gradually imagine their dukkha getting more and more intense, until suicide and/or murder are the end result.

The first part of this meditation sh 1ows us that we are not alone with our dukkha. Many people of all different ages experience the same types of dukkha. This helps us to know that it is not just "me, me, me, I am the only one who has this dukkha!"

The second part of this compassion and loving kindness meditation shows us that our dukkha is not so big, if we compare it to the more extreme dukkha of others. This helps us greatly to let go of our self-pity about our dukkha.

Waking up in the morning

This method is a helpful way to begin the day, as it not only helps us to develop compassion but also motivates us to think of how fortunate we are, for which we give further advice in the next section. This helps to expand our concern from simply ourselves and those we know, to feel more connected with people we do not know and the universality of dukkha.

Upon waking, reflect deeply on a situation in the world where heavy dukkha is occurring. Imagine yourself vividly in such a situation in order to empathise with those involved and wish them all compassion and loving kindness.

Two suggested phrases to use, when wishing compassion and loving kindness, are:

- "May ___ be able to learn, practise and develop methods, techniques and tools of mental development, so that ___ can cope with, understand, accept and overcome the difficulties and challenges of life. May ___ find peace of mind."
- "May ___ be able to let go of anger, fear, worry and ignorance. May ___ also have patience, courage, wisdom and determination to meet and overcome difficulties and problems, challenges of life. May ___ find peace of mind."

How fortunate we are

Simply reflect on all the different ways that you are fortunate, materially and mentally. Watch out for the word "but"—it is not part of this reflection. This reflection is also very good when waking up each morning.

It can be especially helpful to consider the odds of being born human compared to being born another being on this planet. Then consider how many have the chance to read or listen to the Dhamma. Then consider how many have the chance to actually practise the Dhamma. How very, very fortunate we are.

To truly understand how fortunate we are is extremely helpful, in particular, with letting go of self-pity. This then allows more joy, contentment and energy to arise.

Self-pity is a major hindrance for so many meditators. One main reason is because they are not looking at themselves objectively and truthfully. But in this practice we try to be objective with our view of life. We try to see life truly for what it actually is. Thus reflecting on how fortunate we are is a very simple and effective technique to find more inner peace.

Generosity

To reflect on our good generosity is included in the ten "recommended daily recollections," the *anussati*. It is similar to reflecting on "how fortunate we are." Reflect on all of your past generous actions—the times when you used your time, talents, understanding or material resources so others could benefit. Again, this helps us to see ourselves more objectively. Specifically, this helps us to feel positive about ourselves, which aids in overcoming doubt.

One special note here; if you don't feel you've done enough generous actions to feel positive about yourself—then do more!

Dukkha

One way to reflect on dukkha is to think of every single type of dukkha that you can imagine. There are systems that help with this, such as these:

- The alphabet with occupations: What types of dukkha can artists experience? Bankers, carpenters, doctors, etc.?
- Body parts: What kinds of dukkha can occur in the toes, feet, legs, hips, etc.? Internally also, e.g., cancer, diarrhoea, etc.

- Ages: from 0 to 100: What kinds of dukkha can happen to babies, one year olds, two, etc.?
- The alphabet with mental dukkha: aversion, bigotry, craving, etc.

It's also very important to reflect that dukkha is natural and will occur countless times throughout our lives. This is basically due to the fact that everything in and around us is impermanent. All things, including our bodies and our thoughts, have their arising, existing and eventual passing away. This is simply a truth of our existence. Since everything that we know is impermanent, different types of dukkha will arise.

We must take this understanding deep within ourselves, because many people become upset, irritated, angry or agitated when they encounter different types of dukkha, which only causes more and more dukkha. Thus by reflecting that dukkha is natural—that it comes to everyone, to any part of the body, to all age groups and so on—will help us have less resistance to life's difficulties and find more inner peace despite outward conditions.

Impermanence

Contemplate how everything you know is constantly in a state of change—the mind, the body and the world. Using methods similar to the dukkha reflection above can be very helpful. To reflect on impermanence is especially beneficial when experiencing unpleasant situations. It also helps guard us from getting too attached to pleasant situations.

Death

In the Satipaṭṭhāna Sutta the Buddha encourages us to reflect in the following way whenever we see a body in any stage of decomposition:

> "This body, too, is of the same nature, it will be like that, it is not exempt from that fate."

We could also reflect similarly to the dukkha reflection above. Using systems such as ages, occupations or the parts of the body, consider every different way in which people could die.

Specifically, it's important to do this for ourselves, reflect on every possible way we could die right now. So often we believe that tonight will come, tomorrow will come, next week, next year, the future will always come. However, there is only one certain thing that will come, for each and every one of us. That is death. And it may come tonight, tomorrow, next week, next year. We don't know when, yet it is definitely coming. Awareness of death is one of the most important areas of practice lacking in many experienced meditators.

Meditators who use death reflection regularly can often be easily identified by their speech. How many people will say, "See you later?" Whereas, those who regularly reflect on death will say, simply, "Goodbye" or "Hope to see you later." Whenever you think of the future, ask yourself, "What is the only certain thing which will happen to us all?" Death reflection can help us to let go of future desires, worries and fears.

Actions and their results

This is an important subject, which includes kamma and dependent origination. One way of reflecting can be what we call "inward and outward."

Inward is where we look into our past and consider an experience and the results of it. If it was a beneficial action with beneficial results, then we try to remember it so we can repeat it in the future, should a similar experience arise. If it was an unbeneficial action with unbeneficial results, then we try to understand how we could have done it better. We could also consider what others would have done in a similar event. Thinking about what people whom we respect would have done can be especially beneficial.

Outward is where we look at others and experiences that have happened, whether read about or seen. Then we contemplate how the actions were beneficial or unbeneficial as above, and we consider what we would do in a similar situation. By reflecting in these ways, we can develop more understanding of how to react with more wisdom in the future.

Balancing compassion and equanimity

This reflection is part of the previous one. However, in this case we reflect on situations in which a balance of compassion and equanimity was needed. We try to think of times when it was in balance and times when it was not, and reflect how to increase this balance or how to correct the imbalance.

Again, this can be inward and outward. An outward example of balanced compassion and equanimity is Mother Theresa's life story. When she went to India she was filled with compassion, keeping it balanced with equanimity. She did not allow her compassion to turn into grief nor into anger. An example of completely unbalanced compassion and equanimity is the Oklahoma (USA) bombing of a government building some years ago. Apparently, the men who did the bombing had some sort of "compassion" for the USA and wanted to "wake up" the American people. However, their compassion went off into extreme aversion and many people died as a result.

The five daily recollections

This is traditional wise advice from the Buddha to reflect on. It is a very simple practice, often used as a chant, but we must do it over and over to drive this wisdom deep inside.

- I am of the nature to decay; I have not gone beyond decay.
- I am of the nature to be diseased; I have not gone beyond disease.
- I am of the nature to die; I have not gone beyond death.
- All that is mine, dear and delightful, will change and vanish.
- I am the owner of my kamma, heir to my kamma, born of my kamma, related to my kamma, abide supported by my kamma. Whatever kamma I shall do, whether wholesome or unwholesome, of that I will be the heir.

The Four Noble Truths

Take an example of a difficult experience you have had and examine it in light of these four truths:

- What was the dukkha?
- What type of desire did I have which created this dukkha?
- Did the dukkha go away when I let go of my desire?
- What methods did I use to let go of the dukkha?

The eight worldly dhammas

The eight worldly dhammas—praise and blame, fame and obscurity, gain and loss, pleasure and pain—are essential to understand. Yet they are not being taught enough and/or are being inaccurately taught; especially the pair fame and obscurity. We stress the understanding of these eight as an invaluable way to see just what we get attached to and where we create dukkha. One way to meditate on them is by way of the following reflections, adjusting the wording for each pair:

- Considering praise and blame. In what ways do you get stuck, involved, attached to and concerned with wanting praise?
- In what ways do you get stuck, involved, attached to and concerned with not wanting blame?
- Can you remember any times in your life when you received praise and you thought it was very important at the time, making you very happy, yet now you can see it really did not matter?
- Can you remember any times in your life when you received blame and you thought it was very important at the time, making you very sad, yet now you can see it really did not matter?
- Are there any times in your life when you actually do not want praise, times when you would rather have blame, when you would rather people did not think well of you?
- Please reflect on how by attaching to praise and blame, in wanting one and not wanting the other, this can often block you from understanding reality and can give you more dukkha.

The ten perfections

It is said that five hundred lifetimes before our Buddha became enlightened, he made the Bodhisattva vow to become a Buddha, and then meditated on the ten perfections, *pāramīs*, so he could fully understand what his "work" was: generosity, morality, renunciation, wisdom, energy, patience, truthfulness, determination, compassion, loving kindness and equanimity. For the Buddha, they had to become perfect. For us, we have to develop them more and more, so it is important to understand them and learn how to increase them.

To understand the ten pāramīs more, we teach one meditation in which we reflect on the ten in pairs, trying to see how they work together, which ones support the others, which ones comes first, etc.

To help develop them, we teach another meditation with five questions to ask oneself about each pāramī:

- Since starting my meditation/mental development practice, have I grown in ___?
- How much have I grown in ___?
- Reflecting upon my ..., how do I feel about my development of ___?
- Is there more I can grow in___?
- What can I do in my life to help my level of ___ to grow?

Conclusion

I sincerely hope that you will experiment with these techniques, see their value, and practise them regularly; they will help you find more inner peace and happiness.

Walking Meditation

Three Expositions on Walking Meditation

by

Ajahn Ñāṇadhammo,
Ajahn Brahmavaṃso,
and
Dharma Dorje

THE WHEEL PUBLICATION NO. 464

First BPS edition: 2007

About the Essays

"Walking Meditation in the Thai Forest Tradition" by Ajahn Nyanadhammo was edited from two Dhamma talks given at Dhammaloka Buddhist Centre (31st of July, 1992) and Bodhinyana Forest Monastery (22nd of January 2002), Perth, Australia. It was published privately by Wat Pah Nanachat and is republished here with the kind permission of the author.

"Walking Meditation is Wonderful" by Ajahn Brahmavaṃso is an extract (pp. 74–78) from *Mindfulness, Bliss, and Beyond*, Boston, 2006, used with the permission of Wisdom Publications.

The essay "Walking Meditation Practices" by Dharma Dorje (Michael Bell) is first published here.

Discourses

Bhikkhus, there are these five benefits in walking meditation. What five? One endures long (walking) journeys. One endures striving (in meditation). One has little physical afflictions. What is eaten, drunk, chewed, tasted, is well digested. The concentration that has been attained by walking meditation lasts for a long time.

(AN 5:29)

"... Moggallāna, perceiving what is before and behind[1], you should fix attention on walking meditation, with the sense-faculties turned inward, and the mind not going out. ..."

(AN 7:58)

"Bhikkhus, you should train thus: 'We will be devoted to wakefulness; by walking and sitting meditation during the day, ... night, we will purify our minds of obstructive states.'"

(MN 39.10)

I left my dwelling overcome by sleepiness. Going onto the walking path, I fell down on the earth.

Having rubbed my limbs and having gone onto the walking-meditation path again, I did walking meditation and became well composed in mind.

Then wise attention arose in me, the danger in existence became clear, disenchantment was established, and my mind was released.

(Bhagu Thera, Theragāthā 271–273)

---

1. *Pacchāpuresaññā,* which is mentioned in SN 51:11 & 20 as a perception done when developing the *iddhipadas*. Cf. AN 3:89 where this and similar perceptions, said to be limitless concentration (*appamāṇasamādhi*), lead to overcoming the (spatial and temporal) directions (*disā*) or polarities. It seems related to the *ariya-iddhis,* noble powers, whereby the *sekha* transcends the repulsive and unrepulsive polarity (D IiI 112, M IiI 301, S V 119). However, here *pacchāpuresaññā* could simply mean keeping attention confined to the walking path.

Walking Meditation in the Thai Forest Tradition

By Ajahn Ñāṇadhammo

This discourse addresses the how, when, where and why of walking meditation. It includes both practical instructions of the technical aspects of walking meditation and instructions for creating the quality of mind that leads to concentration, insight and wisdom through the physical activity of walking meditation.

The Buddha stressed developing mindfulness in the four main postures of the body: standing, sitting, lying down and walking. He exhorted us to be mindful in all these postures, to create a clear awareness and recollection of what we are doing while we are in any particular posture.

Walking meditation is called *caṅkama* in Pali. If you read about the lives of the monks and nuns at the time of the Buddha, you will see that many obtained the stages of Enlightenment while on the walking meditation path. Walking meditation is an activity in which one can focus and concentrate the mind or develop investigative knowledge and wisdom.

Some people find that they are naturally drawn to walking meditation because they find it easier and more natural than sitting meditation. When they sit they feel dull, or tense, or they are easily distracted. Their mind doesn't calm down.

If this is the case with you, don't just persevere; try a change of posture or do something new. Experiment with standing meditation or try walking meditation. This new meditation posture may give you some other skilful means of applying the mind. All of the four postures of meditation are just techniques, methods for developing and training the mind. Try and develop walking meditation; you may start to see the benefits of it.

In the Forest Meditation Tradition in Northeast Thailand, there is a great emphasis on walking meditation. Many monks will walk for long hours as a way of developing concentration, sometimes as much as ten or fifteen hours a day!

The late Ajahn Singtong used to do so much walking meditation that he would make a rut in the walking path. The sandy path that he used for walking meditation would actually become hollow because he would walk so many hours in a day. Another monk, Ajahn Kum Dtun wouldn't bother to go into his hut at night. When he became really tired after walking in meditation all day and late into the night, he would lay down right there on the meditation path and use his fist as a pillow. He would go to sleep with mindfulness, having made a determination to get up the moment he woke. As soon as he woke, he would start walking again. He basically lived on his walking meditation path! Ajahn Kum Dtun was quick to attain results in his practice.

In the West, there is not such an emphasis on the practice of walking meditation. Thus I would like to describe the process and recommend it to you to complement your sitting practice. I hope these instructions will help you develop your repertoire of meditative techniques—in both formal meditation and in your daily life. As so much of life is taken up with the activity of walking, if you know how to apply awareness to it then even simply walking about in your house can become a meditation exercise.

The Five Benefits of Walking Meditation

The Buddha spoke of five benefits of walking meditation. In the order that he listed them in this Sutta (see frontispiece), they are as follows: walking meditation develops endurance for walking long distances; it is good for striving; it is healthy; it is good for the digestion after a meal, and the concentration won from walking meditation lasts a long time.

Developing Endurance for Walking Distances

The first benefit of walking meditation is that it leads to endurance in walking distances. This was particularly important at the time of the Buddha when most people travelled by foot. The Buddha himself would regularly go wandering from place to place, walking up to sixteen kilometres a day. So he recommended that walking meditation be used as a way of developing physical fitness and endurance for walking long distances.

Forest monks these days still go wandering; it is called *tudong* in Thai. They take their bowls and robes and walk, seeking out secluded places to meditate. In preparation for wandering, they progressively increase the amount of walking meditation so as to develop their physical fitness and endurance. They increase the number of hours of walking meditation a day to at least five or six hours.

Good for Striving

Striving, especially to overcome drowsiness, is the second benefit. While practising sitting meditation, meditators may slip into tranquil states, but if they are "too tranquil," they may start nodding off to sleep. Without mindfulness and awareness, meditation, even though it feels peaceful, can turn into dullness because it has been overcome by sloth and torpor. Doing walking meditation can counteract this tendency.

Ajahn Chah used to recommend us that once a week we stay up all night, sitting and doing walking meditation throughout the night. We tended to get very drowsy around one or two in the morning, so Ajahn Chah recommended we do the walking meditation backwards to overcome drowsiness. You don't fall asleep walking backwards!

Once at Bodhinyana Monastery in Western Australia, I went out early one morning, around five o'clock, to do some walking meditation and saw a layman, who was staying for the Rains Retreat in the monastery, doing walking meditation up and down along the top of the six-foot high wall in front of the monastery. By putting great effort into being mindful of each step, he was overcoming drowsiness by developing a heightened sense of alertness, effort and zeal.

Good for Health

The Buddha said that walking meditation leads to good health. This is the third benefit. We are all aware that walking is considered a very good form of exercise. These days, we even hear of "power walking". Well, we are talking here about "power meditation," developing walking meditation as both a physical and mental exercise. But to get both benefits, we have to bring awareness to the process of walking, instead of just walking and letting the mind wander off thinking of other things.

Good for Digestion

The fourth benefit of walking meditation is that it is good for the digestion. This is particularly important for monks who eat one meal a day. After a meal, the blood goes to the stomach and away from the brain. Thus one can feel drowsy. Forest monks stress that after a meal one should do a few hours of walking meditation, because walking up and down helps the digestion. For lay meditators too if you have had a heavy meal, instead of going to bed, go out and do an hour of walking meditation. It will help with physical wellbeing and provide an opportunity to cultivate the mind.

Good for Sustaining Concentration

The fifth important benefit of walking meditation is that the concentration arising out of walking meditation sustains itself for a long time. The walking posture is a relatively coarse or complex meditative posture compared to sitting. While sitting, it is easy to maintain one's posture. We have our eyes closed so there are no visual sense stimuli, and we are not engaged in any bodily movement. So sitting, in comparison to walking, is a simpler posture in terms of the activities involved. The same is true for standing and lying down, because there is no movement taking place.

If one has developed concentration only in the sitting posture, when one gets up from that position and begins with bodily movements like walking, it is harder to maintain that state of concentration. This is because one is moving from a refined state to a coarser state.

While we are walking there is much more sensory input. We are looking where we are going; thus there is visual input. There is also sensory input from the movement of the body. Therefore if we can concentrate the mind while walking and receiving all this sensory stimuli, then when we change from that posture to a simpler one, concentration becomes easier to maintain. That is, when we sit down the strength of mind and power of that concentration carries over easily to this posture. So walking meditation can help to develop strength and clarity of mind, and a concentration that can carry over into other less active meditation postures.

Preparation for Walking Meditation

Finding a Suitable Place

The place where the Lord Buddha did walking meditation at Bodhgaya after his Enlightenment still exists to this day. His walking path was seventeen steps long. These days the Forest Monks tend to make their walking meditation paths much longer — up to thirty steps long. The beginner may find thirty paces too long because their mindfulness has not yet developed. By the time you come to the end of the path, your mind may have been "around the world and back." Remember, walking is a stimulating posture, and initially the mind tends to wander a great deal. It is usually better for beginners to start off on a shorter path; fifteen paces would be a good length.

If you do a walk meditation outside, find a secluded place where you won't be distracted or disturbed. It is good to find a walking path that is slightly enclosed. It can be a distraction to walk in an open area where there is a view, as you may find that the mind is drawn out to the scenery. If the path is closed in, it tends to bring the mind inwards, into one's self and towards peace. An enclosed area is especially suitable for speculative personalities who like to think a lot; it helps to calm their minds.[2]

Preparing the Body and Mind

Once you have chosen a suitable path, stand at one end. Stand erect. Put the right hand over the left in front of you. Don't walk with your hands behind your back. A meditation master who visited the monastery where I was staying once commented when he saw one of the guests walking up and down with his hands behind his back: "He's not walking meditation; he's going for a stroll." By placing the hands in front, it creates a clear determination to focus the mind on walking meditation, to differentiate from "just walking."

The practice is firstly to develop *samādhi*, a Pali word that means focussing the mind, developing the mind to one-pointedness by gradual degrees of mindfulness and concentration. To focus the mind, one has to be diligent and

2. *Path of Purification* IiI,103.

determined. This requires a degree of physical as well as mental composure. One begins by composing oneself by clasping the hands in front. Composing the body helps to compose the mind. Having thus composed the body, one should then stand still and bring awareness and attention to the body. Then raise your hands together in *añjali*, a gesture of respect, and with your eyes shut reflect for a few minutes on the qualities of the Buddha, the Dhamma and the Saṅgha (*buddhānussati, dhammānussati* and *saṅghānussati*).

Contemplate having taken refuge in the Buddha, the Wise One, He who Knows and Sees, the Awakened One, the Fully Enlightened One. Reflect in your heart on the qualities of the Buddha for a few minutes. Then recall the Dhamma—the Truth that you are striving to realise on the walking meditation path. Finally, bring to mind the Saṅgha, especially those fully Enlightened Ones who have realised the Truth by cultivating meditation.

Then bring the hands down in front of you and make a mental determination on how long you are going to "walk meditation', be it half an hour, one hour, or more. However long you determine to walk for, adhere to it. In this manner you are nurturing the mind at that initial stage of the meditation with zest, inspiration and confidence.

Meditation Objects for Walking Meditation

The Buddha taught forty different meditation objects,[3] many of which can be used on the walking path. However some are more suitable than others. I shall discuss a number of these meditation objects here, beginning with those most commonly used.

Awareness of the Walking Posture

The first method is awareness of the walking posture. While walking, place all your attention at the soles of the feet, on the sensations and feelings as they arise and pass away. As you walk, the feeling will change. As the foot is lifted and comes down again into contact with the path, a new feeling arises. Be aware of this sensation on the sole of the foot. Again as the foot

3. *Path of Purification* III,104

lifts, mentally note the new feeling as it arises. When you lift each foot and place it down, know the sensations felt. At each new step, certain new feelings are experienced and old feelings cease. These should be known with mindfulness. With each step there is a new feeling experienced—feeling arising, feeling passing away; feeling arising, feeling passing away.

With this method, we place mindfulness on the feeling of walking itself, on each step taken, on the *vedanā* (pleasant, unpleasant or neutral sensations). We are aware of whatever type of *vedanā* arises at the soles of the feet. When we stand, there is a sensation, a feeling, of the contact with the ground. This contact can produce pain, heat or other sensations. We place our mindful attention on those feelings, knowing them fully. When raising the foot to take a step, the feeling changes as soon as the foot loses contact with the ground. When we place that foot down, again a new feeling arises as the foot comes into contact with the ground. As we walk, feelings are constantly changing and arising anew. We mindfully note this arising and passing away of feelings as the soles of the feet lift off or touch onto the ground. In this way we are keeping our full attention just on the sensations that arise through walking.

Have you ever really noticed before the feelings in the feet as you walk? They happen every time we walk, but we tend not to notice these subtle things in life. When we walk, our minds tend to be somewhere else. Walking meditation is a way of simplifying what we are doing when we are doing it. We are bringing the mind to the "here and now," being "one with walking when walking". We are simplifying everything, quieting the mind by just knowing feeling as it is arising and passing away.

It is important to remember when walking to keep the eyes cast down about a metre and a half in front. Don't be looking around distracted by this or that. Keep awareness on the feeling at the soles of the feet, and in this way, develop focussed attention, and clear knowing of walking while walking.

How fast should you walk? Ajahn Chah recommended walking naturally, not too slow or too fast. If you walk fast, you might find it very difficult to concentrate on the sensation of feeling arising and passing away. You may need to slow down. On the other hand, some people may need to speed up. You have to find your own pace, whatever works for you. You can begin slowly at first then gradually come to your normal walking pace.

If your mindfulness is weak (meaning your mind wanders a lot), then walk very slowly until you can stay in the present moment of each step. Start by establishing mindfulness at the beginning of the path. When you arrive in the middle of the path, then mentally ask yourself, "Where is my mind? Is it on the feeling at the soles of the feet? Am I knowing the contact here and now, at this present moment?" If the mind has wandered off, then bring it back to the sensations at the feet again and continue walking.

When you get to the end of the path, turn slowly around and re-establish your mindfulness. Where is the mind? Has it wandered off? Does it know the feeling at the soles of the feet? The mind tends to wander elsewhere chasing thoughts of: anxiety, fear, happiness, sorrow, worries, doubts, pleasures, frustrations and all the other myriad thoughts that can possibly arise. If mindfulness of the meditation object is not present, re-establish the mind on the simple act of walking, and then begin to walk back to the other end of the path.

When you get to the middle of the path, again note, "I am now at the middle of the path" and check to see if the mind is with the object. Then, once you arrive at the end of the path mentally note, "Where is the mind?" In this way, you walk back and forth mindfully aware of the feelings arising and passing away. While walking, constantly re-establish your mindfulness pulling the mind back, drawing the mind inward, becoming aware, knowing the feeling at each moment as it is arising and passing away.

As you sustain mindfulness on the sensations and feelings at the soles of the feet, you will notice that the mind gets less distracted. The mind becomes less inclined to go out to things that are happening around you. You become calmer. The mind becomes tranquil as it settles down. Once the mind is calm and tranquil, then you'll find that walking becomes too coarse an activity for this quality of mind. You will just want to be still. So stop and stand to allow the mind to experience this calm and tranquillity.

Walking involves the mental volition to move, and your mind may be too focused on the meditation object to move. Continue the practice in a standing position. Meditation is about the work of the mind, not about any particular posture. The physical posture is just a convenient means to enhance the work of the mind.

This calmness and tranquillity is known as *passaddhi*; it is one of the factors of Enlightenment. Concentration and tranquillity work together with mindfulness; combined with the factors of energy, investigation of Dhamma, joy, and equanimity, they make up the "Seven Factors of Enlightenment." When in meditation the mind is tranquil, then because of that tranquillity there will arise a sense of joy, rapture, and bliss. The Buddha said that the bliss of peace is the highest happiness. A concentrated mind experiences that peace, and this peace can be experienced in our lives.

Having developed the practice of walking meditation in a formal context, then when we are walking around in our daily lives going to the shops, walking from one room to the other, we can use this activity of walking as meditation. We can be aware just of walking, simply being with that process. Our minds can be still and peaceful. This is a way of developing concentration and tranquillity in our daily lives.

From Sitting Meditation to the Walking Path

If while doing sitting meditation, the mind becomes tranquil with a certain meditation object, then you can use that same object in walking meditation. However with some subtle meditation objects, such as the breath, the mind must have attained a certain degree of stability in that calmness first. If the mind is not yet calm and you begin walking meditation focusing attention on the breath, it will be difficult, as the breath is a very subtle object. It is generally better to begin with a coarser object of meditation, such as the sensations of feelings arising at the feet.

There are many meditation objects that do transfer well from the sitting to the walking posture: for example the Four Divine Abidings: Loving kindness, Compassion, Appreciative Joy and Equanimity. As you pace back and forth develop the expansive thoughts based on loving kindness, "May all beings be happy, may all beings be at peace, may all beings be free from all suffering." You can use the walking posture as a complement to sitting, developing meditation on the same object but in a different posture.

Choosing a Mantra

If while walking meditation you find that you are getting drowsy, then activate the mind, rather than calm it, with a mantra so that it becomes more focussed and awake. Use a mantra like Buddho, repeating the word quietly to yourself over and over again. If the mind still wanders, then start saying Buddho very quickly, and walk up and down very fast. As you walk, recite *Buddho, Buddho, Buddho.* In this way, your mind can become focussed very quickly.

Let me tell you a story that illustrates the effectiveness of a mantra. When Tan Ajahn Mun, the famous forest meditation teacher, was dwelling in North Thailand; the hill tribes in the area knew nothing about meditation or meditation monks. However the hill tribe people are very inquisitive. When they saw him walking up and down on his path, they followed him in a line. When he turned around at the end of the path, the whole village was standing there.

They had noticed him walking back and forth with his eyes cast down and had assumed he was searching for something. They enquired, "What are you looking for, Venerable Sir? Can we help you find it?" He skilfully replied, "I'm looking for Buddho, the Buddha in the heart. You can help me to find it by walking up and down on your own paths looking for the Buddha." With this simple and beautiful instruction, many of those villagers began meditating, and Tan Ajahn Mun said they obtained wonderful results.

Contemplation of the Way Things Are

Investigation of Dhamma (*dhammavicaya*) is one of the Factors of Enlightenment. Contemplating the teachings and the laws of nature can be employed while walking up and down the meditation path. This does not mean that one thinks or speculates randomly. Rather, it is the constant reflection and contemplation of the Truth , the Dhamma.

Investigating Impermanence

For example, one can contemplate Impermanence by observing the process of change, and seeing how all things are subject to change. One develops a clear perception of the arising and passing away of all experience. "Life" is a continual process of arising and passing away, and all conditioned experience is subject to this law of nature. By contemplation of this Truth, one sees the characteristics of existence. One sees that all things are subject to change. All things are not satisfactory. All things are not self. One can investigate these fundamental characteristics of nature on the walking meditation path.

Recollecting Generosity and Virtue

The Buddha continually stressed the importance of generosity and virtue. While on the walking path, one can reflect on one's virtue or on acts of generosity. Walk up and down and ask yourself, "Today, what acts of goodness have I done?"

A meditation teacher I knew often used to comment that one reason meditators cannot get peaceful is because they have not done enough goodness during the day. Goodness is a cushion for tranquillity, a base for peace. If we have done acts of kindness during the day—having said a kind word, done a good deed, been generous or compassionate—then the mind will experience joy and rapture. Those acts of goodness, and the happiness that comes from them, will become the conditional factors for concentration and peace. The powers of goodness and generosity lead to happiness and it is that wholesome happiness which forms the foundation for concentration and wisdom.

The recollection of one's good deeds is a very appropriate meditation subject when the mind is restless, agitated, angry, or frustrated. If the mind lacks peace, then recollect your past kind actions. This is not to for the purpose of building up your ego, but a recognition of the power of goodness and wholesomeness. Acts of kindness, virtue and generosity bring joy (*pīti*) into the mind, and joy is a Factor of Enlightenment (*bojjhaṅga*).

Recollecting acts of generosity; reflecting on the benefits of giving; recalling one's virtue; contemplating the purity of harmlessness, the purity of honesty, the purity of propriety in sexual relations, the purity of truthfulness, the purity of non-confusion of mind by avoiding intoxicants—all of these recollections can serve as meditation objects on the walking path.

Recollecting the Nature of the Body

We can also meditate on death and dying, or on the non-beautiful nature of the body, or on the *asubha* contemplations—corpses in various stages of decay. We can visualise taking this body apart, just as a medical student would dissect a body. We "peel off the skin and see" what is underneath, the layers of the flesh, the sinews, the bones, the organs. We can mentally remove each one of the organs from the body so it can be investigated and understood. What is the body made of? What are its component parts? Is this me? Is it permanent? Is it worthy of being called a self?

The body is just an aspect of nature, like a tree or a cloud. The fundamental problem is the attachment to the body; where the mind clings to the view that this body is my body, clings to delights in my body, clings to delights in other people's bodies: "This is me. This is self. I own this."

We can challenge this attachment to the body through contemplation and investigation. For example, we can take up the object of the bones of the body; visualise a specific bone as we are walking meditation, seeing it bleach, break up and return to the earth element. Bone is made up of calcium and other chemicals, absorbed into the body through the consumption of vegetable and animal matter. It comes from earth. Chemicals from the earth come together to form bone, and eventually that bone will return to earth.

We meditate on and break down a bone to its elements and return them back to the earth. We re-establish it again and break it down again, and we carry on this process continuously until clear insight arises. Calcium just is calcium; there is no quality of it being my calcium or someone else's. Earth just goes back to earth, each element returns to its natural form. This is not me; this is not mine; this is not worthy of being called a self.

If you are meditating on the parts of the body and you have not completely broken down the object of meditation into the four elements (earth, air, fire and water) and then re-constituted it, the work of the meditation is not yet finished. The mental exercise is not yet complete; the work is not done. Keep at it. Continue walking. Walk up and down and investigate until you are able to establish the perception in the mind of seeing the *asubha* in the *subha*—to see the non-beautiful, the non-delightful, and the non-attractive in what is assumed to be beautiful, delightful and attractive. We break this body down and turn it back to its natural elements, in order to see it as it really is.

The training of the mind to investigate natural processes leads to wisdom. By repeating these exercises, the mind sees and understands that this is not me, not mine, not self. It sees that the four elements that constitute this body are just aspects of nature. It is the mind that attaches to the view that the body is self. We come to challenge that attachment; we do not accept it blindly, because it is that attachment which causes all our suffering.

Other Contemplations

Another meditation object the Buddha recommended was to reflect on peace, and the nature of peace.[4] Yet another is to consider the qualities of Enlightenment. Alternatively one can walk up and down reflecting on the qualities of the Buddha, the qualities of the Dhamma, or the qualities of the Saṅgha. Or one can recollect heavenly beings (devas) and the qualities needed to become a heavenly being.[5]

Wise Use of Contemplation

There are so many meditation objects in the Buddhist repertoire of meditation. Your meditation object should be chosen carefully. Select a meditation object that stimulates the mind when the mind needs stimulating, or pacifies the mind when the mind needs calming. But a few words of caution are needed when using these contemplations on the walking path. It is very easy for the mind to drift into speculative thought. We have to be very mindful, and to note at the beginning of the path, the middle and the end of the path: "Am I really with my meditation object or am I thinking about something else?" If you are walking up and down on a meditation path for four hours, but there is only mindful awareness for one minute during the four hours, you have meditated for only one minute.

We need to remember it is not how much meditation we do; it is the quality of that meditation that counts. If, while you

---

4. *Path of Purification* III,105, VIII,245f
5. *Path of Purification* III,105, VII,115

are walking, the mind is wandering off elsewhere, then you are not meditating in the sense that the Buddha used the word meditation; as *bhāvanā* or mental development. It is the quality of mind rather than the quantity of meditation which is important.

Conclusion

Throughout the history of Buddhism, monks and nuns have attained insight, wisdom and Enlightenment while on the walking meditation path and practising investigation of the Truth. In the forest monastic tradition, every aspect of our life is treated as an opportunity for meditation. Meditation is not just when seated on our meditation cushions. All the processes of life are opportunities for us to investigate reality. We strive to know things as they are, that things arise and pass away, to understand reality as it actually is.

In this discussion of walking meditation, I hope I have given you something that will extend your repertoire of meditation techniques. Walking meditation is something you can use in your daily life when you are active, as well as when you are doing formal meditation. It is another mode for developing the mind. Walking meditation gives work for the mind to do. If you have problems with drowsiness when sitting, get up and put the mind to work. This is *kammaṭṭhāna*, the fundamental work of the mind.

In the forest tradition whenever a meditation teacher goes to a monastery, one of the first places he goes to are the monks' meditation paths to see how many footprints are on them. And if those meditation paths are well worn, then that is considered a sign of a good monastery. May your walking path be well worn.

WALKING MEDITATION IS WONDERFUL

By Ajahn Brahmavaṃso

Walking meditation is wonderful, especially in the early morning. Often when you get up early in the morning, in particular when you're not used to getting up so early, you're quite tired and the mind isn't bright. One of the advantages of walking meditation is that you can't nod off while you're walking. So if you're tired, walking meditation is very good to do. It brings up some energy, and also you can get very peaceful.

Walking meditation was both praised and practised by the Buddha. If you read the suttas, you find that the Buddha would usually do walking meditation in the early morning. He wouldn't be sitting; he'd be walking.

Many monks and nuns have become enlightened on the walking meditation path. It's a very effective way of developing both calm and insight. For some monks that I know in Thailand, their main practice is walking meditation. They do very little sitting. They do a lot of walking, and many get tremendously powerful insights while they're walking.

Another benefit of walking meditation is that it is especially suitable for those who have physical discomfort when sitting for long periods. If you find it difficult to sit in meditation because of pains in the body, walking meditation can be a very effective alternative.

Don't consider walking meditation as a "second-class" meditation. If you want to spend most of your meditation time this way, please do so. But do it well and do it carefully. See if you can develop the happiness born of serenity as you're walking back and forth.

Setting Up Walking Meditation

Choose a clear, straight path between twenty to thirty paces long. This can be a corridor in a house, a path in the garden, or just a track on the grass. Use whatever is available, even if it's a bit less than twenty paces long. If it's comfortable to do so, walk without shoes, enjoying the contact of your bare feet on the ground.

Stand at one end of your path. Compose the mind. Relax the body and begin walking. Walk back and forth at a pace that seems natural to you. While you are walking, clasp your hands comfortably in front of you, and rest your gaze on the ground about two metres ahead. Be careful not to look around. If you're doing walking meditation, it's a waste of time to look here and there, because that would be distracting.

The Stages of Meditation Apply Here Too

The first four stages of breath meditation apply here as well. But in walking meditation attention eventually comes to rest on the feet rather than the breath.

At first, aim to develop the first stage of present-moment awareness, giving up the baggage of the past and future. Reach the state of just walking, easily, in the here and now. When you feel that you have settled into the present moment, where thoughts concerning the past and future are absent from the mind, then aim to develop the second stage of silent walking in the present moment. Gradually let go of all thinking, let go of the inner commentary. Walk without any inner speech. Develop silent awareness of the present-moment. Make use of techniques such as watching every moment very closely, so that you don't have the time to comment about what has just happened, and attending to the space between thoughts.

Once the inner commentary has slowed to a bare trickle of inner speech, deliberately focus your attention on the feeling of movement in the feet and lower legs. Do so to the extent that you clearly notice every step on the path. Know every left step, know every right step—one after the other without missing any. Know every step as you turn around at the end of the path. The famous Chinese saying that the "journey of one thousand miles begins with a single step" is helpful here. Such a journey is in fact only one step long— the step that you are walking now. So just be silently aware of this "one step," and let everything else go. When you have completed ten return trips up and down the path without missing a single left or right step, then you have fulfilled the third stage of the walking meditation—silent present-moment awareness of walking.

Now increase the attention so that you notice every feeling of movement in the left step, from the very beginning when the left foot starts to move and lift up from the ground. Notice as it goes up, forward, down, and then rests on the ground again, taking the weight of the body. Develop this continuous awareness of the left step, and then similar smooth, unbroken awareness of the right step. Do this throughout every step to the end of the path. And as you turn around, notice every feeling in the turning—around procedure, not missing a movement.

When you can walk for fifteen minutes comfortably sustaining the attention on every moment of walking, without a single break, then you have reached the fourth stage of full sustained awareness of walking. At this point the process of walking so fully occupies the attention that the mind cannot be distracted. You know when this happens, because the mind goes into a state of *samādhi*, or attentive stillness, and becomes very peaceful.

Samādhi on the Walking Path

Even the sound of the birds disappears as your attention is fully focused on the experience of walking. Your attention is easily settled, content, and sustained on one thing. You will find this a very pleasant experience indeed.

As your mindfulness increases, you will know more and more of the sensations of walking. Then you find that walking does have this sense of beauty and peace to it. Every step becomes a "beautiful step." And it can very easily absorb all your attention as you become fascinated by just walking. You can receive a great deal of samādhi through walking meditation in this way. That samādhi is experienced as peacefulness, a sense of stillness, a sense of the mind being very comfortable and very happy in its own corner.

I started my walking meditation practice when I was first ordained as a monk in a temple in Bangkok. I would choose a path and quite naturally, without forcing it, I'd walk very slowly. (You don't need to walk fast, and you don't need to walk slowly. Just do what feels comfortable.) I used to get into beautiful samādhi states during walking meditation. I recall once being disturbed because I'd been walking too long. I hadn't noticed the time pass, and I was needed to go to an important ceremony. One of the monks had been sent to get me. I recall this monk came up to me and said, "Brahmavaṃso, you've got to come to a *dāna*" (an alms offering). I was looking at a space about two metres ahead. My hands were clasped in front of me. When I heard the monk's voice, it seemed as if it came from a thousand miles away because I was so absorbed into my walking meditation. He repeated, "Brahmavaṃso, you have to come now!" It took me more than a minute to actually lift my gaze from the ground and to turn it around to the side where this senior monk was trying to get my attention. And as I met his eyes, all I could say was "What?" It took such a long time to get out of that samādhi and react at normal speed. The mind was so cool and so peaceful and so still.

I hope you experience this peacefulness for yourself when you try walking meditation. Many people who practise walking meditation for the first time say, "This is amazing. Beautiful." Just slowing down gives you a sense of peace. You become calm just by watching the sensations as you walk. So walking meditation is a type of meditation that I suggest you experiment with.

WALKING MEDITATION PRACTICES

by Dharma Dorje

Walking is one of the most adaptable and readily practised meditations found in Buddhism. As one of four postures the Buddha prescribed for the development of mindfulness,[6] walking is a powerful tool used in meditation retreats for establishing mindfulness and for developing energy. It produces and maintains awareness, which in turn helps control fluctuating mind states, even outside of secluded retreats. This paper offers ways to adapt walking as an extension of meditation practice both inside and outside of formal meditation retreats.

All the three main schools of Buddhism[7] use walking as a part of meditation or as a meditation practice. In Theravādin Buddhism a distinction is made between practices that develop "Insight" and "Tranquillity." These two terms, synonymous with wisdom and mental discipline, have a synergistic relationship when it comes to realising Nibbāna[8]. Walking outside of meditation retreats, as presented here, mainly falls under the category of Tranquillity with minor development of Insight. On the other hand, walking within meditation retreats utilises either one or both practices depending upon individual requirements or the aim of the retreat. The goal of this paper is clarification of these two kinds of walking practices and when they should be done.

---

6. The other 3 postures are standing, sitting, and lying down (see MN 119).
7. Namely: Theravada, Mahayana, and Vajrayana. The teachings of all three schools are built upon the development of mindfulness, and walking meditation is often an integral part of that development.
8. Nibbāna, or Nirvāna in Sanskrit, literally means "extinction" and "is the highest and ultimate goal of all Buddhist aspirations" (*Buddhist Dictionary*, p. 125). The tendency to use the word "enlightenment" as a synonym is diminishing amongst Theravādin Buddhist authors because it has been overused and is considered too broad in scope to be a proper definition for what can only be understood after the experience.

Attitudes and Perceptions

Using walking in meditation retreats as a way to increase awareness is often a meditator's first exposure to the benefits to be derived from this practice. Beginners often don't realise just how much walking during retreats can be an integral part of the whole practice. It's not uncommon to hear beginners express views indicating they do not perceive any benefit from the walking other than a break from the sitting practice; that it is little more than a way to stretch and loosen legs and body. They can even develop attachment to walking as a relief or a break from what they see as the formal practice. To the other extreme, some see the periods of walking as getting in the way of the "real" work done while sitting. These meditators end up developing aversion instead of attachment towards the walking. Neither perception is correct and such attitudes need changing if one wants to get the maximum benefit out of meditation exercises. Walking meditation is not a separate practice, but a continuation of the practice in a different posture.

Walking is something that most of us do quite a bit outside of our meditation retreats. As such, mindfulness of the process of walking is a way to carry our meditation practice into our daily lives and thereby derive maximum potential from the exercise. As a daily practice, walking can be adapted so that it is both physically invigorating and mentally tranquillising, which helps to alleviate the strain and stress so many of us experience in day-to-day existence. When used in this way, it's a relief, a break from the daily grind, something quite positive and useful to our well-being. Continued practice will increase mindfulness and act as groundwork or preparation for a retreat. Finding time to go on retreat is often difficult for the laity, and sometimes even for ordained monks and nuns, which makes the limited time within retreat quite precious. So anything that can be done to get us closer to the meditative state of mind prior to a planned retreat is very valuable indeed.

Walking by Itself

Let us start with walking practices not directly connected to sitting practices or retreats. The practices in this section can be used as preliminary work towards going on retreat as well as a daily or anytime practice (meaning that the practice can be done whenever or wherever the opportunity arises). Many of them are adapted from Thich Nhat Hanh's *The Long Road Turns To Joy: A Guide to Walking Meditation,* and I encourage you to read his book, referenced at the end of this paper.

There is a thread or general theme to the following exercises: "Let go and be here now." It is a simple instruction which is hard to do at the beginning. So many of us are too caught up in multi-tasking that we see neither the need nor the benefit to simplifying everyday activities. There is an adage that goes, "It is hard to remember to drain the swamp when you are up to your armpits in alligators." Whenever we start our practice, we bring along a myriad of thoughts concerning our worries, plans, hopes, fears, etc. No matter what thoughts arise while doing walking meditation the correct practice is to simply let go of them. You bring your mind back as soon as you become aware that your attention has wandered away from walking. This should be done without any further contemplation about their content. Regardless of how many times extraneous thoughts arise, just keep letting go of them until you have finished the time set aside to do the walking meditation. You will probably notice thinking is much clearer and more lucid after your walking meditation than before you started.

There are a number of aids which can help you let go and be here now while walking; some are presented in the following paragraphs but the list is by no means exhaustive. Once you have mastered the techniques, feel free to develop some of your own. Although several of these methods can be combined, do not attempt this until you are comfortable doing only one. When you feel ready, go ahead and combine, but take a moment every time you decide to do your walking meditation to ascertain what your capabilities are at that moment. There are a number of factors to consider, such as how energised you feel, what is suitable for the environment in which you walk, the amount of time you have to pull the different methods together, etc. To cover these factors in detail would require quite a few pages and take away from the self-discovery aspect that is so important in Buddhist meditation techniques. Only through mindful repetition and reviewing will you learn what works best. This is a way to practise "clear comprehension" early on; an aspect of mindfulness that is just as important as "bare attention" which is the other aspect of mindfulness in Buddhist meditation.[9]

To be mindful when walking is to be Buddha-like. Take a moment to reflect on how the Buddha is often portrayed. Many Buddha images and paintings show the Buddha with a half smile on his face. This half smile comes naturally to one who is happy and satisfied with being here now. Try to find this state of happiness and satisfaction before you take your first step and smile like a Buddha. The more you let go of extraneous thinking (meaning all thoughts and feelings not associated with the practice), the easier it will be to smile in this way.

Once you have established the Buddha Smile, bring your attention to your feet and start to walk. Be aware of the entire bodily action required to walk. Watch as your foot leaves the ground, remain aware of it as it moves through the air, as it touches the ground, and be aware of the way your body shifts the weight to the now-placed foot as you begin the next step. Try not to break the sequence into parts, but instead try to watch it as a fluid ongoing motion. Do not strain the mind or attempt to hold it on the feet. When you become aware the mind is not attuned to the feet, simply stop thinking about whatever has replaced your attention and return to the feet. Do not fret or be concerned about how many times you have to do this. Your focus will get better the more you practise walking meditation. If you give in to getting concerned or become upset about how poorly you maintain your awareness you will only increase extraneous thinking, which is exactly the opposite of what you are striving to do.[10] Just keep letting go and being here now at the feet.

If you become aware that your smile has gone then simply bring it back and then return to your feet. If you have to turn,

---

9. Bare attention is perception of the initial arising of any phenomena before subsequent reaction or further development is undertaken. It is the starting point for knowing, shaping, and liberating the mind. Clear comprehension builds upon bare attention, determining a course of action or reaction to the initial arising of any phenomena. Clear comprehension is like a sieve that lets pass only that which fits the desired purpose and which is the most suitable given perceived choices. It brings into focus all aspects of daily life as objects for development of mindfulness, and when practiced correctly, rejects all that is not in accord with one's spiritual aspirations. For more on this see *The Heart of Buddhist Meditation* pp. 30–56.

simply be aware as much as you can of the process involved. Again, keep it fluid as much as possible without breaking up the motion. The pace should be just slow enough to be able to watch it all, but not so slow as to make the walk broken or hesitant in any way. Refrain from talking, humming, whistling, or looking around beyond the necessary distance to maintain the direction of your travel.

As you walk in this fashion you will get to the point your mind is filled with all aspects of walking and less and less with mental "stuff" unrelated to walking.[11] You may even start to catch the wandering mind at the point of intention to leave the object and thereby not lose the awareness of the walking. Intention precedes all action, including the mental movement to another thought or to investigate another object of the physical senses.[12] Catching the intention to do something else marks an increase in mindfulness and indicates you are doing well with the practice.

Once you become comfortable with simply walking, increase your awareness to include breathing. This will be an easy transition for those of you who have already been practising preliminary exercises for Mindfulness of Breathing. A recommended method to link the breath to the walk is to count the steps taken during each in-breath and each out-breath. You start by making a mental note of the number of steps you have taken for each in- and out-breath while walking. Simply count 1–2–3 or 5–10–15–20.[13] Each number coincides with a full step

---

10. Conversely, judgments and comparisons leading to such positive thoughts as "I am doing better today" or "The practice is going well" are also extraneous. Let go of all attachments and aversions associated with the practice; work with what "is" rather than what "could be" or what "was". Leave off such dissections until you have completed the exercise itself, which is the only time such an action is of benefit to meditation.

11. The use of the term "stuff" is not idiomatic. It is meant as a conveyance of attitude or approach; a way to quickly perceive extraneous mental activity as not being worthy of further analysis beyond bare recognition before turning away from it back towards the walking itself.

12. It should be noted that in Buddhism the mind is considered to be a sense that results in cognition, in the same fashion as the other bodily sensations of seeing, hearing, smelling, touching, and tasting.

and the duration of the count coincides with a full in-breath. Another count coincides with a full out-breath.

The number of steps for each breath may be different; for example, the count may be 2–3, meaning 2 steps for the in-breath and 3 steps for the out-breath. Do not concern yourself with the discrepancy and be prepared to change the count as you become more comfortable with the exercise or to compensate for changes in terrain you encounter. You can slow down or slightly increase your walking pace as an adjustment when the count and step are not coinciding, but *do not* try to speed up or slow down the breathing. It is very important to let the breathing happen at the rate the body sets. Controlling your breath can tire you quickly.[14] Physically straining in this way is counterproductive, leading to undesirable mind-states such as worry or agitation. On the other hand, slowing or slightly increasing the number of steps will lead to more relaxed physical and mental states which help bring forward tranquillity. Find the rhythm between smiling, walking, counting, and breathing. Let the practice develop naturally without strain and you will find yourself walking in this way spontaneously whenever and wherever it can be done.

Enhancing the Practice

Before discussing other ways of practising walking meditation, let's take a small excursion into ways you can combine breathing and movement to increase mindfulness and tranquillity. These examples may seem a bit off topic, but I am including them to show that mindful use of breathing may be used with a broad range of activities besides just walking to gain beneficial results. Mental exertion will be better if preceded by even a single mindful breath.[15] Weightlifters know you have to

---

13. Using the count of 5–10–15–20 instead of 1–2–3–4 is a matter of individual preference, but it may be of benefit for those who get attached to quantity rather than quality. The former method of counting doesn't lend emphasis to quantity.

14. This cannot be overstated. If you have trouble separating volition and attention, whereby you cannot simply watch the breath without controlling it, then counting and breathing may be counterproductive. Speak to your teacher if problems persist or switch to a different walking practice (see next section on Enhancing the Practice).

exhale when exerting or you can injure yourself. I recall one person telling me how she got into the flow of relaxed mindful breathing while scuba diving. She found that by slightly increasing the amount of air she breathed in, she could rise in the water to clear coral and rocks in her path. Breathing with awareness and not working the legs so much led to less breathing overall. So much so, that when she returned to the boat with the other divers, the impressed instructor pointed out there was a considerably more oxygen left in her tank when compared with the other divers' tanks.

Hatha yoga provides excellent ways to use the breath while doing stretching and exercising. Some of the exercises require you to do them with an inhale or exhale of breath, while some require using both the in and the out breath in one exercise (e.g., Sun Salutations). The length of time to hold a pose, or Āsana, can utilise a breath count.

The same method prescribed in the previous section of combining counting with breathing can be adapted to running, or fast walking, or any repetitive exercise as another way of extending the practice into other activities. In Tai Chi an alternative method called Guo Lin Qigong has been prescribed as a complementary treatment for cancer patients. The method combines tight control of gaze, arm movements, state of mind, and also involves altering the pattern of in-and-out breathing for a specific number of steps to achieve increased vigour while simultaneously increasing concentration.[16]

My teacher, Kema Ananda, recommended another variation for running and cross-country skiing in which you say a mantra just under your breath. The syllables of the mantra act in the same manner as the numbers. He pointed out there was a bonus with this practice because you could only maintain recitation while doing these activities if you weren't overdoing the physical exertion. The mantra was acting like a heart monitor to warn you when you were pushing the activity too far. And let us not forget that some mantras increase wholesome

---

15. For instance in oral presentations, speeches, meetings, etc.
16. A description of this alternative method is in "Daizong's Magic Walking Technique and Qigong." By Lan Blan. *Internal Arts*, Vol. 3, No. 6, November, 1988, p. 38.

mind states like loving kindness. This is extremely beneficial multi-tasking once you develop the skill.

The use of a mantra or a phrase in walking meditation to tie the breath and walk together does require some extra consideration. You should make the syllables in the phrase match the length and rhythm of the breath and steps respectively. But the phrase or mantra can span both the in-breath and the out-breath. As an example, let us use the Thai Buddhist mantra "*Namo Buddhāya, Namo Dhammāya, Namo Sanghāya*" (Translation: "*Homage to the Buddha, Homage to the Dharma, Homage to the Saṅgha*").[17] The entire mantra has a word count of 6 or a syllable count of 15. You could say 2 words on the in-breath and 2 words on the out-breath and 2 words on the in-breath to complete the mantra. Alternatively, you could divide the Mantra across three sets of in- and out-breaths using 5 syllables for each of the three segments: "*Namo*" for the first in-breath, "*Buddhāya*" for the out-breath, "*Namo*" for the second in-breath, and "*Dhammāya*" for the second out-breath and finally "*Namo*" for the last in-breath and "*Saṅghāya*" for the last out-breath.

I personally find varying the speed of parts of a mantra to work quite smoothly: "*Namo*" slowed for one in-breath and a much quicker recitation of "*Buddhāya*" for the out breath. I am very comfortable with a short inhale and a much longer exhale when doing breath meditation and walking. This is why this method works so well for me. I even use this matching of breath, mantra, and movement while I am exercising on a rowing machine (similar to the running with the mantra described above). Each person will need to determine what works for them when expanding their practice. But above all do not fool around with controlling the breath until you are experienced and have good reason to alter its naturally occurring state of flow.[18]

---

17. Not only Theravādin mantras may be used; any mantra that is designed to encourage positive mind states will work. For example, the *Vajraguru Mantra* from the Vajrayana School produces a sense of well-being when chanted and also increases energy.

18. Thich Nhat Hanh points out that once you have been doing the practice of walking meditation for awhile you can try (for a few breaths) to take slightly more air into your lungs and even extend the exhale (pp 22–23 in *The Long Road Turns To Joy*), but I urge caution here for the reasons mentioned earlier.

Another alternative is to form sentences which fit your breath-count. "I smile like a Buddha" fits a 3–3 count, but changing it to "I walk and smile like a Buddha" fits a 4–4 count or "May I smile like a Buddha" fits a 3–4 count. Choose a sentence that aligns you to a wholesome idea.[19] A mettā mantra in English such as "May all beings be happy and free from suffering!" is another example, but the syllable count and word count are an odd number which makes coordination between in- and out-breath more challenging. The challenge however provides the added benefit of greater concentration and more awareness being generated. The benefit is achieved because the exercise becomes more resistant to "running on automatic".[20]

Further Guidelines

If something outside of walking practice requires your attention, then stop the practice momentarily. Do what you need to in order to deal with the situation and then return to the walking meditation. You don't have to be impolite to someone who sees your smiling face and says "Good morning", but you also do not have to do more than reply in the same fashion with mindfulness before returning to the practice. If they persist in an attempt to engage in conversation then politely excuse yourself before returning to practise.

Something very positive may present itself and seem worthy of your attention, such as the beauty of morning dew coating a field of grass or a single exquisite flower encountered on your path. Don't ignore such pleasant mind objects or the wholesome mind states that arise in conjunction with them. Instead, mindfully let them go and return to your walking.[21]

One final point deserves mention. As you develop this way of walking you will find that combining all the elements of

---

19. The term "wholesome" means that which is profitable for your meditation practice, or for your spiritual development. Use clear comprehension to determine suitability of potential phrases or behaviours.

20. The ability for the mind to alternate between tasks so quickly that it appears to be doing two or more things at the same time is what is meant by "running on automatic." The challenge of working with an odd numbered word or syllable count requires sustained attention upon the exercise or you will lose track of the steps, the breath, or the sentence being used.

smiling, walking, counting and breathing will seem to take all your attention, and that it is easy to maintain the mindfulness because the mind is so fully occupied. Such a state will not last long, as the mind is very good at programming behavioural patterns (think about how much can be on your mind when driving a car). Once you establish the practice, boredom arises and the mind will divert its attention and seem to dart around to all kinds of other objects and thoughts. This is simply craving for new stimulation. See it as an opportunity to not respond. Not answering craving when it arises is the first step to undoing or reprogramming conditioned patterns of unwholesome behaviour. Your aim is to let go of whatever arises which is not part of this practice and return to only this practice until the time you allotted for it is over. Do not combat the boredom by changing the phrase or method of practice. The next time you walk you can change something then, but always finish what you start or you risk developing unprofitable habits which will plague you throughout your spiritual development.

Walking Between Sits during Retreats

All sitting practices require mindfulness to do them as well as possible and all sitting practices need energy to keep up the mindfulness required to do them. When you first start sitting and strive to practise meditation, your energy and mindfulness are depleted at a faster rate than they are in more experienced mediators. As a beginner you spend a lot of energy learning what to do and not to do. Conditioned patterns of behaviour which are not conducive to the practice require a lot of effort to detect and correct. Once you know what you are supposed to do, and have developed proper ways and means, the practice itself requires much less energy. As you gain experience, energy lasts longer and mindfulness stays stronger and fuller. For these reasons, walking, the main method of developing energy and

---

21. Joy and tranquillity are factors to be developed, but not at the expense of concentration. Such states are indicators that wholesome states are indeed arising, but taking them as an object to develop further while doing walking meditation is counterproductive. Indulging leads to more and more discursive thinking, or to seeing yet more similar phenomena. This is sense desire clinging rather than a letting go.

mindfulness during meditation retreats, should be adjusted to suit progress in the practice.[22]

Before discussing the different ways to walk between sits, it should be understood that there are different types of meditation practices which dictate the structure incorporated within the walking. In the Theravādin school of Buddhism there are two types of mental development: *Samatha* and *Vipassanā*. Samatha, usually translated as tranquillity, is a synonym for concentration; it is usually used to denote the development of strong concentration, known as jhānas, which allow absorption into the object of contemplation. Vipassanā means insight; it is a synonym for wisdom, and at the height of development has the penetrative ability to make clear the three characteristics of any phenomena perceived (unsatisfactoriness, impermanence, and selflessness). When used together, tranquillity leads to greater penetrative strength for insight, creating the synergy mentioned earlier.[23]

The previous discussion on walking mindfully when not in a retreat describes primarily a tranquillity practice. During a retreat, both types of walking may be used. I shall revisit tranquillity walking as part of a retreat but first I wish to describe walking as part of an insight practice. The guidelines in this section take into account length of practice, type of practice, and the transition between practices designed for Vipassanā development and practices designed to produce Samatha.

---

22. Advanced meditators are sufficiently aware of changes in energy and mindfulness that they walk when they perceive the need to and sit for longer periods between walks than beginners. They are able to perceive how long they need to walk to reach the levels of energy and mindfulness required to maximize the potential of their sitting practice. The time required for each walk and each sit is determined through mindful introspection and not by a prescribed schedule. But prescribed schedules for walking and sitting are beneficial for beginners and should not be abandoned too quickly.

23. *Buddhist Dictionary* p 186 is the main source for the explanation here, but the two types of development are not utilized by all meditation teachers. As well, some meditators are unable to develop jhāna and use only insight meditation practices.

Insight Walking

One of the most common insight practices may be found in the Mahāsi Vipassanā meditation from Burma.[24] There are other variations on Vipassanā meditation, and other Burmese Vipassanā schools, but it serves no useful purpose here to get into differences. Instead, what should be gleaned is the way mindfulness is developed with the walk for the benefit of any sitting practice.

The most common way to practise insight walking is to mentally label the actions and thoughts that arise while walking. Insight walking requires a reflexive placing of the mind, or attention, upon whatever is occupying the meditator's awareness in each moment. The placing of the mind is immediately followed by a directed knowing, or marking, of exactly what it is that is currently occupying the meditator's attention.

You "mark" the awareness with a short mental note, or label, to clearly identify the action or thought process currently present. The practice requires you to know that you are walking when doing so, but that when your attention leaves the bottom of your feet, you know where your attention has gone. And of course, you can only "know" when you come to realise the mind is no longer on the feet and has become occupied with something else. With repeated practice, you can gain the ability to see the mind taking another object as soon as it leaves the object of focus, in this case the feet.

However, no matter how long you practise this exercise or how skilled you become, it will always be a case of "when" the mind leaves your object of awareness and never a matter of "if". It is the nature of the mind to investigate whatever arises at a sense door. So abandon any notion of stopping the mind from doing what it does naturally. The job is to watch the mind, not change the mind. Future frustration can be avoided if this point is clear from the beginning. It is also important not to become dismayed at first sight of the level of detail a matured practice of insight requires. Meditation practice should grow gradually and steadily at the pace natural to the meditator. There is no mandated deadline.

---

24. Two excellent short texts detailing the practice of this form of Vipassanā meditation are Mahāsi Sayādaw's *Practical Insight Meditation* and *Satipaṭṭhāna Vipassanā* (p. 38 has a brief description on walking).

To start, you first note the intention to walk by marking the thought as "intending". If you are sitting, then you will next note the preparation or planning to get up with "planning" or "preparing". The moving of a limb is marked with the mental noting of "moving" and the placing of a hand for balance as "placing". The moving of the other arm is again marked as "moving" or "reaching" and its placement as "placing". Shifting your weight onto your hands is marked as "shifting". If you bend your arm, mark it as "bending". In the same manner mark all actions required for rising to a standing position. This will not be a fluid and continuous motion, but instead will require you to break the action into parts and reflect upon each action-part to determine what to label it. Fully finish the act of marking before proceeding to the next action or thought. Catch everything you can, including all "intending" so that you clearly see each part of the overall task of standing before and as it's attempted.

Here is a list of potential labels which could be used to mark the actions and thoughts you might be aware of when moving from sitting to standing in this manner: intending, planning, preparing, looking, moving, bending, placing, shifting, pushing, straightening, reaching, grasping, pulling, releasing, balancing, stretching, arching. The list is far from exhaustive, so feel free to use whatever comes to mind when doing this practice of insight marking. If thoughts and feelings enter your mind concerning the task then take a moment to note them also with labels such as: reacting, complaining, elation, hoping, wishing, planning, and worrying. If you recognise states of mind, then mark them as well with labels such as: frustrated, sad, happy, agitated, groggy, clear minded, slothful (laziness, indolence), torpid (sluggish, rigid), bright, sharp, and slow.

Do not get overwhelmed by the quantity of examples. Again, these are possibilities which you may or may not see and utilise. I list them to show just how much potential detail may be possible to mark mentally. At first, start by marking what comes to mind and increase marking as more and more becomes evident. You may even get to the point of seeing the intention before each action is started and become able to mark many intentions.

Once you have finished the action of standing, bring your mind to the top of your head. Now move your awareness down through your entire body knowing you are standing. Do this while simultaneously making a mental mark three times slowly, "standing, standing, standing". By the time you finish the third mental mark of "standing" your awareness should be at the bottom of the feet. If you are starting your walk from a standing position,[25] then do this to establish mindfully that you are standing before taking a step. If something happens which interrupts your marking and you lose awareness of the process, then give up marking the "standing" and instead mark the new object which has now become the present object of focus. After marking, do nothing more with it. You simply move your awareness back to the top of the head and start the marking of "standing" three times again. Repeat as necessary until you finish standing.

Start your walk with the right foot.[26] As you lift it, mentally mark the action as "lifting". As you move the foot forward, mark it as "moving" and when you place the foot, mark it as "placing". The heel of the foot you have moved should land no further than the ball of your other foot. If you try to take a longer step, you will lose your balance at some point, so set the distance now and stick to it. As you shift your weight prior to taking the next step with your left foot, mark "shifting" as you shift your weight. Repeat the process of marking "lifting, moving, placing, shifting" with your left foot. Keep marking in this manner until your attention has left your feet.

---

25. For example, you have just finished the dishes and are now going to start walking.

26. Why do I recommend the right foot? I made the decision after contemplating two other points in the practice of Insight meditation: which way to turn at the end of the walk and which side to sleep on. Since turning left is the same direction one turns something to undo it (e.g. the lid of a jar), I thought that turning that way in the walk could be suggestive of undoing conditioning. Starting on the right foot and sleeping on the right side while practicing meditation is utilizing the suggestive quality of "rightness" like "Right Mindfulness" in the "Eightfold Noble Path." As such, my recommendations in this matter are not mandatory, but stay with your choice once made. It is never a good idea to keep changing back and forth on such matters.

When you become aware your attention has wandered, stop walking. In the same manner as previously described, mark where the mind is and what it is doing at that moment with a mental note. If your foot is in mid-air, then put it down. Do not try and balance on one foot while marking or you will lose your balance. If you do try to quickly mark while balancing, and start to fall over, and remember what I said, do mark "remembering" after you regain your balance. You can also mark the "laughing" or "giggling" at yourself if and when that occurs.

When the mind leaves the soles of the feet, it has gone to one of the sense doors. If you catch it right away then you can mark this as simply hearing, seeing, touching, tasting, smelling, thinking. But, if your awareness is not that quick (and often it will not be), then mark what the mind is doing at the moment you become aware of it. Do not attempt to track down when the mind left the feet or what the mind has been doing since it left the feet. If you slip into this cognitive trap, then mark it as "remembering" or "searching" instead. After you have marked what your attention was upon with a mental note or label, bring your attention back to the feet and start the "lifting, moving, placing, shifting" with the foot that is ready to take the next step. With practice, a single action of marking where the mind is or what the mind is doing will be sufficient for returning the attention to the bottom of the feet to take the next step.

Repeated practice of insight walking will reveal the number of movements required to walk are much greater than previously realised. Your first attempts to see each step in four parts soon leads to seeing the intentions that precede each action. Some will see even more actions involved in parts of each step, such as "lifting heel and lifting toes" and "placing heel and placing toes." Resist breaking the walk into more parts in order to mark more. There is little benefit to taking the marking further than the "lifting, moving, placing, shifting" and it can lead to increased frustration from the extra strain. Instead watch all the actions as they occur within each mental knowing of "lifting" using only the label of "lifting" to denote the whole sequence of the rising foot after the intention has been noticed and marked. Likewise use a knowing and grouping together for any other actions seen within "moving" and "placing" the foot, or for the host of actions involved in shifting the weight of the body before taking the next step.

At times you will become aware of a mind state such as agitation or joyfulness, or a physically manifesting state like pain or sleepiness. Treat such occurrences in the same way as mental objects: stop and label them accordingly before returning to the bottom of the feet to resume walking. For example, when you become aware of a painful sensation, first stop, then simply mark "pain" or "painful" without further examination before returning to the feet to resume walking. "Without further examination" means refraining from trying to determine the origin of the pain or from contemplating doing something about it. Only if the pain persists past a few noticing-and-markings, should the meditator stop walking and mindfully contemplate the pain. Often such single-minded examination will result in the pain disappearing as a knowable phenomenon and the walk can be taken up again. If the pain does not disappear, then it is prudent to change posture a little to relieve the painful sensation before returning to the feet to resume walking again.

But be careful not to give in too easily here. I have seen meditators develop a pattern of repeatedly changing their posture only to have the pain continue to bother them or even intensify because they were too quick on altering the practice. Personally, I went through a number of retreats in which I kept changing how I carried my arms in an attempt to deal with pain in my shoulders and lower back. I would clasp my hands behind my back, then cross them in front of me, and then let them hang down. I would keep doing this constant altering throughout the entire walk. I finally tired of having to wrestle with the pain for entire retreats and settled on the choice of leaving the arms always at my side. It took a few walks to break the conditioned pattern of reacting. When I caught myself moving the arms, I put them back at my side. Eventually I was able to mark the intention and desire to move the arms without doing the action. After a couple of days both the pain and the habit of moving the arms ceased.

Pain is probably the most dramatic example for many, but general mind states such as agitation, worry, anger and their opposites such as calm, tranquillity, joy, may present themselves strongly enough to be noticed and marked accordingly. Repeated marking and letting go will eventually result in the mind not returning to phenomena handled in this manner. By this process the mind will become calmer, learning to refrain from continually returning to these states.

On occasions the mind may seem to be less compliant and will not stay at the feet for any length of time. The mind may seem to dart back to a previous thought or object, or may seem to not re-establish on the feet when placed there. When this happens, repeat the mental marking of what is entertaining the mind three times slowly as you simultaneously re-establish the attention upon the soles of your feet. If this doesn't work then you may have to take a closer look at what you are using as a label to mark where the mind has gone or what the mind is doing. When the marking is too general or non-specific, the mind may not let go of the object that is the source of attraction. Nor will the mind return easily or remain upon the intended object of concentration. For instance, if using the label "thinking" doesn't work then look a little deeper and see if you are planning, speculating, projecting, etc. Use a different label that is more specific, then re-establish the mind upon the soles of the feet, and take another step. Be aware and mark if you start "looking" for the very object you just finished marking and thereby causing a returning to that object. Just keep at it and the mind will eventually become more pliant, allowing you to remain attentive on the soles of your feet for longer periods of time. Or, at the very least, you will gain a better understanding of what exactly it is that is exerting such an effect on the mind.

When you reach the end of your walk and take the last step, mark "stopping" three times. Do this slowly so you fill your mind with non-movement. Then start turning to the left, keeping your awareness on the bottom of your feet. Keep the feet close together, heels almost touching, swivel on your heels and mark "turning" three times as you take three sets of left-right combination steps to make a 180 degree turn. Add another left-right combination step if the turn is more then 180 degrees. The amount of detail here is provided to make sure that you complete this action in small steps so that you keep your balance. If your mind leaves the feet during the turn, stop. Mark where or what the mind is doing. Return your attention to the bottom of your feet, and then continue the turn where you left off. After completing the turn, bring your awareness to the top of your head and mark "standing" three times as you bring the awareness down through your body before starting off again on the right foot.

Walk in this manner, continually marking where the mind is until the end of the allotted time. The distance between turns should be somewhere between 5–6 metres (16–20 feet), but this distance can be a less for insight walking. I would recommend a minimum of 15 minutes for an insight walk, and somewhere between 45 minutes to an hour as optimum to develop mindfulness before or between sits. You may also alter your direction or incorporate a diverging path to your seat. Just mark accordingly, meaning the "intention" if you catch it, "turning" and "going" to note the change in direction, and "stopping" when you reach the spot where you plan to stop.

A sit should follow immediately after the walk or you will lose some or all of the mindfulness built-up during the walk. You should also use full awareness and marking in the process of sitting down following the walk. The instruction for getting up from sitting at the beginning of this section is reversed. But after you have completed all the motions, movements and marking required to sit, bring your awareness to the top of your head. In the same manner as was done for standing, mark "sitting" three times as you bring your awareness down through your body knowing that you are sitting.

You are now ready to start your sitting meditation with considerably increased mindfulness. If you were sitting before you started the walk you will notice both an increase in your mindfulness and in your energy as you start the next sit. As you sit and practise your meditation, awareness becomes less keen as time passes and your energy is again depleted. For beginners I recommend no more then an hour of sitting practice without a walk. As your practice becomes more advanced you will find that you can sit longer before the awareness and energy have become depleted to the point of requiring a walk. You will also find that it takes less time with the walk to increase your mindfulness sufficiently to sit again. But don't be too hasty to change. As you work more and more with the insight walk you will know when the awareness has reached its full potential and using set time periods will no longer be required. When you reach this point, walk only as needed.

Changing the Insight Walk

You will know when awareness has reached full potential when it is what I call "brittle awareness." It is like reacting to a soft sound with a fright, a jump, as when you are startled or surprised by a voice when you are unaware another person is present. If you are reaching this level of awareness after 30–45 minutes of insight walking on a consistent basis, then it's time to change your walk. Instead of marking "lifting, moving, placing, shifting" as you walk, change to "walking, walking" with the label of walking coinciding with each full step. After a few walks to get accustomed to the different method of marking, the development of mindfulness will be just as much as before but not so "brittle" as to make you jump from sounds. You still mark whatever the mind is doing or where it has gone when it leaves the feet as before, only the marking of the "lifting, moving, placing, shifting" has been changed.

As you practise insight walking marking "walking, walking" as described above, you will start to catch more and more intentions preceding actions and thoughts. You may glean the "in-sight" that an intention precedes every action and that the act of intending is a separate action from the action following the intention. With repeated practice it is quite possible to develop a loop of seeing intentions. Specifically, as an intention to mark is seen, another intention arises to mark the intention to mark, leading to a series of "intending, intending, intending". If you have developed the practice to this stage, and not everyone does, then you may have to drop the act of mental noting completely. At this level of awareness the meditator's practice becomes a simple knowing where the mind has gone and what it is doing without attaching any labels. Upon realisation that the mind has left the object, the meditator looks and knows where the mind is and what it is doing, then returns to the object. A label is no longer used to denote any part of the walk, but awareness of the entire walk is maintained. The walk stops when something other than the walk has gained one's attention and the walk resumes when one's attention is returned to the feet.

As long as the meditation being practised is insight-based, then no further changes to the walk are necessary (other than shortening the period of the walk and lengthening the periods of sitting as mentioned earlier). However, if there is a shift to a tranquillity-based meditation, then the walk should change to be more conducive to the new method of contemplation.

This paper will now move back towards tranquillity walking, by describing an intermediate walking practice that is quite helpful.

A Gentle Shift from Insight Walking

When doing insight walking, you are developing what is called momentary-concentration, whereby the goal is to observe the arising and passing away of all phenomena. Although this is exactly what you want to develop for Vipassanā meditation practices, it is not conducive for retreats where the aim is to develop samādhi[27] to the point of jhāna.[28] When doing a daily practice with a short walk between sits, insight walking will probably be all you need to develop. But if you are in a retreat where the aim is developing serenity (another term for *samādhi*), the insight walk should only be used at the beginning of the retreat to establish a high level of mindfulness. Once this is achieved, switch to methods that develop and sustain concentration for longer periods of time. This requires dropping the use of labels as well as stopping any investigations where the attention has gone. Such a sudden shift in technique can be quite harsh and it may take a few days to recover from what feels like lost ground. Some teachers of jhāna promote using only a tranquillity-based walk rather than an insight walk to avoid this potential problem in the retreat. But tranquillity walks take longer to develop mindfulness to the same degree that is possible in a relatively shorter period with the insight walk.

There is another method of walking meditation that works very well when changing from insight to tranquillity walking. It is still a form of insight walking, but it replaces the labels of "lifting, moving, placing, shifting" with concepts characteristic

---

27. *Samādhi* in this context means mental one-pointedness or mental unification of the wholesome kind.

28. *Jhānas* are "states of deep mental unification characterized by a total immersion of the mind in its object. They result from the centring of the mind upon a single object with such a degree of attention that the discursive activity of thought is slowed down and eventually stopped." (*The Path of Serenity and Insight*, pp 3–4.)

of the four primary elements: Fire, Air, Earth, and Water.[29] The mind is broken from reliance upon the conditioned pattern of behaviour (previously marking labels), but is still filled with enough work to help keep it engaged.

The meditator starts by seeing the characteristic of the primary element in each of the four stages. The fire element as it heats causes lightness and lifting which corresponds to the lifting of the foot. The feeling along the bottom of the foot as it moves corresponds to the movement of the air element. Placing the foot on the ground or floor is compared to the solidity of earth. Finally, the ways muscles and flesh give way to the shifting weight is representative to the oozing characteristic of water. Thereby, all four elements are represented while walking.[30]

It takes only a few steps to get the knack of dropping the labels of "lifting, moving, placing, shifting", to Fire, Air, Earth, and Water, and substituting with concepts derived from the elements' characteristics. At the same time you also let go of marking when the mind wanders off. When you realise the mind is no longer on the bottom of the feet, simply return to the bottom of the feet. No further investigation is done upon any other phenomena arising during the course of the practice.

So, again and more specifically, as the foot rises up, single out the quality of the rising movement and the lightness of the foot which are both characteristic of things that are heated. This essence of the element of fire is then seen as a process in the walk and not just a concept. In similar fashion, a primary characteristic of Air is movement, so seeing the movement of the foot as the essence of the Air element follows. Touching of the foot to the ground brings out the solidity of the Earth element

---

29. See *The Benefits of Walking Meditation* by Sayādaw U Sīlānanda.

30. The original elemental walking, derived from the commentary to the Satipaṭṭhāna Sutta, uses the following combinations: lifting-fire, moving-air, lowering the foot-water, pressing the foot onto the ground-earth. I have altered this meditation, using water instead to emphasize the shifting of the body between placing and lifting. I believe that the original elemental walk is more conducive to momentary-concentration, which is the aim of Insight meditations. The variation of the elemental walk presented here, by being more fluid, is, I believe, more conducive to developing absorption concentration, which is the aim of Tranquillity meditations.

essence. The essence of the Water element is that it flows out from under things pressed onto it. This process is readily perceived as the full weight of the foot presses down and you feel the muscles and flesh adjust. As you keep walking, the four parts you are focusing upon become filled with new perceptions of the four elements. As stated before, no words are formed, but the mind is nonetheless filled with the watching. When some thought or other stimuli arises to take you away from your observation, you simply let go without further contemplation and return to observing the process of the elements occurring within the walk.

As is often pointed out, "As a thing is viewed, so it appears."[31] The first time I did this meditation I was struck by how easily the concepts were abandoned and replaced with seeing the process. Sayādaw U Sīlānanda states, "By paying close attention to these four stages of walking meditation, the four elements in their true essence are perceived, not merely as concepts, but as actual processes, as ultimate realities." Later he adds, "Only those who practise can ever hope to see these things." So do not give in to doubt, but have faith. Work to surmount the concept and see the process only. It will come if you keep trying.

This walking meditation bridges the gap between Insight and Tranquillity practice because it breaks the yoke of momentary-concentration that was developed through investigating every stimulus noticed. The break is achieved by striving to remain upon a single object and not examining phenomena anywhere else. The concentration builds upon the single object and the mind tends to stay on the object rather than wandering off.

This meditation walk using the elements can still be seen as an Insight practice because continued practice will lead to seeing the four elements comprising everything. Impermanence, perceived through the rise and fall of phenomena is now joined by seeing the body as non-unitary with elemental processes. This knowledge leaves no support for a concept of self. The concept of no-self is the third component of the first Noble Truth of Buddhism which describes all possible phenomena as inherently unsatisfactory, impermanent, and not-self.

---

31. Evans-Wentz's *The Tibetan Book of the Great Liberation*, page 232.

Tranquillity Walking

The intermediate practice of the elemental walk between insight walking and tranquillity walking should help maintain the mindfulness gained from the insight work without requiring marking. For most meditators, a day of practising the elemental walk while in retreat is generally enough time to stop marking without affecting the ability to gain mindfulness in one's walk. Even though the object has changed from developing Vipassanā to developing Samatha, the need for mindfulness remains. The intermediate practice of the elemental walk between insight walking and tranquillity walking should help maintain the mindfulness gained from the insight work without requiring marking. The walk now becomes very similar to the non-retreat walking described at the beginning of the paper, but I shall repeat the instruction and add more relevance where necessary, because this is a retreat and not a walk in the park, so to speak.

To begin tranquillity walking, the meditator simply maintains awareness of bodily movements. This includes knowing that you are walking, that you have stopped walking, that you are turning, that you are sitting down or getting up. Without using any form of marking you simply remain aware of all the motions needed to complete the action. For example, when you stop at the end of your walk, before you turn, feel the sensation of not moving or the lack of motion now that you have come to the end, but do not mark "stopping." Be aware of the shifting of the body and moving of the feet to do the turn, but again do not mark "turning." Before you start to walk again, bring awareness to the top of your head. Bring it down through your body fully experiencing the sensation of standing, but do not mentally mark it as "standing", just know it. When the mind wanders off to another object, stop the physical action. Knowing the mind is not where it is supposed to be is the extent of the investigation. Upon knowing, bring the mind back to the feet and strive to maintain awareness on the feet only. This process is repeated countless times without any marking or labelling of the mind objects, states of mind, or of any other physical activities and sensations. Do not worry about how long the mind stays on the feet or on the walking. The constant bringing of the attention back to the feet will eventually train the mind to stay focused for longer and longer periods of time.

The length of the walk should not be less than 5 metres (16 feet) or development of concentration and tranquillity will be impeded. Walks of 7–8 metres (20–24 feet) would be better. Length was not as important for the insight walking because extended concentration upon an object was not the aim. With the longer walk, there is more opportunity to develop concentration or one-pointedness before stopping and turning. If necessary, the walk may be circular or in a figure eight to gain greater distance, but it is generally a good idea to have a turning point in order to make sure that the mind is not running on for lengthy periods. This is more of a problem if the practice slips into an automatic mode.

The length of time for the tranquillity walk may be increased if necessary. The pace or speed of the walk will probably increase a little, but do not make it so. Let the pace come naturally, as you strive to be aware of the bottom of the feet. Only stop walking when you realise your attention has already left the feet.[32] If you catch the intention of the mind to leave the bottom of the foot but do not act upon the intention, then you have not lost the object and you do not have to stop the walk. As the ability to concentrate for extended periods of time increases, the hindrances are suppressed more and more and the jhāna factors[33] appear. Feelings of tranquillity, happiness,

---

32. This is different from the instruction giving under non-retreat walking. There is no mention there of stopping the walk when the mind wanders from the soles of your feet. The time constraints when walking to work, etc., do not tolerate a lot of stop and go. As well, the onslaught of stimuli is much greater and the ability to resist such stimuli is not as developed as it would be by this point in a retreat.

33. The jhāna factors are mental formations which increase in intensity as the mental hindrances are suppressed. In the first jhāna they are: Applied thought, sustained thought, rapture, bliss, and one-pointedness. The jhāna factors are not the jhāna itself but mental constituents that have increased in intensity beyond normal levels. When these five factors have reached the degree of intensity needed for jhāna, then first jhāna occurs. There are a number of elements, or mental phenomena, that comprise jhāna beside the five mentioned here (up to sixty mental states may be present for first jhāna according to the Dhammasaṅgaṇī of the Abhidhamma, but other sources remove repetitions to reduce the number down to around thirty-three, see *The Path of Serenity and Insight*, p. 69).

and concentration may increase. Resist reacting when these feelings or states are noticed; renew and maintain "awareness without marking" on the feet and on all other activities. At this stage, the length of time required to develop and maintain both faculties of mindfulness and energy may be determined on a per-walk basis, but do not cut the walk too short or the concentration in the sit will wane prematurely.

Benefits of the Practice

The benefits of walking as a meditation practice, whether in or out of retreat, have been shown to be an increase in mindfulness, energy, and concentration. These three are included in the factors of enlightenment[34] needed for ultimate success on the spiritual path. Although walking meditation has benefits that work for both Vipassanā and Samatha practices, it also has a developmental role for attaining jhāna. Walking, as a part of a tranquillity meditation practice, helps to bring forward and intensify the two jhāna factors of Applied and Sustained thought. The focusing of your attention on the feet and remaining there leads to an initial arising of these two jhāna factors which will strengthen the more they are practised.

Skilful use of walking meditation develops and maintains the mindfulness necessary in jhāna work. It is a great aid when trying to reach the razor edge of balance between opposing states as described in the Golden Mean:

> Neither too energetically nor too sluggishly
> Neither too tensely nor too loosely
> Neither too rapidly nor too slowly
> Neither too much determination nor too little
> And with attention that is neither strained nor slack.

There are five faculties to be developed if one wishes to make gains on the spiritual path: Faith, Investigation, Concentration, Energy, and Mindfulness. Mindfulness cannot be overly developed and more is always better, but the first four must be developed in a balanced manner or development will stall until balance is restored. Energy and concentration must be matched for either to work properly. The skill of balancing here is very

---

34. A translation of *bojjhaṅga* (see *Buddhist Dictionary*, p 42).

important and very subtle. When energy outstrips concentration, the result is agitation as the mind bolts from its object with the unrestrained power of energy. In the opposite case, the mind sinks into lethargy and dullness and ends up wandering away. Concentration focuses and disciplines energy, while energy fuels concentration enabling it to remain steadfast and bright.

Practising walking meditation in daily life outside of formal retreats extends the benefits gained from retreats. It can also go a long way in helping you prepare for future retreats. Once you get accustomed to it, walking meditation is adaptable to different physical activities and allows you to combine exercise, mantra work, and breath meditation. Incorporating at least 15–30 minutes of such activity every day aids your spiritual development.

Many teachers and writers of Dhamma books offer similar ways to practise mindfulness outside of formal retreats. No one can predict how long it takes to realise Nibbāna, what practices are going to be required, nor whether it will happen inside or outside of retreat. However when it happens, it will be when mindfulness is present as much as is possible. Therefore it follows that developing mindfulness should be front and centre of your spiritual work. As such, it can be said that the practice of walking meditation could be one of the most valuable exercises that you could ever do.

Bibliography

Brahmavaṃso, Ajahn, *Mindfulness, Bliss, and Beyond*, Boston: Wisdom Publications, 2006

Evans-Wentz, W. Y. *The Tibetan Book of the Great Liberation or the Method of Realizing Nirvana through Knowing the Mind*. London: Oxford University Press, 1968. (1973 reprint quoted).

Gunaratana, H. *The Path of Serenity and Insight*. Delhi: Motilal Banarsidass, 1985.

Mahāsi, Sayādaw. *Practical Insight Meditation: Basic and Progressive Stages*. (BP503). Kandy: BPS, 1971. Reprinted 2006.

Mahāsi, Sayādaw. *Satipaṭṭhāna Vipassanā: Insight through Mindfulness*. (Wheel No. 370/371). Kandy: BPS, 1990.

Ñāṇamoli, Bhikkhu and Bodhi, Bhikkhu, *The Middle Length Discourses of the Buddha* (trans. of Majjhima Nikāya). Boston: Wisdom Publications; Kandy: BPS, 1995

Ñāṇamoli, Bhikkhu. *The Path of Purification* (*Visuddhimagga*), Kandy: BPS, 1999

Nhat Hanh, Thich. *The Long Road Turns To Joy: A Guide to Walking Meditation*. Berkeley: Parallax Press, 1996. This is a newer version of the out of print *A Guide to Walking Meditation*. Nyack, NY: Fellowship Pub, 1985.

Nyanaponika Thera. *The Heart of Buddhist Meditation*. London: Rider and Co., 1962; BPS, 1992.

Nyanatiloka Thera. *Buddhist Dictionary: Manual of Buddhist Terms and Doctrines*. (ed. by Nyanaponika Thera). 1980. 4th ed. Kandy: BPS, 2004.

Sīlānanda, Sayādaw U. *The Benefits of Walking Meditation*. (Bodhi Leaves No. B137) Kandy: BPS, 1995. Available at http://www.bps.lk/onlinelibrary_bodhileaves.asp

THE BUDDHIST PUBLICATION SOCIETY

The BPS is an approved charity dedicated to making known the Teaching of the Buddha, which has a vital message for all people.

Founded in 1958, the BPS has published a wide variety of books and booklets covering a great range of topics. Its publications include accurate annotated translations of the Buddha's discourses, standard reference works, as well as original contemporary expositions of Buddhist thought and practice. These works present Buddhism as it truly is—a dynamic force which has influenced receptive minds for the past 2500 years and is still as relevant today as it was when it first arose.

For more information about the BPS and our publications, please visit our website, or write an e-mail, or a letter to the:

Administrative Secretary
Buddhist Publication Society
P.O. Box 61
54 Sangharaja Mawatha
Kandy • Sri Lanka
E-mail: bps@bps.lk
web site: http://www.bps.lk
Tel: 0094 81 223 7283 • Fax: 0094 81 222 3679